Misconc cience

Misconceptions in Primary Science

Fourth Edition

Michael Allen

McGraw Hill

Open University Press

Open University Press
McGraw-Hill
Unit 4
Foundation Park
Roxborough Way
Maidenhead
SL6 3UD

email: emea_uk_ireland@mheducation.com
world wide web: www.mheducation.co.uk

First published 2010
Second edition published 2014
Third edition published 2020
First published in this fourth edition 2025

Commissioning Editor: Phoebe Hills
Content Product Manager: Graham Jones

A catalogue record of this book is available from the British Library

ISBN-13: 9780335252237
ISBN-10: 0335252230
eISBN-13: 9780335252244

Typeset by Transforma Pvt. Ltd., Chennai, India

O10246 ACL 2025

Praise for this book

"As a teacher educator, I have tirelessly directed beginning teachers to this valuable source of support for over a decade – they and I owe a debt of gratitude to the author. Ensuring that children have a curious mind, and a strong understanding of scientific knowledge and principles, lays the foundations for them to build on throughout their life. This can only be achieved if teachers themselves have good subject knowledge and ambition; the ongoing professional development of both is extremely well supported by the revised and updated version of this excellent book."

Dr Nicola Treby, Associate Professor, University of Roehampton, UK

"As Michael Allen points out, old misconceptions seldom die while new ones are conceived daily. He has made an excellent job of refreshing this fourth edition with up-dated references, post-Covid discussions on disease and inoculations, with common misconceptions on climate change and even the use of infrared devices and artificial intelligence in primary classrooms. It is so much more than a collection of fascinating conceptual 'butterflies', it is a carefully detailed window onto some of children's science-based thinking."

Mike Watts, Professor of Education, Brunel University, UK

"An essential read, an absolute must for any staff room for reference and for students and other practitioners working in primary schools to refresh their memories and learn too. After explaining how to use the text, the author not only discusses how we learn science but also how misunderstandings, misconceptions, occur in learning. He considers the main topics of physics, chemistry and biology, and explains common misconceptions for each topic but how you can reconstruct the concepts. Very useful assessment tools are considered and included. Whilst the topics align with those of the English National Curriculum, this book will be really useful to all across the commonwealth."

Dr Sue Dale Tunnicliffe, Honorary Reader in Science Education, Institute of Education, University College London, UK, and Chair of Commonwealth Association for Science Technology and Maths Educators, UK

"Misconceptions in primary science is a comprehensive account of how children learn science and the common misconceptions they may have. It is a detailed and helpful book that all primary teachers should consult before teaching any aspect of science. Where there's a concept

there's invariably a misconception. The structure of each section sets out the misconceptions and, crucially, how to tackle them so that children do not keep hold of incorrect science.

The layout is easy to navigate, and the inclusion of famous scientists and interesting facts helps teachers construct interesting and accurate science lessons.

The key to correcting misconceptions is the idea of reconstruction, which is a central feature of this book."

Dr James Williams, Reader in Science Education and Communication, University of Sussex, UK

"This 4th edition of **Misconceptions in Primary Science** *is an essential read for all teachers of primary science. Whether a student, trainee, Early Career Teacher or an established teacher, this book offers the clear and concise subject knowledge across the whole science curriculum that will ensure that science is taught with confidence. I particularly welcome the reconstruction sections which help the teacher to plan to address pupil misconceptions, with a wide range of excellent ideas for science in the primary classroom."*

Sarah Hindmarsh, School of Education, Leeds Beckett University, UK

Contents

List of figures

List of planning and assessment sheets

List of tables

List of boxes

Foreword

As a teacher educator, I have tirelessly directed beginning teachers to this valuable source of support for over a decade – they and I owe a debt of gratitude to the author.

Many books discuss learning theory, including the constructivist and social constructivist principles that underpin Michael's writing, without application to a particular area of the curriculum. This means that it can be challenging for beginning teachers to apply theoretical principles in classroom practice. The author tackles directly the challenging issues of teaching parts of the curriculum where the accepted scientific explanation may be counterintuitive to adults, let alone children, and provides suggestions about how this can be done.

The author provides the reader with a clear and concise explanation of how children construct their scientific ideas – stressing the importance of exploring children's conceptions, before going on to carefully explain accepted scientific principles and suggest how a teacher may go about reconstructing children's knowledge. This recent edition includes a helpful focus on assessment, which is essential in knowing whether conceptual change has occurred. Whilst the book can be read in its entirety, it is arranged effectively so that different, relevant sections can be visited and revisited to support the teaching of different areas of the primary science national curriculum. This makes the book particularly helpful for busy beginning and established teachers who may wish to focus on the areas of the curriculum they are imminently due to teach.

Over the years I have talked with many beginning teachers about their experiences of science education when they were children. Sadly, not all prospective primary school teachers join the profession with positive memories of science lessons, or confidence in their subject knowledge. Consequently, much work is undertaken by teacher educators, in various organisations, educational settings and institutions, to help build both confidence and competence. Beyond subject knowledge, for me, this book challenges all educators to remember the sheer joy of talking with children, seeing the world through their eyes and learning more of the experiences that have shaped their understanding. Reconstructing knowledge is not always easy, but this book will provide invaluable support in allowing beginning and established teachers to view this crucial dimension of science teaching as an intellectually stimulating process, rather than a frustration to be avoided.

Science is much more than the acquisition of a body of knowledge and the application of scientific approach – science can change all our lives for the better, which is why it is vital that we foster positive attitudes towards science in childhood. Fostering an interest in science in childhood can benefit children in many ways. It can help children to appreciate and interact with the world around them throughout their lifetime. It can provide them with the knowledge that they need to make informed decisions about matters affecting them as they grow up and gain greater autonomy. Beyond the individual benefits, children who go on to undertake careers in STEM fields can be integral in shaping responses to pressing societal and global concerns as well as contributing to the economy.

Ensuring that children have a curious mind and a strong understanding of scientific knowledge, and principles, lays the foundations for them to build on throughout their life. This can only be achieved if teachers themselves have good subject knowledge and ambition; the ongoing professional development of both is extremely well supported by the revised and updated version of this excellent book.

Dr Nicola Treby BSc (Hons), PGCE, MA, EdD
Associate Professor, University of Roehampton

Preface

I wrote the first edition of this book 15 years ago because I wanted to create something that, as a school teacher myself, I had always wanted to read. Although a plethora of primary science books were available that covered subject knowledge and lesson ideas, none of them gave a very detailed treatment of the problems that children encounter when they learn science. *Misconceptions in Primary Science* filled this vacant niche by focusing exclusively on this aspect of teaching and learning. The rationale of the book over the four editions has remained the same – to help readers become aware of the variety of thought processes that children may be experiencing during lessons and as a result become more confident and effective teachers of science. It is especially aimed at beginning primary teachers who may not have studied science for several years, and it is hoped that readers will find the book clear and concise, user-friendly, readable, bite-sized, and browse-able. The content is at times quite theoretical with links to learning theory but there are over 200 diagrams that support the explanations. With student teachers in mind, each misconception has references to the research literature that will support the writing of assignments.

The concepts that are covered in the book often go beyond **KS2** level to clarify their meanings and, in general, the deeper the understanding a teacher has about a topic, the more likely they are to offer clearer explanations to children. In any case, the level of science taught to children in primary schools in England frequently goes beyond the requirements of the KS2 National Curriculum, embracing such abstract concepts as **particles**. *Misconceptions in Primary Science* also offers tried-and-tested examples of practical and other **pedagogies** that would help bring children's ideas into line with accepted science. Teachers are encouraged to use the principles of constructivist teaching in order to achieve this. To help this process, Part One of the book is essential reading as an introduction to constructivism. Parts Two, Three, and Four have comprehensive content that covers every topic from the Primary Science National Curriculum **Programme of Study**, and as such is useful for student teachers when auditing their own subject knowledge.

This fourth edition has been expanded to incorporate new material. Misconception entries have been 'enriched' with further information that reflects recent scholarship and up-to-date thinking in primary science education. Several new Boxes give supplementary information, including the use of infrared cameras in the classroom, and an account of the history of vaccination. A new misconception entry focuses on using children's experiences of the COVID-19 pandemic in a positive sense. There is now a complete chapter on the causes of global warming and climate change, and a discussion on the future impact of artificial intelligence in primary schools. Alongside these new sections is analysis of the potential influence of online conspiracy theorists on primary children, in particular, the threats they pose to scientific literacy in the form of myths about pandemics and climate change denial. A significant addition are 18 planning and assessment sheets that list the misconceptions from each chapter, providing an easy-to-access teaching resource for use as a reference during lessons (p. xxviii has suggestions on how best to use these sheets). There is a total of 381 separate misconceptions on the sheets, each of which has further information to help when assessing whether children have met the expected standard in science. In the early 2000s I used similar sheets during my teaching, which over time grew in length as I discovered more misconceptions from my reading and eventually evolved into the book *Misconceptions in Primary Science*. In a sense, the material has gone full-circle and returned back to its original form.

As I have emphasized in previous editions of the book, although each misconception entry has a part entitled 'reconstruction', a disclaimer must be made at this point that reconstruction is not always guaranteed! Some misconceptions are very tenacious and children will need lots of time to construct and adapt to new concepts, which often appear to them as entirely non-intuitive. The ideas offered in the book are suggestions that should help these long-term processes. If we as a nation are ultimately to generate a scientifically literate population, primary teachers have a vital part to play by helping children understand science, so laying firm foundations for further learning that they will meet in secondary school and beyond. This can only be achieved if we are able to elicit and recognize children's science misconceptions, then carefully guide their reconstruction.

Acknowledgements

Many thanks to Corinne Simpson who illustrated many of the pictures in this fourth edition – she is a true talent.

How to use this book

How the book is structured

Part One of the book provides a theoretical background, covering misconception research, constructivist pedagogies, and the nature of scientific evidence. Part Two comprises the main body of the book and for ease of reference, is divided into three sections that reflect the traditional organization of school science: biology, chemistry, and physics. Within the three sections are a number of chapters, each dealing with a particular science topic area. Contained in each chapter are the misconception entries, laid out using the following structure:

Misconception. This is a scientifically incorrect statement expressed in words that a child might be likely to use, accompanied by a diagram when necessary.

Scientific conception. This offers a scientifically accurate explanation, again illustrated by diagrams where required. The science concepts discussed here sometimes stray above KS2 level and so are not necessarily to be shared with children in the same detail as given in the text, but instead are there to enhance the reader's subject knowledge. This section may include a short discussion of the origins and thought processes involved in misconception construction.

Reconstruction. Tried-and tested pedagogical approaches are suggested that are likely to enable children to successfully construct accepted scientific concepts. Where possible, they involve practical work with children using scientific enquiry to take control of the learning process and address the misconception themselves.

Sources. Research from the science education literature is cited here. A good deal of the groundwork for misconception research took place during the 1980s and 1990s and so some of the references are taken from this intense period of research activity, although many other citations refer to more recent work. Note that the literature cited is international, with studies having been carried out by researchers from countries around the world, although the vast majority are limited to research that was published in the English language.

The writing is intended to be as accessible as possible – although, unavoidably, scientific terms are frequently used throughout. To assist readers who may have not studied science for a number of years, a glossary can be found towards the end of the book. When a glossary word is first used in the text, it has been highlighted in **bold face**. Figures are used to support and clarify statements in the main text, and are illustrations of correct scientific ideas unless labelled specifically as a 'misconception'.

Readers will find that within each misconception entry there is often cross-referencing to other parts of the book. A misconception rarely exists in isolation within a learner's mind and is instead constructed alongside or 'bolted onto' related misconceptions that all share the same faulty underpinnings. Together, they form part of a complex lattice of understanding called a **meaningful erroneous conceptual network**. Sometimes a teacher cannot successfully address a misconception without first dealing with other, more fundamental, misunderstandings. One tip is to leave a permanent stick-on bookmark at the contents page so that, during reading, other misconceptions in the book can be quickly cross-referenced when they are cited in the text. As an aside to the main narrative, four types of boxes give supplementary information that might appeal to children, or be useful in your planning: *Did you know?*, *Famous scientists*, *Be safe!*, and *Learning technologies*. A fifth type of box, *I think . . .*, offers direct quotations from children who have expressed misconceptions.

Particularly with **KS1** classes, some of the concepts and pedagogies described in the book may not be applicable because they are too advanced for the children, such as some **forces** misconceptions (Chapter 13). Nevertheless, you still might find that younger children have constructed forces misconceptions that need addressing, and the level to which you take your science teaching is up to you. Together with other factors, this is dependent on the general attainment of your class and the science curriculum that is specific to your school. In the main text, whenever a topic is mentioned in association with a specific year group, it refers to the National Curriculum Programme of Study for Science (the 'POS').

Finally, the bibliography provides source material that interested readers might wish to refer to for further information about the misconceptions included in this book. The publications are mainly research reports, some of which might prove difficult to access unless you are a member of a university library. In fact, a driving force that inspired me to write the first edition of the book in 2010 was to open up these 'hidden gems' to a wider audience, instead of allowing them to continue to sit in academic library collections gathering dust. Increasingly, researchers are allowing open access to their work freely on the internet and these can be easily sourced using freely-available electronic bibliographic tools such as the *Education Research Information Center* (ERIC) and *Google Scholar*. If you are a university student, you may have access to more sophisticated databases such as *ProQuest* and *Web of Science* through your library. These allow you to filter hits and narrow your searches. If you are finding it difficult to access a specific article, it is acceptable to email the author directly and request a copy.

Planning and assessment sheets

These sheets are found at the end of each chapter and collate all the misconceptions cited in the chapter in one place, allowing for ease of reference. The intention is for readers to use the sheets as a ready source of the kinds of misconceptions that children might construct when teaching specific topics. Each misconception on the sheets has been categorized using tick boxes to indicate the three levels of attainment pertaining to the expected standard in science: *working towards*, *working at*, and *working above* (*greater depth*). Note that a tick indicates the possibility of that attainment group having that particular misconception. For instance, in the Year 3 topic, Forces and magnets, the misconception that 'all metals are magnetic' is anticipated to be common with children *working towards* and *working at*, while those *working above* are likely to have constructed the more scientific view that some types of metal are not magnetic (see p. 223).

Listed below are suggested ways that the sheets could be used as part of the planning – teaching – assessment cycle:

1. *Planning.* Tailor your planning, bearing in mind the misconceptions on the sheet. For instance, create adapted resources that target the misconceptions that are relevant to each attainment group in the class (as indicated by the tick boxes). Produce resources that elicit the misconceptions, as well as devising tasks to help address them.
2. *Teaching.* During elicitation activities in the classroom, look out for those misconceptions relevant to children's attainment level, e.g. with higher attainers, consider the misconceptions ticked as *working above*. The sheets essentially help recognition (see p. 16), directing your attention to key misconceptions that might be constructed by each different attainment group in your class. Have one printed out in front of you during the lesson as an *aide-mémoire* to remind you what to look out for (photocopied reproductions are permitted for personal use).
3. *Assessment.* Both during and after the lesson, the sheets act as a guide when assessing which level each child has attained, e.g. if a child has constructed the correct scientific variant of a *working above* misconception, this contributes as evidence of them operating at a higher level than the expected standard. After the lesson, you might then choose to return to the main text of the book for ideas to further address any misconceptions revealed during the lesson. To inform assessment on a school-wide basis, the sheets can be incorporated into schemes of work.

One caveat is that the sheets' tick boxes offer general guidance only. Because learners are individuals and come to the classroom with different life experiences, it is sometimes difficult to predict the misconceptions they might have constructed, e.g. a higher attainer may still be stuck on a fundamental misconception. If your school does not adhere to the precise content as given in the

National Curriculum year topics, then some of the misconceptions listed in other year topics on the sheet might be relevant to your teaching. For this reason, I advise reading all the misconceptions on the sheet to inform your planning, teaching, and assessing.

PART ONE
Introduction

A

How do people learn science?

What is constructivism?

Over the course of several million years, **evolution** has provided humans with the ability to develop mental models that help them make sense of the world around them. For instance, the Aztecs 'knew' that the sun was a powerful god who moved across the sky helping crops to grow. The sun god needed to be kept continually pleased through worship and sacrifice, otherwise one day he might fail to rise and cause famine. In everyday situations, people also create mental models that enable them to meet the challenges posed by daily events, such as associating a summer's day with warm temperatures and deciding not to carry an overcoat. People often develop complex models that help when understanding natural phenomena, and go on to reason that the weather is warmer in summer because the Earth is nearer to the sun at this time of the year.

People reflect upon their past life experiences when developing their mental models, or *constructions*. For a new fact or concept to make sense, it needs to fit in somewhere with an already established model that has been previously constructed. If the new concept cannot be incorporated within an existing model, it is less likely that they will be able to remember the new information at a later date. These thought processes take place continually in the classroom, where children do not simply absorb facts like a sponge but instead will subconsciously and automatically search for existing constructions on which to hang new material that is presented to them in lessons. These events illustrate the psychological theory of *constructivism*.

Learners' constructions are always personal. After a teacher has explained a brand-new idea to a class of 30 children, each child will have constructed their own version of that idea that is different to some degree from everyone else's. This is because each learner comes to the classroom with different life experiences, so at the end of the lesson the teacher might be faced with up to 30 different ideas, some of which will be more in line with the teacher's original concept than others. In practice, however, there is usually a small number of specific conceptions that are common, being constructed in the same form by different learners from around the world. An aim of this book is to give readers a greater awareness of the variety of these conceptions.

Historically, and also in many modern contexts, teaching and learning have been seen as the transfer of facts from teacher to learner, with the learner either 'getting it' or 'not getting it'; this is a *transmission* view of learning, with knowledge being passed (transmitted) unchanged from one person to another. The popularity of the positivist theory of behaviourism in the twentieth century has provided a justification for these ideas, with successful learning being linked with practising repeated behaviours, together with suitable stimuli, reinforcements, and punishments. These influences persist today, with students (and curriculum designers) in secondary and higher education commonly following behaviourist beliefs, and successful students tend to be rote learners whose only aim is to achieve high grades. Such learning strategies are used because science in particular is considered to be a collection of facts that need to be memorized and practised. In many cases, learners do not find things out on their own but rely on teachers and peers to 'spoonfeed' them, delivering knowledge that must be absorbed unchanged – and they view science as a constant, with only one correct answer to a problem that will be valid forever.

There have been revolts against behaviourist pedagogies. At the turn of the twentieth century, John Dewey fostered the idea that students learn best from discovery situations, where free interaction with the environment promotes active learning, as opposed to passively receiving unchanged knowledge. About 60 years ago the Swiss psychologist Jean Piaget, the 'father of constructivism', proposed that as children become older, they pass through several developmental cognitive stages, where they reach the next level by building personal theories based on the previous stage. Later thinkers such as David Ausubel extended constructivist theory, emphasizing the importance of linking or scaffolding new material with ideas that learners already have in place. It is thought that constructivist pedagogies (see the *Did you know?* Typical constructivist pedagogies box on p. 19) encourage students to use more meaningful learning strategies, engage in autonomous active learning, and carry out practical work to arrive at answers; science is ever-changing to them, and they seek to connect their different bits of scientific knowledge. Professor Ros Driver at the University of Leeds was one of the first people to introduce constructivist ideas into primary and secondary education in the UK in the early 1980s, largely through her bestselling book *The Pupil as Scientist?* (which I unreservedly recommend to interested readers). However, these earlier constructivist theories have since been criticized as being too limited, formal, and logical, failing to take into account other important factors that affect how children learn science, discussed next.

Learners construct common ideas that researchers have found to reappear again and again in different samples from around the world, showing a commonality in the way people generally think; however, some ideas are specific to certain cultures. Today, in parts of southern Africa scientific ideas are sometimes rejected by children in favour of traditional beliefs based on folk medicine and witchcraft. Cases such as this show that learners do not construct their mental models in isolation but instead are influenced by the ideas of people around them who can play a big part in moulding their thoughts. In the 1930s, the Russian psychologist Lev Vygotsky asserted that all knowledge is socially constructed in this way, and modern scholarly writing on constructivism within the education literature tends to agree with this view. An example is how during group work in science lessons children will socially construct knowledge by discussing and debating how each of them has individually interpreted the results of an experiment, eventually arriving at one agreed shared meaning – this is conceptual convergence.

As discussed, each child brings their own perspective to bear when they construct scientific ideas, which includes personal aspects such as their own emotional involvement with the learning process and how they interact socially with other people. The ideas of Vygotsky have been applied in these contexts, with the *socio-constructivist* view considering that interpersonal interactions are likely to be among the most important factors that govern successful learning. Peers and teachers have a huge influence on children's motivation to learn, in maintaining their interest in science, and generating positive emotional responses that have been shown to significantly enhance learning. In recent years, socio-constructivism has become a major driving force in science education with effective science teaching being linked to approaches that consider the emotional, cultural, and social contexts of a lesson, as well as cognitive aspects.

The socio-constructivist view of science learning is authentic because it reflects how professional scientists go about their work. Contrary to popular opinion, science is not a body of facts, theories, and laws that are written in stone and cannot be challenged. Instead of trying to prove a theory is correct, scientists often purposely set out to try to disprove a theory to test its limits – this is the falsification principle – and if it is found to be weak, it is rejected and replaced by a different theory. This process is done in a social setting where communities of scientists come together to debate and arrive at a consensus, deciding which theories should be accepted and which should be rejected. One example that is described later in the book is Copernicus' and Galileo's efforts to convince fellow scientists of the Renaissance period that the planets revolve around the sun (see Chapter 18); eventually, the evidence became so overwhelming that the old theory (the planets revolve around the Earth) had to be rejected. Therefore, instead of being a set of 'right answers' that cannot be challenged, science is a battle between competing theories where the strongest survives and the weakest fall by the wayside. A constructivist approach involves teachers encouraging an atmosphere where, like scientists, children are given opportunities to test out in practical ways different hypotheses about what the outcome of an experiment might be, and then to decide which hypothesis is best supported by the evidence they collect.

What is a science misconception?

From the discussion so far, it will be clear that children 'know' some areas of science before ever having been taught them at school; a child's constructions are not drawn on a blank slate, but instead build on previously created models. Since the ideas of children gained from both previous experiences in science lessons as well as informal events out of school are of vital consideration, at the start of a topic or lesson, teachers should try to discover children's current ideas that are relevant to the science concepts that are about to be introduced. A major consideration is that constructions which children already have in place that conflict with accepted science can provide a shaky foundation for new concepts. There are vast quantities of constructivist research within the science education literature, much of which deals with these incorrectly constructed scientific concepts, or *misconceptions*.[1] Two different science misconceptions about the nature of the Earth's association with the sun were given at the beginning of this chapter: that the sun is a living god, and that during summer the Earth is nearer to the sun.

In many cases, once learners construct models that make perfect sense to them and have successfully explained a variety of everyday experiences, these models are difficult to change. This is particularly the case if constructed in early childhood, which is clearly a problem if these models reflect misconceptions. Many mental models are the result of informal trial-and-error experiments; for instance, deep-seated knowledge of how forces behave in the real world is thought to be constructed during informal play with toys in the early years, and can be a source of misconceptions that become revealed later on when children are introduced to forces concepts at school. Alternatively, children may never have met certain concepts in their everyday lives before being exposed to them during a science lesson, such as the rules governing food chain diagrams, and so may construct misconceptions during the lesson itself. Constructions can be quite sophisticated where several misconceptions link together in the mind of a child in an apparently sensible way, which has the tendency to strengthen them because each supports the other, becoming a meaningful erroneous conceptual network. Examples include the idea that the lungs' job is to pump air to the heart, and that during exercise the heart beats faster to supply the muscles with more pumped air (see 3.3 and 4.3 in Part Two of the book).

It is well established that science misconceptions present a barrier to learning at all levels of education. The misconceptions contained within this book have been reported in published research articles going back to the mid-1970s; some are commonly seen 'classic' misconceptions, others are less well known. A main aim of this book is to provide teachers with the awareness that their children are capable of formulating their own ideas that are different from those that were intended, exactly what form those ideas might take, and suggested ways to change these ideas into acceptable scientific versions.

How can a misconception be changed?

Identifying children's misconceptions is often the easier part for teachers; addressing them is more complex and less successful in practice. The literature carries a large number of constructivist-inspired attempts to change misconceptions into scientifically acceptable ideas, called *conceptual change*. These approaches can be traced back to Piaget's idea of *accommodation*, whereby new ideas conflict with models the learner has already learned, resulting in a change in those old models, or *equilibration*. More recent explanations have focused less on Piagetian stage theory and more on the nature of learners' ideas with respect to scientific phenomena. Since the early 1980s, research has centred largely on how students construct ideas from observations of natural events, with many studies focusing on Vygotskyian ideas of social constructivism – specifically, constructing knowledge in a social setting.

A successful conceptual change approach reflects the view that if there is dissatisfaction with an idea that is already held, learners will restructure the old idea until it fits the latest evidence as a result of *cognitive conflict*. However, research shows that even if children successfully construct scientific ideas during classroom teaching, they may revert back to their original misconceptions either at a later time, or when a problem is presented to them differently from the way that they learned it. In these cases, the misconception often continues into adulthood. It appears that a child's misconception might never be truly extinguished, instead existing side-by-side with the correct scientific concept, with either of the two being recalled depending on the circumstances. Here, ideas compete with each other for dominance within a learner's mind, and this has been termed *conceptual competition*. The fact that many misconceptions are difficult to deal with is because many accepted scientific ideas, some of which are fundamental to science, are counterintuitive and go against basic common sense. For instance, the previously described misconception that the Earth is closer to the sun during summertime makes more sense than the truth – that during the month of July, the Earth is actually further away from the sun than at any other time of year (see 18.8).

Critics of the conceptual change approach claim that it does not sufficiently explain how children think about science in the real world. Andrea diSessa (1993) argues that when children's understanding of science is carefully probed, they often give answers that suggest they do not have a firm, consistent grasp of scientific concepts; instead, they seem to hold bits of knowledge that are disconnected from each other, which diSessa calls *knowledge-in-pieces*. This view is not compatible with conceptual change theory, which instead assumes children are fully capable of constructing coherent, consistent scientific theories. The idea that children's understanding of science involves them drawing together loosely connected bits of knowledge has gained ground in the literature and serves as a different way to look at how we as teachers can best present science to help children construct appropriate concepts.

What is scientific evidence?

Something that is often a surprise to beginning primary teachers is that during science lessons, we expect children to think slightly differently from how they would do in any other lesson. In fact, in many ways, thinking scientifically is different to thinking 'normally' in everyday life. As will become clear from the following discussion, when we think scientifically, *the standard of evidence* is usually higher than is required in day-to-day situations.

When children are asked to define 'science' they usually have some difficulty. They may, for example, talk about science equipment: 'we do science when we get the thermometers out'. A simple definition of science is 'a way of making sense of natural phenomena'; in children's language, we could say 'science is finding out how things work', although not just how mechanical things like how a bicycle's gears work but the natural world in general. These things would include the **universe**, living organisms and systems, **energy**, and the human mind, and the way a scientist goes about finding out how things work follows a system called the scientific method. The scientific method includes the ideas that any claim the scientist makes must be supported by empirical evidence (i.e. evidence collected by experiment or observation) and that evidence must have been gathered as fairly and objectively as possible. It is not enough for a scientist to just form an opinion – there has to be convincing empirical evidence to support it.

In everyday life, people form opinions all the time based on weak or absent evidence; one example would be the belief that UFOs originate from other planets. It would be socially acceptable in the polite setting of a dinner party for two people to hold opposing views regarding the origin of UFOs. However, such a claim would not be published in a scientific journal because of the current lack of convincing evidence. Opinions, on the other hand, are based on personal judgement and not necessarily objective evidence. They are acceptable in everyday life as statements of free expression and are sometimes necessary for normal social functioning. For example, a manager might have an opinion about a particular employee that they want to promote to a higher grade, and make their decision based partly on subjective 'gut-feelings' about the person, such as they will respond well to taking on extra responsibility. A different manager might hold a different opinion about that same person, believing that the employee would not be able to handle the additional burden. Religious belief is a type of collective opinion, as it does not require evidence to test ideas – faith in the ideas alone is enough. Unlike with science, criticism of fundamental religious ideas is not possible, so the ideas remain unchanged over time, and many religious people see this as a strength, to maintain stable core values that were first passed down thousands of years ago. In contrast, the scientific method requires the interaction of a body of knowledge with new evidence, which may lead to that body of knowledge being reinterpreted. Core scientific theories have changed over time as more convincing models have emerged and will continue to do so in future, and as discussed earlier in the chapter, it is a common myth that once a scientific idea has been 'proved', it is set in stone for eternity. One example is that for 76 years, astronomers considered there to be nine planets in the **solar system**, but recent evidence forced a rethink about classification and there are now officially only eight planets (see 18.9).

Compared with scientific theories, everyday opinions are more likely to be incorrect because they are not always supported by reliable, objective evidence. On the other hand, opinions may be accurate, and everyone has a perfect right to hold any opinion on anything, but it is unscientific to make a claim that is unsupported by evidence. Opinion can become a scientific theory only once there is enough convincing evidence available to support it. The success of science over the past few hundred years has been due to the efforts of scientists actively attempting to prove any existing theory as false, so accepted scientific ideas have been continually scrutinized and challenged by sceptical researchers. Under this withering pressure, only the most convincing and valid ideas survive, with fruitless **pseudosciences** that were once completely accepted, being disproved; these include astrology, alchemy, witchcraft, creationism, and paranormal activity. However, note that, unlike religion, science does not deal in absolutes. It may be the case that, in the future, convincing empirical evidence will emerge in support of some of these pseudosciences, in which case, they may be elevated to the level of accepted science. With science, no idea is dismissed out-of-hand as being invalid forever.

Scientific theory and evidence are considered to be two completely separated things (Figure A.1). The French mathematician and philosopher René Descartes (1596–1650) noticed when travelling by boat that the oars appeared to bend when they were dipped in the water due to an optical illusion.[2] He realized that his senses were deluding him and that, in the case of the bent oars, the outside, real world was different from the way his mind was perceiving it – in

Figure A.1 The basic relationship between theory and evidence

reality, the oars were straight. Taking this line of thinking further, he questioned whether any of his senses could ever give him a correct impression of the world, and he even doubted the existence of the outside world because he could not directly access that world, other than by his unreliable senses. He thought that he was perhaps merely dreaming the outside world. He finally began to doubt that he actually existed himself, but did not take that final step, famously claiming *cogito, ergo sum* ('I think, therefore I am'). Modern ideas within the philosophy of science still carry the essence of Descartes' dualism, that there is an inside world (the mind) that is completely separate from an outside world (reality) and the two are not directly connected other than by senses that are sometimes unreliable.

In the classroom, teachers can explain evidence to children as something in the outside world that they can use to decide if their ideas are correct. It is important to disconnect evidence (something they observe or measure during an experiment) from theory (a prediction, hypothesis, or conclusion, i.e. something they can imagine in their minds). Children need to appreciate that in science it is not enough to believe something in your mind to show it is 'true' or 'accurate' – you have also to collect evidence from the outside world, which needs to be credible.

Scientific literacy of the wider population involves laypeople not only correctly understanding science concepts, but also 'thinking scientifically' – being objective and looking for convincing empirical evidence when considering the claims that others make. The mid-1990s heralded the explosion of the internet as a medium for communication, allowing anyone with access to a device capable of going online to make their views public. Despite the clear advantages of giving people more of a voice by enhancing their freedom of speech, this has also posed threats to scientific literacy in the form of misinformation, especially conspiracy theories that focus on science issues. These include topics as wide in scope as vaccination, **climate change**, the COVID-19 pandemic, flat Earth, and Area 51. Conspiracy theories reflect pseudoscientific beliefs since they present scientific concepts incorrectly and are also baseless in terms of being supported by hard evidence. So far, there has been little research on the effect of conspiracy theories on primary-aged children, but because upper KS2 children, especially, might access these websites, it is possible that they become swayed by their content, much of which comprises of outlandish facts and claims they may find appealing (12.2 briefly summarizes a study a colleague and I recently conducted that demonstrated a proportion of Year 6 children are susceptible to climate change denial). As teachers, protecting the children in our classes from these influences would involve, as discussed earlier in this chapter, emphasizing the value of the scientific method as relying on objective evidence, and also helping them develop generic critical thinking skills to help them sort fact from fallacy. Chapters 1 and 12 further deal with ways to address conspiracy theories when teaching about health education and climate change.

Does artificial intelligence have a place in primary teaching?

As a final point of discussion, readers are likely to have noted that new technologies incorporating artificial intelligence (AI) programs have been a popular topic in recent media reports. The narrative usually takes a negative slant in ways of highlighting the potential threats posed by seemingly all-powerful and mysterious AI algorithms, including their unethical use by governments or criminals to threaten our privacy and security, even the possibility that linked computers might one day collaborate on a plan for replacing humans, aiming for world domination. The use of AI in education has not escaped this emphasis, a well-documented example being university and secondary school students using online chatbots such as *ChatGPT* to generate text and then present it as their own work. AI chatbots have remarkable capabilities but their positive uses in education have so far received little attention in popular media. These include students legitimately using chatbots as information sources (similar to *Wikipedia*), schools and colleges preparing standardized test papers, teachers breaking down communication barriers by communicating with EAL students in their native language, and providing mental health support for students struggling in higher education. In primary schools, teachers are using chatbots for tasks such as confirming their own knowledge in unfamiliar subjects, creating questions for homework, and researching fun ideas for lessons. Primary children, especially, may find chatbots a user-friendly way to source information as the algorithms have been developed to mimic an approachable, friendly human conversational style.

My colleague and I recently published a study into how primary teachers can use *ChatGPT* to generate text that helps them provide clear explanations of tricky science concepts to children – pluses included that the chatbot provided some good analogies, examples, and key words for use in explanations – a minus was some inappropriate, confusing, and unscientific suggestions. The conclusion was that teachers would need to have a secure understanding of the underlying science to begin with, in order to sort the useful from the unusable. Readers could similarly try *ChatGPT* to help explain challenging ideas to children, such as materials dissolving in water, conservation of matter during chemical changes, how the density of materials affects floating and sinking, and categorizing materials into solid, liquid, and gas. Ultimately, it might be the case that AI avatars completely replace teachers at some point in the future, but for the present at least, this remains more science fiction than fact.

Summary

Humans routinely construct mental models to make sense of the world around them (constructivism). If these constructions disagree with accepted scientific ideas, they are misconceptions and act as a barrier, preventing successful learning in science. A good deal of educational research has been geared towards the identification and addressing of science misconceptions by means of conceptual change, commonly using socio-constructivist methods, which are aligned with the learning theories of Piaget, Vygotsky, and others. Attempts to replace learners' misconceptions with scientific ideas have met with mixed success. There are differences between scientific and everyday thinking, and science lessons in school reflect this by requiring any theory, hypothesis, prediction or conclusion to be backed-up by plausible empirical evidence. Conspiracy theories accessed online may pose threats to children's scientific literacy which requires re-emphasizing how to think scientifically. New technologies involving artificial intelligence offer both challenges and benefits to primary science education.

Notes

1 The literature also refers to misconceptions as children's science, naïve conceptions, private concepts, alternative conceptions, alternative frameworks, intuitive theories, preconceptions, and limited or inappropriate propositional hierarchies.

2 This illusion is well known today and can be shown by placing a pencil in a glass of water.

B

How can we elicit, recognize, and reconstruct science misconceptions?

The driving forces behind the initial idea for the first edition of this book in 2010 were an acknowledgement that science misconceptions have been and remain a significant problem at all levels of education, together with a recognition of the importance of 'catching them young' by starting to address misconceptions at the primary stage. An aim of the book is to improve teachers' awareness of the numerous alternative ideas that children may construct either before the formal teaching of science concepts in the classroom, or as a result of that teaching. Once we as practitioners are aware of the misconceptions that we might encounter during the delivery of a particular topic, we will be more equipped to recognize them when children say, write or do something that suggests they hold a misconception. That said, instead of passively waiting for misconceptions to arise during the course of normal teaching, it is preferable that we actively search them out by introducing specialized activities that are designed to highlight them – this is *elicitation.*

Elicitation

This section suggests ways in which teachers could bring out children's ideas to identify both misconceivers and correct conceivers. As well as informing teachers, elicitation will make each learner aware of what they really believe about scientific phenomena, which is an important first step to any future reconstruction.

Ask children directly about their ideas

The most straightforward way in which to find out what someone is thinking is to ask them directly, face-to-face. This can sometimes reap benefits; often, however, asking children directly tends to end up with them giving you the answer they think you want to hear, and not what they really believe. More indirect methods, detailed below, may be necessary to provide a more valid form of assessment. Direct questions can be asked to the whole class and used together with children's mini-whiteboards to check collective understanding, e.g. by using a plenary quiz. Some misconception entries in this book offer specific teacher questions that have been found to be useful when eliciting learners' ideas.

Self-completion exercises

These can take the form of worksheets that ask probing questions about a science concept, written tests, and computer-based quizzes such as found on the BBC *Bitesize* website. There is also an element with these exercises of children not revealing their true beliefs, although less so than with face-to-face questions. If you want to elicit the ideas of all the children, it is best that the class completes these activities as individuals instead of as a group effort, which usually ends up eliciting just the concepts held by the dominant member(s) of each group. An example of a self-completion exercise is a worksheet labelled *Living Things* that has pictures of different plants and animals, and children must decide whether they are indeed living by drawing a smiley face (true) or a sad face (false).

Card sorts

With KS1 classes where some children may have difficulty expressing their ideas in writing, more kinaesthetic tasks are preferred, such as asking them to place cards into different sets. One example of a common card sort activity in primary science is to have a collection of cards with pictures of materials, with the aim of placing them into sets of solids, liquids, and gases. These non-textual approaches also have the advantage of being more accessible to learners with limited literacy skills or who use English as an additional language. One method is to have children first sort their cards into the groups that they think are correct, then swap places with other children so that different arrangements can be compared. The teacher can walk around the room and readily see any misconceptions held by individuals or by the class as a whole. Sorting exercises can also be carried out in front of the whole class using drag-and-drop activities on the interactive whiteboard (**IWB**).

Children' drawings

Asking children to draw pictures of, say, 'different animals' can make the teacher aware of any ideas that are not consistent with the scientific definition of an animal. If the children only draw furry four-legged animals, you could ask them why they haven't drawn other animals, such as a fish or an earthworm. Researchers have used children's own diagrams as a basis for asking questions to explore their scientific ideas in intricate detail.

Story telling

Reading a story can be used as a gateway towards a science concept that the teacher would like to elicit, with learners being asked to draw pictures afterwards that offer imagined scenes of certain events in the story. A familiar example is to use Eric Carle's *The Very Hungry Caterpillar* (1969) to elicit misconceptions related to a butterfly's life cycle. Parts Two, Three, and Four of the book provide many other suggestions of story books to use either as triggers for eliciting children's ideas, or to merely set the scene and give context when first introducing a science topic.

Concept maps

Concept maps are a helpful way to elicit misconceptions in upper KS2 children as well as acting as a revision exercise to assess understanding after the delivery of a topic. There are several concept-mapping techniques, with perhaps the most basic being the version where the teacher provides all the words on a printed sheet. Working in pairs or table groups, children are given a list of key words to cut out. Children then arrange the words onto a sheet of sugar paper and words that link together are glued down and joined with a drawn pencil line. Each line must be accompanied by a written comment explaining why the words are connected, e.g.

Both solids

Sand ____________________________________ Wood

Concept cartoons

Concept Cartoons in Science Education, a popular book by Keogh and Naylor (2014), is written with KS2/**KS3** children in mind. Scientific ideas are presented in pictured scenes where cartoon characters express different views about an illustrated situation. Children then decide which character is correct, or offer their own explanation, so eliciting any misconceptions. One concept cartoon I used regularly is *Snowman*, where three cartoon characters offer different solutions to keep a snowman from **melting** when discussing whether him wearing a coat is a good idea.

Using toys

It is often the case that a more accurate indication of what a person is thinking or feeling is reflected in how they behave and not what they tell you (this forms the basis of the study of body language). When children play with toys, they become relaxed and absorbed in the moment, entering into a different world and dropping their guard, allowing an informed observer the chance to gather valuable information about their scientific beliefs. For instance, children are asked to build a car from Lego that will travel as far as possible down a sloping track and across the floor. Some will go for big wheels, others will add weights, some combine different variables, use different track surfaces, and so on.

Using scientific apparatus

Observing the behaviour of children can be extended from playing with toys to exercises involving scientific apparatus that require them to perform a more formal experiment. An example would be a child who believes all metals are magnetic trying to use a magnet to attract an aluminium drinks can (aluminium is non-magnetic). When the can fails to stick to the magnet, they frantically search for other magnets to try in the belief that theirs must be broken. Watching how children work with equipment such as balls and hoops during PE lessons may be helpful in eliciting misconceptions about forces.

Role play

Children sometimes find it easier to express their true thoughts and feelings when they are pretending to be someone or something else. Research into self-expression by children through hand puppets has suggested that this could be a useful way forward, with the teacher asking the puppet (and not the child who holds the puppet) direct questions relating to scientific concepts, within an appropriate imaginary setting. The child then answers the question while pretending to be the puppet. Interestingly, the same approach is used by the police when talking to children who may have experienced abuse.

Listening to children talking

Eavesdropping on what children say to one another during group work or when engaged with their talking partners on the carpet can be a valuable gauge of their ideas.

Recognition

It is intended that the misconception entries in this book act as prompts for teachers during elicitation so that they can recognize any misconceptions displayed by children as they arise. The rationale is that reading about misconceptions beforehand helps us as teachers to be ready for them should they appear in class. If we are unaware of the variety of misconceptions that are associated with a particular topic or concept, we might overlook them, especially if a misconception is closely aligned with the scientific concept, i.e. is nearly right, but not quite.

Recognition of science misconceptions takes place during elicitation exercises and referring to the methods described in the previous section will help you assess children's ideas. The planning and assessment sheets found at the end of each chapter will assist recognition – each offers a synopsis of the misconceptions to look out for during teaching in the form of a ready-reference aid.

More generic assessment methods that you use during normal teaching are also helpful here, such as the routine marking of books and other written work. Since 2000, *Assessment for Learning* (AfL) techniques have become an integral part of teaching in English schools, and using AfL approaches such as self- and peer-assessment of work can help clarify children's thinking, making them more aware of their own ideas that an elicitation exercise has revealed. However, since many misconceptions are strongly held, they can be overlooked by children, so teacher assessment may be a necessary step during the recognition process. Summative end-of-topic tests are usually very good at revealing misconceptions but take place too late in the process for the teacher to deal with them effectively, so are better suited when assessing whether teaching has been effective in reconstructing the class's misconceptions.

Deciding if a child's idea is a misconception or not depends on the level of the teacher's own subject knowledge of the science topic in hand, and it goes without saying that if there are gaps in our knowledge, children's misconceptions might be missed. However, reading the misconception entries in Parts Two, Three, and Four of this book will help refresh your science knowledge as well as provide more specific information about the different ways to recognize misconceptions.

Reconstruction

Once misconceptions have been elicited and recognized, the next step is reconstruction. Clear ideas for reconstructing specific misconceptions are given in the main body of the book; that said, there are general principles of constructivist pedagogy that are useful for reconstructing misconceptions and they are summarized in this section. The box at the end of this section offers some generic features of a constructivist teaching approach.

A vital starting point for misconception reconstruction is to assess what children know before teaching by using a classroom elicitation exercise and then use this information to guide the lesson. Once you have considered the ideas that children have at the start, you might want to use a reconstruction activity that applies just to the single most common misconception held by your class. This can be done at a simpler level by merely linking an activity with children's familiar experiences, perhaps popular TV science fiction programmes that (incorrectly) show loud explosions in space, or how turning down the volume control on a mobile phone reduces the current in a circuit. As discussed in Chapter A, an important principle of constructivist psychology is that we remember more effectively when we can fit new knowledge into constructions that we already have in place.

Another basic assumption of the constructivist approach is that people often learn best when they are performing a hands-on task; in the case of science learning, this usually means taking part in an experiment. Children in primary (and secondary) schools are taught to act like 'little scientists', planning experiments, observing phenomena, recording and interpreting results, drawing conclusions, and finally, evaluating the whole process by reflecting on what they did. A constructivist teaching method usually follows a particular way of experimenting where, instead of being given a strict 'recipe list' of instructions to follow, children are allowed a certain amount of freedom to plan and perform their practical activities. They begin by making a prediction, then test out that prediction using equipment to see if their prediction was correct. A child may predict that a heavy object will fall through the air more quickly than a light object, though when two different-sized glass marbles are dropped, the child sees them land at the same time. Therefore, their prediction is shown to be false, which triggers cognitive conflict and ideally ends up with the child rejecting their original idea and assimilating the scientific concept in its place – the weight of a marble has no effect on how quickly it falls – i.e. the misconception has been replaced, or *refuted*. A more involved approach is to give children several different outcomes or hypotheses and ask them to carry out hands-on tests to determine which one is correct.

The idea behind constructivist practical work is to allow learners to construct a scientific concept from what they have found out by themselves, and not be told the answer by the teacher. That said, constructivist pedagogies tend *not* to be pure discovery learning where children are left to their own devices with little or no supervision. Instead, there is usually some degree of teacher direction involved so that learners can focus on relevant events during the experiment. Also, practical outcomes need to be reliable – the experiment must produce results that are compatible with the scientific concept you are teaching, otherwise misconceptions will be strengthened, not addressed. Note that it may be the case that reconstruction is not necessary because children already hold the scientific view, so exercises need to reinforce this view as well as challenging any misconceptions.

The familiar stereotype of the professional scientist as a solitary soul who is happy working alone in a laboratory discovering theories is really the opposite of constructivist learning, which assumes people learn science better when they interact in groups and freely discuss the phenomena they observe. In a constructivist classroom, predictions and results are openly expressed and conclusions are freely debated with peers; this is closer to how scientists actually work, since theories have been collectively agreed upon by a community of experts as being a 'best guess'. School science in general should be viewed as a shared activity where the assistance and input of children and teachers are of vital importance, which is consistent with socio-constructivist theory, as discussed in Chapter A.

Over the course of a topic it is sometimes useful to track the ideas of children in order to see how they have changed. Floor books are one way to achieve this, with children sticking down pieces of relevant work, teachers writing down interesting things that children have said, adding photographs of experiments along with predictions and results, and so on. Alternatively, the same result can be achieved using class posters or wall displays.

In the UK, constructivism has stood the test of time and shows no signs of relinquishing its position as the dominant theoretical driver in science (and mathematics) education. For instance, the Education Endowment Foundation (EEF) publishes studies whose aim is to improve teaching and learning in schools by giving teachers access to pedagogies that are more evidence-based, some of which reflect constructivist principles.

Did you know?

Typical constructivist pedagogies

- Helping children's personal construction of knowledge and integrating this knowledge with their original ideas (assimilation).
- Learning involves not only the construction and extension of new concepts but also the reorganization or rejection of old ones (accommodation).
- Providing practical work to help construction of knowledge through personal experience of the physical world.
- Providing experiences such as events that challenge misconceptions using empirical data (cognitive conflict).
- Using a social setting for learning.
- Allowing student autonomy, engagement, motivation, and initiative.
- Using open-ended questions.
- Promoting higher-level thinking.
- Encouraging dialogue with peers and teachers.
- Leaving the final responsibility for learning with the child.

Summary

Science misconceptions are addressed using a socio-constructivist approach by elicitation, teacher recognition, and then reconstruction (ERR). Whenever possible, children should construct science concepts using hands-on activities that allow some freedom in planning, collecting results, and drawing conclusions. The input of peers and teachers is of vital importance during these processes. Activities need to clearly challenge misconceptions and so trigger cognitive conflict in order that children successfully assimilate appropriate scientific ideas.

PART TWO
Biology

1

What makes some things living and others non-living?

Conceptual areas covered in this chapter:

- The distinction between *living*, *dead* (once lived), and *never lived*
- Seeds, fruits, and vegetables as living things
- Microbes as living things
- How microbes cause disease

National Curriculum links:

Year 1: *Plants*

Year 2: *Living things and their habitats; Plants*

Year 4: *Living things and their habitats*

Year 5: *Living things and their habitats*

(PSHE (KS1–2): *Health and wellbeing*)

1.1 When is something 'alive'?

Misconception

Fire is a living thing because it moves, breathes, reproduces, grows, makes waste, and eats.

Scientific conception

Before we can classify something as being alive, it needs to be capable of *all* seven **processes of life** (summarized by the acronym MRS GREN):

Movement
Respiration
Sensitivity
Growth
Reproduction

Excretion
Nutrition

Fire appears to satisfy six of these characteristics but since a fire cannot sense its surroundings, it cannot be categorized as a living thing. Children often incorrectly classify things as living by applying only a few of the seven characteristics, two of the most popular being able to move by itself and **breathing**. For instance, the sun, cars, robots, air (wind), and clouds are thought to be alive simply because they appear to move of their own accord. These are cases of faulty reasoning of the necessary/sufficient type – to be called living, although it is *necessary* for something to be capable of moving, this condition alone is not *sufficient*. A related misconception believed by younger children include that because a plant or mushroom cannot move on its own, it cannot be alive. An example of **reverse causality bias**, where cause and effect are described but in the wrong order, is the assumption that when trees move they cause the wind to blow.

Reconstruction

At the start of a lesson, ask children to list the things that something has to do before it can be considered to be alive. This will reveal any children who have a more restricted view of life when compared to the comprehensive MRS GREN list.

Children may debate with you about the 'living' status of non-living things; for example, they may insist that fire is able to sense its surroundings because it knows where to burn next. One requirement not covered by the MRS GREN acronym is for a living thing to be made from **cells**, which would discount fire, cars, robots, etc. To challenge the misconception that plants are not alive, some of the activities described later in the book would be relevant to show that plants are capable of life processes, e.g. growing broad bean seeds (5.9) and time-lapse photography of tulips' petals over the course of a day (1.2).

When considering robots specifically, it is interesting to note that younger primary children may believe that human-looking robots are living, while non-humanoid robots are not alive. This may be associated with the tendency to apply human-like attributes to **anthropomorphic** objects children have an attachment to, such as teddy bears. For example, when the child speaks to the bear, it listens, it can go to sleep, and it is capable of emotions such as happiness, loneliness, and feeling loved.

Sources: Goldman *et al.* (2023); Ozgur (2018); Piaget (1929); Sere (1983).

Did you know?

Viruses. Viruses are extremely tiny infectious units that appear to meet all the MRS GREN requirements. However, they are not made from cells, which has created debate within the scientific community as to whether they are actually living organisms or not.

1.2 Are fruits and vegetables living things?

Misconception

An apple in a fruit bowl is not alive.

Scientific conception

This idea is common with children and adults alike and can include any piece of plant material that has been cut away from where it was first grown, such as fruit or vegetables for sale in a shop, or a bunch of daffodils. Even if learners have accepted that an apple tree is a living thing, they believe that once part of the tree is removed, such as the fruit, then that part is no longer alive. With animals it is certainly the case that if a part of an animal's body is taken away, then under normal conditions that part cannot survive independently, such as when a dog's tail is 'docked'. However, if part of a living plant such as an apple is removed, that part is able to continue to survive away from its main body, for a time at least. Research has shown that vegetables found at the greengrocer are able to sense light and release different chemicals according to the time of day. Fruits, vegetables, and cut flower stems all contain living cells, which, in addition to the seven MRS GREN criteria, is another requirement that needs to be met before something can be called 'alive' (1.1). Of course, once a fruit or vegetable has been cooked, then this kills the cells and so it can no longer be considered a living thing.

Reconstruction

Show children a tray of potatoes such as King Edwards with 'eyes' (axillary buds) and ask whether the potatoes are alive. Children then place the potatoes on a paper towel in a light area of the classroom – it is important that any eyes on the potato are placed face up. After several weeks the potatoes should begin to 'chit' and green shoots appear from the eyes, which shows that something that was apparently dead was actually alive but in a **dormant** state. Children can carry out the same activity but using cut carrot tops in place of potatoes. A more sophisticated experiment is to grow new plants from cuttings taken from older plants. Taking a small cutting from common garden species like dahlia or geranium and allowing it to grow in its own pot will surprise children who believe that pieces removed from the main body of a plant cannot survive. Explain that this only works with plants – removing a part from an animal's body would kill that part very quickly. There are, however, some exceptions to this; for instance, **sperm cells**, **embryos**, and **stem cells** can be frozen and survive in a dormant condition for long periods away from an animal's body. Younger children in particular may not consider any plant as being alive (1.1),

Table 1.2 Examples of living, dead, and never lived

Living	*Dead (once-lived)*	*Never lived*
Cut daffodil in a vase	Wood from a pencil	Paper clip
Potato	Fossil	Nylon sweater
Seed	Bird's feather	Ceramic teapot
Carrot	Coal	Gold ring

which will need to be addressed prior to any teaching about detached plant material such as apples and cut daffodils.

In Year 2, the basic distinction between living and non-living is extended as children decide whether something is *living*, *dead* (once lived), or has *never lived* (Table 1.2). If you visit www.bbc.com/bitesize there is an interactive activity for KS1 children where they are presented with a series of objects in a park scene and must choose which ones are alive. A challenging example is a bird's feather (Table 1.2) since it is made from protein **keratin**, essentially a dead material, but the keratin was originally manufactured by living cells in the bird's skin.

Source: Allchin (2017).

Learning technologies

Time-lapse photography. The use of tablet computers is commonplace in primary classrooms, with schools typically purchasing a set of devices that can be booked out by a class when needed. Modern tablets have excellent cameras that enable children to capture high-definition images of their work, such as a set-up of their experiment during a science lesson, or a picture of their results that can be used later by the teacher to assess their work. Tablet cameras have other functions aside from taking still pictures, one of which is to take a series of photographs at pre-set intervals over an extended time period. An example of this *time-lapse photography* is to take a photographic record of a plant moving very slowly over the course of a day – children often have a problem believing that plants are living things because they do not appear to be capable of movement (see 1.2). Tulips provide a dramatic example of this since they open and close their flowers on a regular basis; they close their petals during cloudy or cold weather, and at night, to protect pollen from becoming damp. A tablet camera programmed to take a single image every 20 minutes over a period of 12 hours would record this movement, which in real-time occurs too slowly for people to notice. This helps persuade children that plants are capable of both sensing changes in their environment and then reacting to these changes by moving. As an alternative, teachers can use the camera on their own mobile phone, which will usually have similar time-lapse functions (although this would of course mean normal use of the phone during this period would not be possible because it needs to be kept perfectly still).

1.3 Seeds

Misconception

Seeds are not alive.

Scientific conception

Children often believe that a seed only becomes alive once it has been planted and begins to grow. It may be the case that they have applied the MRS GREN characteristics (1.1) to a seed and concluded that it is 'non-living' – in this case, the normally useful MRS GREN method, in effect breaks down. A seed that has yet to **germinate** does not respire, grow, etc.; however, because given the right conditions it is capable of these things, it is alive but dormant. Dormancy is a very effective way for a plant (in the form of a seed) to survive unfavourable conditions for long periods; for instance, a 2000-year-old date palm seed recovered from King Herod's palace in Masada, Israel, was in recent times successfully germinated and grown into a tree several metres tall.

Children who think seeds are not alive have a problem understanding that during a plant's life cycle there is no time when it is *not* alive, instead believing that a seed is dead then comes back to life again when it starts to grow. A related misconception is the belief that although a caterpillar is alive, when it becomes a pupa (chrysalis) it dies, then when it appears as a butterfly it becomes alive again.

Reconstruction

Just using the MRS GREN characteristics would do little to convince children that seeds are alive. As in 1.1, explain that since a seed contains living cells that are 'sleeping' (dormant), the seed itself can be considered a living thing. Also emphasize that any breaks in a life cycle would mean an organism dies permanently. The familiar primary school activities of growing broad bean seeds or incubating butterfly pupae help children to understand that a life cycle needs to be continuous with no breaks. Other seed misconceptions can similarly be addressed by referring the children to real-world examples. For instance, if they believe that a small seed always grows to become a small plant, discuss how an acorn that weighs only a few grams develops into an oak tree of several tons.

Sources: Stavy and Wax (1989); Wynn *et al.* (2017).

1.4 Microbes

Misconception

Microbes inside our bodies are alive, while microbes in the environment are not.

Scientific conception

Many upper KS2 children can begin to appreciate that **microbes** such as bacteria that are infecting a human body and causing a disease are living things because of ideas such as the 'battle' between the immune system and the invading microbes. They may also understand that those same microbes are also present in the environment outside our bodies and that we need to guard against infection, e.g. by cleaning wounds; however, they do not necessarily see these environmental microbes as living things. They instead imagine something with the potential of causing an infection whose appearance and behaviour they find difficult to describe. A similar misconception is that mouldy bread comes about due to non-living environmental action, similar to how iron rusts, instead of living fungi.

Whether microbes are present inside or outside the body does not make any difference to their status as living things. Confusion might develop from the knowledge that some bacteria and fungi in the environment produce spores. Although spores are inactive and dormant, they are still alive and when reactivated become fully-functioning microbial cells, similar to how a germinating seed becomes an active plant in the right conditions (see 1.3).

A related misconception is that all microbes are harmful to humans because they are associated with causing disease, being seen as 'bugs' or 'germs', or are responsible for **food spoilage**. These views are perhaps reinforced by lessons devoted to personal hygiene as a preventative measure to avoid infective disease, and vaccination.

Reconstruction

Remind children that microbes that are currently infecting a human body originally came from outside the body (from the environment). When the microbes were in the environment, they must have been alive because the cycle of life can never be broken unless the microbes die; microbes are alive regardless of whether they are causing an infection (also see 1.5). Showing pictures from the internet of the same microbe both in the body and in the environment would help here, particularly time-lapse sequences of bacteria in the environment such as *E. coli* growing and dividing. If your class has access to a microscope, prepared slides are available of real bacteria and fungi that will help generate further interest (see Chapter 11 for more on using microscopes in the classroom). Interestingly, the experience of living through the COVID-19 pandemic of the early 2020s appears to have increased children's appreciation that living microbes are a constant presence in the environment.

An experiment to study how yeast (a microbial fungus) grows under different conditions (temperature, sugar/no sugar, light, etc.) reminds children that microbes can live outside the human body. The yeast is placed together with a little water in a small bottle and then covered with a balloon. As the yeast cells become active, they produce carbon dioxide gas, making the balloon slowly inflate.

Remind children about the useful roles that microbes play in our lives. For instance, bacteria and fungi have widespread uses in the food and pharmaceutical industries, as well as in nature, helping rid the environment of dead plant and animal material through **decomposition**. Bacteria living inside the human gut have vital functions including the **digestion** of **food** and the production of vitamins. There is a current trend for taking fermented 'biotic' health drinks and live yoghurts for purported health benefits, and children can be reminded that these actually contain living bacteria. Practical activities such as making bread or yoghurt underline the ideas of microbial usefulness.

Sources: Edelsztein (2023); Ruiz-Gallardo and Paños (2018); Sequeria and Freitas (1986).

1.5 How do we catch a disease?

Misconception

You automatically catch a virus when you come into close contact with an infected person.

Scientific conception

Whether an infection spreads from one person to another is not automatic and depends on a number of factors. Some diseases are easier to catch than others; for instance, the common cold is extremely contagious, the virus being able to pass from person to person in exhaled air without the need for physical contact; on the other hand, leprosy is extremely difficult to catch even after prolonged contact. Microbes that cause disease (**pathogens**) can enter (infect) a person's bloodstream without causing a full-blown disease because either insufficient microbes infect to cause the onset of symptoms, or the immune system is rapidly mobilized to fight and destroy the invaders. If pathogens are not given the opportunity to multiply to sufficient numbers inside a person's body, then symptoms will not appear. Therefore, a person can come into very close contact with an infected patient and not necessarily catch what they have, although with extremely infectious or potentially harmful diseases such as mumps, isolation from others is usually recommended. Even if disease does occur after infection, it is rarely an immediate event as pathogens need time to multiply and overcome the host's immune defences – different conditions have different incubation periods – with the common cold, symptoms can appear within 24 hours of infection by the virus, while rabies can take up to two years to materialize.

COVID-19 is caused by a coronavirus called *Sars-CoV-2* and is a typical example of a disease that is readily passed between people and very easy to catch. Like the common cold, the coronavirus is transmitted via airborne droplets in exhaled breath, usually by an infected person coughing, sneezing, or by touching a surface covered with droplets. Preventative measures include hand washing to remove infected droplets and wearing a face mask to catch the droplets when you cough or sneeze. In common with many other infectious diseases, the ultimate prevention with COVID-19 is vaccination (see Boxes p. 31 and p. 32). The pandemic of the early 2020s revealed that people had misconceptions about how COVID-19 is spread between people, including: face masks do not help in preventing transmission; drinking alcohol stops you catching it; you can catch it from a letter or parcel from an infected person; it can be transmitted from person-to-person in a mosquito bite; there is a higher probability of developing it in a cold climate; taking a hot bath or drinking hot water will kill the infection; and the flu vaccine protects against COVID-19.

Other misconceptions include the idea that all diseases are contagious, and you catch a common cold by wearing insufficient clothing in winter.

Reconstruction

Following on from the previous misconception entries on the living status on microbes, a good place to start would be by establishing that bacteria, viruses, and fungi that infect our bodies are actually alive, and not some abstract agents, so they can be killed by depriving them of their essential life processes. Next, teaching an upper KS2 class, at a relatively simple level, the scientific concepts relating to how microbes infect the human body would be appropriate for addressing the misconceptions described above, particularly that infection is not automatic and depends on several factors. The myths about COVID-19 transmission are often fuelled by conspiracy theory and children can readily access them via the internet. Safeguarding children against pseudoscientific online influences is further discussed in 10.8.

An activity suitable for understanding disease transmission and personal hygiene involves rolling a small foam ball in multi-coloured glitter. Pass the ball around the class until all children have touched it and glitter has been transferred onto their hands. Explain that some microbes are passed from person-to-person in the same way, but because they are tiny they are invisible and a person would not know that they were carrying microbes. Ask children to wash their hands and then check to see if all glitter has been removed – this can be linked to the importance of regular handwashing, and correct washing techniques. Apart from COVID-19, another example of a microbe easily transmitted by touch is the rhinovirus (common cold) although the virus is more commonly spread via airborne droplets created during sneezing. Simple ideas about the nature and transmission of contagious disease can be explained to KS1 children by reading the story book *Germs* by Ross Collins.

The story of Edward Jenner's development of vaccination has been traditionally taught in primary schools and can be used as a vehicle to explain exactly how microbes infect, multiply, and then are destroyed by the immune system (Box p. 31). Children's own experiences of the COVID-19 pandemic can be reflected on when teaching about the transmission and treatment of diseases, and vaccination; however, this must be done with sensitivity as it may trigger memories of past events about family members who suffered during the pandemic.

Sources: Collins (2005); Rodríguez (2006); Simard (2023); Tang *et al.* (2021).

Did you know?

The origins of vaccination. In the late eighteenth century smallpox ravaged much of Europe, carrying with it high levels of mortality. Edward Jenner, an English country doctor, noticed that milkmaids who had caught the similar but far less dangerous disease cowpox from cows, did not contract smallpox. Understanding that cowpox must be carrying something that gave immunity, Jenner infected a young boy called James Phipps with cowpox. He later infected the boy with smallpox – fortunately, and as Jenner had predicted, James did not develop smallpox. This experiment laid the foundations for modern immunology and today we routinely inoculate young children with inactive or less virulent strains of serious diseases, such as polio and tetanus. Jenner's apparently ruthless methods have been challenged on ethical grounds. However, the practice of introducing a small amount of infected material to people with a view to them contracting a lesser form of the disease and building up immunity, was an accepted practice of the day.

Famous scientists

Dame Sarah Gilbert. Achieving national fame in the wake of the COVID-19 pandemic as team leader of the research group that helped develop the Oxford–AstraZeneca vaccine, Sarah had relatively humble beginnings, attending state school in Kettering, Northamptonshire in the 1970s. After gaining a PhD in microbiology Sarah worked in industry and academia, which proved a firm foundation for her later successes in vaccine development. At the start of the COVID-19 pandemic Sarah was employed as a professor at the Jenner Institute (affiliated with the University of Oxford) and was tasked with leading the immense challenge of rapidly creating a new vaccine that would protect people against the virus, which at the time was beginning to claim a significant number of lives. This feat was widely recognized and appreciated as a key scientific endeavour in both academic and everyday circles – so much that the US toy manufacturer Mattel produced a Sarah Gilbert Barbie doll in acknowledgement of her status as a role model for girls.

Planning and assessment sheet 1 What makes some things living and others non-living?

(For suggestions on how to use this sheet, see p. xxviii.)

Misconception	*Attainment re. expected standard*		
	Working towards	*Working at*	*Working above*
Year 2: *Living things and their habitats*			
Fire, the sun, cars, robots, air (wind), and clouds are living things because they move of their own accord (1.1)	✓	✓	
Plants and mushrooms are not living things (1.1)	✓	✓	
Human-looking robots are living, while non-humanoid robots are not alive (1.1)	✓		
Fruit and vegetables for sale in a shop are not alive (1.2)	✓	✓	✓
A bunch of flowers is not alive (1.2)	✓	✓	✓
A bird's feather is an example of a material that has *never lived* (1.2)		✓	✓
Seeds are not alive (1.3)	✓	✓	✓
A seed is dead but it comes back to life again when it starts to grow (1.3)	✓	✓	
A caterpillar is alive, when it becomes a pupa (chrysalis) it dies, then when it appears as a butterfly it becomes alive again (1.3)	✓	✓	✓
Microbes inside our bodies are alive, while microbes in the environment are not (1.4)	✓		
Year 2: *Plants*			
A small seed always grows to become a small plant (and vice versa) (1.3)	✓		
Seeds are not alive (1.3)	✓	✓	✓
A seed is dead but it comes back to life again when it starts to grow (1.3)	✓	✓	
When trees move, they cause the wind to blow (reverse causality bias) (1.1)	✓		
Year 5: *Living things and their habitats*			
A caterpillar is alive, when it becomes a pupa (chrysalis) it dies, then when it appears as a butterfly, it becomes alive again (1.3)	✓	✓	

(continued)

(*continued*)

PSHE (KS1–2): ***Health and wellbeing***			
Mouldy bread is caused by non-living environmental action, similar to how iron rusts, and not living fungi (1.4)		✓	
All microbes are harmful to humans (because they are solely associated with causing disease and food spoilage) (1.4)	✓	✓	
You automatically catch a disease when you come into close contact with an infected person (1.5)	✓	✓	
Myths about how COVID-19 is spread from person to person (1.5)			✓
All diseases are contagious (1.5)	✓	✓	
You catch a common cold by wearing insufficient clothing in winter (1.5)	✓	✓	✓

2

How living things are classified

Conceptual areas covered in this chapter:

- Defining the terms 'animal' and 'plant'
- Scientific rules of animal and plant classification
- Differences between vertebrates and invertebrates
- How children naturally classify living things

National Curriculum links:

Year 1: *Plants; Animals including humans*

Year 4: *Living things and their habitats*

Year 5: *Animals including humans*

Year 6: *Living things and their habitats*

2.1 What is an animal?

Misconception

All animals are furry and have four legs.

Scientific conception

The animals that children tend to talk about the most are land mammals, especially those found in the home, the zoo or on farms, or played with as soft toys. They have fur or hair, walk on four legs, and make their own particular noise. Children may not consider anything else to be an animal – this is especially the case with **invertebrates**[1] such as insects, earthworms, jellyfish, snails, and crabs. Also, **vertebrates** that are not furry, do not live on land, or have fewer than four legs may not be thought of as animals, e.g. fish, snakes, and birds.

The scientific definition of 'animal' is much wider than this everyday meaning that children use. For a living thing to be categorized as an animal, it must be able to consume food (plants instead make their own food by **photosynthesis**), be capable of free movement, and usually consist of more than one cell (**multicellular**). Therefore, all the organisms that have been mentioned in this paragraph are animals.

Taxonomically speaking, living organisms are categorized into five kingdoms (Figure 2.1). Note that protoctists are often simple, single-celled life forms, such as an amoeba, while prokaryotes are bacteria. All living things belong to one of the five kingdoms, so by a process of elimination, if a child is not sure whether an organism (such as a shark) is an animal , if it cannot easily be placed in any of the other four kingdoms, then it must be part of the animal kingdom.

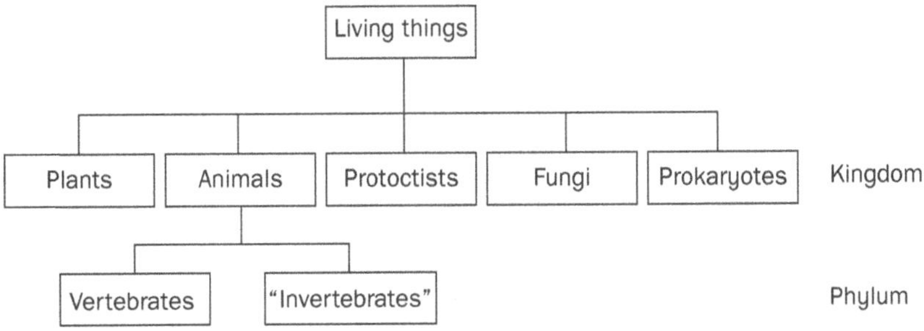

Figure 2.1 The taxonomy of living things

Reconstruction

Misconceptions can be elicited by asking children to write down what they think something must be like before it can be called an animal. Alternatively, they can draw 'some animals' to see if they exclude any particular types of organisms.

At primary level, the **taxonomy** can be simplified if teachers only reveal four 'kingdoms' to the class: plant, animal, fungus, and 'single cell' (so merging protoctists and prokaryotes). Having these four kingdoms permanently on display in the classroom as a poster helps remind children of the choices they have to make when categorizing a living thing. Ask them, *could a shark be called a plant, a fungus or a 'single cell'?* Sharks clearly cannot be placed in any of these three kingdoms, so by default the only remaining group left is 'animal'. This could be extended to a whole-class sorting exercise with Venn-type models that use plastic hoops and photographs of species (2.2). The Venn model approach could be used with any classification concept to make the taxonomic system as visually clear as possible for children. Alternatively, a cut-and-paste paper worksheet or a drag-and-drop activity with the interactive whiteboard could be used. Giving children a wide variety of examples (and counter-examples) will help them to realize that the boundaries of the animal set are wider than they first thought. A good source of interesting animal photographs to use in sorting tasks is the National Geographic website: https://www.nationalgeographic.com/animals/topic/photos

There is evidence to show that some children with English as an additional language may have less of a problem accepting non-typical species such as earthworms and birds as belonging to the animal kingdom. Spanish dictionaries do not list different definitions for 'animal' – there is no alternative, everyday meaning for the word as there is in English. Similarly, in Setswana and Malay, 'animal' has a broad definition, helping to explain why children who speak these languages make fewer errors when categorizing animals.

Sources: Allen (2015); Hast (2022); Patrick and Tunnicliffe (2011); Trowbridge and Mintzes (1985, 1988).

Famous scientists

Carl von Linné. Known better by his Latinized name *Linnaeus*, this eighteenth-century Swedish botanist devised his own system of classifying living things that biologists still use today (in an adapted form), two-and-a-half centuries after his death. He also created the binomial taxonomic naming system that can be applied to every species; for example, humans are ***Homo sapiens***. Unlike the five kingdoms we accept today, Linnaeus initially recognized only three – the animal, vegetable, and mineral kingdoms.

2.2 Is an insect an animal?

Misconception

A bee is not an animal ... because it is an insect.

Scientific conception

A bee is indeed an insect, though children making this statement do not recognize that the set 'insect' is part of a bigger 'animal' set. It needs to be made clear that a bee can be both an insect and an animal at the same time.

Reconstruction

Using Venn-type models helps children appreciate the system – these diagrams are simplifications, but easier for younger children to understand than the more complex 'tree of life' drawings of animal classification. They could be asked to sort animal picture cards into sets using different-sized plastic hoops (Figure 2.2).

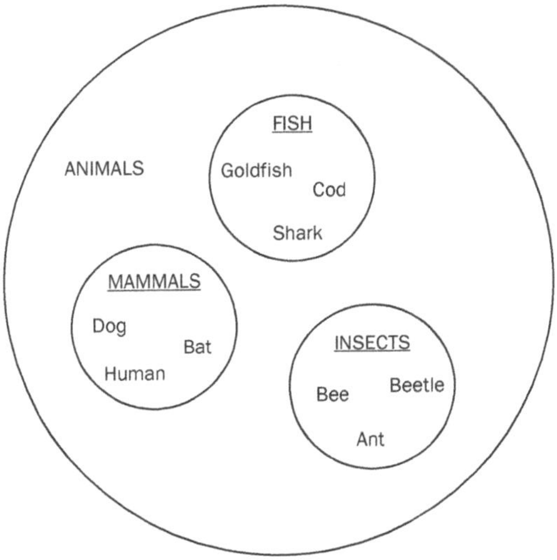

Figure 2.2 Taxonomy of classification using Venn-type models

Sources: Allen (2015); Leach *et al.* (1992); Schlegel *et al.* (2015).

2.3 What is the difference between a vertebrate and an invertebrate?

> **Misconception**
>
> *A crab is a vertebrate because it has a hard shell on its back.*

Scientific conception

Upper KS2 children typically know that animals with backbones are called vertebrates and those without a backbone are invertebrates (Figures 2.3a, 2.3b, and 2.3c). Despite appearances, crabs do not possess a backbone; in fact, their bodies do not contain bones at all. When children are deciding whether a particular animal has a backbone, they tend to look only at its outward appearance,

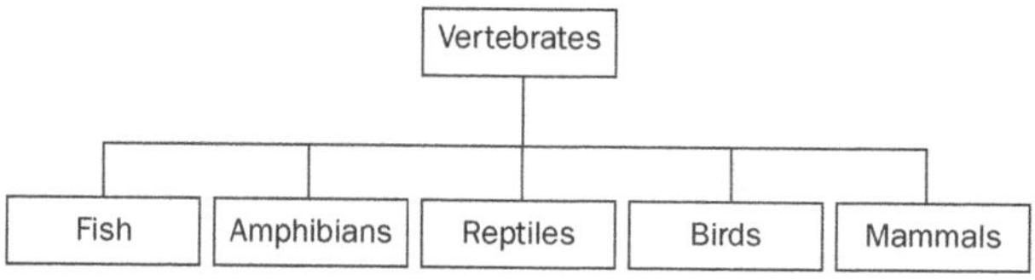

Figure 2.3a Vertebrate classification

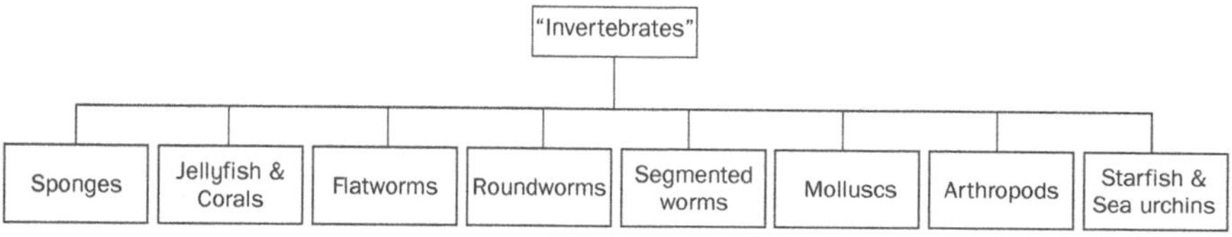

Figure 2.3b Invertebrate classification

Figure 2.3c Some examples of common invertebrates

particularly its overall body shape, texture, and the flexibility and curvature of its back. Some children think that animals with soft bodies are entirely boneless, so do not possess a backbone. They commonly consider the turtle to be an invertebrate because they imagine a soft, boneless body underneath its shell, and for that reason it needs its shell to provide support. In a similar way children describe animals that are very flexible when moving, such as eels and cats, as invertebrates because they are 'too bendy' to have a backbone. For the same reason, they know that snakes can coil up tightly because they are flexible and so must be invertebrates, or are too long and thin to contain something as substantial as a backbone (also see 2.4). However, turtles, fish, and snakes are all vertebrates. In contrast, children (correctly) believe animals with noticeably curved backs, such as elephants and gerbils, are vertebrates. They may also mistakenly think that **arthropods**, such as crabs and centipedes, are vertebrates because the backs of their bodies are protected by a hard **exoskeleton**, and frequently draw these animals with bones underneath their external 'armour'.

Reconstruction

Research has shown that children who have seen skeletons of fish and snakes in museums and elsewhere quickly realize that they are vertebrates. Children who have eaten bony fish, such as trout, whose parents have dissected the backbone and ribs before eating can be reminded that fish are indeed vertebrates.

Sources: Braund (1998); Prokop *et al.* (2008); Trowbridge and Mintzes (1985, 1988).

2.4 Snakes and earthworms

Misconception

Earthworms are invertebrates, so snakes must be too.

Scientific conception

In many cases, this misconception is the result of the visual similarity of snakes and earthworms – both are bendy, have tube-shaped bodies with no limbs, and crawl on the ground. Some children who have correctly learned that earthworms have no backbones and so are invertebrates go on to automatically include snakes in the same category. However, snakes do have backbones because they belong to the reptile class, which is part of the bigger vertebrates **phylum** (Figure 2.3a).

As seen previously in 2.3, related misconceptions include the belief that animals such as eels (fish) and turtles (reptiles) are invertebrates. Children can make these errors if the outward appearance of an animal does not obviously suggest that a backbone or even any bony structure exists.

Reconstruction

Show the class a picture of a snake skeleton, or if possible a real snake skeleton, and it should become clear that the animal is a vertebrate because the whole skeleton seems to consist of backbone and ribs. Compare this with a photo or diagram of the inside of an earthworm, which has no bones; an earthworm's insides are mainly soft and liquidy. The outward (hydrostatic) pressure of this liquid helps the worm maintain its shape, keeping it 'inflated' like a water balloon, and also enables the worm to move. In contrast, as is also the case with other vertebrates including humans, a bony skeleton supports a snake's body, which also is important in movement.

Remind children that according to the rules of taxonomy, snakes belong in the reptiles set because they have scaly skins and lay leathery eggs, and that reptiles are included within a larger vertebrates set (Figure 2.3a). As well as having no backbone, earthworms have moist, smooth skins, and so are neither reptiles nor vertebrates.

A model backbone can be made by children in the classroom by cutting a drinks straw into short lengths and then threading them through with string. This can help demonstrate that although the human backbone has only limited flexibility, vertebrates such as snakes and cats are able to coil their bodies tightly because their backbones are very bendy.

Sources: Trowbridge and Mintzes (1988); Yen *et al.* (2004).

2.5 What exactly is an insect?

Misconception

All 'creepy crawlies' are insects.

Scientific conception

The above statement reflects a common over-generalization of the 'insects' set and can emerge when animal classification is first introduced in Year 1. As well as proper insects, children often incorrectly place other arthropods in the insect category, such as arachnids (e.g. spiders, mites, and scorpions), myriapods (e.g. centipedes and millipedes) or crustaceans (e.g. woodlice).

In taxonomy, insects are different from other arthropods because they have three body sections (head, **thorax**, and **abdomen**), one pair of antennae, and three pairs of legs (Figure 2.5). Spiders, in comparison, have only two body sections and four pairs of legs; myriapods such as centipedes and millipedes have a large number of body sections (a 'myriad') with one or two pairs of legs on each. Crustaceans have a variable number of body parts and legs. When presented with unfamiliar arthropods children may automatically call them 'insects' and not use these taxonomic rules. For instance, a frequent error is to call the wingless daddy long legs an insect, although it is actually a type of

Figure 2.5 Comparing insects (left), arachnids (middle), and crustaceans (right)

arachnid called a harvestman. Also, children can think that a woodlouse is an insect when it is in fact a crustacean.

Reconstruction

In keeping with other classification misconceptions covered in this chapter, try to encourage children to get into the habit of referring to the criteria that are unique to individual sets; for instance, for something to be called an insect, it must have six legs. Having live arthropods such as locusts, giant cockroaches, or giant millipedes as class pets would aid this process.

The use of taxonomic **keys** will help children differentiate between different arthropod groups by comparing their physical characteristics. These can be done as paper exercises or by using real animals captured from soil samples. Such activities can be extended by research-style lessons where the class is asked to find out about a particular arthropod using library books or the internet with a view to producing an information poster.

KS1 children can capture insects and other small soil-dwelling animals by using pitfall traps. Dig a hole in the soil so that a small tub or cup can be placed inside, making it deep enough so that the lip of the tub is flush with the surface of the ground. Cover the trap with a small roof made from plastic or wood to keep the rain out, remembering to leave a gap at the lip of the cup to allow animals to enter. Use a little sugar or fruit as bait, then wait overnight. Any captured animals can be taken to the classroom and studied using magnifying glasses. Ask children to treat the animals with respect, and at the end of the lesson return them to where they were captured, removing your pitfall traps. Fulfilling the same purpose, in the summer term a bug hunt can be carried out in the school grounds by children equipped with jam jars, small nets, and magnifying glasses.

Children can have negative attitudes towards insects and other arthropods generated by a 'yuk factor' and be reluctant to work with them up close, or even see them as a kind of vermin that need to be exterminated. It has been shown that children's empathy towards them can be stimulated if arthropods are purposely attracted to the school garden, by cultivating pollinator plants such as thistles, nettles, garlic mustard, and dandelions. Building compost heaps and providing shaded areas using stones, logs, and old tiles will attract ground-dwelling species. Children can observe the garden on a regular basis, keeping a checklist of the variety of arthropod visitors at different times of the year.

For KS1 classes, books such as *The Very Hungry Caterpillar* by Eric Carle are good for helping to explain the complex life cycle that many insects undergo.

Sources: Carle (1969); Jones and Hill (2023); Schlegel *et al.* (2015); Shepardson (2002).

2.6 What is an amphibian?

Misconception

If an animal lives on land and in water, it is an amphibian.

Scientific conception

As with the other misconceptions in this chapter, when children classify animals they use non-scientific reasons; in this particular case, where an animal lives. The incorrect idea that **habitat** needs to be considered when classifying organisms leads children to think that a variety of animals are amphibians when they are not, such as seals, penguins, sea turtles, and water snakes. Figure 2.3a shows the five vertebrate classes of fish, amphibian, reptile, bird, and mammal. For something to belong to the amphibian class, it needs to be able to breathe underwater and also in air, have a smooth moist skin, lay soft eggs, and typically have a complex life cycle consisting of several distinct stages. Animals such as frogs, toads, newts, and salamanders meet all these criteria and so are true amphibians – where they live is unimportant when making classification decisions. Everyday expressions such as an 'amphibious car' that can drive on both land and water would reinforce this misconception.

Children can encounter other problems when conceptualizing amphibians, including differentiating them from reptiles. Newts are amphibians but are frequently confused with lizards, which are reptiles. Most children are aware that frogs and toads are amphibians but they sometimes draw them with clawed toes, which is a reptilian feature. A related misconception common in lower KS1 children is that any animal that lives in water is a fish even if it does not belong to the fish class, e.g. crabs, tadpoles, squids, dolphins, and whales (also see 2.7). In contrast, preschool children tend to correctly categorize crabs, tadpoles, and squids as *not* being fish because they do not look like a typical fish such as a cod – they are less fixated on habitat and more on the outward shape of the organisms.

Reconstruction

In Year 1, children have to know the five vertebrate classes and start to compare the structure of familiar animals that belong to each set. A table that provides the different criteria when placing animals into the vertebrate classes is useful (Table 2.6), although a more constructivist approach would be to allow the children the opportunity to discover the criteria themselves by giving them examples of animals from each set from which they then identify similarities and differences. Specific examples can be discussed using animals that they already know. For example, a penguin is not an amphibian because it has feathers, and although it spends its time on land and in the sea, it cannot breathe both in air and underwater.

With KS1 children who are new to the idea of placing things into sets based on taxonomy, they might find trying to classify complex things like animals too challenging. Before they first start placing animals into sets, ask them instead to place familiar objects into sets based on how they look. These objects could be the contents of a pencil case or stationery kept on their class table such as paper, rubbers, and glue. Tell them that when assigning an object to a particular set it must have at least one thing in common with every other member of the set. This exercise is followed by the more usual tasks where children place pictures of living things into sets such as plant/animal. This would encourage them to categorize using the observable features of living things instead of their habitat or behaviour.

Play the game *Who am I?* where a volunteer secretly thinks of the name of an animal and answers questions from the class based on physical appearance by answering either 'yes' or 'no', with the class having to guess which animal the child is thinking of from the responses. Introduce amphibians and their

Table 2.6 Criteria used to categorize vertebrates

Fish	*Amphibian*	*Reptile*	*Bird*	*Mammal*
Cold-blooded	Cold-blooded	Cold-blooded	Warm-blooded	Warm-blooded
Scaly skin	Smooth, moist skin	Scaly skin	Feathers	Fur
Breathes using gills	Breathes using gills, skin, or lungs	Breathes using lungs	Breathes using lungs	Breathes using lungs
Lays soft eggs in water	Lays soft eggs usually in water	Most lay leathery eggs	Lays hard-shelled eggs	Gives birth to live young
Has fins	Typically has a complex life cycle	Has clawed toes	Has a beak	Feeds milk to young

complex life cycles to KS1 by reading the story book *Oscar and the Frog* by Geoff Waring.

Sources: Allen (2015); Rittig and Scheuch (2022); Waring (2009).

2.7 Sea-dwelling mammals

Misconception

A whale is a fish because it lives in the sea.

Scientific conception

When classifying an animal, children sometimes base their decision on habitat instead of the physical features of the animal itself, such as thinking that seals, penguins, and turtles are amphibians because they live both on land and in the sea (2.6) and that a bat is a type of bird because it flies (also see Box p. 45). These ideas may be reinforced by the fact that the physical features of some of these animals do not make correct classification easy; for example, whales and bats are not typical mammals, penguins are not typical birds, and turtles are not typical reptiles. Early-years children have particular difficulty in classifying reptiles and mammals, though they perform better with the fish, amphibian, and bird classes.

With a related type of misconception, children are distracted by an animal's name and think that starfish and jellyfish are types of fish, when they are in fact invertebrates.

I think . . .

How birds are classified. *'[An ostrich is not a bird because it] has a long neck so it can't fly'* (5-year-old child; Allen, 2015, p. 124).

Reconstruction

Remind children that classification is based largely on how an organism's body is put together, not where it lives. Recapping the characteristics of vertebrate and other taxonomic groups can help address the above examples: a whale is not a fish because it does not have gills or a scaly skin; a bat is not a bird

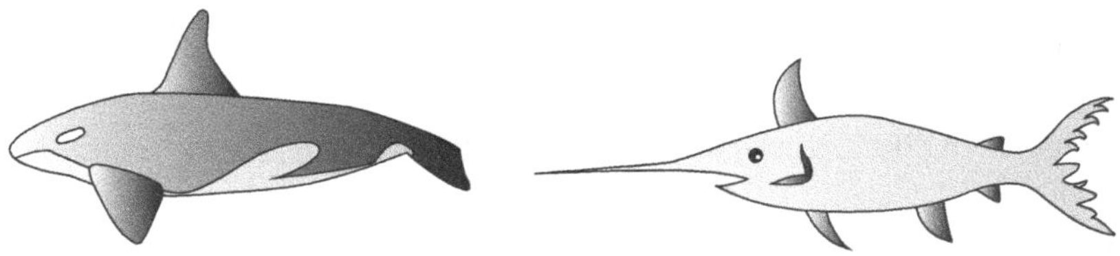

Figure 2.7 Comparing the tails of a killer whale (left) and a swordfish (right)

Table 2.7 Tick list for observable features of different animals belonging to the same taxonomic group (fish)

Animal	*Scales?*	*Gills?*	*Fins?*
Shark			
Goldfish			
Puffer fish, etc.			

because it has fur instead of feathers (Table 2.6). A simple rule of thumb when deciding whether a sea animal is a whale or a fish is to look at the tail – whales and other cetaceans such as dolphins have their tail fins oriented in the horizontal plane and move up-and-down, while fish have theirs in the vertical plane and move side-to-side (Figure 2.7).

For an exercise in observation, children can be asked to compare pictures of a variety of animals that look different but are classified within the same taxonomic group, e.g. different fish. Using a tick list, they can look at the pictures and try to spot as many of these features as possible (Table 2.7). Conclude by explaining for something to be called a fish, it needs to tick *all* these boxes. Note that a problem of using such simplified taxonomy means that exceptions sometimes crop up, such as the fact a seahorse has no scales but is still technically a fish. Nicola Davies' *Big Blue Whale* is a good story book with which to introduce the concept to KS1 children.

Sources: Davies (1997); Trowbridge and Mintzes (1988).

2.8 Are humans animals?

Misconception

We are not animals because we are people.

Scientific conception

It is a widespread belief among children and adults alike that humans are not animals. Some of the reasons given are because humans do not match the four-legged/furry model expected of animals (see 2.1). Other reasons centre around a child's ethical or religious experience; for instance, an animal is thought of as something less than human and beast-like. In contrast, human beings are believed to be a unique kind of living thing that occupy a special place in the world and exist outside the rules of classification (see Box p. 47). When we call another person 'an animal', it is usually meant as an insult, referring to something non-human and degenerate. This type of anthropocentric thinking lies at the source of several other misconceptions discussed in this book.

All living things have their place within a biological taxonomic system, including our species *Homo sapiens*, which is classified alongside similar species such as chimpanzees and gorillas in the family Hominidae (great apes). This family is included within the primate order, mammal class, vertebrate phylum, and the animal kingdom; therefore, humans are taxonomically classified as a type of animal.

A related misconception is that death does not happen with other living things, just human beings.

> ***I think . . .***
>
> **People as animals.** *'[The little girl is not an animal because] she lives at home, she picks flowers in the garden ... and she is human too'* (7-year-old child; Chen and Ku, 1998, p. 60).

Reconstruction

As with other taxonomic misconceptions, making children aware of the place that human beings occupy within the animal kingdom can be done by offering them a view of exactly where our species fits into the 'big picture'. Teaching the five (or more simply, four) kingdoms, perhaps alongside a tree-of-life picture, should make it clear that humans are indeed a type of animal. Discussing similarities between humans and other great apes can lead into a discussion about human evolution and how all great apes (including humans) have evolved from a common ancestor that is now extinct (see 7.8 for more).

Sensitivity may be needed because some young children will be surprised or even taken aback to hear that they are actually a type of animal, with all the negative connotations associated with the everyday, beast-like meaning. In addition, bear in mind that with any discussion about human evolution, the scientific view may conflict with the beliefs of children from families with strong religious ideals. A study from Botswana found that pupils were generally accurate when classifying animal species. but because of their strong Christian faith were adamant that people were not part of the animal kingdom. Similarly, children in Saudi Arabia subject to an Islamic worldview where creationism is a fact, rejected humans as animals. However, some Saudi children were able to compartmentalize their thoughts: they affirmed the religious view while at the same time agreeing with the scientific position that humans are mammals.

Sources: Alanazi (2018); Chen and Ku (1998); Papadopoulou and Athanasiou (2015); Tema (1989); Yen *et al.* (2007).

2.9 What is a plant?

Misconception

All plants have flowers with coloured petals, green leaves, and a stem. They can be grown in a plant pot.

Scientific conception

Indeed, many plants meet the criteria as laid out in the above misconception statement. Others may not be judged by children as being plants, e.g. trees, grass, vegetables, and non-flowering plants, such as mosses and ferns. These ideas may be underpinned by the related misconception that 'a flower' is the whole plant, including petals, stem, and leaves, as in 'a bunch of flowers'. The origins of these misconceptions lie partly in the fact that domestic plants in pots and gardens are the most familiar to children and tend to have large, attractive coloured petals because they serve an ornamental function around the home. These ideas are sometimes held in parallel with the belief that plants are not living things (see 1.2). An associated misconception is that in a garden there are two types of things that grow – plants and weeds, the difference being that for something to be called a plant, it needs to be purposely cultivated by humans.

Taxonomically, there is a wide variety of organisms in the plant kingdom (Figure 2.9). An important criterion that must be met before something is called a plant is that it uses sunlight to make its own food, a process known as photosynthesis. So as a rule of thumb, anything that looks plant-like and is green is likely to be a plant because plants have the green photosynthetic pigment **chlorophyll**. That said, there are a small minority of plants that do not photosynthesize (the myco-heterotrophs) and instead are parasites, gaining nutrients from other living things.

Some learners classify fungi as plants because on first inspection they appear to be plant-like and many are rooted in the soil. In the past, fungi used

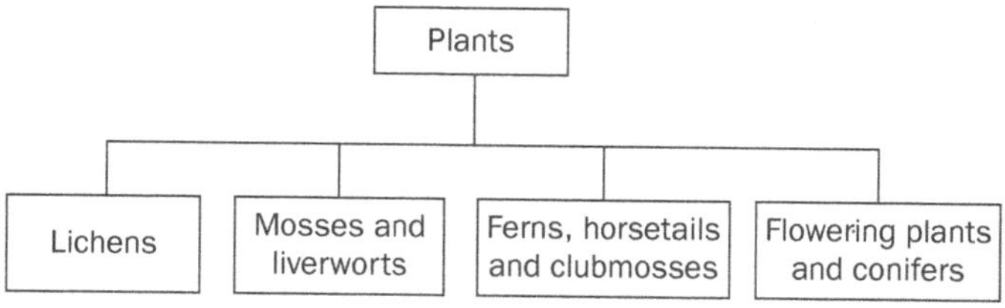

Figure 2.9 The plant kingdom

to be classified as plants but modern taxonomy has allocated them their own kingdom because they are all non-photosynthetic, which is why mushrooms, toadstools, and yeasts are rarely green. Some tiny single-celled creatures such as *Chlamydomonas* are not plants but can still photosynthesize, falling within the protoctist kingdom (single-celled, not bacteria), which serves to further complicate the situation (see Figure 2.1).

Did you know?

The algae. These include the seaweeds and phytoplankton and are perhaps surprisingly not classified as plants even though they can photosynthesize. Because they lack the proper roots, stems and leaves that are normally associated with plants, algae instead belong to the protoctist kingdom (2.1).

Reconstruction

As with 2.1, the four kingdoms of animal, plant, fungi, and 'single-cell' could be shown to the class who are then asked, *which set would a fern best fall into?* In addition, although the material is beyond KS2, if the taxonomy in Figure 2.9 can be successfully explained to children, this would help them appreciate the variety of life found in the plant kingdom. This could be extended by asking children to classify a collection of pictures or living examples of a variety of plants belonging to the different phyla.

Sources: Bell (1981); Villarroel *et al.* (2018).

Note

1 'Invertebrate' is not an official taxonomic term, but a name used to collectively describe several groups (phyla) of animals without backbones (see 2.3). In primary schools, invertebrates are often called 'mini-beasts'.

Planning and assessment sheet 2 How living things are classified
(For suggestions on how to use this sheet, see p. xxviii.)

Misconception	*Attainment re. expected standard*		
	Working towards	*Working at*	*Working above*
Year 1: *Animals including humans*			
Humans are not animals (2.8)	✓	✓	✓
All animals are furry and have four legs (2.1)	✓	✓	✓
Invertebrates such as insects and earthworms are not animals (2.1)	✓	✓	✓
Vertebrates such as fish, snakes, and birds are not animals (2.1)	✓	✓	✓
'Creepy crawlies' such as woodlice, centipedes, and spiders are insects (2.5)	✓	✓	
A bee is not an animal because it is an insect (mutual exclusivity errors) (2.2)	✓	✓	✓
Year 4: *Living things and their habitats*			
Crabs and centipedes are vertebrates because they have a hard covering on their backs (2.3)	✓	✓	✓
A turtle has no bones, so is an invertebrate (2.3)	✓	✓	✓
'Flexible' animals such as eels, snakes, and cats have no backbones (2.3)	✓	✓	
Earthworms are invertebrates, so snakes must be too (2.4)	✓	✓	
All plants have flowers with coloured petals, green leaves, and a stem (2.9)	✓	✓	
All plants are grown in a plant pot (2.9)	✓		
'A flower' is the whole plant, including petals, stem, and leaves (as in 'a bunch of flowers') (2.9)	✓	✓	
In a garden there are two types of things that grow – plants and weeds (i.e. weeds are not plants) (2.9)	✓	✓	✓
Mushrooms and toadstools are plants (2.9)	✓	✓	✓
Year 5: *Animals including humans*			
Only humans die; other living things cannot die (2.8)	✓		

(continued)

(continued)

Year 6: *Living things and their habitats*			
Animals such as turtles, penguins, and seals that live both on land and in water, are amphibians (2.6)	✓	✓	
Newts are reptiles (2.6)	✓	✓	✓
All animals that live in water are fish (e.g. crabs, tadpoles, squids, dolphins, and whales) (2.7)	✓	✓	
A bat is a type of bird (2.7)	✓	✓	
Starfish and jellyfish are types of fish (2.7)	✓	✓	✓
Ostriches and penguins are not birds because they cannot fly (2.7)	✓	✓	

3

Blood circulation

Conceptual areas covered in this chapter:

- Anatomy of the circulatory system
- How the heart and blood vessels work together to keep body cells alive
- The importance of blood in moving different materials around the body

National Curriculum links:

Year 6: *Animals including humans*

3.1 Where is the heart?

Misconception

The heart is at the left side of the chest.

Scientific conception

Children often draw the heart as a valentine cartoon shape ♥ and think it lies on the left side of the chest (Figure 3.1a).[1] The common practice of people holding the left side of their chest at the nipple level when doing a 'broken heart' or 'I love you' action shows the widespread nature of the myth, as do comic strips and animated cartoons.

The heart lies at the centre of the chest, behind the breastbone, and is about the size of a clenched fist (Figure 3.1b). The shape of the human heart *approximately* resembles a valentine heart shape, having a pointy bottom and a minor indentation at the top (separating the two top chambers, called atria), though it

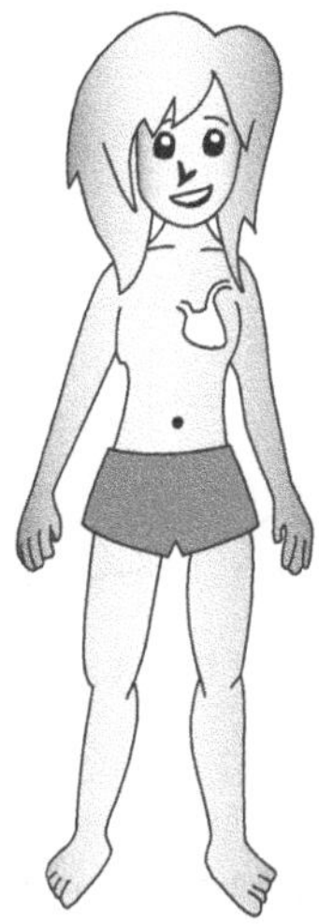

Figure 3.1a My heart lies at the left side of my chest (misconception)

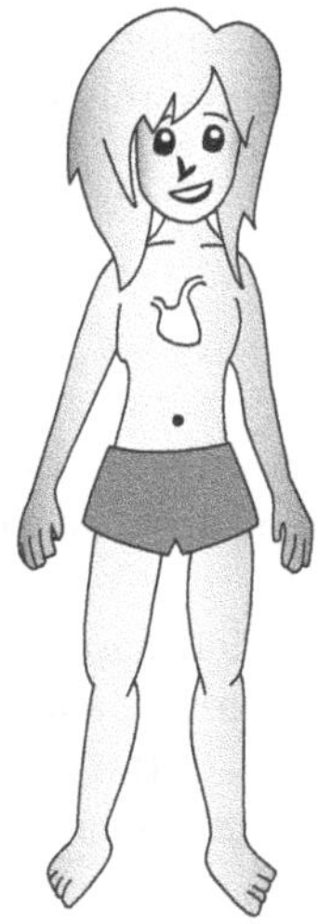

Figure 3.1b True anatomical position of the heart

should be made clear to children that drawing a valentine heart is scientifically inaccurate; a non-symmetrical pointed oval is a better simple representation at primary level (Figure 3.1c). Note that the bottom of the heart points over

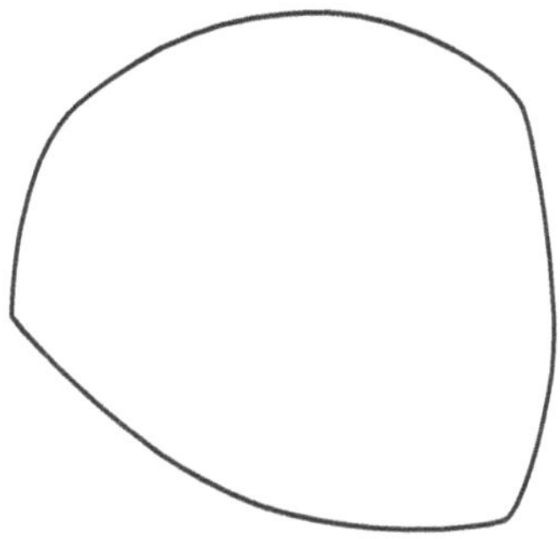

Figure 3.1c A simple way to draw the heart

towards the left and so slightly more of the heart's mass is actually in the left half of the chest (Figure 3.1b).

The heart is one of the first internal organs that young children become aware of. The 'heartbeat' (pulse) can be felt if the palm of the hand is pressed firmly just below the left nipple; if you place the hand over the breastbone where the heart actually lies, there is no discernible pulse. This is one likely source for the misconception, although what you can feel on the left side of the chest is not the heart itself beating, but instead the pulse **wave** travelling through the great **arteries** that leave the heart on the left side.

Reconstruction

As discussed later in Chapter 5, posters or organ vests are useful for the elicitation of ideas, end-of-topic assessment, or to reinforce previous learning. Commercial plastic anatomical models are quite expensive but very effective at demonstrating the heart's true position as well as the location of other internal organs.

Ask children to feel with their left hand where the bottom of their breastbone ends, just where the squashy abdomen begins, and keep the left hand at that position – exactly in the middle of the torso. Make a clenched fist with the right hand and sit it on top of the left hand – this will locate the position and the fist gives the approximate size of the heart. Mention that during cardiopulmonary resuscitation (**CPR**) the heart is massaged by pressing onto the breastbone and not on the left side of the chest.

Sources: Bartoszeck *et al.* (2011); Osborne *et al.* (1992).

3.2 Blood vessels

Misconception

Blood is not found in blood vessels, it sloshes around freely inside the body.

Scientific conception

KS1 children especially may not appreciate that there are blood vessels inside the body, instead believing that blood is held in by the skin in a similar way to how a party balloon can be filled with water. Their blood is free to splash around and when they move their bodies, this makes the blood inside them move as well; this is one type of *hollow body model* (Figure 3.2). (See Chapter 5 for similarities to hollow body models of digestion.) If a child has an accident and cuts or scrapes their skin, blood seeps slowly out, giving the illusion that the skin acts as a 'bag' for blood and, when broken, this allows blood to escape or spill out.

Blood inside the body is contained in tubes called blood vessels, of which there are three main types: arteries carry blood away from the heart and towards body tissues; **veins** do the opposite, carrying blood away from tissues and towards the heart; while **capillaries** are tiny, **microscopic** blood vessels that join arteries to veins.[1] With minor cuts to the skin, the bleeding that occurs is due to broken capillaries, which are so small they cannot be seen with the naked eye, giving the illusion of blood seeping out just because the skin itself has been broken.

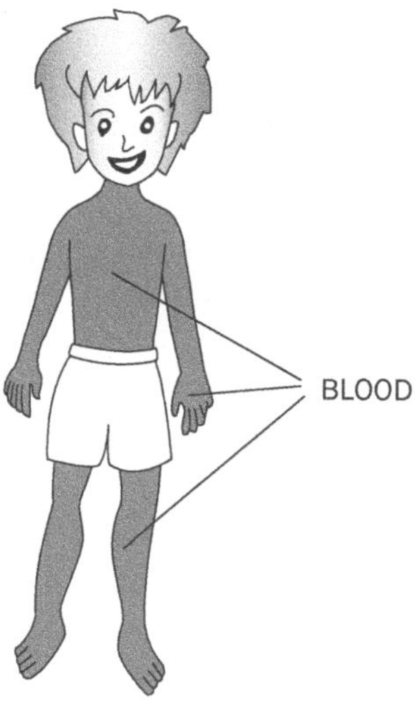

Figure 3.2 Hollow body model of blood circulation (misconception)

Reconstruction

Children's attention can be drawn to the fact that their own bodies have blood vessels that can be seen or felt. With paler skins, blue veins are clearly visible where the skin is at its thinnest, for example, at the inside of the wrist, the ankle, and the temple (although veins are not really blue, see 3.5). Parts of the body where a pulse can be felt are the sites of major arteries, and include the wrist, the neck, the armpit, and at the top of the inside of the thigh. Using a stethoscope to listen at these sites allows children to hear the sound of the pulse, and sometimes blood can be heard rushing through the arteries like water through a pipe. These can be linked with an activity that investigates how pulse rate changes with exercise (3.4). A simple task for KS1 children can help orient their thinking towards blood circulation, especially the link between exercise and heart rate. In an open space such as the playground or school hall, ask the class to run around vigorously for about a minute, then stop – they will be able to hear the pulse throbbing in their ears.

The circulatory system appears in the National Curriculum in Year 6 and some children may not naturally associate the heart with blood, instead seeing the two as completely different body systems. When asked to draw the body's internal structures, if they do include blood vessels on their pictures, they rarely draw them connected to the heart. Explaining that the heart's job is to pump blood around the body through 'pipes' or 'tubes' would be an appropriate starting point for describing the role of blood vessels. By looking at circulation as a holistic system in this way would make it easier to understand and can be accompanied with video animations that show the general circulation of blood around the body. Although the content is well beyond KS2, the website www.visiblebody.com has a variety of animations of body systems that are useful visualizations.

As a demonstration that blood moves around the body in arteries, first ask a child to locate the radial pulse at their right wrist. Place a tennis ball under their right armpit and if they squeeze it fairly tightly, they will no longer be able to feel their radial pulse; this is because the brachial artery in their armpit is being compressed, stopping the flow of blood down the arm. Importantly, the tennis ball should only be squeezed for a few seconds at most, enough to stop the radial pulse, then be immediately released. First aiders apply pressure in this same spot to stem severe bleeding in the hand or aim.

Sources: Dameraua *et al.* (2022); Osborne *et al.* (1992); Westman and Karlsson (2016).

Did you know?

The length of the human circulatory system. If all the blood vessels from a single human body were removed and placed end-to-end, their total length would reach about 100,000 km, which is equivalent to 2½ times around the Earth. This is because capillaries are so tiny that many millions can be squeezed into small spaces within body tissues.

3.3 Are the heart and muscles joined together?

Misconception

Our heart beats faster during exercise to work our muscles.

Scientific conception

Some children believe that the heart pumps air (not blood) around the body down narrow tubes to make the muscles move during exercise, as part of a kind of **pneumatic**-style machine system. The idea might be constructed from experience with bicycle pumps, where if you put work into the system at the hand pump end, air is forced through tubes and the tyre is inflated at the other end. Many Year 6 children are aware that oxygen is a gas that we **breathe** in and is necessary for survival, but may extrapolate that knowledge to reason that the heart pumps oxygen *gas* around the body to keep cells alive.

The heart pumps liquid blood and not gaseous air around the body. As blood moves away from the heart and towards muscles, it contains oxygen and food that the muscle cells need to sustain themselves (for use in **cellular respiration**). During exercise, our muscles work harder and so need a greater supply of oxygen and food. To meet these extra needs, the heart beats more quickly and with greater force to speed up blood flow and deliver these much-needed materials to muscles at a faster rate. Blood also removes wastes such as dissolved carbon dioxide from muscle cells – during exercise more waste material is produced and because blood is moving faster, it can be removed more quickly.

A related misconception that may form part of a meaningful erroneous conceptual network is that we breathe more quickly and deeply during exercise to supply the muscles with 'more air' (also see 4.3). Other misconceptions regarding the role of the heart are that its job is to cleanse the blood, it is where the blood is reoxygenated, and it is the site of our emotions.

Reconstruction

As mentioned in 3.2, when the circulatory system is taught in Year 6, some children may not link the heart with blood, so first establishing the heart's job as a

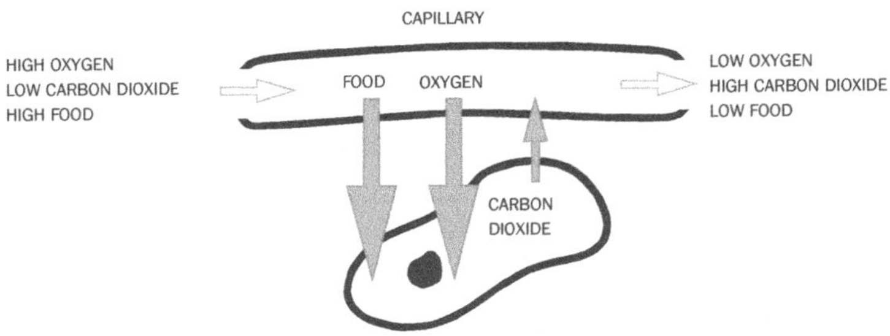

Figure 3.3 A simple model showing the exchange of materials between blood in a capillary and a cell

pump for blood circulation is essential. To extend this concept, and although beyond the simple ideas laid out in the Programme of Study, a basic understanding of the exchange of materials between cells and the blood would help children to construct an appropriate mental model: the blood system delivers oxygen and food to muscles and takes away dissolved carbon dioxide and other wastes (Figure 3.3). Integrating these ideas into a wider picture of circulation, including the role of the lungs, would provide a more holistic explanation that may make more sense to children (see Chapter 4). This model of the exchange of materials can be practised through a role-play exercise where children circulate around the classroom acting as 'the blood', dropping off and picking up substances at appropriate points in the room that represent different parts of the body. This role play of the exchanges at body cells can be used simultaneously with role plays involving other bodily processes such as **gaseous exchange** at the lungs, and the addition of food to the general blood circulation at the liver. It is helpful if children understand that although blood contains oxygen and carbon dioxide, they are not carried in their true gaseous state. Oxygen is chemically joined to haemoglobin in red blood cells, while carbon dioxide is dissolved in the liquid part of blood (**plasma**) in a similar way to how carbon dioxide gas is dissolved in carbonated soft drinks.

This work can be linked with teaching the muscular system in Year 3. Commercially available anatomical models show how the biceps and triceps muscles contract and relax to move the arm. However, because these model muscles are driven by an air pump system, this can reinforce the misconception, so if a model is used, children must be reminded that muscles are not in reality driven by air. Comparisons can also be made with the 'circulatory system' of a flowering plant. Plants do not contain blood but still transport vital materials by means of tubes called xylem and phloem that run throughout their roots, stem, leaves, growing tips, etc.

Sources: Chavan and Khandagale (2022); Westbrook and Marek (1992); Westman and Karlsson (2016).

3.4 What makes your heart rate increase?

Misconception

The only time my heart beats more quickly is when I exercise.

Scientific conception

Children who believe misconceptions such as 'the heart pumps just to make the muscles work' (3.3) can further reason that if the muscles are not working vigorously, as during exercise, there is no need for the heart to beat any faster, no matter what the circumstances. However, during periods when the body is at rest, a person's heart rate may still become elevated. Drugs such as caffeine, nicotine, and asthma medicines all increase heart rate even when a person is not exercising. Being ill can also elevate heart rate, such as having a thyroid abnormality, anxiety disorder, high blood pressure, or simply having a raised body temperature due to infection.

Humans (and vertebrates generally) have evolved bodily responses to any expected threat that help them deal with dangerous situations – these are called *fight-or-flight* **adaptations**. When we feel threatened, the body prepares itself for immediate physical action by increasing the supply of blood to the muscles so they can work more effectively to fight the threat or run away. Blood pressure becomes raised, breathing is deeper and more rapid to increase oxygen levels in the blood, more sugar is released into the blood to provide food for muscles, and the digestive system is shut down to allow more blood to be diverted to muscles. The fight-or-flight response can also be triggered by relatively non-threatening situations such as anxiety during a job interview, riding a roller-coaster, or watching a scary film.

A related misconception is that during exercise, heart and breathing rates increase to keep the whole body at the same temperature.

Reconstruction

A traditional activity is to have children measure their resting heart rates using stopwatches, then take part in some vigorous physical activity such as dancing or doing steps on a bench. Immediately after the activity stops, measure the heart rate again to see how much it has been raised, and repeat the measurement every two minutes until the resting rate is regained. The speed at which the resting rate is reached after exercise has finished is a measure of physical fitness and is called the 'recovery rate'. Children often have difficulties finding their pulse and it is generally easier for them to locate their carotid pulse (neck) and not their radial pulse (wrist). The quickest way to find the carotid pulse is to make a cup shape with your hand, then place the fingers and thumb either side of the Adam's apple (larynx) touching it on both sides. Press the hand gently inwards around the sides of the larynx and the pulse should be felt. Do not press directly onto the larynx at any time. Note that contrary to popular belief, girls also have an Adam's apple but it is less pronounced. Alternately, use an electronic pulse meter that children can wear on a finger or the wrist – these can be purchased for about £10 each (see Box pp. 60–61).

To address the misconception that only exercising can affect heart rate, it will be necessary to have a child experience a short period of mild psychological stress. Find a paper dot-to-dot puzzle but use correcting fluid to mask one of the numbers near to the end of the sequence, then photocopy the puzzle so that it is not obvious that the number has been erased. Have a child wear an electronic pulse meter, preferably one that can be connected to a computer so that pulse rate can be visually displayed for the rest of the class to see. Have the child start the puzzle but say that this will be a timed exercise where the object is to finish as quickly as possible. When the child cannot find the missing number they will experience a brief period of anxiety as they search frantically for something that is not there. Pulse rate should increase during this time as the body senses a threat and reacts with a fight-or-flight response. After pulse rate elevation has been demonstrated, stop the activity and let the child in on the secret, explaining when people's hearts beat more quickly this is sometimes caused by things other than exercise.

Sources: Pasco and Ennis (2015); Westman and Karlsson (2016).

Learning technologies

Heart rate monitors. When children carry out a science activity that requires them to record heart rate (see 3.4), they need to be able to take their own or another child's pulse. However, children frequently have difficulties with first finding the pulse, and then performing an accurate count of the number of pulses per minute (they miss some beats). Electronic heart rate monitors are a good alternative to having to take a pulse manually and are cheaply available online, starting from around £10. The monitors are simple to use and just require a child to clip them onto the end of their finger. They work by shining a bright **LED** at the skin, detecting the pulse through the movement of blood in tiny vessels in the finger, then calculating heart rate. The display is easy for children to read, though many monitors also have a function that measures the blood's oxygen saturation level at the same time, so users will need to pay attention to the correct numbers on the output display. One disadvantage of these monitors is that they sometimes provide inaccurate results if the user is physically moving around, so heart rate needs to be measured while sitting quietly. Over recent years, activity trackers such as *Fitbit* have become common, which are worn on the wrist and measure heart rate in the same way. More reliable heart rate monitors are expensive and designed for use during exercise – these are worn as a band around the chest and detect the electrical activity of the heart. Datalogger equipment is available that is designed for educational use where a child's heart rate can be linked to a computer and displayed for the whole class to see on the interactive whiteboard, although they only allow one child to be tested at a time, unlike a class set of the cheaper heart rate monitors (see Chapter 16 for more on dataloggers).

3.5 The colour of blood

Misconception

The blood in our veins is blue.

Scientific conception

It is commonly believed that blood in the arteries is red while blood in the veins is blue. Higher-attaining upper KS2 children can assume that blood rich in oxygen is bright red, and as this blood travels around the body, oxygen levels are reduced as cells take oxygen and dump waste carbon dioxide into it (Figure 3.3). This low-oxygen (deoxygenated) blood then enters the veins, being dark blue or purple in colour. They may also believe that when **venous** blood makes contact with the air, for instance, as a result of injury, the blue blood turns immediately bright red as it absorbs oxygen from the atmosphere.

In fact, venous blood is not blue, it is deep red – as can be witnessed when a doctor draws a blood sample from a vein using a transparent syringe; arterial blood is a brighter red because of increased oxygen levels. The chemical haemoglobin gives blood its red colour, changing its shade depending on whether oxygen is present or absent. The blue colour of veins as seen through paler skins acts as a source for this misconception, which is further reinforced by diagrams in textbooks that show, for reasons of ease of understanding, the arterial system in red and the venous system in blue.[2]

Despite venous blood being dark red, veins appear to be blue due to a false impression of colour – the bluish tinge of veins is merely an optical illusion (partly caused by a phenomenon known as *Rayleigh scattering*). As light is reflected from dark red deoxygenated blood in veins and up through the skin towards an observer's eyes, the blue parts of the reflected light spread out and penetrate the most, so that only blue light leaves the surface of the skin, making the veins appear blue (see Chapter 16 for more on how we see different colours). This effect can also be seen during *cyanosis* – blue lips and skin – a symptom of low blood oxygen that occurs during asthma attacks, heart failure, asphyxiation, and other conditions.

Reconstruction

Even though the study of blood and blood vessels appears in the Year 6 Programme of Study, an explanation of the science behind the illusion of blue venous blood is probably beyond what most teachers would deem appropriate to introduce at KS2. However, showing a video clip of venous blood being drawn from a patient would help children realize that the blood in veins is actually red. This can be readily sourced using an internet search; be aware of sensitivity issues – some children may find this uncomfortable viewing.

Sources: Loukas *et al.* (2018); Schoon and Boone (1998).

Notes

1 The anatomy is more complex than described here and well beyond KS2. Small arteries are called arterioles and small veins are venules – capillaries actually link arterioles to venules, not arteries to veins.

2 With the pulmonary artery and pulmonary vein this convention is reversed, with textbooks (appropriately) showing the former as blue and the latter as red. This is because the pulmonary artery takes blood away from the heart but is unusual because the blood is deoxygenated, and vice versa for the pulmonary vein.

Planning and assessment sheet 3 Blood circulation

(For suggestions on how to use this sheet, see p. xxviii.)

Misconception	*Attainment re. expected standard*		
	Working towards	*Working at*	*Working above*
Year 6: *Animals including humans*			
The heart lies at the left side of the chest (3.1)	✓	✓	✓
Drawing the heart as a valentine cartoon shape ♥ (3.1)	✓	✓	
Blood is not contained in blood vessels; it sloshes around freely inside the body (hollow body model) (3.2)	✓		
Our heart beats faster during exercise, pumping air (or oxygen gas) to make our muscles work (3.3)	✓	✓	
We breathe more quickly and deeply during exercise to supply the muscles with more air (or oxygen gas) (3.3)	✓	✓	
The heart's job is to cleanse the blood (3.3)		✓	✓
Blood is reoxygenated in the heart (3.3)		✓	
The heart is the site of our emotions (3.3)	✓	✓	
The only time my heart beats more quickly is when I exercise (3.4)	✓		
During exercise, heart and breathing rates increase to keep the whole body at the same temperature (3.4)			✓
Girls do not have an Adam's apple (larynx) (3.4)	✓	✓	✓
The blood in our veins is blue (3.5)	✓	✓	✓

4

Breathing

Conceptual areas covered in this chapter:

- Anatomy of the respiratory system
- How the lungs and heart are connected
- The respiratory and circulatory systems work closely together to maintain oxygen and carbon dioxide levels in the blood
- How the air we breathe in is different to the air we breathe out

National Curriculum links:

Year 6: *Animals including humans*

4.1 Why do we breathe?

Misconception

We just breathe air in and out – air has no further purpose.

Scientific conception

KS1 children are aware of the sensation of breathing and know that if they stop breathing, this leads to feelings of discomfort. However, prior to KS2 they receive little formal instruction about the role of the human respiratory system and may not realize that they need to breathe air to survive. Some will associate breathing with the lungs, being able to locate these organs somewhere in the chest, neck, or abdomen (see 4.2). They may have little understanding of the reasons for breathing and if they do know that it is an essential process for staying alive, they rarely consider that the air they breathe in is different to the air they breathe out.

As will be explained later in 4.4, the differences between inhaled and exhaled air are not as stark as is commonly expected. The differences reflect the processes of oxygen being absorbed into the blood together with carbon dioxide and water being excreted from the blood, again discussed later (4.3). A related misconception is the idea that after air is inhaled, it remains inside the head, merely circulating around briefly before being immediately breathed out, without change. Children can incorrectly attribute human-like characteristics to the respiratory systems of other animals; for instance, thinking that earthworms breathe using lungs (they do not breathe in the formal sense – gaseous exchange occurs through their moist skins). Although this is beyond the primary curriculum, it is worthwhile addressing such misconceptions if they arise.

Reconstruction

Although the respiratory system does not appear in the primary Programme of Study, its workings are closely connected with the circulatory system (Chapter 3) and so children will need some understanding of the physiology of breathing to fully comprehend blood circulation. An activity previously mentioned (3.2) and suitable for KS1 is to ask the children to run around quickly in the playground for a minute and then stop, feeling how their breathing has changed from rest, and listening to their blood pumping in their ears. Explain that during exercise our muscles need extra oxygen and food, and the heart and lungs provide these by working harder. Any sense of vagueness that children might have about the reason why they breathe air needs to be addressed in the wider context of the role of the respiratory system as an absorber of oxygen, and a remover of carbon dioxide and water. Demonstrating that there are differences between inhaled and exhaled air will help children understand that there are changes taking place deep within their lungs. Place a burning candle under an inverted tall glass containing normal (atmospheric) air, and time how long it takes for the candle flame to be extinguished (Figure 4.1). Repeat the process, this time with exhaled air in the tall glass. The candles go out because all the oxygen within the sealed glasses is used up and carbon dioxide is produced in its place. In the glass with exhaled air, the flame splutters a little and goes out well before that in the glass with normal air, because the air we breathe out has higher levels of carbon dioxide and lower levels of oxygen.

Be aware that showing inhaled and exhaled air are different can act as a trigger for the misconception that exhaled air is mainly carbon dioxide, which may need to be addressed separately (4.4).

Sources: Arnaudin and Mintzes (1985); Gellert (1962); Pasco and Ennis (2015); Sarwanto *et al.* (2021).

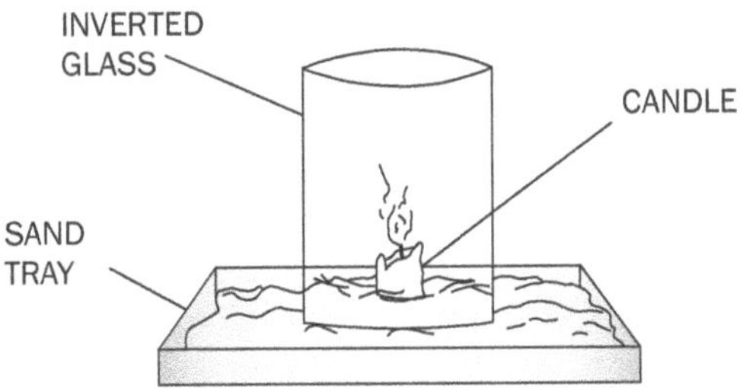

Figure 4.1 Using a candle and an inverted glass to compare exhaled air with normal air

4.2 Where are the lungs found?

> **Misconception**
>
> *The lungs are in the 'stomach'.*

Scientific conception

Typically, primary children are aware that breathing involves a part of their body called the lungs, though they often have difficulty in correctly identifying exactly where their lungs are located. A common idea is that they are found in the abdomen, which in humans is the area below the ribs and above the pelvis that children call the stomach, tummy, or belly (Figure 4.2a). The lungs are actually located in the chest area of the body, just below the collarbone and above the bottom of the ribs (Figure 4.2b). However, when we breathe normally while at rest, our chest does not move very much but our abdomen is seen to noticeably rise and fall, which is a likely source of this misconception. When we inhale, our lungs expand and a sheet of muscle called the diaphragm pushes down on the organs below the ribs, making the abdomen swell; the opposite happens when we exhale and the abdomen shrinks back.

Children may also think that the stomach itself is responsible for breathing and do not consider the lungs at all. They understand that the body needs food and this is collected in the stomach, and similarly the body needs air, which is collected in the same place. A related misconception is thinking the lungs are in the neck area, linked with the idea that air is breathed in, remains in the head and neck and is then breathed out, serving no further purpose (see 4.1).

Even if children know that the lungs are located within the chest, they frequently draw them too small, when in fact the lungs fill the entire chest cavity from collarbone down almost to the bottom of the ribcage (Figure 4.2b).

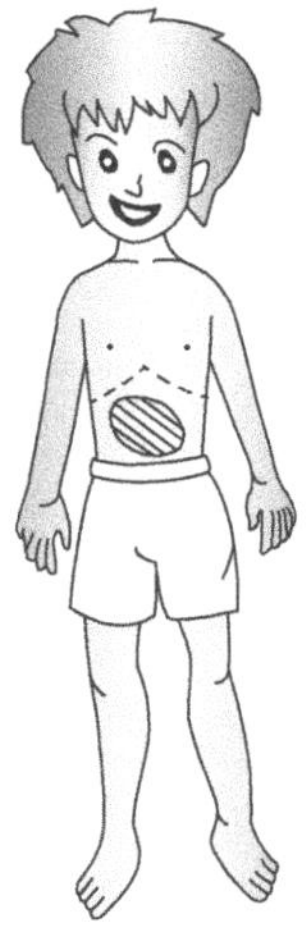

Figure 4.2a The lungs are in the abdomen[1] (misconception)

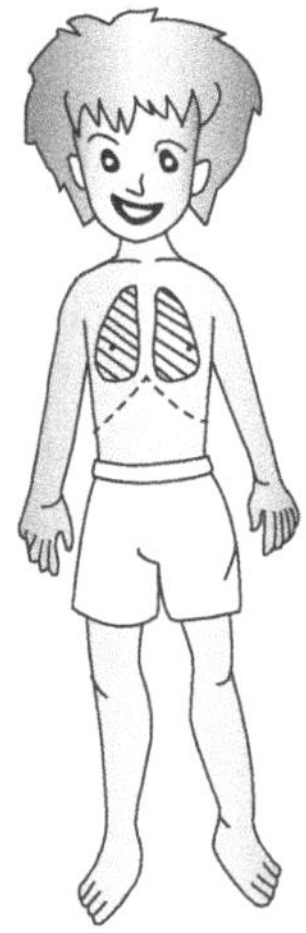

Figure 4.2b Actual location of the lungs

Reconstruction

A straightforward way to show the location of the lungs is to use an anatomical 3D plastic model. These are quite expensive but worth purchasing if possible because children find them fascinating and I have found them to be an excellent learning tool. Although during normal breathing the chest does not move noticeably, when we take vigorous exercise our breathing becomes much deeper (and faster) and the rise and fall of the chest are very clear as we 'get out of breath', revealing the true position of the lungs.

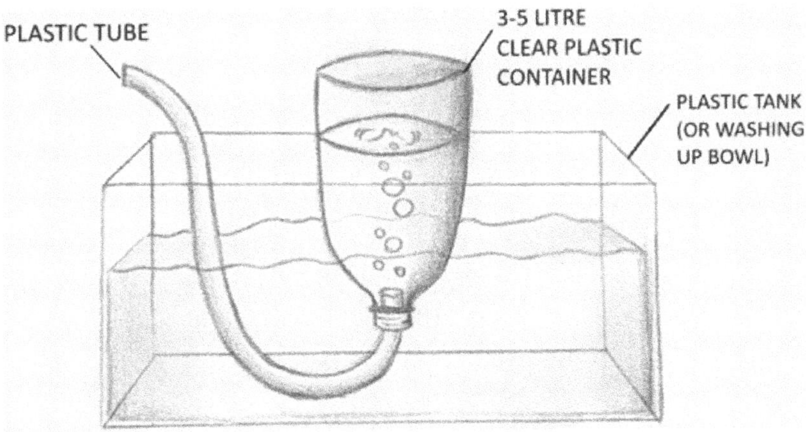

Figure 4.2c Measuring the lungs' vital capacity

Even if children are aware of the rise and fall of their chest, they may not automatically link this with the true cause – the lungs expand and contract during breathing. As mentioned, children often draw the lungs smaller than their actual size; if they comprehend the true size and position of the lungs, including the fact they expand during inhalation, this will help them link the chest's rise and fall, with the lungs' expansion and contraction. A traditional activity is to measure the lungs' vital capacity using a plastic tube, a washing-up bowl ¾ filled with water, and a 3–5-litre clear plastic container (Figure 4.2c). Fill the container with water and place it inverted into the washing-up bowl, ensuring the container's mouth is underwater. Children take a deep breath and blow though the tube, emptying their lungs' **volume** of air into the container; it is surprising how much air even a child's lungs can hold. Hygienic considerations include having children use disposable plastic mouthpieces that have been sterilized in Milton fluid beforehand.

Source: Dameraua *et al.* (2022); Fokides and Mastrokoukou (2018).

4.3 How are the heart and lungs connected?

Misconception

The lungs send air to the heart, then the heart pumps air around the body.

Scientific conception

At primary level, children learn that when they breathe, air enters the body through the nose and mouth and travels down the 'air tubes'[2] to the lungs. They

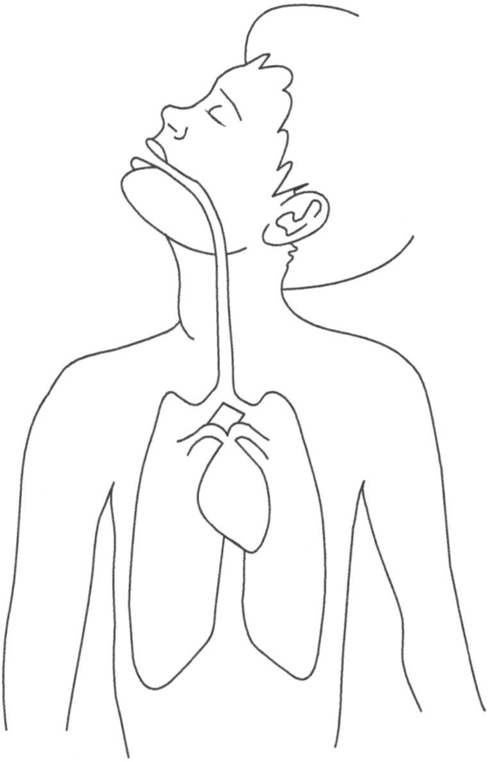

Figure 4.3a Air tubes lead directly from the lungs to the heart (misconception)

may also learn that oxygen from inhaled air enters the blood, which then transports the oxygen around the body (along with other materials, such as food). For many, the movement of oxygen gas from the air into the liquid blood is a mysterious process, and they may rationalize it by assuming that the air that they breathe into their lungs travels directly to their heart through further air tubes and then enters the bloodstream at the heart (Figure 4.3a; see also child's comment in Box on p. 69).

I think . . .

Linking circulation with breathing. *'[Your heart] helps you to breathe'* (9-year-old child; Osborne *et al.*, 1992, p. 33).

In reality, the process is more complex. After a breath of air is inhaled, it eventually ends up in air sacs (**alveoli**) deep inside the lungs. At the alveoli, oxygen in that air sample passes into the blood across tiny thin-walled blood

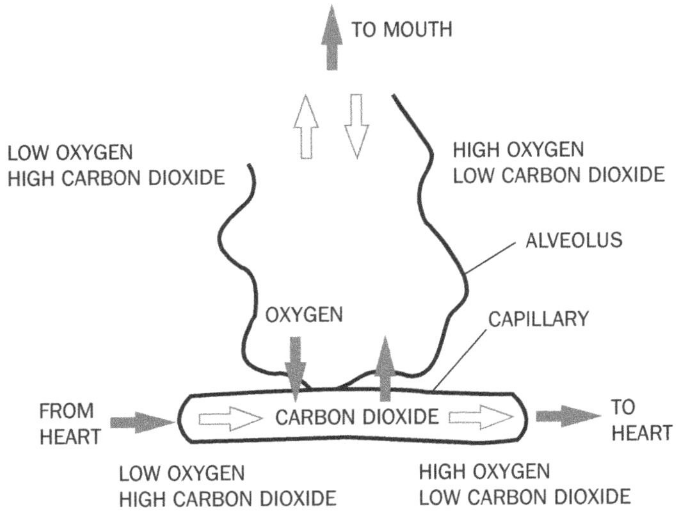

Figure 4.3b Gaseous exchange in the lungs

vessels called capillaries (see Chapter 3 and Figure 4.3b). At the same time, carbon dioxide – a waste gas produced by all body cells – leaves the blood and enters the alveoli, ready to be breathed out and removed from the body in exhaled air. Blood is pumped continuously through the capillaries in the lungs, and when this blood leaves the alveoli, it is 'refreshed', being rich in oxygen and low in carbon dioxide. Equally, the air that leaves the lungs when we exhale is 'spent' and is higher in carbon dioxide and lower in oxygen.

The heart really does two separate jobs. The first is well known – to pump blood around the body to deliver oxygen to cells and remove carbon dioxide from those same cells (Figure 4.3b). Its second job is to replenish the blood's oxygen and get rid of the carbon dioxide, which it does by sending blood on a separate journey around the lungs (Figure 4.3c). As this diagram shows, the circulatory system can be thought of as two separate circuits that meet in the heart. 'Used' blood low in oxygen and high in carbon dioxide enters the heart after a trip around the body. This blood needs to be refreshed, so is sent to the lungs; when the blood returns to the heart, it is now high in oxygen and low in carbon dioxide, and so ready for another trip around the body. These ideas were first put forward by the English physician William Harvey in the seventeenth century (Box p. 72).

Considering the complexity of the double circulation, it is not surprising that some children try to make sense of how oxygen enters the blood by thinking open tubes exist so that air can pass from the lungs to the heart, allowing oxygen to directly enter the blood (see Figure 4.2a). Related misconceptions include the heart is where oxygen enters the blood, and the heart makes the muscles work by pumping air into them (3.3).

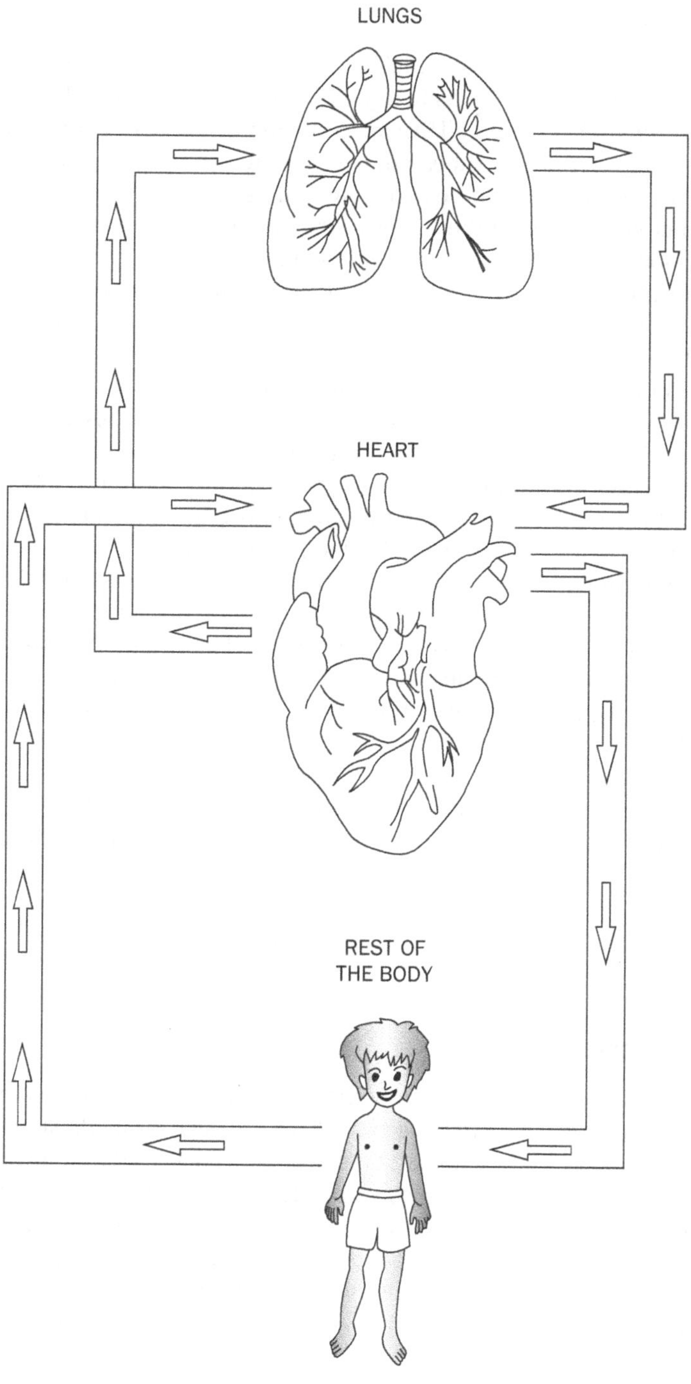

Figure 4.3c Simple diagram of the double circulation

Reconstruction

In children's drawings of the body's interior, the circulatory and respiratory systems are rarely depicted as being linked together, despite the two in reality being intimately connected. An anatomical plastic model of a human torso will help to show that air tubes connect the mouth to the lungs, but not the lungs to the heart. This can be supported by useful animations sourced from the internet showing how the lungs' blood supply connects to the rest of the body's blood circulation (try searching for 'animation pulmonary circulation'). Traditionally, a lamb's heart and lungs dissection has been used to show how the circulatory and respiratory systems are linked, although in some schools there may be ethical issues with using this pedagogy. Higher-attaining children may be able to figure out the basics of how the double circulation works by themselves. You can scaffold this understanding by first reminding the group that the heart pumps blood that is high in oxygen to body cells, then that blood returns to the heart low in oxygen because the cells have taken it away. Also say that the lungs add oxygen to the blood. Set the group the task of creating a drawing that explains how these two processes link together. This is a good example of a socio-constructivist activity where complex ideas are shared and debated before a consensus is reached. The double circulation is a difficult concept, and your own personal study of human biology in general can be supported by, for example, accessing free TV documentary programmes streamed from the BBC website: https://www.bbc.co.uk/programmes/

Sources: Arnaudin and Mintzes (1985); Chavan and Khandagale (2022); Dameraua *et al.* (2022); Garcia-Barros *et al.* (2011); Osborne *et al.* (1992); Symons *et al.* (1994); Tracana *et al.* (2012).

Famous scientists

William Harvey. Before Harvey proposed his double circulation model in 1628, physicians believed the teachings of Galen, a medical scientist who had lived in Ancient Roman times. Galen had judged that the human arterial and venous systems were completely separated and that the job of the lungs was merely to cool the blood, while the heart heated the blood. These beliefs were blended with mystical views of the heart as the place where the human spirit was located. Many physicians at the time did not accept Harvey's theory despite clear anatomical evidence, since medical thinking was generally very conservative and new ideas were not readily accepted.

4.4 What is in the air we breathe out?

Misconception

The air we breathe out air is mainly carbon dioxide and very low in oxygen.

Scientific conception

This is a common misunderstanding, often expressed as *we breathe in oxygen and breathe out carbon dioxide*. Children learn that the job of the lungs is to take in oxygen and get rid of unwanted carbon dioxide, so it makes sense to them that most or all what humans breathe out will contain this waste gas. This idea may link to the related misconception that inhaled air is pure oxygen, to form a meaningful though erroneous conceptual network.

In fact, exhaled air only contains around 4% carbon dioxide; this compares with about 0.04% carbon dioxide in inhaled air. Furthermore, the air we breathe into our lungs (atmospheric air) has an oxygen content of 21% and, contrary to popular opinion, our lungs do not absorb all this oxygen, only around a fifth of it. It could be argued therefore that the air we breathe out is not hugely different to the air we breathe in, even though carbon dioxide is 100 times more concentrated in exhaled air (Table 4.4). The gas that makes up most of both inhaled and exhaled air is neither oxygen nor carbon dioxide, but nitrogen, which enters and leaves the lungs at the same concentration (78%). Note that the values given in Table 4.4 are for dry samples of air – inhaled air will normally contain **water vapour**, the amount of which depends on environmental humidity, which can be up to 5% of the total volume of air. Because the surface of the respiratory system is very moist, exhaled air is saturated with water, making up around 5% of its total composition – this is why on cold days we can see water droplets as a fine mist when we breathe out.

This misconception is not helped by a popular diagram that children are generally good at recalling, which implies that trees give out only oxygen and humans give out only carbon dioxide (Figure 4.4).

Table 4.4 The compositions of inhaled and exhaled air (by volume of dry samples)

Gas	*Inhaled air, %*	*Exhaled air, %*
Carbon dioxide	0.04	4
Oxygen	21	17
Nitrogen	78	78
Others	1	1

Figure 4.4 Humans give carbon dioxide to trees and trees give oxygen to humans (misconception)

Reconstruction

Ask children to carefully waft a gentle breeze onto a **glowing splint** using a piece of stiff material such as a piece of A4 card. Why does it glow more brightly? The answer is that we are 'feeding' the smouldering fire with a stream of atmospheric air that contains 21% oxygen, which increases the rate of burning, so causing the splint to glow. Next, ask them to gently blow at the splint using a straw – as before, the splint will glow more brightly. When we blow on something, we pass exhaled air from our lungs over it so the splint glows brightly because this air still contains significant levels of oxygen, which at 17% is just 4% less concentrated than atmospheric (inhaled) air. If we breathed out pure or highly concentrated carbon dioxide, the glowing splint would be extinguished because something cannot burn when doused with carbon dioxide (which is why carbon dioxide fire extinguishers work so well).

To reinforce this idea, mention to the class that mouth-to-mouth resuscitation would not work if exhaled air was high in carbon dioxide and low in oxygen.

Source: Yip (1998).

Notes

1 Note that the dotted 'Λ' shape in some of the anatomical drawings represents the bottom of the ribs.

2 The term 'air tubes' is a simplification; more anatomical terms are the trachea, bronchi, and bronchioles.

Planning and assessment sheet 4 Breathing

(For suggestions on how to use this sheet, see p. xxviii.)

Misconception	*Attainment re. expected standard*		
	Working towards	*Working at*	*Working above*
Year 6: *Animals including humans*			
We just breathe air in and out – air has no further purpose (4.1)	✓		
After air is inhaled, it remains inside the head, merely circulating around briefly before being immediately breathed out, without change. Therefore, the lungs lie in the neck area (4.1)	✓		
Like humans, earthworms breathe using lungs (4.1)		✓	✓
The air we inhale is pure oxygen (4.1; 4.4)	✓	✓	✓
Exhaled air is mainly made up of carbon dioxide, and is very low in oxygen (4.1; 4.4)		✓	✓
The lungs lie within the abdomen ('belly') (4.2)	✓	✓	
The stomach's job is to breathe air (4.2)	✓		
The lungs send air to the heart, then the heart pumps air around the body (air tubes lead directly from the lungs to the heart) (4.3)	✓	✓	
Blood is reoxygenated in the heart (4.3)		✓	
Our muscles work because our heart pumps air (or oxygen gas) into them (4.3)	✓	✓	
Drawing the respiratory system unconnected to the circulatory system (4.3)	✓	✓	
Trees give oxygen to humans, while humans give carbon dioxide to trees (4.4)		✓	✓

5

Plant and animal nutrition

Conceptual areas covered in this chapter:	*National Curriculum links:*
• Anatomy of the digestive organs • The different functions of the digestive and urinary systems • The importance of considering food groups when planning a balanced diet • Photosynthesis in plants	Year 2: *Animals including humans; Plants* Year 3: *Animals including humans; Plants* Year 4: *Animals including humans* Year 6: *Animals including humans*

5.1 Where is the stomach located?

Misconception

My stomach is around where my navel is.

Scientific conception

In Figure 5.1a, the stomach has been drawn as a large organ that lies around the level of the navel. This popular idea originates from the everyday use of the word 'stomach' to describe the whole area at the front of the body that lies below the ribs and above the pelvis – for instance, stomach/tummy/belly ache is discomfort emanating from this area of the body.

The stomach actually sits at the level of the bottom of the ribs on the left side of the body and is much smaller than people generally realize (Figure 5.1b). The shaded area in Figure 5.1a, understood by most children to be the stomach, is anatomically part of the abdomen and contains several organs,

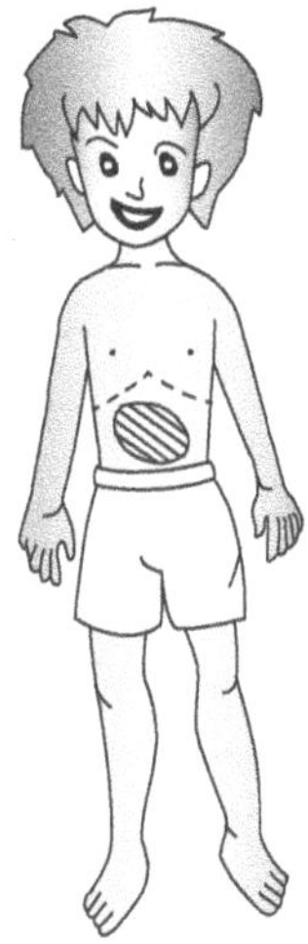

Figure 5.1a The stomach is a large organ situated around the navel area (misconception)

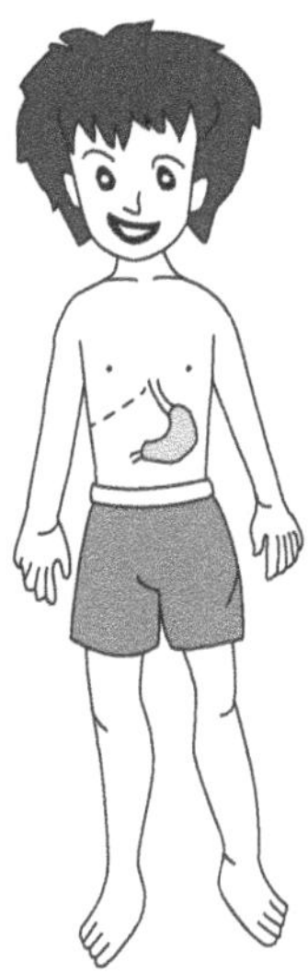

Figure 5.1b The actual anatomical position, size, and shape of the stomach

including the intestines, liver, spleen, bladder, pancreas, and the stomach itself. One source of the misconception is that after a large meal the stomach pushes downwards into the abdomen, which itself swells and makes the clothing around our waist feel tighter, giving us that feeling of being full.

There are misconceptions related to other organs in the digestive system. When children are asked to draw the internal structure of their bodies, while some will include the intestines and correctly locate them in the abdomen, they rarely differentiate between small and large intestines. They instead draw a single wiggly tube labelled 'intestines'. However, many children correctly draw different digestive organs as being joined together, e.g. oesophagus to stomach, and stomach to intestines; this linkage suggests some understanding of digestion occurring in a set sequence through a series of organs.

Reconstruction

Ask children to produce a life-sized poster of their body outline on a large piece of paper with stuck-on paper organs in the correct position. Alternatively, a fabric 'vest' can be made; this will require different organ shapes to be cut out of spare pieces of material and glued/sewn onto an old T-shirt, with the finished article worn by the children as an item of clothing. These activities can be used at the beginning of a topic to elicit misconceptions; at the end of the topic, the process may be repeated allowing children to be aware of how their learning has progressed. A common problem is that children tend not to overlap organs when they create a two-dimensional poster or drawing, which results in errors in the size and position of organs. For instance, in reality, the stomach overlaps or is overlapped by the large intestine and the left lung, the heart overlaps the lungs, and the kidneys are tucked away at the back of the body, overlapped by several organs.

Have the children physically locate their own stomachs by feeling for the bottom of their ribs just to the left of the breastbone. A commercially available plastic anatomical model of the human torso will prove very useful, helping to reinforce the real position and size of the stomach.

Sources: Dameraua *et al.* (2022); Mintzes (1984); Stears and Dempster (2017).

5.2 How the digestive system deals with food and drink

Misconception

The digestive system is made up of two separate tubes – one for faeces, the other for urine.

Scientific conception

Before they are formally taught any concepts of digestive processes, some children believe that any food they eat passes down a 'solids' tube inside their body,

Figure 5.2 The digestive system is two separate tubes (misconception)

and anything they drink travels down a separate 'liquids' tube (Figure 5.2). The solids tube is directly connected to the anus where faeces leaves the body as waste once the goodness has been absorbed from food. Similarly, the liquids tube is connected to the urinary system, which disposes of what is left over once the body has extracted all it needs from what the person has drunk.

These misconceptions are a result of children's attempts to construct a rational explanation to link the processes of eating with defecating, and drinking with urinating. They realize that there is a cause-and-effect relationship between what goes into and what leaves their bodies, particularly the knowledge that the desire to urinate often follows after taking a drink. They have a clear understanding of the start and end events, but the intervening processes are a mystery to them, taking place inside the unfathomable 'black box' of their bodies.

In fact, anything that is swallowed, whether food or drink, follows the same pathway through the digestive system. Many children appreciate that solid food goes on a journey from the mouth to the anus with nutrients ('goodness') being absorbed from the food into the bloodstream at several points during this trip. Ingested liquids such as drinks, soups, and yoghurts normally have a high water content yet travel precisely the same route as solid foods, with water being absorbed into the blood at the stomach, large intestine, and other sites. The brain detects that there is now too much water in the blood and 'tells' the kidneys to get rid of this excess water, so redressing the balance and producing the familiar feeling of the need to urinate after drinking liquids (Box p. 81). As is the case with solid foods, any nutrients contained within the liquids are absorbed by the digestive system and enter the blood, e.g. sugar in soft drinks and protein in milk (although these proteins are first broken down into simpler units, or digested).

A fuller appreciation can be gained if children understand the role of the urinary system, which clarifies the point that urine is not just the end-product of liquids that have been drunk (Box p. 81). Related misconceptions include that the body melts food during digestion, and that the stomach acts as a filtering organ sorting out the goodness from the useless parts of food.

Did you know?

The urinary system. School children and adults alike tend not to fully understand the reasons why they urinate, although there is an obvious connection between drinking liquids and urinating. Blood enters the kidneys which then act as filters, extracting waste substances the body does not need, especially urea (a by-product of protein metabolism) and drugs such as alcohol. It is acceptable to say in simple terms that the kidneys clean the blood. For these waste materials to be removed from the body, they must be dissolved in water, which is why urine is a liquid. There is more sophistication to the process, as the kidneys can adjust the amount of water they excrete according to the body's needs. For instance, on hot days we lose lots of water as sweat through the skin and so we urinate less because the body needs to conserve water to avoid dehydration. If both kidneys fail, then death will be imminent due to the build-up of waste toxins in the blood.

Reconstruction

The original misconception of there being a food tube and a liquid tube is partly accurate, and so can be used as a foundation on which to build more correct scientific ideas. Tell the children that if they reject the idea of a liquid tube, they are on the right lines, and that all swallowed material – whether liquid or solid – follows the path of the 'food tube' and is treated in a similar way by the digestive system.

Mention that the colour of urine does not usually change in response to any liquid they drink – it does not matter whether you drink water, cola, or milk, urine is still yellow. Incidentally, if large amounts of milk are drunk, faeces often takes on a whiter shade due to having a higher fat content, which supports the scientific view of a single food tube for both liquids and solids. Further discussion could cover some simple ideas about water balance. For example, urine can change its shade not because of the colour of liquids drunk, but in response to whether the body is conserving or shedding water – on hot days, our bodies lose less water in urine because of the large quantities lost as sweat, so urine has a more concentrated deep yellow tone because it contains less water.

Sources: Brinkman and Boschhuizen (1989); Equit *et al.* (2013).

5.3 What happens to food after we swallow it?

Misconception

When we eat food, it stays inside our body forever.

Scientific conception

Some Reception and younger KS1 children think that all the food that they eat stays within their body, disappearing without trace into the 'black hole' of their stomach. This is called the *stomach as storehouse model* because children are unable to imagine any further processes taking place in the digestive system once food reaches the stomach. Children who *do* understand that food travels to places beyond the stomach, and some nutrients ('goodness') are absorbed by the body, sometimes think that the material left over once digestion is complete stays in the body permanently. With this *fixed container model* children have not made the connection between the food they eat and the waste they defecate when they visit the toilet. With both the stomach as storehouse and fixed container models, children have not conserved **mass** – i.e. what goes in must come out – the mysterious disappearance of the food they have eaten is not a problem for them.

Related misconceptions include the ideas that weight gain occurs when undigested food sits permanently in the stomach, making it swell, and that food left over after digestion turns into fat in the intestines. Some children believe misconceptions that have opposite meanings to the fixed container model, where food is never stored in the body but is completely used up to provide energy (see 5.5), or that *all* the food they eat eventually passes out of the body in faeces. The Box on p. 82 highlights one child's statement about digested food that is only partly correct.

I think . . .

Food distribution. *'[The stomach] changes [the food] into blood what is good. What is not good goes down to the intestine. The heart transforms [the food] into blood, then pumps it through the body'* (10-year-old child showing partial understanding of the distribution of absorbed food through the body; Teixeira, 2000, p. 515).

Reconstruction

As children become older and move through KS2, many will come to realize that the stomach as storehouse and fixed container models do not make sense, partly because they become more adept at conserving mass – they realize that the food they eat cannot just disappear or keep on accumulating inside the body. In Year 4, children can be taught as a story the journey of food from the mouth to the anus and begin to understand that the digestive system is basically a long, continuous tube. There is an engaging and messy demonstration called 'gums to bums' where real food is passed through a model gut to show children what happens to it at the various stages (videos are available on the internet that explain how to do this).

A deeper understanding of structure and function can be gained by creating a giant model of the digestive system on the floor of the school hall. Draw out a route that correctly reflects the journey of food through the body, with props representing events that occur in each organ. Children start to walk themselves through the model starting at the mouth, carrying a piece of 'food' (several Duplo or Lego bricks stuck together). As they pass through each organ, pieces of food detach and enter the blood. Food that the body does not need passes out through the far end of the model (anus).

Sources: Allen *et al.* (2019); Ozbas and Kilinc (2015); Uskola *et al.* (2022).

5.4 The body's interior

> **Misconception**
>
> *The entire inside of the body is a hollow bag where blood, food, and wastes are contained.*

Scientific conception

Even though they understand that the human body contains a variety of things, KS1 children in particular may not realize that there are specific areas inside their bodies where life processes such as digestion and excretion are carried out. To them, the whole body is a large bag where food that has been eaten floats around, mixing freely with the other things. For instance, some children have drawn food entering this bag and then slowly making its way downwards to the legs, which are also hollow areas (Figure 5.4).

Since the interior of their bodies cannot be directly seen, it is not surprising that children use their imaginations in attempts to construct rational explanations of how the things inside of them might look (also see 3.2 and 5.1).

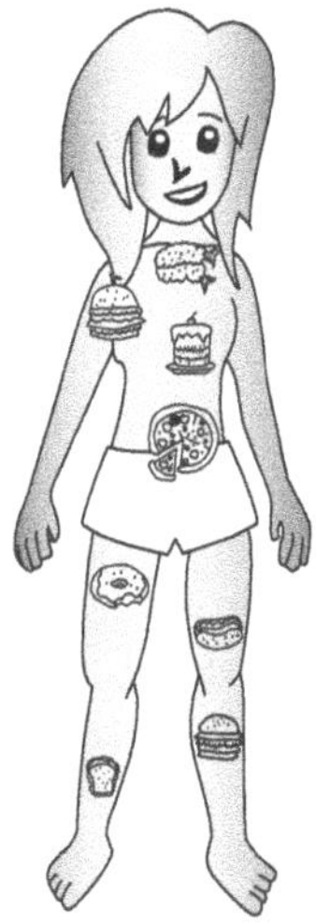

Figure 5.4 The body is a hollow bag (misconception)

Reconstruction

When children are taught the locations of their major body organs it becomes difficult for them to sustain a hollow bag model. The lesson ideas used in 5.1 can be used to clarify the correct locations of internal body organs, especially three-dimensional representations such as plastic models that challenge the idea of an empty space inside their bodies. Note that using a skeleton during teaching may actually reinforce the hollow bag misconception, since knowledge of the presence of the ribs, spine, and pelvis would be consistent with the incorrect view of an empty internal space.

Sources: Allen *et al.* (2019); Fraiberg (1959); Osborne *et al.* (1992).

5.5 Why do we need to eat food?

Misconception

The only reason we eat food is to give us energy.

Scientific conception

Like a fuel, food provides the body with the energy needed to carry out life processes (1.1), with the amount of energy in a food being given in kilojoules (kJ) or kilocalories (kC, usually just called calories).

Children can forget, however, that many nutrients have functions within the body other than providing energy. After proteins and fats in the diet have been digested and absorbed into the blood, they are often reassembled into new protein and fat **molecules** that then become a lasting part of our body structure. For example, amino acids from proteins in a burger can end up becoming part of our biceps muscle; animal fats from the same burger may eventually be used to make new cells within the lining of our lungs. Food is therefore important during the growing years as a source of raw material for building our bodies, though it is still vital after we stop growing because the body is continually repairing itself due to losses of cells during everyday wear and tear, as well as illness.

In contrast, the carbohydrates that we eat – found, for example, in fruits, bread, rice, and sugar – are normally broken down by the digestive system into glucose, which does not necessarily become a permanent physical part of our body. Instead, glucose is 'burned' as a fuel to provide energy for the body, although if carbohydrates are eaten in large quantities, glucose can become converted into body fat and stored under the skin, around the abdomen, etc. The same occurs when we eat an excess of dietary fat. **Minerals** can also become integrated into bodily structures, such as calcium in bones and teeth, and vitamins are important for certain chemical reactions inside the body. The body is unable to digest dietary fibre contained in foods such as wholegrain bread, carrots, and nuts, though fibre is needed for the effective movement of material through the intestines.

Reconstruction

Primary children are generally aware that their bodies will not grow if they do not eat enough of the 'right' food, a belief that is reinforced by reminders from parents at mealtimes. At the same time, they are warned that eating an excessive amount of the 'wrong' food can make them overweight. These are good starting points from which to introduce the idea that nutrients not only supply energy but also can become a physical part of our bodies – or, *we are what we eat.*

Babies increase in size rapidly during the first months of life, with growth then continuing at a slower pace up until the mid to late teens. Ask the class the question, *where has all this extra body mass come from?* It cannot have just appeared from nowhere! If science were more advanced, we perhaps might be able to look inside our bodies and link every piece of ourselves to a particular meal that we ate on a specific day in the past.

Source: Smith and Anderson (1986).

5.6 Why is eating protein important?

> **Misconception**
>
> *It is important to eat protein because it is the body's main source of energy.*

Scientific conception

This idea is related to the misconception that the only reason humans eat food is as a source of energy to drive life processes (5.5). It is often forgotten that food can also act as raw material for growth and repair. The importance of protein as a vital component of a healthy diet is well known and reinforced by the media and government health education programmes. A child making the statement above has merged a (correct) understanding that proteins are a necessary part of the diet with the (correct) concept that we eat partly to provide our bodies with energy. However, the role of protein is not as a source of energy and is discussed further in 5.5; instead, it is carbohydrates and fats in the diet that act as the main sources of energy for the body. Note that in certain circumstances, for instance, during starvation, fasting, or intense exercise, the body *is* able to use proteins as an emergency energy supply in the place of carbohydrates, but this process is far from the norm.

Related misconceptions include the ideas that water and vitamins are important sources of energy for the body.

Reconstruction

The pedagogies described in 5.5 are also applicable here in explaining the idea that proteins are important for body growth and repair.

Sources: Boyes and Stanisstreet (1990); Opitz *et al.* (2017).

5.7 Can eating fat be good for you?

Misconception

Eating any fat is bad for you.

Scientific conception

A major focus of public health education is the problem of increasing levels of overweight and obesity in the developed world. Health issues associated with weight gain such as heart disease (and other cardiovascular illnesses), type II diabetes, arthritis, cancer, and lowered self-esteem act as a significant drain on medical resources; in the UK, more than 80% of conditions treated by GPs are obesity-related. The recent COVID-19 pandemic further highlighted the link between overeating and illness – obese patients with the virus experienced disproportionately more serious symptoms than those patients who had a healthy weight. Eating excessive amounts of animal fat from foods such as meat,

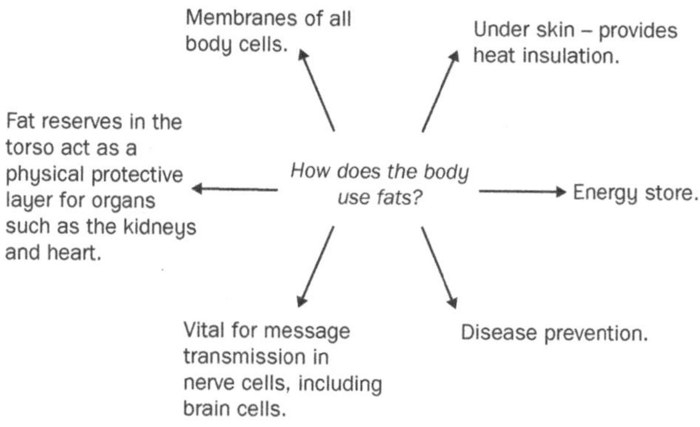

Figure 5.7a The importance of fats inside the body

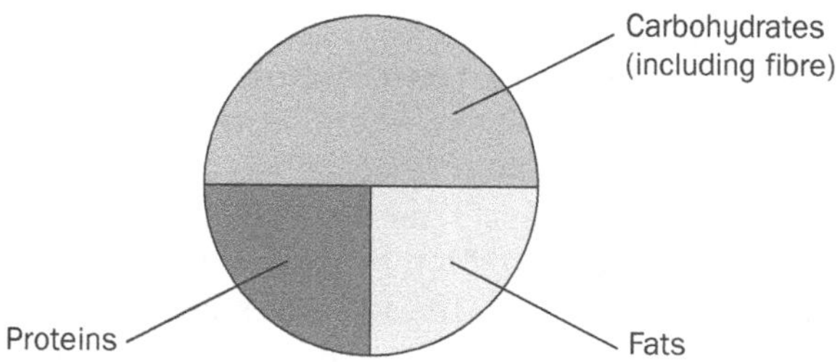

Figure 5.7b A simple diagram of the approximate proportions of nutrients recommended for a balanced diet

butter, and other dairy products has been singled out as a factor in the onset and maintenance of obesity, which has led to the current popularity of preventative measures such as low-fat diets.

These contributary factors are well established in the public domain, which has led to the mistaken belief that *any* intake of dietary fat is a bad thing. In fact, fats are vital for maintaining life processes (Figure 5.7a) and if we were to completely stop eating fats, we would become ill. Sources vary, but it is usually recommended that a balanced diet should contain 45–65% carbohydrates, 10–35% proteins and 20–35% fats (Figure 5.7b). Nutritionists advise that to maintain a healthy body weight, we should not exceed the recommended intake of fats as part of a balanced diet. As is the case with carbohydrates, the main reason why we eat fats is to provide the body with energy; in fact, the same mass of fat provides twice the amount of energy as carbohydrate, and it is this high calorific content that contributes to the obesity problem. Some types of dietary fat are less healthy than others, for instance, saturated fats (e.g. dairy products, red meat) have been linked to cardiovascular conditions and cancer. Unsaturated fats (e.g. fish oils, olive oil, nuts) are associated with fewer health problems, with the exception of unsaturated trans-fats (e.g. butter, some cooking oils) which have been strongly linked to heart disease.

Reconstruction

In primary science, healthy lifestyles are taught alongside concepts of how the human body works. As part of a discussion on healthy eating teachers should make children aware of which foods are rich in particular nutrients – for example, meat, fish, and eggs contain proteins. This can be presented as a pie chart using pictures of different foods to show the proportions that should be eaten as part of a balanced diet (Figure 5.7b gives a simple depiction). The Food Standards Agency in the UK has published its own version, the *Eatwell Plate*. These ideas can be extended by using the nutritional information labels found on packaged food to plan an 'expedition menu', where children must decide which foods to take on a three-day expedition to the desert, bearing in mind the requirements of a balanced diet.

Using the library or the internet as a resource, ask children to produce a poster of the human body that shows where fat reserves are found and also where fats play an important role in healthy body functioning.[1] Well-known low-carbohydrate programmes such as the Atkins Diet recommend a long-term intake of high percentages of fat that appears to have no lasting harmful effects – this would form the basis for an interesting discussion on how different scientists' views are sometimes at odds. The Food Standards Agency website provides further information and advice on healthy diets, including diagrams of the *Eatwell Plate* that can be used in class: https://www.food.gov.uk/

Ask children to list characters from books or TV who they think are following an unhealthy diet and give reasons why. They might consider Garfield (lasagne), Augustus Gloop (chocolate), Paddington Bear (marmalade sandwiches), and Jabba the Hutt (insatiable appetite). Althea Braithwaite's book *Lunch Boxes* focuses on the variety of foods that children bring to school for their lunch and can stimulate discussions about considering different food types when planning a balanced diet.

Sources: Althea (1999); Linfield (2021); Turner (1997); Xu and Jones (2016).

5.8 Which foods contain fats?

Misconception

Food only contains fat if the fat can be seen.

Scientific conception

Some meats have obvious fatty parts (e.g. bacon rind, lamb joint, pork chops, ham) that are often removed by health-conscious diners and left uneaten. Children may believe that other foods, which are actually rich in fats but without any visible fatty areas, are fat-free (e.g. crisps, nuts, cheese, cream, pastries).

Reconstruction

Having an *Eatwell Plate* type poster (Figure 5.7b) on display in the classroom will help children understand that a wide variety of foods are rich in fats, and not just meats with visible fat. If they were to read the information given on food nutrition labels, this would help to reinforce these ideas. A rule of thumb is that if your fingers feel greasy after eating a particular food, then it contains comparatively high levels of fats (e.g. crisps, chips, peanuts, spare ribs).

Teachers can demonstrate the energy content of different foods by burning equal masses of samples and measuring the temperature rise of a small container of water held over the flame (Figure 5.8). Foods like crisps and cashew nuts **heat** the water more intensely than crispbreads or pasta owing to their higher fat contents, because fats contain twice as much energy as carbohydrates.[2]

Source: Turner (1997).

Be safe!

Using naked flames in the classroom. Naked flames in the form of candles are potentially both a fire and burns hazard and so require a little thought before they are used in the classroom. The long, thin shape of many traditional candles makes them unstable and capable of being easily knocked over. Before lighting candles, place them in a small sand tray consisting of a disposable foil baking dish approximately 20 cm in diameter. Make sure the base of the candle is sunk well into the sand so that it will not fall over easily. Tea light candles have a low centre of gravity and are the safest type of candle, so should be used whenever possible. Tell children of the dangers of working with naked flames, including the risk of burnt fingers and clothing. Know where the fire extinguisher is in the room and how to use it correctly (read the instruction label beforehand) and have it close by during these activities. The decision about whether to use candles with your class is a matter for risk assessment, but generally they are quite safe with well-behaved upper KS2 children. It is good practice not to let children light their own candles with matches or splints; instead, the teacher should go around the class and light the candles.

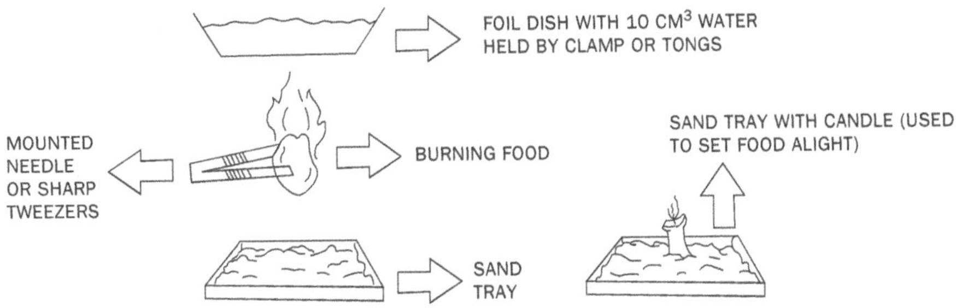

Figure 5.8 An experiment to show the energy values of different foods

5.9 Do plants need food?

Misconception

Plants get their food from the soil.

Scientific conception

This idea makes sense to children because they have made a link between two pieces of knowledge – a plant's roots take in water and goodness from the soil, and the plant is constantly growing. It is correct to say that some substances vital for life processes are absorbed into a plant through its roots, e.g. water, nitrates for making proteins, and magnesium for chlorophyll production. However, even though the plant takes in these nutrients (in a similar way to an animal eating), they are not 'food' in a strictly scientific sense. For a chemical to be classed as food, it must be able to supply energy to the organism during cellular respiration, so in plants only carbohydrates such as glucose and starch are technically food. Carbohydrates are made during the process of photosynthesis, where the plant converts carbon dioxide and water into glucose (food) and oxygen in the presence of sunlight. A plant does not take in food directly from the environment as an animal would, but instead is a kind of food factory, making its own glucose from raw materials and storing it as starch (Figure 5.9).

In an everyday sense, to say that plants absorb food from the soil is true since 'food' is commonly understood to be anything an organism takes in for nourishment, so any nutrients absorbed from the soil would fall into this category. This is an example of how scientific and everyday meanings sometimes clash and create confusion; the commercial availability of garden fertilizers labelled 'plant food' unfortunately reinforces this scientifically incorrect meaning.

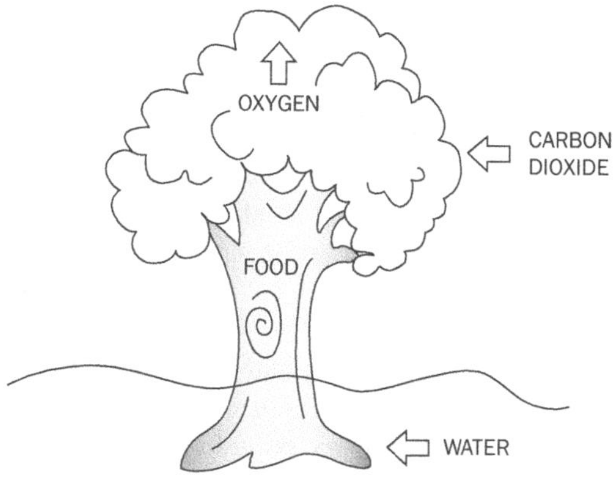

Figure 5.9 The materials involved in photosynthesis

The misconception can be elicited from the class with questions such as: *over many years this tree has grown from an acorn to become a mighty oak . . . where did all this extra mass come from?* It is important to remember that some of the plant's mass did in fact originate from the soil in the form of water absorbed by the roots that is converted into carbohydrate, and also remains as water within the plant's tissues. However, this water cannot be called 'food' because in the form it is absorbed, it cannot act as a source of energy for the plant. A related misconception is that as a young plant grows taller, all its new material comes from what was originally contained within the seed.

Reconstruction

One way to address the misconception is to ask children to plant a **seedling** such as a broad bean in a pot containing soil. At the beginning, weigh the soil and pot together without the seedling, and then the seedling on its own. Allow it to grow for a few weeks keeping it well watered in a bright area of the classroom, then reweigh both soil/pot, and plant, again separately. The plant will have significantly increased in mass though the mass of the soil and the pot will have remained fairly constant. Point out to children that obviously the soil could not have been responsible for the plant's large increase in mass, even if the soil/pot ends up being slightly lighter than before. Also, if soil is directly converted into the plant's mass, you would expect there to be a crater-like hole around the roots where soil was absorbed. Demonstrate that soil is not essential for growth by showing air plants and aquatic plants, or how cress seeds can grow on a piece of damp tissue. Use these ideas as a starting point to explain that water in the soil and carbon dioxide in the air were responsible for the extra mass.

Hydroponics refers to growing plants in a liquid solution without the need for soil, and is helpful in dispelling the misconception that plants use soil as their food. Commercially-available hydroponics kits developed for use in primary schools can be used to grow crops such as tomatoes, strawberries, and spinach, in as little time as three weeks. Evidence suggests that children take more interest in what they eat if they grow their own food, personally tending to the plants over a period of time before harvesting, so this activity would link well with a topic on healthy eating (see 5.6, 5.7, 5.8). Self-grown crops are a good example of how sustainability can be used as a solution to environmental problems associated with supermarket foods such as packaging, fair trade, accumulated air miles, etc.

A traditional KS1 activity is making leaf prints. Use leaves as a template by painting one side and then pressing them down firmly onto sugar paper to make striking patterns. This can be extended by labelling anatomical regions of the leaf prints using scientific terms including veins, stalks, and lobes.

The story book *Fran's Flower* by Lisa Bruce can provide an appropriate introduction to the subject of plant nutrition for young children.

Sources: Bell and Brook (1984); Bruce (2000); Smith and Anderson (1984); Temple Clothier (2019); Wandersee (1983); Yong (2017).

Notes

1 Note that discretion and sensitivity should be exercised, bearing in mind that many primary-aged children are within overweight and obese limits.

2 With upper KS2 classes, and only after appropriate risk assessment, you could consider allowing children to carry out this experiment themselves.

Planning and assessment sheet 5 Plant and animal nutrition

(For suggestions on how to use this sheet, see p. xxviii.)

Misconception	*Attainment re. expected standard*		
	Working towards	*Working at*	*Working above*
Year 2: *Animals including humans*			
The only reason we eat food is to give us energy (5.5)	✓	✓	✓
Eating any fat is bad for you (5.7)	✓	✓	✓
Year 3: *Animals including humans*			
The only reason we eat food is to give us energy (5.5)	✓	✓	
Eating any fat is bad for you (5.7)	✓	✓	✓
Food only contains fat if the fat can be seen (5.8)	✓	✓	
It is important to eat protein because it is the body's main source of energy (5.6)		✓	✓
Water and vitamins are important sources of energy for the body (5.6)		✓	✓
Year 3: *Plants*			
Plants get their food from the soil (5.9)	✓	✓	✓
As a young plant grows taller, all its new material comes from what was originally contained within the seed (5.9)		✓	✓
Year 4: *Animals including humans*			
My stomach is around where my navel is (5.1)	✓	✓	✓
The intestines are drawn as a single wiggly line in the abdomen (not differentiating between the small and large intestines) (5.1)		✓	✓
Not overlapping organs when drawing the body's internal structure (resulting in errors in the size and position of organs) (5.1)	✓	✓	✓
The digestive system is made up of two separate tubes – one for faeces, the other for urine (5.2)		✓	✓
The body 'melts' food during digestion (5.2)		✓	
The stomach is a filtering organ sorting out the goodness from the useless parts of food (5.2)		✓	✓

(continued)

(*continued*)

When we eat food, it stays inside our stomach forever (stomach as storehouse model) (5.3)	✓		
Food travels to places beyond the stomach, with some nutrients being absorbed by the body, while the material left over stays in the body permanently (fixed container model) (5.3)	✓		
We gain weight when undigested food sits permanently in the stomach making it swell (5.3)	✓		
Food left over after digestion turns into fat in the intestines (5.3)		✓	✓
Digested food is never stored in the body but is completely used up to provide energy (5.3)		✓	✓
All digested food eventually passes out of the body in faeces (5.3)	✓	✓	
The entire inside of the body is a hollow bag where blood, food, and wastes are contained (hollow body model) (5.4)	✓		
The food we eat eventually falls down to our legs and makes us taller (hollow body model) (5.4)	✓		

6

Food chains and webs

Conceptual areas covered in this chapter:

- Defining basic ecological terms, including ecosystem, population, community, and interdependence
- How populations of species are dependent on other populations as food sources
- If the size of one population changes, this usually affects other populations in the same ecosystem

National Curriculum links:

Year 1: *Animals including humans*

Year 2: *Living things and their habitats*

Year 4: *Animals including humans*

6.1 Food chain rules

Misconception

An arrow in a food chain means 'eats'.

Scientific conception

As shown in Figure 6.1a, children often draw a food chain with the arrows reversed which incorrectly implies that a rabbit is a **predator** of a fox, although when questioned they will tell you that the opposite is true. The error is due to the widely accepted meaning of an arrow in any diagram to show the direction of an action; the thing having the action done to it is placed at the pointed end of the arrow. In physics, for instance, a **force arrow** is drawn away from the source of the force and towards the object being pushed; in cartoons, arrows represent the movement of a character or object from one place to another.

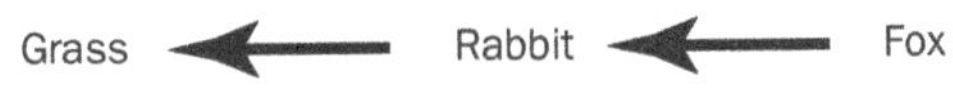

Figure 6.1a Reversed arrow food chain (misconception)

Figure 6.1b Food chain with correct arrows

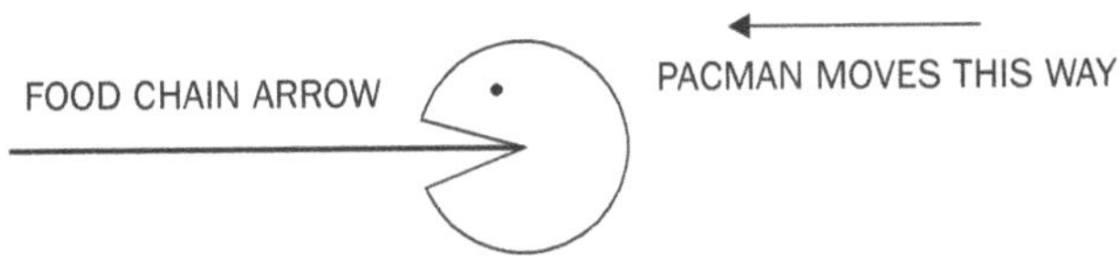

Figure 6.1c Pacman rule

Figure 6.1d Using pictures to illustrate a food chain

With food chain and food web diagrams, we are asking children to mentally reverse this familiar rule and instead remember that an arrow means 'is eaten by'. A food chain with the arrows pointing in the correct direction is shown in Figure 6.1b. Children will usually spot their mistake if they are asked to think about whether the food chain they have just drawn makes any sense: do rabbits actually eat foxes? However, if at least one of the organisms is unfamiliar to them, errors may go uncorrected; for instance, although commonly included in food chains, many children do not know what a thrush or an aphid are.

Reconstruction

This issue is sometimes difficult to address since it requires rote learning a rule that goes against the familiar meaning of a drawn arrow, and children tend to remember the correct direction one day but forget it the next, reverting back to the misconception. As with all rote learning, repetition and practice will help.

One tip is to use the 'Pacman rule', referring to the well-known video-game character (Figure 6.1c). Get children into the habit of using a pencil to lightly draw a 'Pacman' on the ends of their food chain arrows and imagine the character is moving – they only munch in one direction, where the 'mouth' is facing. Therefore, the organisms in the food chain eat in the same direction as 'Pacman' munches. Remind children not to forget to rub out their 'Pacmen' before handing in a piece of work.

It is a good idea when possible to use photographs or drawings of organisms when constructing food chains, and not just words, as some organisms may be unfamiliar to children (Figure 6.1d). When each organism is shown in this way, it is more obvious which is the predator and which is the **prey**. The same pictures that are used for classification exercises (e.g. 2.2) can double up as useful food chain plants and animals.

Sources: Biffi *et al.* (2016); Schollum (1983).

6.2 Food chains and population numbers

Misconception

If lots of caterpillars die, this has no effect on the numbers of hedgehogs or nettles.

Scientific conception

Children can find it tricky to appreciate the wider effects of **population** changes within an **ecosystem**. The misconception statement above suggests that if the numbers of one living thing are reduced in a food chain, this has no effect on the others in the same chain. In the example given, if the number of caterpillars was to decrease, the number of hedgehogs would be expected to decrease also, as caterpillars are a source of food for hedgehogs (Figure 6.2). Another consequence of less food being available is that hedgehogs would tend to reproduce less, further contributing to the fall in their numbers. A second effect of fewer caterpillars in the ecosystem would be that nettles would tend to thrive, given that there are fewer caterpillars to eat them.

Nettle → Caterpillar → Hedgehog

Figure 6.2 A simple food chain

In reality, the situation would be more complex, since another animal that competes with caterpillars for food may flourish and start to eat more nettles, keeping the nettle population constant. Also, hedgehogs have a varied diet and after the caterpillars' demise, might start to hunt a different prey to avoid starvation. However, since the only evidence put before us is a single food chain, we need to base any predictions regarding population changes on these three organisms alone.

Other misconceptions similarly involve not considering the food chain as a holistic system, where a change in the numbers of one organism will have an effect on all the rest. Children who can successfully predict an effect of a population change on a predator–prey relationship, e.g. hedgehog–caterpillar, sometimes forget to include the **producer** (the plant). Children usually expect producer numbers to remain constant, something that has been called **plant blindness**. Alternatively, they think changes in predator numbers will affect prey numbers, but not the other way around, e.g. if hedgehogs die, then caterpillars thrive, but if caterpillars die, this will not affect hedgehog numbers. A different misconception is the idea that when the population of an organism changes, this only affects other organisms immediately next to it in the chain, e.g. fewer nettles would affect the numbers of caterpillars, but not the hedgehog population. Anyone unable to fully appreciate the far-reaching impacts of changes to a single population may trivialize a media report about an endangered species, only believing that species alone is under threat, when the likelihood is that many members of an ecosystem will be adversely affected. A related misconception is that children only think about feeding relationships between single organisms, e.g. one lion eats one zebra, and do not consider that a food chain represents entire populations of species.

Did you know?

The cane toad. Cane toads were introduced to Australia in the 1930s to control cane beetles that were ruining sugar cane plantations. As planned, the beetle population fell after the introduction of the toads; however, the toads' presence influenced other food chains – for instance, crocodiles and other animals that hunted the toad died after eating its poisonous skin. Today, the toad itself has become a pest and measures to control its numbers include the introduction of ants that prey on the toads.

Reconstruction

The topic can be introduced by asking children to think about differences between a variety of different ecosystems such as tropical rainforest, coral reef, desert, wetland, and temperate forest. Working in small groups in the library or computer room, allocate each group one ecosystem, asking them to research questions such as: *Which plants and animals live there? What are the environmental factors affecting the ecosystem (e.g. climate, humans)? How are plants and animals adapted to living there? In what ways do the plants and animals depend on each other for survival?*

More practice answering questions about food chain population changes in different ecosystems would help children understand that a food chain represents an **interdependent** system and not just isolated pairs of predator–prey or animal–plant relationships. A starting point could be observing local wildlife within the school grounds and thinking about what the animals eat to survive (e.g. wild cherry → blackbird). Once children know about these simple feeding relationship pairs, they can be extended to three-step food chains. Talking to the class about real-world examples of population changes within food chains and webs could include pest control, e.g. introducing ladybirds into an ecosystem to reduce the population of aphids that are destroying crops.

Making the jump from simple food chains to more complex food webs can be problematic. Using an ecosystem that contains familiar living things such as African grassland can help this process. One socio-constructivist activity would involve children working in small groups to arrange lion, zebra, crocodile, locust, antelope, acacia tree, grass, leopard, etc. into several linear food chains. These can then be converted into food webs by joining the chains together with more offshooting arrows. Children then move around the room to compare other groups' food webs with their own. Finally, run a whole-class peer discussion session where children put forward arguments as to whether their food webs make sense (i.e. carnivores, herbivores, and producers have been correctly identified) and if the webs would be sustainable in a real ecosystem (see 6.5). A food web wall display in the classroom that shows pictures of organisms can also be useful, using lengths of coloured string for the arrows. There are free interactive food chain games available on the internet that are fun and pitched at primary level, e.g. http://www.sheppardsoftware.com

Further discussion of how humans can affect the delicate balance of ecosystems can include accounts of how culling animal populations can sometimes go wrong (also see cane toad, Box p. 98). Past initiatives have involved removing the **top predator** or **apex predator** in an ecosystem to increase the populations of other species; examples include hunting whales to boost fish numbers, and culling magpies in the UK to protect songbirds. However, these operations can create unforeseen events that have the opposite effect of what was intended. If whales are hunted to excess, tiny organisms called phytoplankton that depend on the whales' faeces for nutrients will reduce in number. Since the phytoplankton are producers that occupy the bottom **trophic level** of the ocean food web, this also reduces the numbers other oceanic organisms, including the fish populations that the hunting was originally intended to increase.

Sources: Gotwals and Songer (2010); Leach *et al.* (1992); Tyler (2020); Yoon *et al.* (2018).

6.3 Predators in food chains

Misconception

A sparrowhawk is a predator of thrushes, ladybirds, and aphids.

Scientific conception

The above statement reflects the idea that an animal placed higher in a food chain is a predator of all others placed below it. This may be due to thinking the food chain represents a kind of power hierarchy, like roles in human organizations; for instance, with the army ranks of private, lance corporal, sergeant, etc., each rank holder has authority over all those lower in the chain of command. It cannot help when we (correctly) tell children that the sparrowhawk is the top predator, a term which suggests that it has complete dominance over all other predators in the food chain.

Each arrow in a food chain represents a single feeding relationship – Figure 6.3 shows that sparrowhawks eat thrushes, thrushes eat ladybirds, and so on. Note that food chains are diagrams that show only a single pathway, so are simplified and do not tell the whole story. Within an ecosystem, a sparrowhawk may indeed eat ladybirds as well as thrushes, which could be represented by drawing an additional arrow from ladybird to sparrowhawk. However, the diagram could no longer be called a simple food *chain*, and instead is the beginnings of a more complex food *web*.

Figure 6.3 A food chain with more than one predator

Reconstruction

Explain to children that within a food chain only organisms immediately next to each other have a feeding relationship. These relationships cannot 'skip' over trophic levels. Remind children that when an animal is the top predator, this simply means that it is not the prey of any other animal and this has nothing to do with any overall dominance over the other living things in a food chain.

Day trips to woodland centres provide a useful context for teaching the ideas that underpin ecological feeding relationships, providing a natural setting with direct access to organisms that make up food chains and webs.

Sources: Barman *et al.* (1995); Yoon *et al.* (2018).

6.4 What is interdependence?

Misconception

Wild animals never go short of food.

Scientific conception

Young children can think that food is always plentiful for wild animals, which live together peacefully because they have similar needs – they do their best to get along with each other. They can also think of plants and animals as individual and isolated, instead of understanding that different species live as members of populations in a **community** that are dependent upon each other for survival. In any ecosystem, there is life and death competition between organisms for scarce resources; some species triumph over others in these competitions, which may result in outcompeted species disappearing from an ecosystem. The idea that organisms do not exist in isolation but are vitally dependent upon each other is important in **ecology**, and termed interdependence, usually taking the form of one organism being food for another. However, some dependences are nothing to do with feeding, as in the sparrow who needs the oak tree to nest in; other dependences involve connections with non-living features of the environment, as when plants absorb essential minerals from the soil. The idea of infinite resources within an ecosystem is a problem as it will prevent children from developing a correct understanding of sustainability.

Another form of interdependence that children tend not to consider is the vital role played by species that feed on dead organisms. For example, bacteria and fungi in the soil feed on the carcasses of dead animals such as foxes and help keep the ground free from organic debris. During this decomposition, carbon **atoms** are released from the carcass into the atmosphere as carbon dioxide gas, which in turn is absorbed by grass plants during photosynthesis and converted to carbohydrate in the grass; this recycling is an essential stage within the **carbon cycle**. Although the role of decomposition within an ecosystem is beyond the primary curriculum, it can help children construct a holistic understanding of ecology as involving 'circles of life' (Figure 6.4).

Related misconceptions include the idea that wild animals are cared for and fed by humans so never go hungry, and that a food chain exists purely to provide food for humans. A similar idea is if one member of a food chain is reduced in numbers or disappears, then this is not a problem because animals have varied diets and can always find something else to eat.

Figure 6.4 Introducing decomposition into a simple food chain[1]

Reconstruction

When children consider simple food chains, it is not always obvious that different organisms are competing with one another for the same resources. Presenting them with food *webs* would help them to understand how food chains are interlinked in the real world, and that populations can rise or fall depending on whether one organism outcompetes another (see 6.2 and 6.5). It is better to start children off thinking about carnivore–herbivore before herbivore–producer relationships, since it is easier for them to imagine a lion competing with a leopard for an antelope, rather than an antelope competing with a wildebeest for grass. Basic ideas relating to supply and demand would be necessary for children to fully appreciate interdependence – for example, globally, resources are finite and so can become scarce within an ecosystem; this would have the effect of increasing demand, and to satisfy that demand the number of competitors would need to be reduced.

Sources: Kharrazi *et al.* (2018); Leach *et al.* (1992, 1996); Melis *et al.* (2020); Munson (1994).

Famous scientists

Dian Fossey. A primatologist by discipline, Dian studied the social behaviour of mountain gorillas in Rwanda during the 1960s and 1970s. Her research became well known outside of her field and led to the gorilla being considered less an aggressive, dangerous 'beast of the jungle', and more an intelligent, gentle, and socially complex ape species which shares many behavioural traits with humans. Part of her work established how gorillas play a vital, interdependent role in their ecosystem by recycling nutrients; in fact, maintaining the gorillas' habitat became important to her in later life and she became a prominent environmentalist. Dian's life and work were celebrated in the 1988 film, *Gorillas in the Mist*.

6.5 Pyramids of numbers

Misconception

There are always more carnivores than herbivores in a food chain.

Scientific conception

With a simple food chain such as grass → rabbit → fox, some children believe that there are always more foxes than rabbits because the foxes are stronger and can kill rabbits easily. One way to illustrate the number of organisms in a food chain is to use a **pyramid of numbers**. Figure 6.5a shows a pyramid that reflects the misconception that foxes outnumber rabbits. In reality, this would not be sustainable because food supply would not be able to keep up with demand. Considering the different numbers of organisms within the pyramid in Figure 6.5a, if each fox needed to eat one rabbit per week, then after one week all the rabbits would be eaten and 900 foxes would be starving. Equally, the rabbits would eat all the 10 grass plants very quickly and themselves starve. Figure 6.5b shows the pyramid inverted with numbers decreasing up the food chain, which is a more ecologically sustainable model. In this case, the 10 foxes could each eat one rabbit each per week and leave 90 rabbits. The following week 10 more rabbits would be eaten, and so on, though the rabbits would be able to keep their numbers constant because they are able to produce many offspring. The same would happen when the rabbits eat the grass plants, with the grass reproducing and re-growing to replace losses. Therefore, a fine balance of numbers is necessary to make a stable, sustainable food chain. However, this balance can be easily upset. For example, if the foxes over-reproduce and increase their numbers to 15, this would have a large impact on rabbit numbers. But it would also create competition between the foxes, some of which would die because there would no longer be enough rabbits to go around, and the number of foxes might drop to below 10, which would give the rabbits a chance to recover. Eventually, a balance of numbers would be restored.

Related misconceptions include the belief that food is always plentiful in the wild instead of there being fierce competition for resources (see 6.4). The Box on p. 105 shows an example of anthropomorphic thinking, in that the child has imagined a rabbit having caring feelings towards other rabbits that are in fact competing with it for the same food supply. A different misconception is thinking that carnivores are always large, aggressive animals and herbivores are smaller, more peaceful creatures.

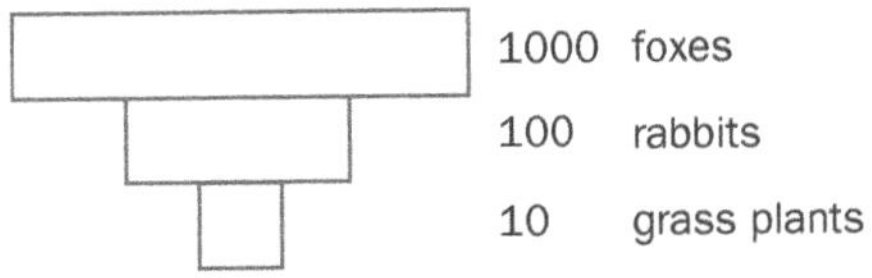

Figure 6.5a Pyramid of numbers: population size increases up the food chain (misconception)

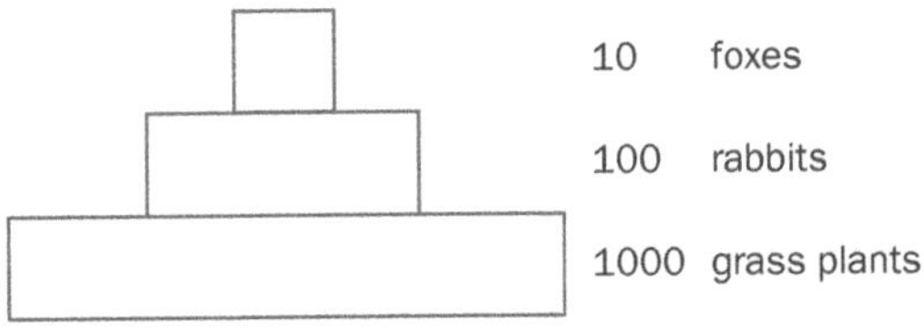

Figure 6.5b Pyramid of numbers: population size decreases up the food chain (correct)

I think . . .

Non-competitive species. *'[The rabbit was happy because] more rabbits might like to eat [the grass]'* (5-year-old child describing the feelings of a rabbit in a food chain if more grass became available. This response reflects the idea that rabbits share resources and have empathy with other members of their species; Allen, 2017, p. 1502).

Reconstruction

Learning about pyramids of numbers is beyond the primary curriculum but some upper KS2 children would be quite capable of understanding the basic concepts, which will help generate a deeper understanding of sustainability in the wild. Learning about real feeding relationships in the local environment can help to bring food chains to life, e.g. dandelion → ground beetle → garden spider. If you have access, pond dipping is an engaging way to collect and identify wild species, and think about how organisms living in close proximity depend on each other for survival. Alternately, a woodland walk can fulfil the same purposes while also providing more of a variety of habitats to consider, including the different layers of the forest (canopy, understorey, shrub, herb, floor).

Any misconceptions about all carnivores being large and aggressive can be addressed by giving examples such as the domestic cat, and if herbivores are thought to be small and passive, mention the rhinoceros.

Sources: Allen (2017); Gallegos *et al.* (1994).

Note

1 This is a simplified diagram that gives children a basic idea of the role of decomposition; for instance, decomposers would also consume rabbit carcasses and dead grass plants.

Planning and assessment sheet 6 Food chains and webs

(For suggestions on how to use this sheet, see p. xxviii.)

Misconception	*Attainment re. expected standard*		
	Working towards	*Working at*	*Working above*
Year 1: *Animals including humans*			
Carnivores are always large, aggressive animals, while herbivores are smaller, more peaceful creatures (6.5)	✓	✓	
Year 2: *Living things and their habitats*			
An arrow in a food chain means 'eats' (6.1)	✓	✓	✓
Wild animals care for each other (instead of there being fierce competition for resources) (6.5)	✓		
Wild animals never go short of food (6.4; 6.5)	✓		
Wild animals are cared for and fed by humans so never go hungry (6.4)	✓		
A food chain exists purely to provide food for humans (6.4)	✓		
Year 4: *Animals including humans*			
An arrow in a food chain means 'eats' (6.1)	✓	✓	✓
A food chain only represents the feeding relationship between single organisms, e.g. one lion eats one zebra, not considering that it represents entire populations of species (6.2)	✓		
Plants and animals living in the wild are individual and isolated (not appreciating that different species live as members of populations in a community that are dependent on each other for survival) (6.4)	✓		
If one member of a food chain is reduced in numbers or disappears, this is not a problem (animals have varied diets and can always find something else to eat) (6.4)	✓	✓	
There are always more carnivores than herbivores in a food chain (6.5)		✓	✓
An animal placed higher in a food chain is a predator of all others placed below it (e.g. a top predator eats everything else in the food chain) (6.3)	✓	✓	
If the population numbers of a living thing increase or decrease, this has no effect on the population numbers of other living things in the same food chain (6.2)	✓	✓	

(continued)

(continued)

If many prey animals die, this will not change the numbers of predators or plants (6.2)	✓	✓	
Changes in predator numbers will affect prey numbers, but not vice versa (6.2)		✓	✓
Children who correctly predict the effect of population changes with a predator–prey relationship expect the plant numbers to remain constant (plant blindness) (6.2)		✓	✓
When the population of a living thing changes, this only affects other living things immediately adjacent to it in the chain (6.2)		✓	✓

7

Reproduction, inheritance, and evolution

Conceptual areas covered in this chapter:

- Sexual reproduction in plants and animals
- Life cycles
- Plant and animal adaptations
- Darwin's theory of natural selection

National Curriculum links:

Year 2: *Living things and their habitats; Animals including humans; Plants*

Year 3: *Plants*

Year 4: *Living things and their habitats*

Year 5: *Living things and their habitats*

7.1 How do plants reproduce?

Misconception

Fruits are always soft, sweet, and fleshy.

Scientific conception

Like some other misconceptions in this book, this idea arises from confusing two different definitions of the same word. In everyday life, we use the definition reflected by the misconception statement, and the fresh fruit section of a supermarket stocks foods such as apples, pears, bananas, cherries, melons, and pineapples. Scientifically, all of these foods are indeed types of fruit but the scientific definition also includes things that people do not generally consider to be fruits. In simple terms, a fruit is *a structure in a flowering plant that contains seeds.*

Animals sexually reproduce when a male and female mate, allowing sperm cells to **fertilize** egg cells (**ova**) which eventually become embryos. In a similar way, plants undergo sexual reproduction within their flowers when pollen grains fertilize ova to make seeds, which are embryonic plants. With animals, embryos are laid in eggs that hatch out as new offspring that are then free to move around (although mammals give birth to live young). Plants, however, have evolved a different method to move their seeds about – they produce fruits. Once ova have been fertilized and new seeds made, the place within the flower where the seeds are kept (the ovary) begins to change, usually swelling to a larger size or changing its shape completely. This occurs as preparation for **seed dispersal** because it is better for seeds to come to rest well away from the parent plant, otherwise they will compete with the parent for water and nutrients from the soil, and light from the sun. With plants such as an apple tree, the ovary swells and becomes sweet and fleshy to produce the apple fruit that we are familiar with. Passing animals are enticed to eat the apple fruit and seeds, which are digested and eventually pass out in the animal's faeces in a place some distance from the parent. With dandelion plants, the fruits are small, light, and parachute-shaped to catch the air and are dispersed away when the wind blows.

Essentially, if a structure from a plant contains seeds, then it is a fruit. Some unexpected fruits include walnuts, hazelnuts, green beans, acorns, cucumbers, and tomatoes. Rice, wheat, and other cereals are a type of fruit with a very thin wall called a caryopsis. Cultivated bananas are fruits that do not contain seeds because they reproduce with human help by cuttings, which is not sexual reproduction (but bananas sometimes have tiny black dots inside which are vestigial seeds – see 7.5 for more about **vestiges**). Although most children know that fruits contain seeds, they may not automatically make the link to understand that a fruit was once part of a flower.

Other misconceptions about plant reproduction include mixing-up the processes of pollination and **fertilization**, e.g. the transfer of pollen from one flower to another is called fertilization. Some children associate reproduction only with animals and are surprised when they first learn that plants are also capable of reproducing themselves, which is a form of plant blindness (also see 6.2). This echoes a reluctance to accept *per se* that plants are living things (1.2); even when children do acknowledge the living status of plants, some believe them to be 'less alive' than animals.

Reconstruction

A good starting point when introducing plant reproduction to a class is to make it clear that the flower contains the organs of reproduction. Many children find it odd that unlike in animals, both male and female reproductive parts are found on the same flower. A very common misconception is to call the whole plant a flower, including leaves, stem, roots, and the flower itself, as in 'a bunch of flowers' (2.9). Children can act out a role play of plant reproduction in the context of bees flying out from a hive to visit flowers and collect nectar; this can cover the concepts of pollination, fertilization, fruit formation, and seed dispersal. Dissections of plants such as daffodil flowers are very engaging, allowing children to see for real, reproductive anatomy including petals, anthers, stigmas, styles, pollen, and ova.

Ideas can be elicited by presenting a table of a wide variety of real fruits, including the unexpected examples mentioned above, and asking children to divide them into fruits and non-fruits. They may want to create a different set consisting of savoury foods called 'vegetables', though 'vegetable' is less a scientific word and more a culinary term. Both KS1 and KS2 children can use coding activities to create interactive animations of plant reproduction (see Box p. 110).

Sources: Amprazis and Papadopoulou (2023); Schussler (2008); Zacharia *et al.* (2016).

Learning technologies

Computer programming. With the introduction of the current National Curriculum in 2014 came the requirement for KS1 and KS2 children to learn how to write simple computer programs. In primary schools, this is known as 'coding', the aim being for children to extend their computer skills beyond those of merely users of software such as word processors, spreadsheets, and internet search engines, and become actual creators of programs. One example of a programming language is *Scratch*, which is especially designed for children, being user-friendly and easy to access online. Children do not write code by typing in words as a professional computer programmer would; instead, they drag and drop blocks of code from a menu that link together to form an algorithm, so creating a simple animation, game, quiz, etc. They quickly become familiar with the concept of a computer program being a logical series of linked codes, and how these codes can be fitted together in different ways to perform a variety of functions. Once written, the programs provide an interactive experience for users where links can be clicked that lead a 'story' in different directions. The topic of reproduction lends itself well to this approach because life cycles are quite complicated stories that tell how plants and animals pass through different stages as they mature. For example, a *Scratch* animation about the life cycle of a flowering plant can include the journey of pollen of a variety of different plant species, some wind-pollinated, others pollinated by insects. This can lead on to seed and fruit formation, fruit dispersal by animals or wind, and so on. Similar animations can be created about the life cycle of a frog or a butterfly and the experience of writing the programs helps children to better understand these complex sequences of events.

7.2 Same-sex-only inheritance

Misconception

Sons take after their fathers, and daughters take after their mothers.

Scientific conception

Even at preschool age, children are aware that they physically resemble their parents in some ways. However, they may believe that they have inherited features from only one of their parents – the parent who is the same biological sex as them. All organisms that reproduce by sexual reproduction, from grass plants to humans, contain genetic material in the form of equal numbers of **chromosomes** from each parent (Figure 7.2). Children therefore inherit characteristics from both their mother and father, including hair and eye colour, body size and shape, as well as a tendency to develop certain diseases later in life. Children notice, for instance, that boys share more obvious sex-specific features such as genitals with their fathers and then go on to assume that their whole body is completely inherited from just that one parent. In a similar way, children who correctly think that features can be inherited from both parents mistakenly conclude that boys inherit the majority of them from their fathers, and girls from their mothers.

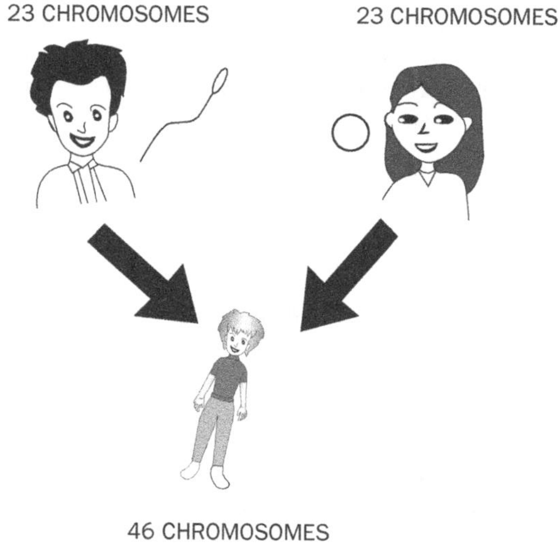

Figure 7.2 Children inherit an equal number of chromosomes from each parent

Table 7.2 Recording physical features

Physical feature	*From father*	*From mother*	*Not sure who from*

A related misconception is the belief that children of both sexes inherit most of their characteristics from their mothers, since **gestation** takes place within the mother's body.

Reconstruction

Ask children to complete a table (Table 7.2) that lists physical characteristics they think they may have inherited from their fathers and mothers. If children bring in photographs of their parents, this can help others in the class appreciate these observations (or, a teacher can ask the class to email photographs that can be displayed on the IWB). If there are sensitivity issues related to children not knowing or living with one or both biological parents, this activity could instead be carried out using the photographs of celebrity couples and their children.

Similarly, children can construct their own family trees going back a couple of generations to grandparents or great-grandparents to see physical features such as eye colour being directly passed down, or even skipping generations to appear only in grandchildren. Simple ideas about inheritance can be taught to KS1 children by referring to experiences set in familiar contexts, such as a black cat having black kittens, and the puppies of two purebred dogs will be the same breed as the parents – for example, if a pair of labradors mate, they do not produce bulldog puppies. Children need to correctly appreciate how inheritance works before they can understand the concept of evolution (see 7.3).

Sources: Engel-Clough and Wood-Robinson (1985); Ibourk *et al.* (2018).

7.3 Why do giraffes have long necks?

Misconception

Modern giraffes have long necks because their ancestors' necks grew longer as they stretched to reach leaves high in trees.

Scientific conception

Children and adults alike commonly believe that adaptations appear because of changes that occur during an organism's lifetime. For instance, in the distant past, giraffes had short necks and could only reach leaves on a tree that were close to the ground; as they strained to reach the higher branches, their necks became slightly longer. This adaptation was passed to the next generation where the process was repeated, and after several generations giraffes ended up with very long necks.

This commonly held idea is *Lamarckian*, after Jean-Baptiste Lamarck, the founder of a now outdated theory of evolution. Modern scientists instead accept *Darwinian* evolution, which is based on the idea of natural selection. Charles Darwin proposed that instead of the giraffe ancestor having a short neck, there existed a variety of giraffes with different neck lengths living together during the same time period. Due to some environmental event such as drought that caused the disappearance of most **flora**, plants that lived close to the ground became scarce because of overfeeding and the shorter-necked giraffes died out due to starvation, while their longer-necked competitors survived because they were able to reach the higher vegetation. This is the basic principle behind Darwinian evolution, that modern organisms have a particular adaptation because at some time in the past that adaptation gave some advantage to an ancestor over its competitors, a process known as *survival of the fittest.*

Of course, body changes can occur in individual organisms due to lifetime events, including changes in bone length due to physical stress such as the stretching of an animal's neck. However, as is the case with other misconceptions in this chapter, these changes cannot be passed to the next generation because the information is not contained within **genes**.

A related misconception is that before being taught Darwinian evolution, children can believe that all living things have been made by a creator and so their adaptations are creations that are unchanging over time. This is not helped by their difficulty in imagining time in a geological sense, over millions of years, and so they cannot appreciate gradual changes in species over long time spans.

Reconstruction

While learning about evolution in Year 6, children need to understand the fundamental concepts behind Darwinian theory. Lamarckian misconceptions can also surface during lessons that deal with plant and animal adaptations, so a typical teaching sequence is to ask children to note the physical characteristics of different organisms and then link those characteristics with each organism's habitat, explaining why they might be suited to living in that environment. For example, a polar bear is well adapted to living in the cold Arctic because it has thick white fur, large paws, etc. This provides an ideal opportunity to feed in the idea of natural selection, describing how an organism's characteristics may appear to have been purposely 'sculpted' to fit their habitat, when in fact their adaptations are the result of chance events long ago in the past.

Lamarckian ideas can be addressed by encouraging the understanding that information will only cross from parent to child if it is present within the genes, and that genetic information cannot change in response to life events (7.4). Therefore, it did not matter how much the ancestor giraffes stretched their necks because this stretching could not have entered the genes and so was unable to be passed on to their offspring.

Evolution concepts are typically taught in schools using only large, familiar animals as exemplars, such as humans, giraffes, polar bears, and horses. However, this limited approach can generate misconceptions such as evolution always produces descendants which are larger, more complex, and have a higher intelligence than their ancestors. One suggestion is to supplement these larger animals with invertebrate exemplars, which although might be less attractive to children, offer a more comprehensive model of evolution. For instance, modern barnacles and tapeworms are highly successful species but have smaller brains than their prehistoric ancestors; the bodies of some parasitic wasps have decreased in size as they evolved over millions of years; and sponges are much simpler organisms now compared with how they were in the distant past.

There are commercially available computer simulations of natural selection for use in schools. Although they tend to go well beyond the primary curriculum, they include some relevant games and activities that would be useful for younger children. The Natural History Museum website has resources and videos that support the teaching of natural selection: http://www.nhm.ac.uk/

Sources: Adeniyi (1985); Czekanski-Moir and Rundell (2020); Deniz *et al.* (2008); Jensen and Finley (1995).

Did you know?

Creationism in schools. Since the early 2000s, there have been attempts by creationist religious groups to raise the profile of the pseudoscientific idea of intelligent design (ID), seeking to include it within the school curriculum alongside genuine science theories. ID takes a position that opposes Darwinian natural selection, suggesting that organisms' adaptations arose because of the intervention of a creator, and some children may argue the case for ID in the classroom motivated by religious belief, or innocent curiosity. As teachers of science we need to make it clear to children that ID is not a scientific theory, i.e. something that is backed by convincing evidence, and as such is inappropriate for discussion during science lessons, although as a religious viewpoint it can be considered alongside other belief systems.

7.4 The bodybuilder's child

Misconception

The son of a bodybuilder will have big muscles.

Scientific conception

Children can be aware from an early age that they inherit certain characteristics from their parents, informed by comments such as 'hasn't he got his father's eyes!' Some children assume that almost any characteristic can be passed down to offspring even if that characteristic is the result of lifetime events such as a hairstyle, the loss of a limb or, as in the case of the example given above, muscle growth as a consequence of gym workouts.

To be inheritable, a characteristic needs to be encoded genetically, i.e. be present in the genes. Features such as eye colour and facial features are examples of such *genetic variation*. Physical changes that take place owing to exposure to a person's surroundings, such as developing a suntan, undergoing cosmetic surgery, or breaking a bone, are termed *environmental variation* and are not passed on to children because this information is not in the genes. Discussions related to these ideas are called nature vs. nurture debates, though children sometimes merge the two and lump all characteristics together as being inheritable. Note that many characteristics occur due to a combination of environmental and genetic factors, such as height and body weight.

Reconstruction

Children need to be able to tell the difference between changes that happen solely due to life events and those that they have no control over because of their parents' genetic heritage. Explain that for something to be passed on to a child it needs to be already there within the parents' genetic make-up; more specifically, it needs to be present in the genes of the sperm cell or ovum that combine to make a new individual. People cannot change, add to, or take away information that is already in their genes, so it does not matter what you do to your body during your lifetime because this will not affect your offspring.[1]

Asking children to make a simple family tree going back a couple of generations will help show how some characteristics such as hair and eye colour are inheritable. If there are sensitivity issues related to any children not knowing the family history of one or both of their biological parents, the teacher can create a 'model' family tree that the whole class can refer to, based on members of a family the teacher knows.

Although it is beyond KS2, drawing a simple picture of a chromosome will help children visualize what a gene actually is, that it is made from **DNA**, and that it duplicates itself, with one copy being given to offspring (Figure 7.4). Say that we are born with these genes, and then in time pass them on to our own children. During our lifetime they do not change, we are merely their custodians. If we build up our bodies in the gym, this does not change the genes and so we cannot pass on this characteristic to our children.

Figure 7.4 A simple diagram of a gene on a chromosome

As is sometimes the case in school science, reality is at odds with the simple concepts we teach to primary children because exceptions to the rule do exist. Genes *can* change due to exposure to hazardous environmental effects such as UV light, X-rays, and certain very toxic chemicals. These changes are **mutations** and nearly always have devastating consequences; for instance, excessive exposure to UV light causes mutations in epidermal cells that trigger skin cancer. However, only mutations in sperm cell or ovum DNA would be inheritable.

Sources: Ibourk *et al.* (2018); Nehm and Schonfeld (2008).

> ***Did you know?***
>
> **Epigenetic inheritance.** Recent advances in **epigenetics** have shown that changes in chromosomes can take place during a parent's life in response to exposure to something in the environment, and then be passed to offspring. These changes mean that genes are 'expressed' differently, thus affecting children's characteristics. For example, male mice given doses of morphine fathered baby mice with hormone problems, showing that life events (in this case, exposure to a drug) can indeed have consequences for later generations. It is important to note that with epigenetic alterations, the genes themselves do not change, merely the chromosomes where the genes are located, which causes genes either to 'switch on' or 'switch off'.

7.5 Are certain human characteristics dying out?

> **Misconception**
>
> *Our little fingers are getting smaller because we no longer use them.*

Scientific conception

The idea that not using a characteristic will make it surplus to requirements and cause it to disappear is another version of the Lamarckian misconception – that life events influence what parents can pass down to their offspring (7.4).

If having a smaller little finger offered an evolutionary advantage, then humans with this feature would out-compete others with larger little fingers and through natural selection the proportion of people in the population with smaller little fingers would increase (7.4). However, since there appears to be no significant disadvantage to having a larger little finger this is unlikely to happen.

The human body has leftover features we no longer find useful that we have inherited from distant ancestors, called vestiges (see Box p. 118). We still have the genes for these characteristics even though they are now redundant. Having thick body fur is important for hairy great apes such as gorillas because it helps insulate their bodies in cold temperatures, similar to how humans use clothing. The common ancestor of humans and other great apes was probably hairy like modern gorillas but at some point in history along the human evolutionary branch of this tree of life it must have been advantageous *not* to be hairy, since hominids (human-like species) lost their hair and evolved into the nearly hairless modern human. A few scientists have speculated that our ancestors took to living in coastal marine or freshwater environments where thick fur would produce considerable water **drag** during swimming, so being hairless would have been a significant advantage (the aquatic ape hypothesis). Others suggest that having little body hair is just one clue that early humans were adapted to run long distances in hot climates without overheating, perhaps to run down prey over a period of many hours as part of a cooperative hunting group (the endurance runner hypothesis).

Did you know?

Vestiges. The human body has leftover signs that suggest that we share common ancestry with a variety of creatures. The human coccyx is a short, redundant tail. The vestigial presence of human hair has been discussed in the main text and a related vestige is piloerection (goose bumps) in reaction to cold, which serves a useful function in hairy animals by increasing the thickness of their fur coat, improving heat insulation. Another fur-related vestige is how the hair on the back of our hands and wrists always grows away from the thumb and towards the little finger, supposedly because when our ancestors walked on all fours the thumb formed the leading edge of the forelimb, so that grass brushed their hands 'with the grain' of the hair as they moved forwards.

Human ancestors' loss of fur was therefore not due to it no longer being useful, but instead having fur must have offered some evolutionary disadvantage that caused hairy hominids to die out. Similarly, human little fingers could not shrink over generations just because they are not used very much. In fact, in the developed world the little finger plays an increasingly important role – the IT explosion that began in the 1980s has made most of us into keyboard operators, and a proportion of us are touch typists who use all our fingers.

Reconstruction

If children think that with each new generation the little finger is becoming gradually smaller, then similar interventions as detailed in 7.3 and 7.4 are necessary that help them construct the scientifically acceptable idea that only information passed in genes is inherited, including the shape or size of body parts. This genetic information is with us from the time of our conception and does not change before we pass it on to our own offspring, no matter how often we may use a specific body part during our lives.

Sources: Bishop and Anderson (1990); Tuomisto *et al.* (2018).

7.6 Why are organisms adapted to living successfully in their habitats?

Misconception

Polar bears grow thick warm coats because they live in a very cold environment.

Scientific conception

Some children believe that an animal reacts to its immediate surroundings by producing an adaptation during its lifetime, e.g. polar bear cubs sense the cold at a very young age and react by growing thick fur coats. This is like the giraffe neck misconception covered in 7.3 but differs as the polar bear's adaptation is not thought to be inheritable, with each new generation of polar bears reacting similarly and producing its own adaptations in response to cold environmental conditions. Another example of this misconception is the belief that cheetahs run fast merely because they have learned how to do so – if they ran slowly they would not catch any prey and starve. This is an example of reverse causality bias, where children mix up the cause of something with its effect.

As discussed in 7.3, adaptations such as a polar bear's thick fur exist because there was once variation within the population of an ancestor of polar bears where different individuals had a variety of fur thicknesses. The climate turned colder, so the bears with thicker fur had an advantage over others in the population and the disadvantaged shorter-haired bears either migrated to warmer places or died of cold. Therefore, in the region we now call the Arctic, modern polar bears have thick fur because their ancestors were the only individuals in the population equipped to survive, with this adaptation being passed down the generations via the genes.

A similar misconception is that all variation between individuals arises only due to an organism reacting to its immediate environment (environmental variation), such as overeating results in an increased body mass. It must be remembered that some variation is inheritable and is caused by differences in the genetic make-up of organisms (genetic variation), where the mixing of genes during sexual reproduction produces a variety of offspring. Different children in the same family are never completely alike despite the fact they may have the same parents (as long as they are not identical twins); these differences are due mainly to gene crossover and chromosome mixing when sperm and egg cells are made. Polar bear cubs born in zoos in hot countries will still grow thick fur despite the warmer weather because their genes 'tell' their body to do so; however, the fur may become thinner due to moulting in response to the hot temperatures, which is a further adaptation that helps the animal survive.

A different set of misconceptions are goal-driven; for instance, evolution creates organisms that are perfectly adapted to their habitat, and an organism chooses to evolve to help it survive.

Reconstruction

Apart from polar bears, other exemplar species used in primary science when teaching adaptations include camels and cacti, since their anatomical and physiological features are easy to understand and relate to their desert habitat. Since the polar bear misconception is a Lamarckian variant, the pedagogies that encourage the construction of concepts that help explain natural selection as described in 7.3 and 7.4 are appropriate. Modern selective breeding involves farmers only allowing plants and animals to breed if they have certain desirable features such as resistance to disease or large size. Disease-prone and smaller individuals are not allowed to breed, so any genes responsible for these undesirable features disappear when the organisms die. Teaching this idea can help children understand how the selection of useful adaptations has happened in the past due to accidental natural events.

Beany Beetles is a game that can be sourced online that is a simple simulation of natural selection. Children cut out paper beetles, some green and others brown, which are placed in 'a field in summertime' (a piece of green sugar paper). A bird appears and starts to hunt for beetles (children throw dice) which results in more brown beetles being eaten because they are less camouflaged. The process is repeated, this time 'in autumn' (brown sugar paper) where more brown beetles survive compared with green ones.

Sources: Budden (2018); Deadman and Kelly (1978); Dennis *et al.* (2015).

Famous scientists

Gregor Mendel. Called the 'father of genetics', Mendel was born in Austria in 1822 and was an unconventional scientist, living most of his adult life as a monk. He experimented with growing pea plants and discovered that certain features such as the colour of flowers, the plant's height and seed shape were being inherited from parent to offspring in very predictable ways. Mendel realized that there must be something physical being passed on between the generations, which later scientists called 'genes'. This research was vitally important, since it laid the foundations for the science of genetics, and evolution. The true value of Mendel's work, however, was not realized until years after his death and so he never personally received the accolades he deserved.

7.7 Biological variation

Misconception

A dog looks different to a cat – this is an example of variation.

Scientific conception

The misconception statement reflects an understanding that the scientific word 'variation' means that animals belonging to different species do not look the same. However, the school science definition states that only differences between individuals of the *same species* count as 'variation'. There is great variation in body size, shape, coat colour, and other physical characteristics between different breeds of dog; however, all dog breeds belong to the same species because they can interbreed successfully to produce pups that themselves will one day be capable of reproducing (Figure 7.7). It is common for children to use the wider, everyday definition of 'variation', i.e. any differences between any organisms.

Although children can list observable examples of variation, they typically find it difficult to explain using concepts of heredity why different members of the same species do not look the same; they suggest different ages, genders, or eating different foods as reasons.

Figure 7.7 Noticeable variation exists within the species *Canis familiaris* (domestic dog)

Reconstruction

Comparing human physical features can help children appreciate what variation means. Ask children to compare themselves with the person sitting next to them and write down five examples of variation, i.e. how they look different from each other. Tell the class not to make personal or nasty comments about their partners. Taken further, surveys that involve measuring children's heights, shoe sizes, or hand spans to create bar charts or frequency charts will help develop maths skills.

This work can be linked to discussions about adaptations by explaining how variation can be vital for the survival of a species. The fact that individuals within the same species are different means that if their environment changes, some individuals will be more suited than others and survive, so the adaptation becomes more common within the whole population (see 7.3).

With younger children, observing variation within the same species can be achieved by visits to farms (do all hens and sheep look the same?), growing plants from seed (if sourced from the same seed packet, do they all grow as tall?), and comparing photographs of children's pets (why do cats look different if they are all the same species?).

All the above can help children understand variation but it may not prevent them from incorrectly believing that diversity between *different* species can also be called variation. In the end, it might merely be a case of children remembering by rote learning that variation means only differences within the same species. A deeper discussion involving genetic and environmental variation will help ground their understanding and improve memory (see 7.4).

Sources: Gormley *et al.* (2022); Hackling and Treagust (1982); Russell and McGuigan (2019); Stern and Kampourakis (2017).

7.8 If we evolved from apes, why are there still apes?

Misconception

Humans evolved from chimpanzees.

Scientific conception

This common idea reflects a linear model of evolution where at some point in history chimpanzees evolved directly into humans. The misconception is Lamarckian, with species able to physically change during the period of their lifetimes and then giving birth to offspring that inherit these changes. A logical extension of this idea is that because ancestors change directly into descendants, i.e. when one species evolves into another, both cannot exist during the same time period.

Although *Homo sapiens* and *Pan troglodytes* (chimpanzees) are very closely related genetically, there is no direct lineage between the two species. Both species did, however, evolve from a common ape-like ancestor that lived approximately 15 million years ago. It is true that chimpanzees did evolve before humans – the first chimp appeared around 4 million years ago, while humans are a very young species, with the first anatomically modern *Homo sapiens* appearing only a quarter of a million years ago. Nevertheless, chimpanzees were not our great, great-(etc.) grandparents; they are more like our evolutionary cousins (see 'Reconstruction' below).

Even if humans were directly descended from chimpanzees, the two species could still potentially exist together today. Just because one species has evolved from another does not mean that the ancestor species will automatically die out and be replaced by the descendant species. For instance, the domestic dog evolved from the grey wolf around 20,000 years ago, yet both species are still in existence today. The question *if we evolved from apes, then why are there still apes?* has been used incorrectly by creationists in attempts to disprove Darwinism and make the case for Intelligent Design (see Box p. 114).

Reconstruction

Meikle and Scott (2010) suggest using the idea of cousins to address this misconception. We are related to our cousins but we are not directly descended from them in a linear way; instead, we share common ancestors, our grandparents. If we consider chimpanzees as evolutionary cousins, then the situation is the same – both species had a common ancestor that lived many millions of years ago, which means humans and chimpanzees are distantly related. Just as we could not have evolved from our family cousins, humans could not have evolved from chimpanzees (Figure 7.8a).

This could be taught as part of a discussion on human evolution in Year 6. To help illustrate the idea, introduce the theme of how the human skeleton has adapted from the time our species split from other primates. One feature to highlight would be the move to bipedalism, when our ape-like ancestors first began to walk on two legs instead of four. To walk efficiently on two legs, certain adaptations to the skeleton were necessary (Figure 7.8b). Feet developed an arch, and toes became smaller to help bipedal walking because they were no longer necessary for grasping trees during movement through the forest. Knee

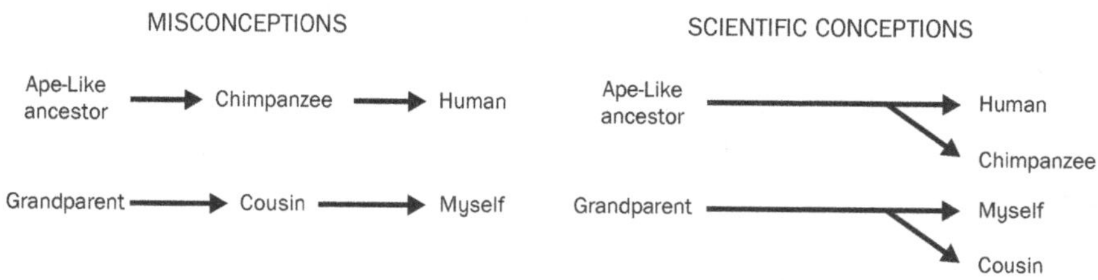

Figure 7.8a Using cousins as an analogy
Source: Adapted from Meikle and Scott (2010).

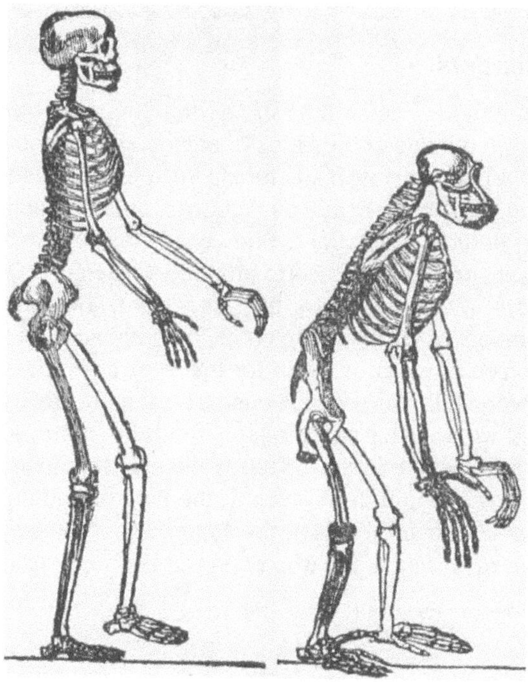

Figure 7.8b Comparison of modern human and chimpanzee skeletons to illustrate skeletal changes necessary for bipedalism
Source: Adapted from Huxley (1890), p. 70.

joints became bigger to support the entire weight of the body during upright walking and running. The shape of the backbone changed to give a more upright stance which allowed sustained running over long distances. The upper leg (femur) turned inwards from the hip to the knee to allow comfortable standing for long periods. Legs became longer, and arms – no longer needed for moving around – became shorter. These adaptations allowed our bipedal ancestors to stand erect and so have their hands free to manipulate tools, an adaptation thought to be vital in allowing the development of human technology. These discussions can be part of a more general treatment of evolution, with fossils of human ancestors being offered as evidence to support Darwinian theory (see Chapter 11 for more about fossils). A useful story book for introducing KS1 children to fossils and simple ideas about evolution is *Gumdrop and the Dinosaur* by Val Biro. Similarly, *Dinosaur* by Meredith Hooper is a good text for upper KS1/lower KS2 children.

Sources: Biro (2004); Hooper (1996); Meikle and Scott (2010).

Famous scientists

Mary Anning. Although celebrated in her day, in recent times Mary has been little known outside of the fields of palaeontology and fossil collecting. Born into a poor working-class family in 1799, she had only a basic education and did not become qualified as a professional geologist, instead being entirely self-taught. She is credited for unearthing many important fossils from the sea cliffs around Lyme Regis, Dorset, including the first ever plesiosaur (an extinct sea lizard). Her work led directly to the development of important scientific theories such as the extinction of species, which provided a basis for the later claim that there was a prehistory before humans when dinosaurs roamed the Earth, an idea that conflicted with biblical teachings of the time. Mary achieved all of this despite the social barriers of her humble background and the fact that she was a woman, both of which at the time barred her from following an academic career. In 2010, the Royal Society recognized her as among the ten most influential women in the history of British science.

Note

1 An exception to this is exposure of a pregnant mother to environmental influences that may affect a foetus, such as drugs or pollutants; however, this is not genetic inheritance. Recently, geneticists have begun to achieve a degree of success in genetically modifying the sperm cells of animals such as pigs and rabbits to produce viable offspring; however, attempting the same in humans for the purposes of disease prevention is still some years away.

Planning and assessment sheet 7 Reproduction, inheritance, and evolution
(For suggestions on how to use this sheet, see p. xxviii.)

Misconception	*Attainment re. expected standard*		
	Working towards	*Working at*	*Working above*
Year 2: *Living things and their habitats*			
An organism reacts to its immediate surroundings by producing an adaptation during its lifetime (7.6)	✓	✓	✓
Modern giraffes have long necks because their ancestors' necks grew longer as they stretched to reach the leaves high up in trees (7.3)		✓	✓
Polar bear cubs grow thick warm coats because they have to live in a very cold environment (7.6)	✓	✓	
Cheetahs run fast because they have learned how to do so (if they ran slowly they would not catch any prey and starve) (7.6)	✓	✓	
All living things have been made by a creator and so their adaptations are creations that do not change over time (7.3)	✓	✓	
Year 3: *Plants*			
The transfer of pollen from one flower to another is called fertilization (7.1)		✓	✓
Only animals are capable of reproduction, not plants (plant blindness) (7.1)	✓		
'A flower' is the whole plant, including petals, stem, and leaves (as in 'a bunch of flowers') (7.1)	✓	✓	✓
Fruits are always soft, sweet, and fleshy (7.1)	✓	✓	✓
Year 6: *Evolution and inheritance*			
Sons take after their fathers, and daughters take after their mothers (7.2)	✓	✓	
Both boys and girls inherit most of their characteristics from their mothers (because mothers give birth) (7.2)	✓	✓	
Modern giraffes have long necks because their ancestors' necks grew longer as they stretched to reach the leaves high up in trees (7.3)		✓	✓

(continued)

(*continued*)

All living things have been made by a creator and so their adaptations are creations that do not change over time (7.3)	✓	✓	
Evolution always produces descendants which are larger, more complex, and have a higher intelligence than their ancestors (7.3)			✓
The child of a bodybuilder will be born with big muscles (7.4)	✓	✓	✓
A person's characteristics are all inherited from their parents (i.e. ignoring environmental variation) (7.4)	✓	✓	
A person's characteristics only appear when they are reacting to their immediate environment, e.g. overeating results in an increased body mass (i.e. ignoring genetic variation) (7.6)	✓		
Our little fingers are getting smaller because we no longer use them (7.5)		✓	✓
An organism reacts to its immediate surroundings by producing an adaptation during its lifetime (7.6)	✓	✓	✓
Polar bear cubs grow thick warm coats because they have to live in a very cold environment (7.6)	✓	✓	
Cheetahs run fast because they have learned how to do so (if they ran slowly they would not catch any prey and starve) (7.6)	✓	✓	
A dog looks different to a cat – this is an example of variation (7.7)		✓	✓
Variation is due to factors such as different ages, genders, or eating different foods (i.e. ignoring that characteristics can be inherited) (7.7)		✓	✓
Humans evolved from chimpanzees (7.8)	✓	✓	✓

PART THREE
Chemistry

8

Chemical changes in materials

Conceptual areas covered in this chapter:	*National Curriculum links:*
• Defining scientific terminology (material, combustion, dissolving) • Differences between chemical change and physical change • Conservation of mass	Year 1: *Everyday materials* Year 2: *Uses of everyday materials* Year 5: *Properties of everyday materials and reversible change*

8.1 What is a material?

> **Misconception**
>
> *A material is something used for building, clothing or writing.*

Scientific conception

Children are familiar with the word *material* in its everyday sense, e.g. bricks are a form of building material, fabrics are clothing material, and stationery is writing material. Other non-scientific meanings include information (research material), and a material being something solid, worldly, and physical ('Jesus appeared in material form'). Children can think that anything outside of these examples is not a material.

In science, a material is something that is made from **matter**, i.e. from atoms, molecules, or **ions**. Therefore, liquids and gases are materials, though children often think they are not because they restrict the meaning to just solids. Non-materials are things not made from matter, e.g. energy.

The term *raw materials*, as in the starting substances for an industrial process, may also act as a source of confusion even though all raw materials are still *materials* in the scientific sense.

Reconstruction

These misconceptions may crop up when the term 'material' is first introduced to children in Year 1. During this and other primary chemistry topics that children experience, teachers use the word 'material' extensively in many classroom contexts, including activities that involve liquids and gases. It would be hoped through this repeated exposure, that children come to construct the scientifically wider meaning of the word and understand that this is different from any everyday definition that they know. This process can be helped during classification exercises such as the placing of objects into solid, liquid, and gas sets, by teachers repeatedly referring to all the objects as materials (see Chapter 10).

Source: Bouma *et al.* (1990).

8.2 When something burns, why does it disappear?

Misconception

When an object burns, parts of it disappear and no longer exist.

Scientific conception

When a piece of wood burns, flames appear to eat away at the wood, which turns into something different that is much smaller, i.e. ashes. Some children find it difficult to explain both why this size reduction takes place, and where the original wood may have gone. They may think that through the action of burning, the flames convert some of the wood into ashes, while the rest of it is completely destroyed and no longer exists. Others might conclude that the missing wood becomes smoke, which is nearer to the truth, although when questioned further, they insist the smoke then 'disappears into the air', also ceasing to exist.

As with any **chemical change**, during **combustion** (burning), the mass of materials is always conserved – if you weigh what you start with and what you end up with, these values will be identical because matter can neither be created nor destroyed – this is the *law of conservation of matter.* When wood burns it reacts with oxygen in the air, and the particles that make up wood and oxygen are rearranged to make new materials – carbon dioxide and water (Figure 8.2). When a piece of wood is burning, children think there is an obvious loss of mass as the wood shrinks and turns to ashes. But since combustion produces carbon dioxide gas and water (as **steam**), these gaseous products invisibly rise up in heat currents and spread out into the surrounding air – the gases have not ceased to exist, they are just difficult to detect. To complicate matters, it is likely that not all the wood burns completely and so other 'wood' + oxygen ⟶ carbon dioxide + water

Figure 8.2 Simple word equation for the complete combustion of wood

products will be created, such as gaseous carbon monoxide and solid carbon. Some of this carbon is lost as smoke (soot) and the rest becomes part of ashes, which also includes minerals in the wood that cannot be burnt. If burning takes place within a sealed container, none of these products of combustion can escape; if the container and its contents are weighed before and after combustion, there will be no loss in mass.

Related misconceptions are that during combustion the wood disappears because it turns into heat energy, or that the ash produced is still wood but has just changed its appearance, with nothing new being made.

Reconstruction

While burning a candle, ask children *why does the candle eventually become smaller? What has happened to all the wax?* This will help elicit some of the misconceptions discussed above. Then, place a candle into a sealable transparent container such as a large jam jar or similar. Weigh the candle plus container. Light the candle, being sure to quickly seal the top and leave it to burn until it extinguishes itself – this will take less than half a minute with a large jam jar. Keeping the jar sealed, reweigh the contents, explaining that although it might be surprising that the weight has not changed, this conservation of mass occurs because the gases produced by burning have been trapped within the jar. These products normally drift away from the flame and escape into the surrounding air. Conclude by saying that burning does not destroy the wax, which then ceases to exist; the wax merely changes into something else, mostly carbon dioxide and water (see 8.3 for other misconceptions about candles).

Although some children may predict a loss of mass within the closed container, others might believe the burning will result in an increase in mass, possibly because the smoke being produced is thought to add its mass to the final value. Like the main misconception, this type of thinking reflects a failure to conserve mass during a chemical change.

Sources: de Andrade *et al.* (2017); Watson *et al.* (1997).

8.3 What happens when a candle burns?

Misconception

Candle wax does not burn, it just melts.

Scientific conception

A lighted candle will melt the wax around the wick and also burn the wax as a fuel. The melted wax that does not burn runs down the outside of the candle and becomes solid again, which may give the impression that the flame just melts the wax. A chemical change has taken place because something new has been produced – the products of combustion, which include carbon dioxide, and water, escape as gases (see 8.2).

Reconstruction

Burning a candle on an electronic balance will show a slow and steady decrease in mass since the products of combustion escape as gases into the air. If the candle was only melting, then its mass would stay the same. Keeping an eye on a tea light candle as it burns over the course of an hour will first show the wax melting, becoming completely liquefied. As the candle continues to burn, the liquid wax gradually disappears, which can help children understand that the wax is converted to invisible gases during combustion which escape into the surrounding air. Be aware that because the melted wax is a clear liquid, some children may think it has turned into water.

Children may also believe that liquids are always lighter than solids (10.4), so the decrease in mass of a burning candle is to be expected because the wax melts to become a liquid. If you weigh a burning tea light candle while the wax is completely liquefied and immediately blow out the flame, reweighing it a little later after the wax has re-solidified will show that wax weighs the same whether it is in solid or liquid form.

Traditionally in primary science, chemical change is demonstrated using the reaction between vinegar and bicarbonate of soda. One product of this chemical change is carbon dioxide gas which is easily detectable as it fizzes within the vinegar. For an engaging demonstration of this reaction, source several plastic photographic film canisters – these are obsolete, but still available to buy online. Using Blu Tack, children press an Alka Seltzer tablet into the lid of the canister so that it does not fall out (which is a perfect size fit), then pour about 1cm depth of vinegar into the canister itself. Place the lid onto its canister, pressing firmly to ensure an airtight fit. Turn the canister upside down which mixes the vinegar and Alka Seltzer (contains bicarbonate of soda), generating carbon dioxide gas resulting in a build-up of pressure within the canister. After a few seconds the canister pops open with sudden bang and flies into the air. Remind children to wear safety spectacles and step back at least 1 metre once they invert the canister; with my class I used to call this activity *Vinegar Surprise* because it produces quite a jump scare!

Another variant of the same reaction is to mix the juice from a jar of pickled red cabbage (contains vinegar) with baking powder (contains bicarbonate of soda). This is a slower reaction than *Vinegar Surprise*, and after about a minute the mixture will push-up a large froth which threatens to overflow its container. Red cabbage is a type of natural indicator that turns a different colour in acids and alkalis – the red cabbage juice is red because vinegar is acidic, but when baking powder is added, it turns blue because bicarbonate of soda is alkaline.

There are spectacular examples of chemical changes available as Graphics Interchange Format files (GIFs) that can be downloaded free from the internet that demonstrate how a chemical change involves new materials being made, e.g. www.giphy.com. GIFs are useful animations because the files can be copied and pasted into programs such as Microsoft PowerPoint to help enliven a visual presentation.

The children's book *Burn: Michael Faraday's Candle* by Darcy Pattison and Peter Willis helps to consolidate concepts relating to the conservation of matter.

Sources: Fotou (2014); Meheut *et al.* (1985); Pattison and Willis (2016).

8.4 Confusing the terminology of reversible and irreversible changes

Misconception

When burning paper shrinks to leave ash, part of it has evaporated.

Scientific conception

A Year 5 practical lesson familiar to primary teachers involves children observing the changes that take place when a variety of everyday materials such as paper, twigs, and fabric are carefully burned over a candle flame. These observations are then used as a basis for discussions about differences between **reversible** and **irreversible changes** in materials, with combustion being held up as an example of a process that is irreversible – once something has burned, you can never get back what you started with. A child having the above misconception has grasped the correct idea that the paper has undergone change, and bits of what the paper changes into (ashes) have drifted away during burning. As with many related examples in school science (e.g. 8.1), the way in which the child has chosen to describe the escaping process reflects the literary and not the scientific meaning of 'evaporate'. The everyday definition is to disperse or disappear, e.g. 'on the arrival of the police, the crowd evaporated', so in this sense the ashes have indeed evaporated. But in science, **evaporation** has a more specific meaning: the change of a liquid into a gas below the **boiling** point, as in 'during the course of the day the puddle evaporated'. When the paper burns, it does not evaporate because it is not a liquid.

Many people find it surprising that one of the substances made when most things burn is water (8.2), which is usually associated with extinguishing flames. When paper burns, water is produced, although as soon as the water appears it immediately boils due to the high temperature of the flame and escapes into the air as gaseous steam. However, strictly speaking, this is still not evaporation because the change into gas takes place above the boiling point of water, which is 100°C – so scientifically, the correct word to use is 'boiling'. Note that the process of melting and evaporation may indeed occur when some substances burn, e.g. parts of a burning piece of chocolate melt; with a lighted candle, wax melts, then evaporates. However, this is not the case for all examples of combustion.

Children have been known to substitute the word 'melt' in a similar way, confusing it with its literary meaning of mysterious disappearance, as in 'she melted away into the night'; therefore, a child might say a burning piece of wood in a campfire slowly melts to become ashes. As with evaporation, the scientific meaning of melting is quite precise: the changing of a solid into a liquid. Another reason why children might use an inappropriate word is that there is uncertainty regarding the scientific definitions of words that are involved in similar contexts. For instance, during a **state changes** topic, the words melting and **freezing** are confused with each other and then used interchangeably, as are evaporation and **condensation**, because children have not yet fully understood exactly what these words mean, and may have merely attempted to rote-learn them.

Related misconceptions include that a candle melts but does not burn (8.3), and confusing physical and chemical changes (children may lump all changes into the same category without differentiating between the two processes).

Reconstruction

Frequent use of scientific terminology by the teacher helps children to successfully learn the correct definitions of words. If words such as burning, evaporation, and melting are presented in a variety of scientific contexts, including practical work, then their definitions are reinforced and children become more adept at using them correctly. Referring to the differences between reversible and irreversible changes will help to remind children that burning, evaporation, and melting are three quite different processes.

The concept of irreversible chemical change can be introduced to KS1 children through the simple activity of baking bread. Make up a dough and give out a handful to children to knead and then shape as desired. Place in an oven for 20 minutes at 150°C to produce little parcels of bread, which can lead to discussions about whether they can ever reverse the process and get back the dough.

Sources: Hadenfeldt *et al.* (2016); Papageorgiou *et al.* (2010).

8.5 What happens when a material dissolves?

Misconception

When salt is dissolved in water, it no longer exists.

Scientific conception

It is surprising the number of children who think that when a substance such as salt or sugar is completely dissolved in a glass of water, that substance ceases to be present in the resulting mixture. One common reason for this is the fact that the salt or sugar starts off as a powder that is clearly visible but then magically vanishes when it is stirred into the water, and so is now 'out of sight, out of mind'. Variants of the same misconception include that when salt is dissolved in water, there is no increase in mass – i.e. the salt solution weighs the same as the original water – or that simply the salt disappears because it turns into water.

The chemical name for table salt is sodium chloride, having the chemical formula NaCl. A sample of solid salt grains is made from sodium ions (Na^+) and chloride ions (Cl^-) arranged in a 3D structure, but when mixed with water this structure starts to break up (Figure 8.5). The sodium and chloride ions split from each other and become attracted to water molecules which then surround the ions. This breaking up of the solid structure together with water molecules surrounding the ions means that the salt becomes very finely divided within the water so that you can no longer see any salt – the individual ions are too small to be visible. The salt is still there but is too spread out within the water. It is like taking an aerial photograph of a crowd of people – when they are clumped together they can be easily seen because they are a large mass, but if the crowd disperses and individuals move off in different directions, they are more difficult to spot. Another analogy is to imagine that you sprinkled a trail of black pepper while running across a sandy beach – it would be very difficult to go back and find each individual pepper grain in the sand. A different dissolving misconception is that when you pass salt water through filter paper, the salt is removed.

Both children and adults alike tend to believe that when you dissolve a solid in water the volume remains the same, when in fact the level of liquid does rise slightly. Some children have the opposite misconception, believing that when salt dissolves in water, the solution becomes lighter due to the salt acting like a sponge and absorbing some of the water's weight, and so the level drops. Learners sometimes believe that dissolving is a chemical change because it appears that new materials are created.

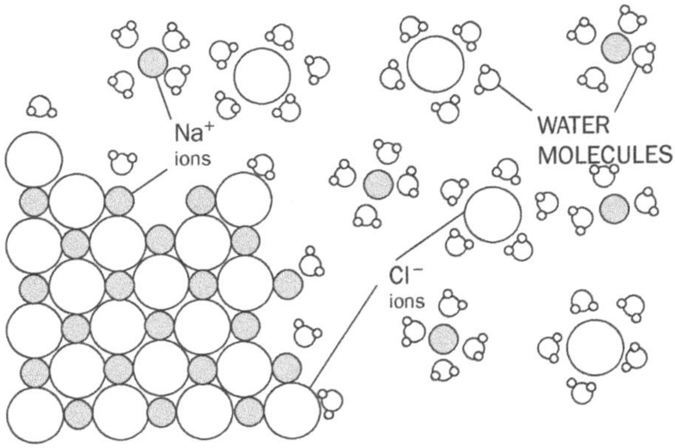

Figure 8.5 Salt dissolving in water

Reconstruction

Dissolving is a **physical change** that is reversible.[1] For example, primary children traditionally dissolve table salt as part of practical work on separating techniques; the salt and water are mixed together and then separated by placing the solution in a warm place, which makes the water evaporate, leaving solid salt. Carrying out this activity helps to persuade children that the salt never disappears completely when it is mixed with water. With KS1 children, if salt and water are mixed in hygienic conditions, the children could dip their fingers into the salt solution and taste it to prove that the salt is still there. This can be linked to memories of seaside holidays – the sea tastes salty because it is also a salt solution. With older children who drink tea or coffee, you can remind them that dissolving sugar in hot drinks would be pointless if the sugar just disappeared. A demonstration using a coloured solid such as bath salts in place of table salt would help children appreciate that when something becomes part of a solution, its particles are still present. Alternately, dissolving different-coloured boiled sweets in transparent containers of hot water placed in a row, makes an attractive display that refutes the same misconception. A similarly engaging demonstration of dissolving is to arrange a circle of *Skittles* sweets at the rim of a saucer then add hot water – the food colourings dissolve then mix together to create an interesting swirling pattern.

For upper KS2 children, understanding diagrams such as Figure 8.5 helps them appreciate that the particles are still there in a solution but finely divided. A good demonstration is to carefully fill a small cup right to the brim with hot water from a kettle, then pour the water into a larger cup before dissolving 4 teaspoonfuls of sugar into it (stir well). Pour the sugar solution back into the original small cup, which will now overflow due to the added sugar, which is invisible but clearly still there because it has increased the volume of the water.

A similar experiment that children can do is to weigh a fizzy drink, then allow it to go flat over a couple of days by leaving the top off before weighing it again. The flat drink will be lighter because the dissolved carbon dioxide gas adds weight to the fizzy drink.

Sources: Angeloudi *et al.* (2018); Cosgrove and Osborne (1980); Holloway (2019); Panagiotaki and Ravanis (2014).

Note

1 Although dissolving is not a chemical change and so does not directly fit in with the chapter's theme, it links with other material in the chapter that discusses physical changes.

Planning and assessment sheet 8 Chemical changes in materials

(For suggestions on how to use this sheet, see p. xxviii.)

Misconception	*Attainment re. expected standard*		
	Working towards	*Working at*	*Working above*
Year 1: *Everyday materials*			
Liquids and gases are not materials (8.1)	✓	✓	
A material is something solid, worldly, and physical (8.1)	✓	✓	
Year 2: *Uses of everyday materials*			
A material is something used for clothing, building, or writing (8.1)	✓		
Year 5: *Properties of everyday materials and reversible change*			
When an object burns, parts of it disappear and no longer exist (8.2)	✓	✓	
When wood burns, it disappears because it turns into heat energy (8.2)			✓
Ashes produced when wood burns are still wood – it has just changed its appearance with nothing new being made (8.2)		✓	
Candle wax does not burn, it just melts (8.3; 8.4)	✓	✓	
The clear liquid at the top of a burning candle is water (8.3)	✓		
When burning paper shrinks to leave ashes, part of it has evaporated (8.4)	✓	✓	
A burning piece of wood in a campfire slowly melts to become ashes (8.4)	✓	✓	
When salt is dissolved in water, the salt no longer exists (8.5)	✓	✓	
When salt is dissolved in water, the salt disappears because it turns into water (8.5)	✓	✓	
When you dissolve salt in water, there is no increase in mass (i.e. the salt solution weighs the same as the original water) (8.5)	✓	✓	✓

(continued)

(*continued*)

When you dissolve salt in water, there is a reduction in mass (i.e. the salt solution weighs less than the original water) (8.5)	✓		
When you dissolve salt in water, there is no increase in volume (i.e. the volume of the salt solution is the same as the original water) (8.5)	✓	✓	✓
When you dissolve salt in water, the level drops (i.e. the volume of the salt solution is less than the original water) (8.5)	✓		

9

Particles

Conceptual areas covered in this chapter:

- How particles are arranged in solids, liquids, and gases
- The internal structure of particles
- A gas inside a container can be under pressure (compressed), or at atmospheric pressure

National Curriculum links:

Year 4: *States of matter*

Year 5: *Properties of everyday materials and reversible changes*

9.1 Particles within solids and liquids

Misconception

Particles in a liquid are further apart than particles in a solid.

Scientific conception

Although not part of the primary curriculum, many schools introduce simple **particle** theory as part of topics that deal with **states of matter**. After teaching, children are typically able to correctly recognize particles as arranged in solid and a gas (Figures 9.1a and 9.1c). However, particles in a liquid are usually inaccurately drawn as being further apart than those in a solid, midway between the arrangements of particles in the solid and gaseous states (Figure 9.1b).

A reason for this may be confusion around how particles behave when a liquid boils or evaporates. Children learn that when a liquid becomes a gas, the liquid particles are heated to such an extent that they become excited enough to escape from the surface of the liquid and spread out into the room.

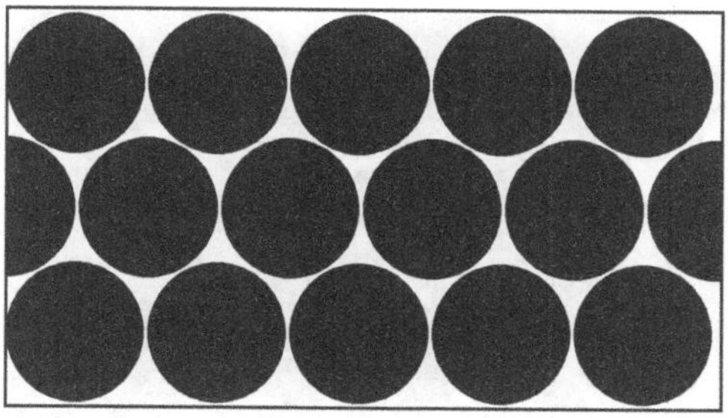

Figure 9.1a Particles in a solid

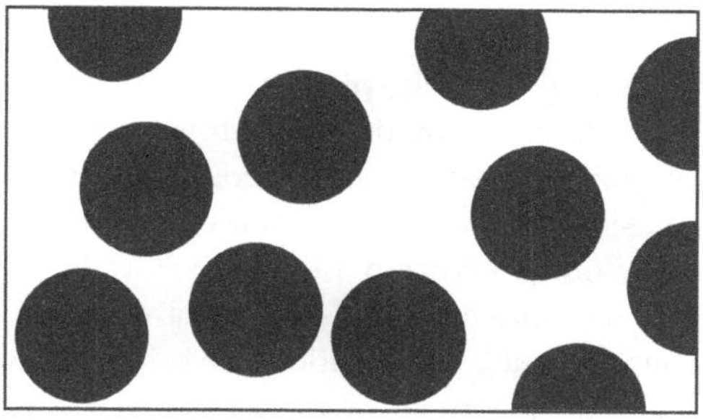

Figure 9.1b Particles in a liquid (misconception)

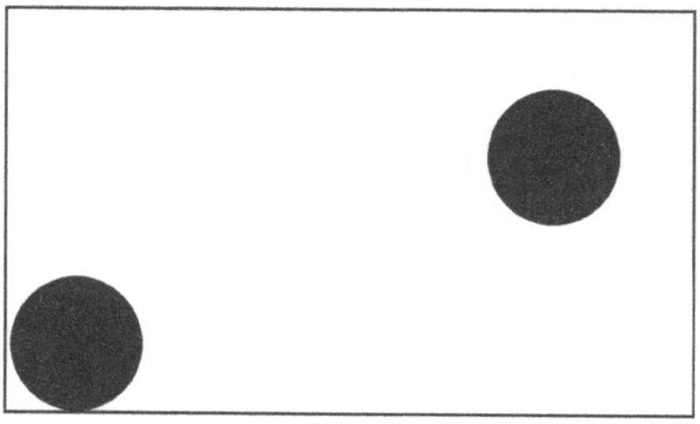

Figure 9.1c Particles in a gas (distances between particles are not to scale)

A common illustration of this process is boiling a kettle, with children tending to remember that particles of a gas are much further apart than they were when in the liquid state (Figure 9.1c). They understand that a cupful of water inside a boiling kettle becomes a mist they call 'steam' that can fill an entire room (this is not steam, but water droplets and water vapour – see 10.5). Children may extend this explanation to melting and assume that when a solid becomes a liquid, the solid particles also become excited and break apart (correct) and then move further away from each other to form a liquid (incorrect).

Figure 9.1d Correct drawing of particles in a liquid (particles are overlapping in three dimensions)

Figure 9.1d gives a more accurate picture of the arrangement of particles in the liquid phase. The particles in liquids remain touching each other as in a solid but have lost their regular arrangement and exist in a random and overlapping pattern in three dimensions. Since liquid particles are no longer fixed in position, they can roll over each other, allowing a liquid to flow, be spilled, and take the shape of the bottom of its container. Solids, on the other hand, have a fixed shape because their particles are stuck into position like bricks in a wall, although they do vibrate. Therefore, it does not matter whether particles of the same material are in the liquid or solid state, they remain the same distance apart, in close contact with each other (but see the unusual case of water, next paragraph).

The belief that liquid particles are further apart can also lead to the mistaken idea that a liquid takes up more space than a solid. Water is an odd material since the opposite happens – solid ice takes up *more* space than liquid water, which is why it is often difficult to remove ice cubes from a freezer tray; the particles in ice are further apart than in water so the ice expands when it freezes. Ice expanding is also the cause of burst water pipes in sub-zero temperatures and the reason why we mix antifreeze into the water inside a car radiator.

Did you know?

Thermal expansion. Although it is correct to say that the distance between particles in a material remains constant when a solid becomes a liquid or vice versa (water being an exception), this must not be confused with the fact that heating a material without it changing state can cause it to expand because the particles actually do move further apart. For instance, if a steel key is heated strongly in a flame, it will expand so much that it will become too large to fit its lock. If the steel is heated until it melts (around 1400°C), and then the liquid steel is heated further to, say, 2000°C, the liquid will continue to expand directly in response to the input of extra heat.

Reconstruction

This is a difficult misconception to overcome, as the (correct) idea of liquids being an intermediate stage between solids and gases makes perfect sense to children who then go on to assume that the spreading out of particles that occurs with boiling or evaporation, also takes place when a solid melts. Physical models are a useful way to introduce the concepts of particle arrangements, particularly *Molymod* and similar products, although glass marbles are a cheaper option. Using these models as props, emphasize that when a solid melts, the particles do become more excited and break free of their physical bonds, but they do not move any further apart. A good analogy for liquid particles that will be familiar to children is the colourful plastic ball baths that are found in public indoor play areas, where the balls are touching one another, are free to move (so can flow) and settle into the bottom of their containing box. A further example that would be familiar to KS1 children is how breakfast cereals such as *Rice Krispies* settle into the bottom of a bowl and can be spilled, poured, etc.

When addressing this misconception, water might be considered a poor example to use because it expands when it freezes to become ice, as mentioned above. A better material is a piece of candle wax, which can be carefully melted in a small glass beaker, metal eggcup or a similar heatproof container, using another candle as a source of heat. Once melted, the height of the hot liquid wax is carefully marked off on the side of the container using a pen and the wax then allowed to cool. Once solid, the level of the wax should not dip to below this mark showing that both solid and liquid wax occupy the same volume, so the solid and liquid particles must be similar distances apart. In contrast, water is useful to show that there are no gaps in between the particles of a liquid because it is impossible to squeeze a plugged syringe that contains water.

Sources: Papageorgiou *et al.* (2010); Shallcross *et al.* (2016).

9.2 What is the best way to draw particles?

> **Misconception**
>
> *An object is made from particles that look and behave like tiny bits of the larger material.*

Scientific conception

The diagrams in Figure 9.2a are the kinds of imaginative yet inaccurate pictures children may produce when asked to draw 'particles'. These drawings show that children can keep the **macroscopic** identity of the whole material (copper, aluminium, or air) right down to the particle level.

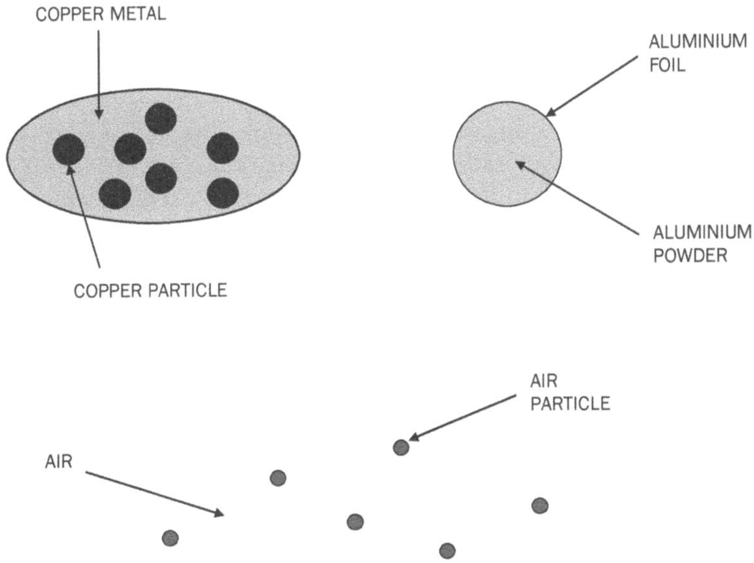

Figure 9.2a Children's drawings of particles (misconceptions)

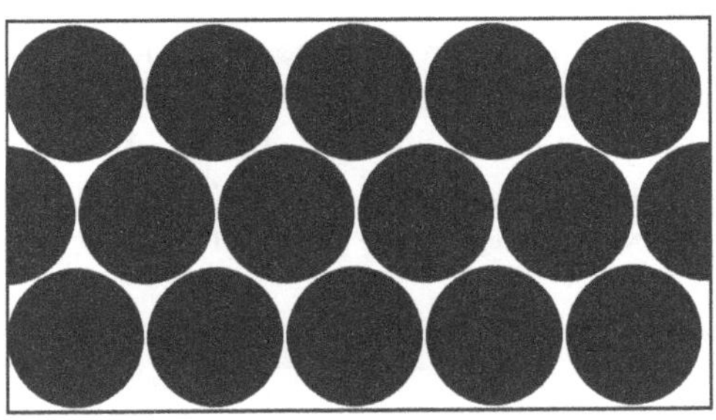

Figure 9.2b Atoms in a typical solid, e.g. copper

The copper diagram in Figure 9.2a has been called the 'currant bun' model, where copper particles (atoms) exist within a bed of copper. In reality, copper atoms are not embedded in a larger material, instead they are tightly linked to each other in a regular pattern (Figure 9.2b). The gaps between the atoms are filled with nothing, i.e. are a **vacuum**.

In Figure 9.2a, the child has drawn an aluminium atom as being made from different types of aluminium material (foil and powder), which conflicts with what scientists believe is inside an atom. As with all atoms, a single aluminium atom is made up of smaller building blocks, or **subatomic** units, called **neutrons**, **protons**, and **electrons** (Figure 9.2c). Each of these units is thought to consist of even tinier subatomic pieces such as quarks, leptons, and gluons; one

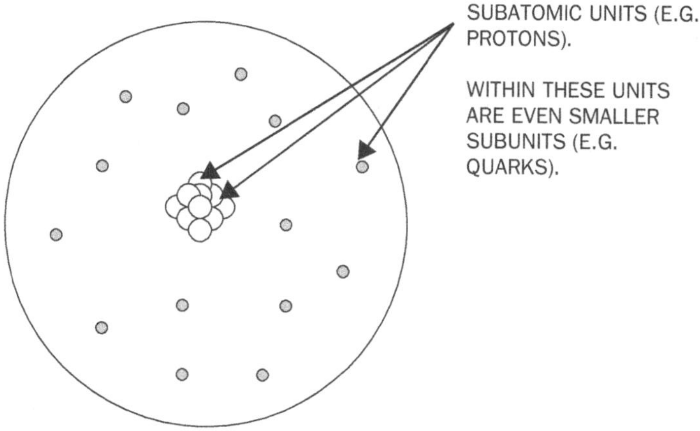

Figure 9.2c A simple diagram of a whole atom

theory proposes these small pieces are made from even smaller things called superstrings. Therefore, atoms of every material are built from these same kinds of basic building blocks whether that material is aluminium, copper, oxygen, carbon, or anything else. It is like how the same Lego bricks can be arranged in different ways and used in different amounts to build a variety of different objects. To say that an aluminium atom is made from aluminium is not correct and is practically the same as saying that the bricks that make up a house are house-shaped.

In Figure 9.2a, the air picture is a version of the currant bun model where particles exist within a surrounding substance made from the same material. As with the copper picture, the space between the 'air particles' is a vacuum and contains no matter.

There are several very common misconceptions where children similarly apply macroscopic features to particles (see 9.3).

Reconstruction

If children have constructed misconceptions where the macroscopic nature of the whole material continues at the particle level as in Figure 9.2a, challenge their thinking by asking questions such as *what is the aluminium foil/powder made from? What is the copper metal in which the copper atoms sit made from?* An aluminium atom is the smallest piece of aluminium that can exist, so it does not make sense to say that the foil/powder in the drawing must itself be made from aluminium atoms. The same argument can be made with the copper bed and the continuous air medium.

At primary school level, a detailed discussion of subatomic particles is beyond the curriculum; that said, the simple knowledge that particles such as atoms are made of even smaller particles may help children visualize a more scientific model. Use of the Lego analogy as mentioned above would be likely to help their understanding. Comparing the **densities** of different materials can be linked to the internal structure of atoms; for instance, a piece of iron is heavy compared with a same-sized piece of wood, in part because iron atoms contain more protons and electrons than the atoms in wood.

The London Science Museum has interactive exhibits that help children understand the particulate nature of matter and is well worth a visit. Its website has downloadable resources for use in the classroom: www.sciencemuseum.org.uk

Other approaches to engage children with particle structure include showing images of real atoms captured by electron microscopy, and using *Molymod* to build reproductions of the particles that make up common substances such as carbon dioxide, oxygen, water, and sugar (sucrose). There are YouTube video clips available to help teach atomic theory at primary school level, although some are beyond the curriculum (search for 'Atomic School').

Sources: Nussbaum (1985); Renstrom *et al.* (1990); Rips and Hespos (2015); Stuart (2021).

Famous scientists

Marie Curie. Born in Poland in the mid-nineteenth century, Marie spent most of her adult life in France studying and researching chemistry and physics. She was especially interested in what atoms were constructed from, and her work helped prove that inside atoms there are even smaller particles, such as protons, neutrons, and electrons. She is more famous for her important discoveries about the nature of radioactivity and, as a result, became the first woman to be awarded the Nobel Prize. However, the dangers of exposure to **radiation** were not well known when Marie was conducting her experiments, and working with highly dangerous entities such as X-rays and radium were likely responsible for her poor health in later life, and her death from a rare form of anaemia. In fact, Marie's original research papers are now considered too radioactive to handle and are stored in protective lead-lined containers at the Bibliothèque Nationale in Paris.

9.3 How do particles behave?

Misconception

When a solid is heated, its particles melt.

Scientific conception

When children are taught that materials are made from particles, there is often a tendency to apply macroscopic qualities to them that match those of a larger piece of the material. For instance, when a piece of ice melts, children believe that the water particles that the ice is made from, also melt. As is detailed in 9.2, a particle (or more correctly an atom, a molecule, or an ion) is the smallest piece of a material that can exist. If ice melts, it becomes a liquid because its water particles are no longer attached to each other and become free to move around, which means that water can flow, be spilled, etc. (9.1). The water particles have merely become rearranged within the material; the particles themselves have not changed at all. Therefore, particles cannot melt, it is just the macroscopic material (ice) that has melted. There are similar misconceptions where learners of all ages believe particles expand, contract, or heat up, and also have properties such as being hard, soft, transparent, and possessing texture. Some learners think particles are a kind of living thing that can grow, reproduce, and exhibit other life processes. One caveat to this is that in some cases when children make these claims, they are simply making a language error and do not really believe that particles can melt – they have just been careless and used the wrong scientific term to describe a material's behaviour.

Related misconceptions include that because a liquid is motionless, then its particles must be fixed in position and do not move around, particles have the same colour of their macroscopic material, particles of solids are hard while those of liquids are soft, and particles of solids are always larger than those of liquids and gases.

Reconstruction

This misconception is quite difficult to address at primary level because it requires children to think in an abstract way to consider what exactly is happening to a material at the particle level. Using commercially available models of particles such as *Molymod* (though glass marbles would do) are good because each particle is a rigid plastic sphere that cannot be altered. Explain to children that a particle cannot melt, expand, etc. because it is like a piece of plastic *Molymod* – it can only change its position inside the structure of the whole material. Using the activities covered in 9.1 and 9.2 would also be relevant here.

As discussed in 9.2, the belief that all particles are fixed in position is not correct since liquid particles are free to flow over each other, gas particles move around randomly at high speed, and although solid particles have a fixed, regular arrangement, they are constantly vibrating. *Thermoscope*, an educational app, allows children to place a temperature probe inside a material that is linked to a tablet or PC. As children heat and cool the material as part of a practical experiment, a visual animation of how the particles are behaving can be viewed onscreen. *Thermoscope* has been shown to be effective in helping younger children especially, construct scientific models of particle behaviour.

Sources: Hadenfeldt *et al.* (2016); Harrison and Treagust (1996); Samarapungavan *et al.* (2023).

9.4 How much air is in a flat tyre?

Misconception

Flat tyres contain no air.

Scientific conception

If a bicycle tyre or a football deflates because of a puncture, in an everyday sense it is acceptable to say that *all the air has been let out.* Once the puncture has been repaired, to re-inflate the tyre we then need to *put some air in.* However, to say that a tyre does not have any air left suggests that there is nothing at all inside, i.e. a vacuum exists within the tyre, which is scientifically incorrect.

The air particles inside an inflated tyre are closer together – that is, more concentrated – than the surrounding air particles outside the tyre (Figure 9.4, left). This is because when the tyre was inflated, air has been pumped into the tyre under pressure so becoming **compressed air** inside the tyre. This is why when we press an inflated tyre with our fingers, it feels springy and firm – the air particles at high concentration inside push out against the tyre wall. It is as though the particles are pushing outwards because they want to escape into the surrounding atmospheric air because they are too crowded inside the tyre. Indeed, if the tyre gets a puncture, the particles rush out through the hole, causing the pressure to drop inside and the tyre to deflate (Figure 9.4, right). Note that with the totally deflated tyre, not all the air particles have escaped – some of them will remain inside the tyre. This is because when the tyre is punctured, air only continues to escape until the concentration of particles inside the tyre is exactly the same as the concentration of particles in the surrounding air (Figure 9.4, right). When we press a deflated tyre, there is no firm springiness because it does not contain air under pressure, just air at normal atmospheric pressure. Therefore, a deflated tyre may appear at first sight to have no air inside when in fact it has plenty, and the particles inside are at the same concentration as the surrounding air.

Reconstruction

Air is invisible and in everyday contexts we rarely acknowledge its presence, including the air that fills an 'empty' cup. Only when we are able to sense air do we acknowledge it, such as when we squeeze an inflated party balloon and feel its

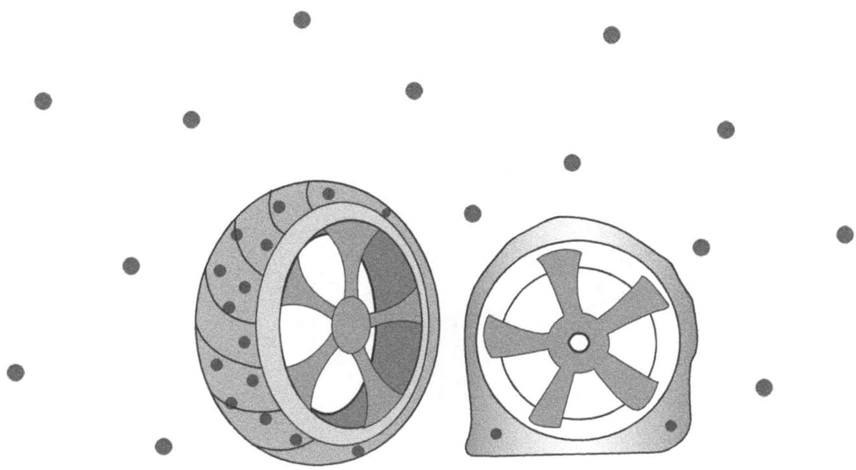

Figure 9.4 The concentrations of air particles inside and outside an inflated tyre (left) and a totally deflated tyre (right)

pressure pushing outwards, being aware of a draught of cold air coming in through the open door of a house, or when we hear air escaping from a punctured tyre. Giving children these examples to think about will help remind them that air is constantly present around us. At KS1, show children an 'empty' cup with a piece of screwed-up paper lodged tightly in the bottom, then turn the cup upside down and dunk it in-and-out of a bowl of water. The paper inside stays dry because although the cup looks empty, it actually contains lots of air, which stops water entering and keeps the paper dry. Although beyond the primary curriculum, teaching a model that includes particles would be helpful and be within the grasp of higher-attaining upper KS2 children, laying the foundations for work in Year 7.

Sources: Sere (1985); Smith and Plumley (2016).

9.5 Lighter than air?

Misconception

When a party balloon is inflated with air, the balloon becomes lighter.

Scientific conception

An inflated party balloon appears to have little or no **weight** and can be effortlessly bounced around a room, sinking gently to the ground when let go.

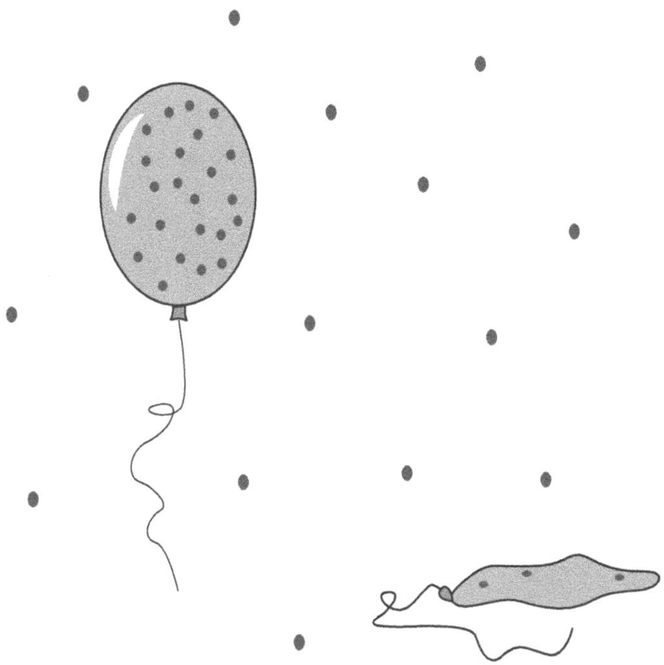

Figure 9.5a The concentration of air particles in an inflated balloon (left) and deflated balloon (right)

A deflated balloon, on the other hand, behaves like a thin piece of rubber, falling quickly to the floor when dropped. These observations can lead to the mistaken belief that once a balloon is blown up, it becomes lighter because it contains air (also see 9.4).

It usually comes as a surprise for children when they learn that the inflated balloon is actually heavier than the deflated one. This is because when we inflate a balloon, we force air in under pressure, which makes the air particles inside the balloon more concentrated than in the surrounding air (Figure 9.5a, left). Each individual air particle has a weight of its own, so air is not weightless, and the greater concentration of air particles inside the inflated balloon means it will be heavier than a deflated balloon. This is referred to as a *heavier than air* situation. This is the reason why scuba divers know that a full air cylinder is noticeably lighter once empty. The concentration of air particles inside a *deflated* balloon[1] is the same as that in the surrounding air (Figure 9.5a, right), so it contains fewer air particles than an inflated balloon and weighs less.

These ideas can also be explained using the idea of **density** (see Chapter 14 for more about density). Imagine the Earth's atmosphere as a 'sea of air', and we live at ground level, at the bottom of this 'sea' An inflated balloon weighs more than an identical volume of surrounding air, so is more dense; therefore,

Figure 9.5b The concentration of air particles inside and outside of a hot air balloon

when it is dropped it **sinks** to the floor of the sea of air, as would a piece of solid metal when dropped in water. A balloon full of helium, however, weighs less than the surrounding sea of air because of the very light weight of helium particles, so is less dense. A released helium balloon therefore rises in an attempt to **float** on the surface of the sea of air, as would a piece of expanded polystyrene released under water. This is a *lighter than air* situation.

Hot air balloons can be a source of further confusion. The reason why a hot air balloon rises is because the air inside expands as it is heated and the air particles inside are less concentrated than those in the surrounding air, so the parcel of air within the hot air balloon is less dense, or lighter than air (Figure 9.5b).

Reconstruction

Some children may have heard the story *Winnie the Pooh and the Honey Tree* in which Pooh borrows a party balloon from Christopher Robin and uses it to float up a tree to steal honey. The story can be used as an introduction to an investigation where the aim is to make an object rise using balloons inflated with air. Children soon realize that this is impossible, which addresses the misconception that balloons inflated with air are lighter than air. Air balloons can be compared with helium balloons, which *are* lighter than air.

Carbon dioxide balloons can be prepared by stretching a party balloon over a small bottle that contains vinegar and bicarbonate of soda. First, pour a 3cm depth of vinegar into the bottle. Add about two teaspoons of bicarbonate of soda powder inside the deflated balloon (this is fiddly), then seal the balloon over the neck of the bottle. Shake the bottle plus balloon to cause mixing, and the balloon will dramatically inflate. The carbon dioxide gas that is produced during the chemical reaction will be collected in the balloon, which can then be removed and tied off. Carbon dioxide balloons fall to the floor quite quickly, demonstrating that not every gas is lighter than air.

Ask children to predict what will happen to the weight of a party balloon when it is blown up, then get them to test their hypotheses by using an electronic balance to compare the masses of a deflated and an inflated balloon (the balance needs to be sensitive to differences of 0.1g).

Sources: Sere (1985); Smith and Plumley (2016).

Be safe!

Safety with balloons. It is advised that adults supervise the blowing-up of party balloons owing to the risk of choking. Balloon hand pumps are commercially available to help with the quick inflation of large numbers of balloons. Also consider any children who might have an allergy to latex rubber.

Note

1 As is the case with a flat tyre (9.4), a deflated balloon also contains air inside.

Planning and assessment sheet 9 Particles

(For suggestions on how to use this sheet, see p. xxviii.)

Misconception	*Attainment re. expected standard*		
	Working towards	*Working at*	*Working above*
Year 5: *Properties of everyday materials and reversible changes*			
Particles in a liquid are further apart than particles in a solid (therefore a liquid takes up more space than a solid) (9.1)	✓	✓	✓
An object is made from particles that look and behave like tiny bits of the larger material (9.2)	✓	✓	
'Currant bun' particle model (9.2)	✓	✓	
When a solid is heated, its particles melt (9.3)	✓	✓	
Particles can expand, contract, or heat up (9.3)	✓	✓	
Particles have properties such as hardness, softness, be transparent, and have a texture (9.3)	✓	✓	
Particles are a kind of living thing that can grow, reproduce, and exhibit other life processes (9.3)	✓		
Because a liquid is motionless, then its particles must be fixed in position and do not move around (9.3)	✓		
Particles have the same colour as their macroscopic material (9.3)	✓	✓	
Particles of solids are hard, while particles of liquids are soft (9.3)	✓		
Particles of solids are always larger than those of liquids and gases (9.3)	✓		
Flat tyres contain no air (9.4)	✓	✓	
When a party balloon is inflated with air, the balloon becomes lighter (9.5)	✓	✓	✓
A large balloon filled with air will rise upwards (9.4)	✓	✓	

10

Solids, liquids, and gases

Conceptual areas covered in this chapter:

- Categorizing materials as solids, liquids, or gases
- State changes
- Conservation of mass during state changes
- The water cycle

National Curriculum links:

Year 1: *Everyday materials*

Year 4: *States of matter*

Year 5: *Properties of everyday materials and reversible changes*

10.1 Can something be hollow and solid at the same time?

> **Misconception**
>
> *A football is not a solid because there is space inside.*

Scientific conception

During the primary years, children learn to think about the properties of materials to help sort them into the sets of solid, liquid, and gas. These sets are mutually exclusive and so children are taught that any material cannot belong to more than one set. There is sometimes difficulty deciding which set some objects belong in, such as a football, which children often consider not to be a solid because it is hollow. With this particular example there has been a clash of meanings with the literary definition of 'solid' as something that is non-hollow, as in 'the castle wall was solid'. Children similarly believe other objects cannot be solids because they have hollow spaces, such as a feather, cotton wool, fabric, items made from a wire frame, a bathroom sponge, powders, and so on.

With hollow objects such as a football, the inside space contains a gas (air) but the football itself is made from a solid material, typically plastic, leather, or rubber. Other examples are metal scuba-diving cylinders and inflated balloons, which are solid objects that also happen to contain a reservoir of trapped air inside. This is comparable to foams such as the froth on a glass of beer, or shaving foam, which are liquids that contain some air. Occasionally, children classify objects they are unsure about, such as footballs, into an imaginary intermediate set of solid/gas (see 10.2).

A second reason why materials might not be considered as solids is that they are thought to be liquids instead. Soft solids such as plasticine and Blu Tack go against some children's expectations that all solids must be hard and rigid, and because they can be moulded into new shapes are mistakenly classified as liquids. Candle wax and butter are other soft solids that children believe are liquids because they melt easily. On the other hand, some children think liquid treacle is a solid because it is more **viscous** (thicker) than water. Jelly is frequently considered not to be a solid because it is too soft and has been made by adding water, which is a liquid. Some children believe that powders like sand are liquids because they can be poured, spilled, and take the shape of the bottom of their containers, even though each individual grain of powder is in the solid state (Table 10.1). The Box below summarizes a brief discussion between early years children who have difficulty placing talcum powder into an appropriate set.

I think . . .

Unclassifiable material. *'[Talcum powder] is a kind of liquid, but it isn't liquid.' 'It's a bit solid, but it isn't'* (children in a Reception class; Russell *et al.*, 1991, p. 120).

Table 10.1 Properties of the three states of matter

Solid	*Liquid*	*Gas*
Has its own shape	Takes the shape of the bottom of its container	Fills its container
Cannot change its volume	Cannot change its volume	Volume can be changed (can be compressed)
Particles very close together and fixed in position in a regular pattern	Particles very close together but not fixed in position	Particles far apart, free to move randomly at high speed
	Can flow	Can flow
	Can be spilled	

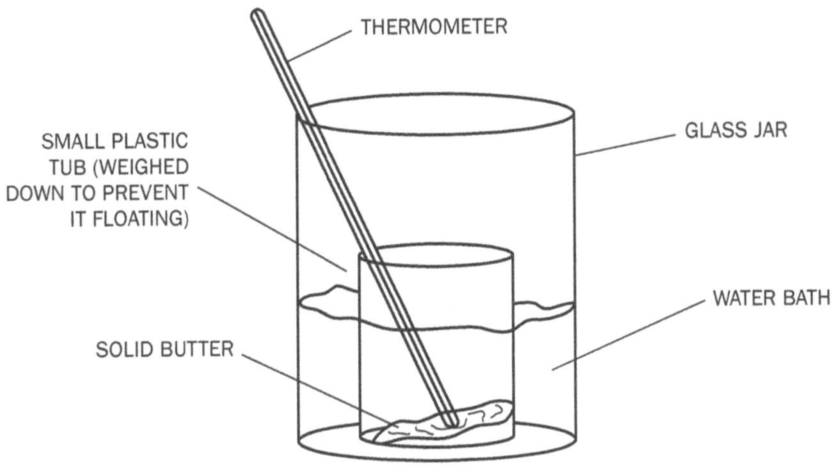

Figure 10.1 Finding out the melting point of butter

Reconstruction

In addition to using the arguments already presented in this section, a good way to begin to deal with some of the misconceptions is by introducing the idea of state changes. Explain to children that materials are not permanently solid, liquid, or gas but can change state depending on the temperature.[1] An experiment designed to discover the melting point of butter will help to clarify this, and can be done, with care, using hot water added to a water bath (Figure 10.1). Start with water straight from the cold tap in the water bath, then carefully add water from a hot kettle a little at a time, which will slowly increase the temperature of the butter. When the butter liquefies around the thermometer bulb, then this is the melting point temperature; note that butter melts at around 30°C and so a very hot day would not suit this activity because the butter would be runny to begin with. Conclude by saying that we decide on whether a material is a solid, liquid, or gas by looking at its state *at room temperature*, and although butter melts easily, when we use it in the kitchen to make a sandwich it is in the solid state. The same ideas can be reinforced using the activity of making jelly.

A key to understanding state changes is to differentiate between the properties of materials in different states of matter (see Table 10.1). Although beyond the primary curriculum, properties can be more easily appreciated once children compare the particle structures of solids, liquids, and gases (see Chapter 9). Activities such as working with 3D particle models of the same material existing in three different states, watching animations of moving particles during state changes, or participating in role play with children acting as particles in solids, liquids, and gases, will help consolidate ideas of what happens when materials change state.

KS1 children can begin to describe materials using a 'feely box'. Place objects secretly in the box one at a time and ask children to use adjectives that best describe each object, before guessing what each object is. Use a variety of materials including hard and soft solids, an open tub of salt, an open cup of washing-up liquid, etc. Shallcross *et al.* (2016, p. 39) explain how children in the early years can be asked to sort simple everyday materials into groups of their choosing; they recommend '. . . a paper plate, a jelly cube . . . jelly babies, a sugar cube, coloured rubber bands and cocktail sticks'.

Sources: Adams and Feagin (2017); Baji and Haeusler (2022); Jones and Lynch (1989); Russell *et al.* (1991); Shallcross *et al.* (2016); Stavy (1994).

10.2 What is a colloid?

Misconception

A soap bubble is like a liquid and a gas and so belongs in its own set, in-between these two states.

Scientific conception

It can be tricky to categorize some materials into solid, liquid, and gas sets. A soap bubble that appears when washing-up liquid and water are mixed together consists of a liquid outer coating with air inside, and children understandably are in two minds when deciding which set a bubble belongs in. One approach they use is to hedge bets, inventing an in-between set called liquid/gas and placing it there. Other materials that children might place in this intermediate liquid/gas set are shaving foam, the froth on a glass of beer, aerosol sprays, and fizzy drinks. In a similar way, children create a solid/gas intermediate set for materials such as a football and a feather (see 10.1), or a solid/liquid intermediate for jelly and toothpaste. Table 10.2 gives some examples of materials that children think need an intermediate set.

Scientifically, a soap bubble is neither a liquid or a gas, nor does it belong in an intermediate liquid/gas set. Because two states of matter are present simultaneously, it is an example of a mixed-phase material, or **colloid**. The name of the type of colloid depends on which state of matter is containing the other; in a soap bubble, air is contained within a small amount of soapy water so is a gas-in-liquid colloid. Shaving foam is mostly liquid containing a little gas and is also a gas-in-liquid colloid. The state of the part of the colloid that is being contained can exist as tiny bits that are spread out evenly throughout the containing state. Therefore, in milk, which is a liquid-in-liquid colloid,

Table 10.2 Classifying colloids in primary science

Material	*Type of colloid*	*Primary science classification*
Soap bubbles	Gas-in-liquid	Gas
Dirty river water	Solid-in-liquid	Liquid
Milk	Liquid-in-liquid	Liquid
Aerosol	Liquid-in-gas	Gas
Froth on a glass of beer	Gas-in-liquid	Liquid
Whipped ice cream	Gas-in-solid	Solid
Expanded polystyrene	Gas-in-solid	Solid
Fog	Liquid-in-gas	Liquid (see 10.6)
Hair gel	Solid-in-liquid	Solid
Smoke	Solid-in-gas	Gas
Mayonnaise	Liquid-in-liquid	Liquid
Toothpaste	Liquid-in-solid	Solid

minute fat droplets are dispersed within a larger volume of water, and this fat content gives milk its white colour. Table 10.2 summarizes different types of colloid alongside examples of their constituent materials. Note that there is a fine semantic distinction between a child's intermediate set and a colloid – with an intermediate set the material is not solid, liquid, or gas, while a colloid belongs in two states at the same time.

Reconstruction

Year 4 children are required to place different materials into the definitive categories of solid, liquid, and gas and so no intermediate sets are allowed. Although we frequently give children challenging examples such as colloids to think about, I advise sticking to the three familiar sets of solid, liquid, and gas, and avoiding placing colloids into mixed-phase sets. Many primary children find it difficult to cope with having a large number of categories to work with and the introduction of colloid categories would give them potentially 12 different sets to juggle. If children are ever in doubt about which state a material such as a colloid is in, ask them which set they think it belongs in the most. Get them into the habit of judging a material to be solid, liquid, or gas with no intermediate or mixed-phase sets. Table 10.2 gives examples of colloids together with which solid, liquid or gas set they are best placed in when teaching at primary level.

Non-Newtonian **fluids** (sometimes called smart materials) are engaging substances for children to work with. Cornflour slime can be made with two parts cornflour to one part water, and children will have great fun finding out that the slime can act either like a solid or a liquid, depending on the forces being applied. For instance, when stirred quickly, the mixture will harden and become solid, but if spooned gently it will flow like a liquid. Discuss how quicksand behaves the opposite way, being a solid until you apply a force by stepping on the surface, at which point it liquifies and you begin to sink. Tomato ketchup is similar; inside a plastic bottle it is a thick liquid and difficult to shake towards the mouth of the bottle, but once you squeeze the bottle and apply a force, it becomes very runny and spurts out. Footballers' shin pads and goalkeeper gloves are available that behave as non-Newtonian materials, being flexible and soft until a force is applied and then they harden instantly.

Sources: Samarapungavan *et al.* (2017); Stavy (1990).

10.3 Does turning a solid object into a powder change its weight?

Misconception

If something is made into a powder, it will be lighter than it was before.

Scientific conception

Children may believe that if an object is ground down into tiny pieces to make a powder it naturally becomes less heavy. The idea can be triggered by the correct observation that many familiar powders such as salt, sugar, flour, sand, and coffee feel relatively light if picked up by the handful.

This familiar sensation has some basis in truth. If you hold some powder in one hand (e.g. iron filings) and a similar sized whole piece of the same material in the other (e.g. a 10g iron mass), the powder will indeed feel and weigh lighter. This is because the powder is less dense than the solid piece of material owing to air spaces between the powder grains. The solid piece has no air spaces and is more dense, making the same volume of material heavier than the powder (Figure 10.3). However, it must be remembered that a single grain of powder is made from exactly the same substance as a larger piece of material, so each grain has the same density as that larger piece. Therefore, if a large bit of material is first weighed and then completely filed down to powder, and the grains are collected then weighed again, they should weigh exactly the same as the original large bit because there has been no loss of mass. Just because the solid now exists as a powder, it does not mean that it has become any lighter.

The more insubstantial nature of a powder may reinforce this misconception, e.g. the fact it can slip through the fingers easily. For this reason, it is difficult to grab much of a powder in a single handful, so you are unlikely to be able to hold enough material for it to feel appreciably heavy.

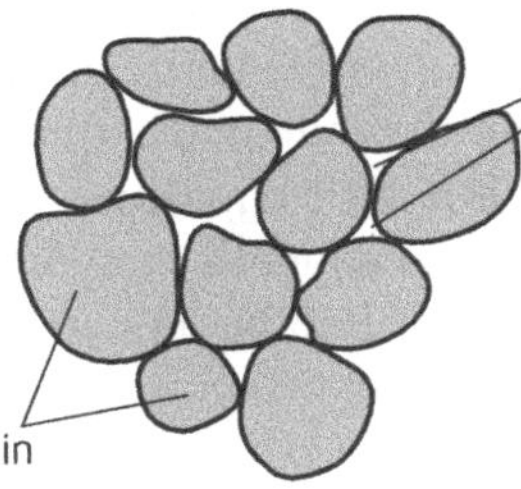

Figure 10.3 A microscopic picture of how the grains of a powder fit together

Reconstruction

Weigh a small piece of wood. Using a file, grind the piece down a little bit, carefully collecting all the filings, then reweigh the filings together with the original piece to show that no loss of weight has occurred. There is a possibility of some loss as dust during the filing process, so practice may be required to prevent a significant reduction in weight that would show up on the balance. Passing a jar of iron or copper filings around the class is a useful way to demonstrate that not all powders are light and insubstantial – the metal filings feel surprisingly heavy.

Sources: Bar *et al.* (2016); Galili and Bar (1997).

10.4 Which is heavier, ice or water?

Misconception

If you melt a solid, it becomes lighter.

Scientific conception

If an ice cube is weighed, left in a cup at room temperature to melt completely into liquid, then the melted water weighed again, some children will predict a loss of weight. They expect this because water, when compared with ice, appears to be less substantial, softer, and less tangible. Others might expect that when ice melts to become water, its *volume* decreases to a large extent because an ice cube takes up more space than melted water (Figure 10.4), or that because water expands when it freezes to become ice, the weight of ice will be reduced after melting because it has contracted. Similarly, children may believe that if candle wax is melted to form liquid wax, it too would become lighter.

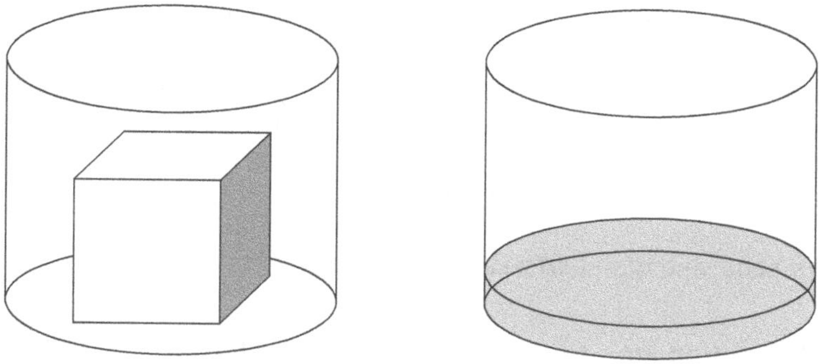

Figure 10.4 The illusion of a large reduction in volume when ice melts

When any material melts, its mass remains the same. This is because although there has been a change in state, the number of particles in both the solid and liquid forms is the same (see 13.6 for more on weight and particles). This conservation of mass occurs despite obvious changes in the volume of water during melting or freezing. For instance, some children will be aware that it is difficult to remove ice cubes from the freezer tray because the water has expanded during the freezing process (although they may incorrectly believe that the mass of water has increased during its transformation into ice). Because ice expands during freezing, it is less dense than cold water and so when equal volumes are compared, ice is actually *lighter* than cold water, which is why ice floats.

The misconception might be linked to the incorrect idea that solid particles are closer together than liquid particles and so liquids must weigh less because there are fewer particles in a given space (9.1). Other contexts in which children have problems conserving weight include the belief that running water weighs more than still water, and when a liquid boils to become a gas, it has no weight. Similar misconceptions involving the conservation of matter are discussed in Chapter 8, such as the belief that when wood burns, smoke disappears into the air and is lost forever (8.2). As with other particle misconceptions, animations of what happens during state changes are good visual tools and can be sourced from the internet, e.g. www.youtube.com

Reconstruction

This misconception can be challenged experimentally in a straightforward way by asking children to weigh a sealed jar containing an ice cube, waiting for it to melt at room temperature, then reweighing the jar to show that its weight does not change. Be sure to wipe the outside of the jar just before each weighing to remove any condensation from the outside of the glass.

As in 10.3, remind children that water is a substantial and heavy material by asking them to carefully try to lift a 10-litre filled container of water. This needs to be done under close supervision to ensure the children do not hurt themselves. A fun KS1 activity that demonstrates one factor that influences melting is to give teams of children an ice cube at the start of a lesson and ask them to think of a way to stop it melting by the end of the lesson. Allow them to wrap the ice cube in materials such as fabrics, bubble wrap, aluminium kitchen foil, cling film, and expanded polystyrene.

Sources: Galili and Bar (1997); Leite *et al.* (2007).

10.5 What happens to water once it has boiled?

Misconception

Boiling and evaporation are irreversible processes.

Scientific conception

In Year 5, children are introduced to the concept of reversible changes, whereby materials can be altered but are able later to be changed back into their original form. These are usually taught this in the context of state changes, often using water as the material (Figure 10.5).

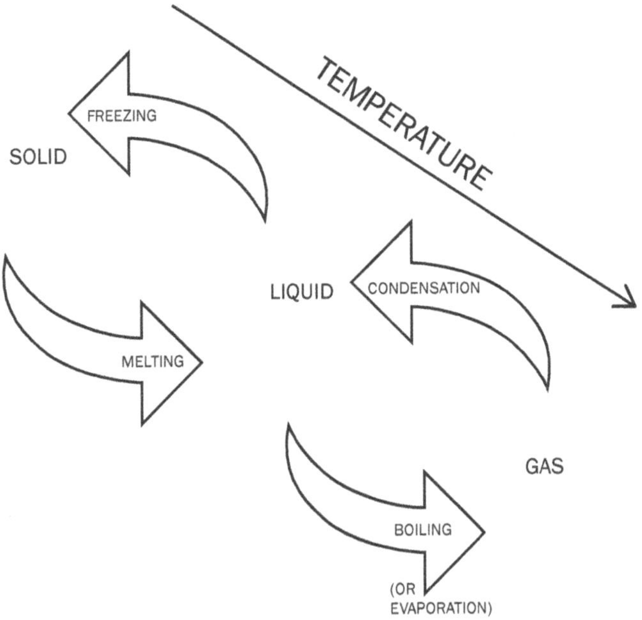

Figure 10.5 State changes

Year 5 children are also introduced to the concept of irreversible changes, where materials are transformed into something new but cannot be returned to their original form, e.g. burning wood, cooking a fried egg. The misconception statement above reflects the belief that when liquid water is heated and changes into steam (liquid → gas), the steam can never revert to water. However, since state changes such as boiling are reversible, the steam can be cooled and condensed to become liquid water once more (Figure 10.5). The misconception is reinforced when children see the clouds from a boiling kettle disappear into the air, apparently lost forever.

Reconstruction

Introduce a familiar occurrence by asking children *why do the insides of kitchen windows sometimes become wet when someone is cooking?* Explain that when water is boiled in pans on the hob, it becomes steam and rises into the air. As the steam floats away from the boiling water, it cools in the kitchen air and condenses back into liquid water to make a cloud of mist, some of which ends up on the cold window panes making them wet. A good analogy is that when a child changes their clothing, say, out of their school uniform when they arrive home in the evening, they look different, and may even behave differently, but are still the same person; that child is always able to change back into their school uniform. When liquid water boils and becomes steam, it too changes its appearance and behaviour – it has 'changed its clothes' – but is essentially the same thing, since condensing the steam allows it to again become the liquid water that it once was.

Have the children hold a glass containing ice and liquid water (carefully) above a cup of just-boiled water to see how the glass becomes dripping wet on the outside. Asking the children where the drips came from can elicit some surprising responses, including the idea that the icy water from inside has seeped through the solid glass to the outside (see 10.9). The discussion should eventually be steered towards the scientific idea that condensation has taken place because the rising hot water has hit the cool glass surface (gas → liquid); this shows that evaporation is reversible. A further complication is that the white clouds that we see above boiling water are not technically in the *gaseous* state (as steam or water vapour) but instead are in the *liquid* state in the form of water droplets (see 10.6 and 10.7 for further discussion of this frequently misunderstood point).

Water is typically used as the exemplar to demonstrate state changes in primary science, which may result in children compartmentalizing their learning, finding it difficult to transfer the concepts to other materials. An engaging alternative is to demonstrate state changes using liquid nitrogen. Visits into school from organizations such as the National Physical Laboratory can be arranged where children can see dramatic phenomena such as the rapid boiling of liquid nitrogen when exposed to room temperature, freezing of apples (which are then smashed with a hammer), shrinking an inflated balloon, and instant ice cream.

Sources: Ahtee and Varjola (1998); National Physical Laboratory (2024); Wang and Tseng (2018).

10.6 The disappearing puddle

Misconception

Liquids that evaporate or boil disappear forever.

Scientific conception

When asked to explain what happens when a puddle evaporates on a warm day, some children will simply say that it has vanished in the heat. Similar responses are forthcoming with a boiling kettle scenario (10.5), with some children believing that water becomes steam before disappearing off, never to be seen again. Other children may suggest that the missing water has 'disappeared into the air', which is nearer to the truth.

Boiling is the state change that takes place when a liquid becomes a gas at its boiling point, which in the case of pure water is 100°C at normal atmospheric pressure – the gas produced by boiling is *steam*. On the other hand, evaporation occurs when a liquid becomes a gas below its boiling point; the gas produced in this case is *water vapour*, which is gaseous water below 100°C. A puddle disappears on a warm day not because the sun boils the water to 100°C; instead, the puddle is only heated to, say, 25°C and then slowly evaporates as water vapour. This water vapour then becomes part of the air around us, contributing to humidity; some water vapour will rise up and upon reaching a certain height, will cool down and condense back into liquid water, forming a cloud in the sky.

The fact that when water evaporates – as from a puddle, for example – it is invisible, is likely to be a source of this misconception. Because it is quite an abstract idea many children struggle to imagine the unseen water vapour as still being here in the air around us, rising to form clouds in the sky, maybe falling as rain at some point. A different misconception is that a puddle on a concrete surface disappears because the water has soaked into the ground. The Box below shows how one child rationalized the disappearance of a puddle.

I think . . .

Disappearing puddle. *'I think the water has dissapeard [sic]. I think the air around us sucked the water up and the air made it into nothing because the air is stronger than the water'* (9-year-old child; Russell and Watt, 1990, p. 15).

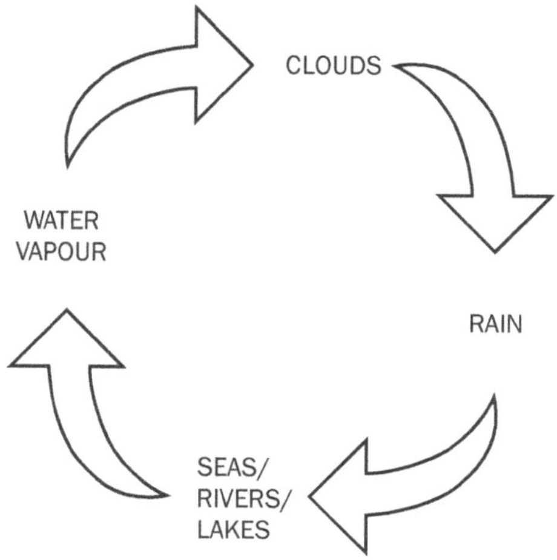

Figure 10.6 Simple representation of the water cycle

Reconstruction

Understanding the water cycle (Year 4) is a good way to address this misconception. Children will become familiar with the 'story of water' as it takes on different forms within the water cycle (Figure 10.6), something they can act out as a classroom role play. One way to elicit misconceptions or check learning in a socio-constructivist way is to use sets of dice called story cubes, which have different pictures of random images on their faces. Working in small groups, children throw the set of nine dice to produce nine different images. The aim is for the group to work together to create a story that mentions all the images, in this case to explain what happens during the water cycle. Their conversations will involve debate and negotiation as they work out between them the scientifically correct sequence of events.

Start a discussion about the uncomfortable 'muggy' feeling that is associated with a hot, humid day being due to the air being 'very wet', i.e. lots of invisible water vapour is present in the air. Place a container of water covered by clingfilm in the classroom in direct sunlight or on a radiator to catch evaporated water vapour, making it visible again in liquid form on the inside of the clingfilm, showing that as water evaporates it does not disappear forever. Having a control container without clingfilm for comparative purposes is helpful, as the water will simply appear to vanish. This activity can be used to support explanations of the evaporation → condensation part of the water cycle. The fact that Earth's water has been recycling itself in this way for billions of years helps generate feelings of wonder, as well as an appreciation of deep time – the puddles that they see in the playground today likely contain the same water particles from puddles that the dinosaurs drank from.

Since this misconception is closely related to the misconception that boiling is irreversible, use of the pedagogies described in 10.5 would facilitate the construction of acceptable scientific ideas.

KS1 children can create puddle prints. Make up batches of different-coloured water with food colouring. Have the children use droppers to make small coloured puddles on an A4 plastic page protector, then leave this on the windowsill in direct sunlight or close to a heat source such as a radiator. When the water evaporates, coloured patches will be left on the plastic. Take care with this exercise if your classroom has a carpet that stains easily.

Sources: Bar (1986); Holloway (2019); Paik (2015); Russell and Watt (1990).

10.7 What are clouds made from?

Misconception

Clouds are made of gas.

Scientific conception

This misconception is relevant to all water clouds, including clouds in the sky, above a boiling kettle or those associated with weather conditions, such as mist or fog. Water clouds appear gaseous and seem to behave as a gas would – they float in the air, can flow, are able to fill a container, and appear to have no physical substance. However, these clouds are made of water in the *liquid* state and not the gaseous state. Under a microscope they appear as very tiny water droplets that can float in the air. Because they are so minute they have a very low weight and can be lifted by the rising air currents that exist above a boiling kettle or a pan of water on the hob. Since they rise and swirl around in these air currents, the water droplets appear to behave like a gas – floating, flowing, etc. Clouds in the sky contain water droplets that move around in very turbulent conditions, colliding with each other and joining together, becoming progressively larger until they are so big that their weight can no longer be supported, and so fall as rain.

The misconception is reinforced by the everyday name we give to the clouds of water produced by a boiling kettle or a hot bath – *steam*. Scientifically, steam is water in the gaseous state at or above its boiling point (100°C with pure water under normal conditions) and because water clouds exist below this temperature, they are not gases – they are in the liquid state as water droplets (Figure 10.7). Therefore, in the classroom it is best to get into the habit of referring to them as 'clouds' or 'mist', instead of using the colloquial term 'steam'. If you watch a boiling kettle there is a small transparent area just above

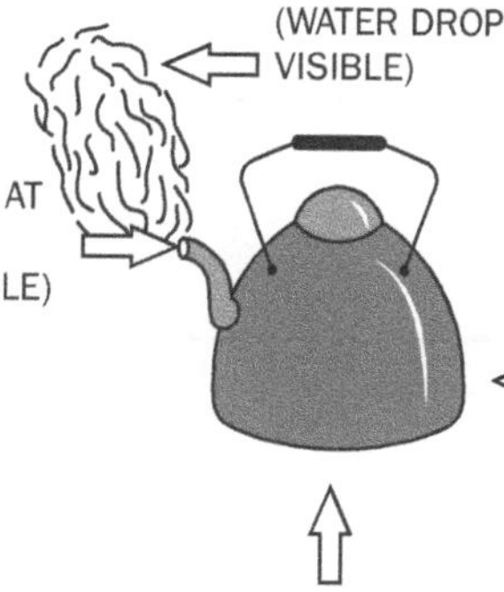

Figure 10.7 The different states of water associated with a boiling kettle

the spout, below where the clouds begin to form – this is true gaseous steam, which is invisible. The white clouds that are visible above this area are condensed water in the liquid state (Figure 10.7).

A related misconception is the belief that powders are liquids when in fact they are tiny bits of solids (10.1). Powders seem to behave as a liquid –they flow, can be poured, spilled, and so on – but each individual bit is in the solid state.

Reconstruction

As with 10.6, the state changes discussed here form part of the water cycle so an understanding of the processes involved in the cycle would help children appreciate that clouds are made from liquid water. You could demonstrate how (with care) using tongs to hold a piece of tissue within the cloud above a boiling kettle makes the tissue damp as the water droplets are absorbed onto the tissue. Note that this is *not* an example of condensation (gas → liquid), since the drops in the cloud are already liquid, not gaseous.

Remind children of familiar examples to help them understand that clouds are actually liquid water; for instance, how a car windscreen quickly becomes wet when driving through fog, or cycling through fog can make your hair wet. Similarly, water can often be seen collecting on the outside of aircraft windows when descending through cloud.

Finally, it should be noted that, in reality, the situation is slightly more complex since the white cloud produced by a kettle will actually contain *some* water in the gaseous state in the form of water vapour (see 10.5). Weather clouds in the sky also contain some water vapour and even some water in the solid state, as ice or snow. Whether this information should be taught at the primary level is a matter for debate – although it reflects correct science, it might be the source of further confusion.

Sources: Dove (1998); Paik (2015).

10.8 Moving heat

Misconception

Heat always rises.

Scientific conception

The idea that heat always rises is commonly held by children and adults alike. Familiar experiences such as seeing smoke travelling upwards, rising hot air balloons, and shimmering heat haze during a hot summer's day support this view. However, in these three cases it is actually *hot air* that is rising – but what makes hot air rise, and also cold air sink?

A block of wood that is held underwater and then suddenly let go always rises to the surface of the water because wood is less dense than water (see Chapter 14 for a detailed discussion of density). When the wood is released, water rushes underneath it, undercutting the wood, pushing it upwards until it floats on the surface. The wood and water have separated into different 'layers' because they have different densities. Figure 10.8a shows two 'parcels' of air that are next to each other, one warm and the other cold. Because cold air is denser than warm air, the cold parcel will push underneath the warm parcel, making the warm air rise. The same processes also cause **convection currents** to be created (Figure 10.8b).

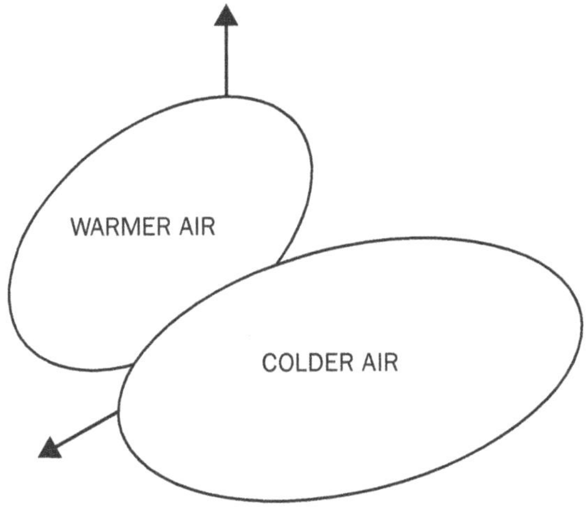

Figure 10.8a Parcels of air at different temperatures have different densities

Figure 10.8b The different ways that heat can move away from a cup of hot tea: 1. radiation; 2. convection; 3. conduction

Scientifically, heat is defined as a type of energy that moves from hotter to colder places. At primary level, however, energy is not in the science Programme of Study because it is an abstract idea that children find difficult to conceptualize. Instead, although it is technically wrong, children can think about heat at a simpler level by imagining it to be something inside a material that can move from warmer to cooler places, for instance, along the solid handle of a hot cup of tea (**conduction**, see Figure 10.8b).

Because it moves from warmer to cooler areas, heat can move in any direction, not only upwards. As stated above, the concept of heat energy is not taught at KS2 although the fact that warm air rises is (e.g. during the water cycle) and children may think it is heat that is rising, not the air.

Another common misconception about heat is the belief that if a glass of water at room temperature is wrapped with an insulating material such as wool, this causes the water to heat up. If the wool is also at room temperature, then there is no temperature difference between it and the water. Thus, there is no transference of heat and the water's temperature will not change. A different misconception is that if an ice cube is placed in the classroom and covered with insulating material such as bubble wrap, it will melt more quickly. In fact, the opposite happens because the material insulates the ice from the warmer air in the room, so the ice heats up more slowly than if it were unwrapped.

Reconstruction

At primary level it is not necessary to introduce the concept of energy. However, a picture of the cup in Figure 10.8b can be used to show that heat is able to travel in all directions, not just upwards. Pouring hot water from a kettle into a metal camping cup will make the cup handle heat up very quickly because

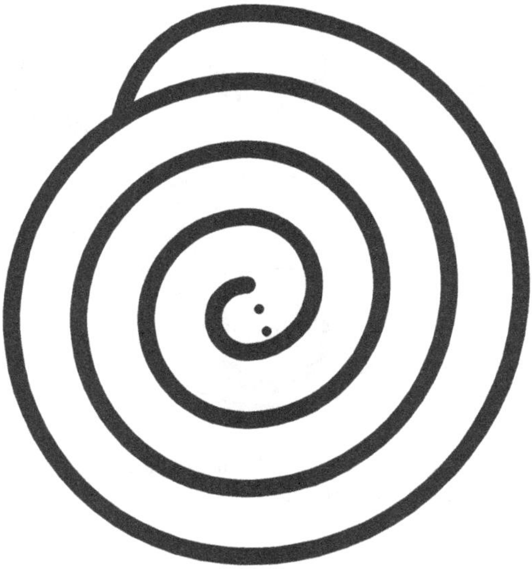

Figure 10.8c Heat snake

metals are efficient heat conductors, which is a good illustration of heat moving sideways away from the body of the cup.

Showing hot air rising helps children to understand that cold air undercuts warm air, causing it to lift. Examples include 'heat snakes' and model hot air balloons. Create a heat snake as in Figure 10.8c by cutting along the thick black lines to form a spiral, then make at small hole in the head in the middle of the spiral. Thread a length of cotton through the hole and tie the snake above a heat source such as a hot radiator. The snake will whirl in the rising air current.

Holding inflated party balloons underwater and then letting them go is a good way to model warm air rising. These ideas can be introduced together with other experiments on floating and sinking (see Chapter 14). However, it must be made clear that it is 'hot air' and not 'heat' that is rising. At primary level, it might simply be a case of correcting children who say 'heat always rises' to instead say 'hot air rises'.

For a simple demonstration of heat moving from a warmer to a cooler area, carefully pour hot, just-boiled water into a metal can (such as an old baked bean tin), filling the can to about ¾ full. Place the can in a small bowl of cold water, then insert thermometers inside both the can and the bowl (you will need to add some mass to the can to stop it floating in the bowl). Over a period of time the water in the can will become cooler and the water in the bowl becomes warmer as heat moves from the can to the bowl. Eventually, both containers will be at the same temperature – this is **heat equilibration**. The activity can be extended by wrapping the can in different materials to act as insulators, slowing down the movement of heat.

Using 'ice hands' is an engaging way to perform experiments that test the speed of melting at room temperature when they are wrapped in different materials. To make an ice hand, fill a rubber washing-up glove or latex disposable glove with tap water, tie off at the wrist with string and place in the freezer. The basic ideas underlying heat insulation can be explained to KS1 children by reading the story book *The Emperor's Egg* by Martin Jenkins.

Sources: Jenkins (2008); Opitz *et al.* (2015); Stylos and Kotsis (2021); Tiberghien *et al.* (1983).

10.9 Why do objects sometimes become moist when taken out of the fridge?

Misconception

When taken out of the fridge, a drink can feel wet because liquid from inside the can seeps through to the outside.

Scientific conception

Most children will be familiar with this common experience, especially on a warm day when containers of cold drinks become moist on the outside. However, they are usually unable to explain why the water appears. As with other misconceptions in this chapter, water vapour plays a vital part in the process. Invisible water vapour in the gaseous state is present in the air outside the fridge, and when it comes into contact with the cold can, the water vapour cools and condenses into water in the liquid state. We say that the cold temperature of the can is below the **dew point**, causing the water vapour to condense or 'become dew', therefore the can acquires moisture as the liquid water becomes visible. In hot, arid countries where humidity is very low, there is little water vapour in the air and this may not occur.

The mist that comes from inside the family freezer when we open the door appears for the exactly the same reason – the freezer temperature is below the dew point and so water vapour in the air outside the freezer condenses into water droplets, visible as mist. At dawn, cold surfaces such as the ground or the metal body of a car can be wet with dew even if rain has not fallen during the night because temperatures have dropped to below the dew point.

Reconstruction

Children should be reminded that drinks cans made from aluminium are both waterproof and airtight, so it is impossible for anything from the inside to seep through. A good illustration of how water vapour is present in the air as humidity is to wait for a rainy day when the children enter the classroom. The windows will quickly mist up because liquid water from their wet clothes will evaporate, becoming invisible water vapour in the air, creating a humid atmosphere. This water vapour then condenses on the cold surfaces of windows to produce the misting. Children who wear glasses will be familiar with this experience.

Sources: Allen and Kambouri-Danos (2017); Osborne and Cosgrove (1983).

Note

1 Pressure also has an influence on state changes, although this concept is probably best left until the secondary years.

Planning and assessment sheet 10 Solids, liquids, and gases
(For suggestions on how to use this sheet, see p. xxviii.)

Misconception	*Attainment re. expected standard*		
	Working towards	*Working at*	*Working above*
Year 4: *States of matter*			
Objects that contain air spaces are not solid (e.g. a football, a feather, cotton wool, fabric, items made from a wire frame, a bathroom sponge, powders) (10.1)	✓	✓	
Soft materials such as plasticine, Blu Tack, and butter are liquids because they can be easily moulded into new shapes (10.1)	✓		
Candle wax and butter are liquids because they melt easily (10.1)	✓	✓	
Treacle and syrup are solids because they are much thicker than water (10.1)	✓		
Jelly is a liquid because it has been made by adding water (10.1)	✓	✓	
Powders such as sand, flour, salt, and talcum powder are liquids because they can be poured, spilled, and take the shape of the bottom of their containers (10.1)	✓	✓	
A soap bubble, shaving foam, aerosol sprays, and fizzy drinks exist in an in-between state of matter called liquid/gas (10.2)	✓	✓	✓
A football and a feather exist in an in-between state of matter called solid/gas (10.2)	✓	✓	✓
Jelly and toothpaste exist in an in-between state of matter called solid/liquid (10.2)	✓	✓	✓
If something is turned into a powder, it will be lighter than it was before (10.3)	✓	✓	
If you melt a solid, it becomes lighter (10.4)	✓	✓	
When ice melts to become water, its volume decreases to a large extent (10.4)	✓	✓	
When ice melts to become water, it will be lighter than it was before because ice contracts as it melts (10.4)		✓	
When candle wax melts to form liquid wax, it becomes lighter (10.4)	✓	✓	
Running water weighs more than still water (10.4)	✓	✓	✓

(continued)

(*continued*)

When a liquid boils to become a gas, it no longer has any weight (10.4)	✓	✓	✓
Boiling and evaporation are irreversible processes (10.5)	✓	✓	
Condensation on the outside of a cold can of drink is liquid that has seeped through from the inside of the can (10.5; 10.9)	✓		
Liquids that evaporate or boil disappear forever (10.6)	✓	✓	
A puddle disappears on a hot day because the sun has boiled it away (10.6)	✓	✓	
A puddle on a concrete surface disappears because the water has soaked into the ground (10.6)	✓		
Clouds are made of gas (10.7)	✓	✓	
The clouds of water produced by a boiling kettle or a hot bath are steam (10.7)	✓	✓	
Heat always rises (10.8)	✓	✓	✓
If a cup of water at room temperature is wrapped in wool, the water becomes warmer (10.8)	✓	✓	
If an ice cube is insulated with bubble wrap, it will melt more quickly (10.8)	✓	✓	
Year 5: *Properties of everyday materials and reversible changes*			
Solid particles are closer together than liquid particles, so liquids must weigh less because there are fewer particles in a given space (10.4)		✓	✓

11

The Earth

Conceptual areas covered in this chapter:

- Definitions of rock and mineral
- Concepts of 'up' and 'down' based on personal frames of reference
- Soil structure
- Fossils and dinosaurs

National Curriculum links:

Year 1: *Seasonal changes*

Year 2: *Use of everyday materials*

Year 3: *Rocks*

Years 3 and 6: *Light*

Year 4: *Living things and their habitats*

Year 5: *Earth in space*

11.1 Is there a difference between a rock and a stone?

> **Misconception**
>
> *'Rocks' are large, heavy, and jagged. If smaller, they are 'stones'. If smooth, they are 'pebbles'.*

Scientific conception

During the teaching of a primary Earth science topic, children work with a variety of actual **rock** and **mineral** specimens. Some may think that any pieces smaller than the palms of their hands are too small to be called rocks – instead, they are stones. The roots of this misconception probably lie in everyday language use, since to many children 'a stone' is any rock-like object that is small enough for them to be able throw it a fair distance (see Box p. 180). It is problematic if children construct mutually exclusive sets in this way, since if a fragment of material is thought to be a stone because of its small size, it cannot be a rock. This is likely to result in classification problems where children think small fragments of rocks such as granite or slate are not rock. Children may also give the name 'stones' to small pieces of materials that are not technically rocks, for instance, human-made materials such as brick or concrete (see 11.2).

For the same reasons of size, a boulder may not be thought to be a rock because it is too big. In addition, children may classify any smooth sample as being a pebble and not a rock. A rock can be defined scientifically as *any natural material that is a product of geological processes and consists of more than one mineral.* Therefore, whether an object is a rock has nothing to do with its size, which means both a very small fragment and an entire cliff face are classified as rock.

I think . . .

Categorization by size. *'A rock is bigger than a stone. A stone is dead small . . .'* (Year 2 child; Russell *et al.*, 1993, p. 33).

Reconstruction

A useful approach is to encourage children's semantic use of the word *rock* to be more scientific. Instead of using the word to describe a particular object as 'a rock', explain that scientifically the object is 'made from rock' or simply the object 'is rock'. When deciding whether to classify something as 'rock', physical properties or qualities need to be considered irrespective of size or smoothness. For example, you might want children to sort specimens into rocks and minerals, so an activity may involve inspecting samples and deciding on whether they are made from one pure substance (mineral) or several substances mixed together (rock) (see 11.2 and 11.3 for further clarification of this difference). Including a range of different samples that have a variety of sizes, shapes, densities, smoothness, etc. would help children appreciate that the scientific definition of rock is different from any everyday meaning.

Did you know?

Semantic differences in other cultures. Interestingly, in everyday American English use, size is less important when distinguishing between a rock and a stone. In the US, a rock can be a smaller piece, reflected in the American expression *people in glass houses shouldn't throw rocks.*

Sources: Ford (2005); Russell *et al.* (1993).

11.2 What exactly is a rock?

Misconception

Brick and concrete are examples of rocks.

Scientific conception

A brick looks and feels very rock-like; indeed, a small fragment from a damaged brick that has its flat sides and corners broken away looks very similar to a piece of rock such as sandstone. However, rock is a natural material (see 11.1) whereas a brick is not a natural material – it has been artificially manufactured by firing clay in a kiln, often together with additives such as lime to produce a hard and fairly brittle solid ideal for use as a building material.

Similarly, concrete is not a natural material, being a hardened mixture of cement, sand, gravel, and water. Once liquid concrete has been poured into place (e.g. on a garden pathway), it sets due to a chemical reaction that binds the mixture together to form a dry, hard-wearing solid. A piece of broken concrete can look very similar to rock such as conglomerate.

A related misconception is that a polished piece of marble or a granite paving stone is not a rock because it has been worked and so is no longer natural. Even if children accept that a rock has natural origins, they may believe misconceptions such as all rocks were made billions of years ago when the Earth was first formed, that all rocks have been created by volcanoes, or very ancient rocks are always soft and crumbly.

Reconstruction

Encourage children to avoid automatically calling anything that looks rock-like 'a rock', reminding them that along with appearance and physical properties, the source of a material also needs to be taken into consideration. Sometimes the flat sides or corners of a brick or piece of concrete can reveal its artificial origin. A sorting exercise requiring children to separate a variety of objects into synthetic and natural sets would help, while KS1 children can inspect a rock collection and describe each specimen, commenting on its colour, texture, attractiveness, etc. Children can also use Microsoft PowerPoint to make a slideshow that depicts a collage of things in the local environment that are made from rock such as drystone walls, driveways, patio floors, roofs, and statues. The National Geographic Kids website has some engaging resources relevant to learning about rocks and fossils: www.natgeokids.com/uk

The class could host a 'museum event' focused on rocks and fossils. inviting other classes and parents into the school. Children construct wall displays to show how different rocks are formed (igneous, sedimentary, metamorphic), and include exhibits such as clay models (cross-curricular links with art) and rocks and minerals children have brought from home. Cross-curricular connections can also be made with design and technology and computing, with children creating animations of dinosaur fossils that can be rotated in 3D.

Sources: Ennis (2023); Happs (1985); Russell *et al.* (1993).

11.3 What exactly is a mineral?

Misconception

Minerals are precious small stones.

Scientific conception

Minerals are typically thought to be attractive, shiny, rare, and used extensively in jewellery, e.g. diamonds, rubies, sapphires, and emeralds. Indeed, many minerals are jewels because of their beauty and rarity and are called *gemstones*; other minerals such as quartz are not rare and have low monetary value. So although the misconception statement is correct on one level, it excludes other minerals that are less rare, attractive, and expensive.

In contrast to minerals, children usually consider rocks to be dull, commonly available, and not worth a great deal of money. In fact, some rocks such as the igneous hornblendite are quite rare, and rocks that have high crystal content such as schist are naturally shiny and attractive. It is therefore sometimes difficult to tell the difference between rocks and minerals when only considering their attractiveness or cost. Minerals are naturally occurring, 'pure' materials that have been formed by geological processes and *are made of just a single chemical*, for example, pyrite (fool's gold) is a chemical called iron disulphide (FeS_2). Rocks, on the other hand, are natural mixtures of more than one mineral, so *contain more than one chemical* (Figure 11.3).

The distinction between rocks and minerals is confused by the colloquial use of the word 'rock' to describe mineral gems such as diamonds and sapphires when set in an expensive engagement ring. Interestingly, some gemstones are not only natural but can also be produced synthetically in the laboratory, for example, rubies can be artificially made for use in industrial lasers – these are not technically minerals.

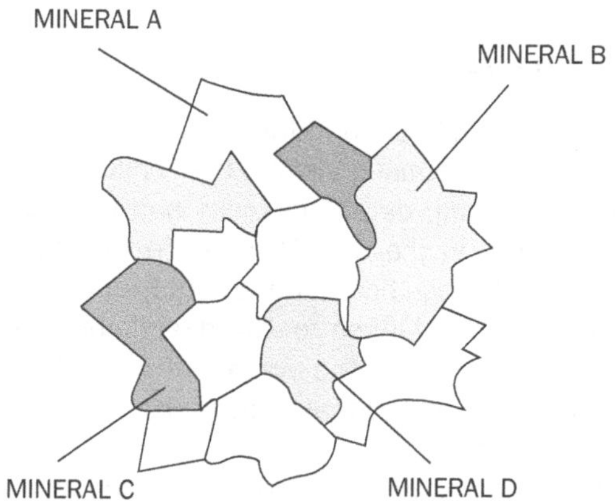

Figure 11.3 Microscopic view of a rock sample made up of four different minerals

Related misconceptions include that a rock is made up from a single substance only, all rocks are heavy, and rocks or minerals that are attractive are called crystals. Children have also been known to mix-up the geological and nutritional meanings of 'mineral'; for example, they may think a mineral such as quartz is a type of vitamin.

Reconstruction

When children examine rock and mineral samples to study their appearance and properties such as hardness, be sure to include quartz, calcite, and other inexpensive minerals to show that not all minerals are gemstones.

To help children distinguish between rocks and minerals, use a photograph (e.g. sourced from the internet) to show the microscopic rock structure of granite. Point out the individual minerals in the picture, which are usually interlocked like a jigsaw puzzle (as in Figure 11.3). Careful examination of an actual sample of granite using a magnifying glass or microscope would also reveal this pattern. Inform children that each piece of the jigsaw is a small bit made from a pure chemical called a mineral. To help reinforce this, use the classroom geology collection to show children larger pieces of the same minerals that are found in granite (e.g. feldspar, quartz). Some children may have their own rock and mineral collections at home that they could bring into school for the day and can be used in the same ways as described in this chapter. Providing examples of less dense rocks such as pumice will help dispel the idea that a rock has be heavy.

Sources: Ford (2005); Fröyland *et al.* (2016); Happs (1985).

Learning technologies

Digital microscopes. Children are fascinated when introduced to an 'inner world' that is not normally visible. KS1 children can use magnifying glasses to explore tiny details of rocks and minerals, flowers, and small animals that live in the soil. However, extremely minute objects require more powerful magnification and, until fairly recently, were not possible for young school children to view directly because microscopes were very expensive and solely the domain of secondary science classrooms. These days, a decent digital microscope that is fit for purpose in primary schools can be as cheap as £20. Some of these microscopes are marketed as 'toys' and designed for use by children at home; nevertheless, many can be connected to a computer and projected onto the IWB for the whole class to view, and digital images saved as photos and videos. They are capable of magnifying material such as pollen grains, the scales on butterfly wings, a human hair, and even individual cells in a potato or onion (these last two are difficult to see without iodine stain). Sets of prepared slides can be purchased cheaply and include fish scales, the hairs of different animals, plant leaves, and root tips, as well as insect wings. In relation to this chapter, digital microscopes can be used to view mineral grains in rocks such as granite, and compare the sizes of particles in different soils, for example, sandy soils have larger particles than clayey soils. Some microscopes are top-lit so can be detached and carried around by hand, even taken outdoors to record interesting events like an aphid feeding on a leaf. An alternative is to buy a cheap magnifier for a couple of pounds that clips onto a tablet or mobile phone camera and enables photos to be taken, although these are not as powerful as microscopes. At the other end of the scale, if your budget allows, a professional digital microscope costing several hundred pounds will have excellent optics that generate very clear images at high magnifications, beyond the range of the inexpensive 'toy' versions.

11.4 Which way is down?

Misconception

The heaviest materials in the Earth are found at the South Pole.

Scientific conception

Children may have the idea that heavy (dense) materials inside the Earth such as iron have settled over time and filtered 'down', coming to rest at the 'bottom'

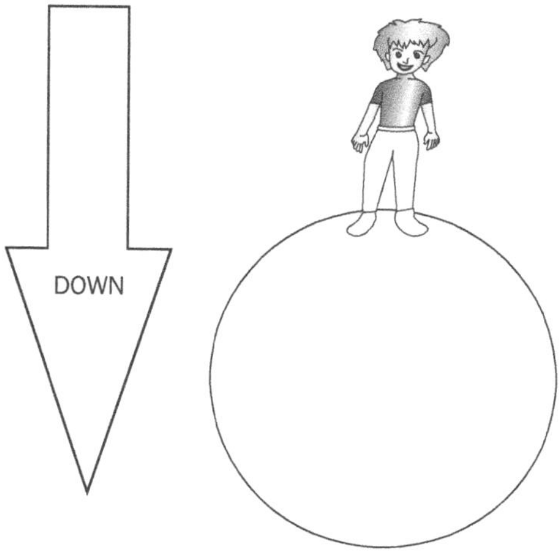

Figure 11.4a 'Down' is in the direction of the surface of the Earth where I am standing (misconception)

of the Earth. This misconception is related to the common acceptance of 'up' being directly overhead and 'down' in the direction of our feet (Figure 11.4a). However, if you look at the Earth from space, there is no ultimate frame of reference, i.e. up and down are meaningless because it depends on which way up your body currently is. If you are standing on the Earth's surface, since gravity pulls towards the centre of the Earth and not the geographical South Pole, this is the true direction of 'down' if the Earth is the frame of reference (Figure 11.4b). Billions of years ago when the Earth was forming, because of gravity, the denser materials sank towards its centre, which is why the Earth's core today is made of the heavy **elements** iron and nickel (Figure 11.4c).

Stories, often exaggerated, of a wealth of natural resources such as metals and oil in Antarctica might further reinforce this misconception. A geography misconception that is also linked to a naïve concept of up/ down is that on a 2D map of Antarctica the direction *north* is always at the top of the map; however, north actually radiates in all directions away from the geographical South Pole like the spokes of a bicycle wheel (this can be shown using a globe).

Reconstruction

A first step is to address the naïve concept of 'down' that acts as a source of the misconception, explaining that 'down' for anyone standing on Earth is towards the Earth's centre, not the South Pole. Children' beliefs regarding which way they consider to be 'down' can be elicited by using Figure 11.4d, asking *where would the balls go if the three people were to drop them at the same time?* This can be a challenge for many children, who find it difficult to understand why a person who lives in Australia does not fall off the Earth, 'downwards' into space.

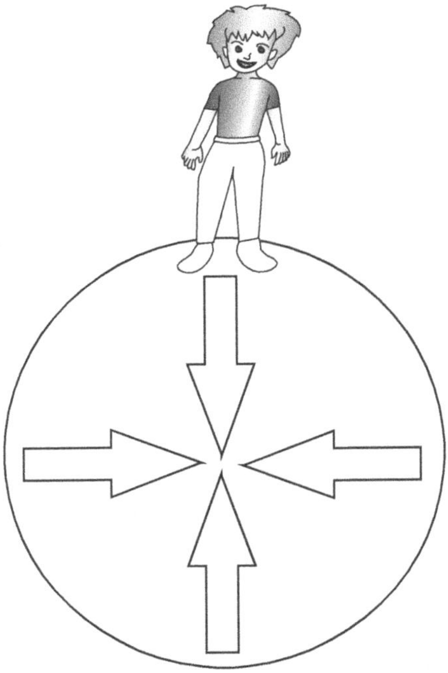

Figure 11.4b The true direction of 'down' (when the frame of reference is standing on the Earth's surface)

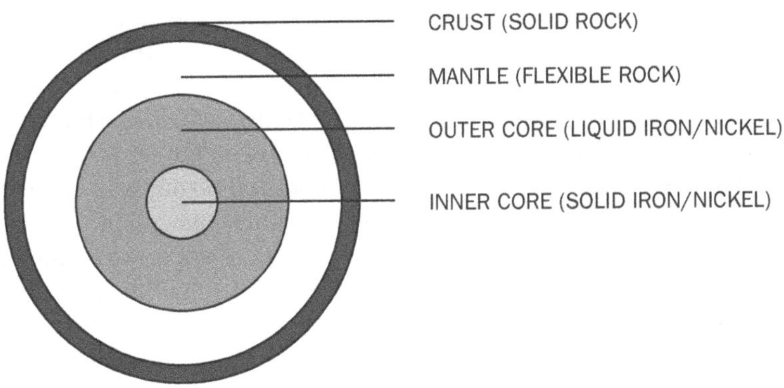

Figure 11.4c Internal layers of the Earth (not to scale)

Although the inside structure of the Earth is beyond the primary science National Curriculum, children could be introduced to the idea of the Earth consisting of different layers and that the heaviest (densest) layers are found at the core, not the South Pole. Explain that this is because gravity pulled them there when the Earth first formed (see Chapter 13 for other misconceptions concerning gravity).

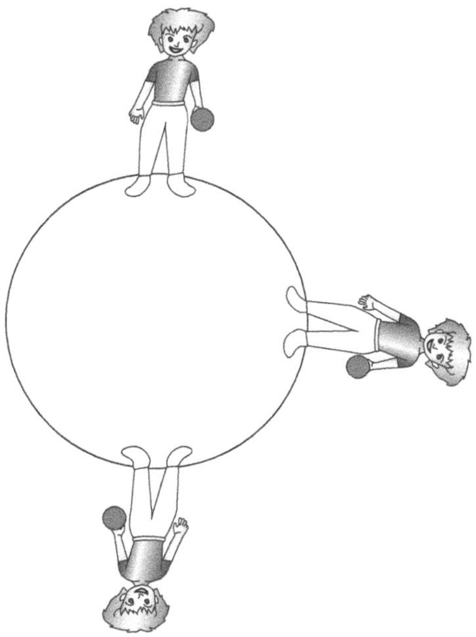

Figure 11.4d How to explore children's ideas of 'down' (see main text)

Sources: Marques and Thompson (1997); Nussbaum (1985); Schoon and Boone (1998); Turkmen (2017).

11.5 What is soil made from?

Misconception

There is no air in soil, so underground creatures need to come up to the surface to breathe.

Scientific conception

Children may have watched animals in their gardens such as ants, ground beetles, or centipedes suddenly appearing on the surface of the soil, crawling around for a short time and then disappearing underground again. This can lead them to believe that the animals come up to breathe air, in the same way that a whale, being a mammal, has no gills and so needs to regularly come to the surface of the sea to breathe.

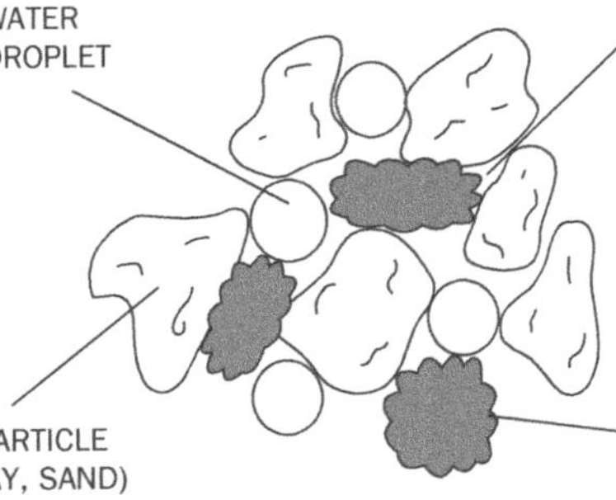

Figure 11.5 The basic structure of soil (showing air spaces)

Like whales, soil invertebrates do not have gills, so to survive they need direct contact with air to absorb oxygen. However, it is not usually necessary for them to surface above the soil to breathe because there is plenty of air underground. Soil is not a compact solid mass; instead, it contains many air spaces within its structure. These tiny pockets of air mean that soil animals can breathe quite adequately while underground (Figure 11.5).

During rainy weather, earthworms appear on the surface of soil, which can act as a source or reinforcer of the misconception. Worms absorb oxygen through their skins and when soil becomes waterlogged due to rain, they find it difficult to extract the oxygen underground, so surface in search of air. Therefore, in this particular case the worm does indeed surface in order to 'breathe'.[1]

A related misconception is that soil has always been there, and not created over time by the erosion and weathering of rock.

Reconstruction

The idea that soil does not contain any air spaces lies at the root of this misconception. It can be shown that soil is not a solid mass by asking children to spoon some soil to fill a small container such as an eggcup to the brim, then predict how much water they will be able to pour into the filled container before it overflows. It is surprising how much water can be added – soil contains lots of air spaces that the water can squeeze into. This can be linked to more general discussions about the structure of soil having four main parts: (1) tiny rock particles, weathered down from larger lumps of rock – these give soil that gritty feel; (2) humus, mostly dead plant material; (3) water droplets; and (4) air spaces (Figure 11.5).

This activity can be extended by comparing different soils. Clayey soils placed in an eggcup will accept less water than sandy soils before overflowing because the clay particles are small, fit together more closely and so have far fewer air spaces. When soils are placed in a funnel[2] and water is poured over them, sandy soil will hold scarcely any water, letting it run straight through; however, clayey soil will let hardly any water pass through and instead slowly absorbs it, becoming sticky in the process. Farmers who grow crops usually prefer an intermediate soil between clay and sand so that some air spaces are present, and also some water is held in the soil.

A spring or summer activity that is suitable for KS1 classes is to ask each child to study a 'circle of earth'. Cut pieces of string into 2-metre lengths and ask children to make a circle with the string over an area of grass or dirt. Children then watch for any animal activity within their circle, for instance, ants or ground beetles coming to the surface. If the ground is sprinkled with a very diluted washing-up liquid solution, earthworms are likely to appear.

Sources: Brass and Duke (1994); Frankel-Hauser (1998); Koba and Mitchell (2011).

11.6 When did the dinosaurs become extinct?

Misconception

Dinosaurs lived at the same time as humans.

Scientific conception

Sometimes called the 'Flintstones fallacy', this idea has its origins in story books, cartoons, and films that show people co-existing alongside dinosaurs such as *Tyrannosaurus*, *Brachiosaurus*, and *Pterodactylus*. Cavemen and women can be seen hunting dinosaurs, being chased by them, or keeping them as pets. Such media sources provide entertaining stories about humans interacting with these mysterious, now-extinct creatures, but conflict with what the fossil record tells us. The last non-bird dinosaurs died 66 million years ago due to a cataclysmic incident that changed the Earth's climate called the Cretaceous–Tertiary (C-T) extinction event. The most likely cause was a giant asteroid crashing into the Earth, creating a huge dust cloud in the atmosphere that blocked out sunlight, causing the onset of a prolonged winter. The darkness and cold meant that photosynthesis was greatly reduced and plants started to die out. This affected food chains worldwide and many living things became extinct, including non-dinosaurs such as fish, reptiles, and invertebrates. However, some dinosaurs did survive – theropods eventually evolved into modern-day birds, and it is not widely known that scientists classify today's birds as a type of dinosaur. The first early human species (hominids) only appeared 6 million years ago, 60 million years after tyrannosaurs and the other well-known dinosaurs disappeared from the Earth.

Other misconceptions are that all dinosaurs were very large creatures that lacked intelligence, lived in jungles, and were smooth-skinned (in fact, many had feathers). Fossil misconceptions include the idea that if there is a fossil, then that organism must now be extinct, which ignores the fact there are fossils of plants and animals that are still alive today. Many of these species were living at the time of the dinosaurs, for example, ferns, crocodiles, sharks, and honey bees. Another common belief is that fossils are made from bone, when many are actually made from rock that was once bone millions of years ago but slowly changed over time due to a process called fossilization. Some children think that the older the fossil, the less complex it is, which has echoes of the misconception that evolution always ends up producing more sophisticated living things (7.3).

A conceptual extension of the main misconception is that humans are responsible for the dinosaurs becoming extinct due to over-hunting; this idea has been used by creationists to refute scientific explanations of the C-T extinction event.

Reconstruction

As part of a Year 3 rock topic, children learn that fossils are the remains of species that lived in the ancient past, and in Year 6 this learning is linked with the theory of evolution (see Chapter 7). From a young age, children are interested in learning about dinosaurs and this enthusiasm can be tapped into by means of activities such as creating posters or MS PowerPoint presentations about different species of dinosaur. Field trips to places such as Lyme Regis in Dorset can provide opportunities for fossil hunts.

A significant problem is that children often find it difficult to comprehend the huge spans of time involved when learning about the Earth's natural history. Therefore, these ideas need to be secure before attempting to teach the concept of a 60-million-year gap between the commonly known dinosaurs and early humans. *A time-line in your own backyard* is an activity freely available on the internet that involves erecting a string across the classroom, using pegs to place pictures of events from Earth's history along the string in the correct sequence as they occurred historically. These events include first land plants, first dinosaurs, and first mammals; there are obvious links here to evolution misconceptions such as humans are descended from chimpanzees (7.8).

A different issue is that creationists reject the idea of a long prehistory before humans, instead believing that the Earth is only 6000 years old, so children from some religious families may have different beliefs to the concepts you will be teaching (Chapter 7). There is a fundamentalist Christian museum in Kentucky in the US that has displays showing dinosaurs and humans happily living alongside each other, reflecting the creationist belief that all animals, including dinosaurs, were created at the same point in time.

If the Dinosaurs Came Back, a book by Bernard Most, helps KS1 children appreciate that dinosaurs became extinct a very long time ago before humans appeared on the Earth.

Sources: Guffey and Slater (2020); Most (1978); Russell and McGuigan (2015); Trend (2001).

Notes

1 Although technically this is not breathing, see the Glossary definition.
2 The cut-off neck of a 2-litre plastic drinks bottle makes a good funnel.

Planning and assessment sheet 11 The Earth

(For suggestions on how to use this sheet, see p. xxviii)

Misconception	*Attainment re. expected standard*		
	Working towards	*Working at*	*Working above*
Year 3: *Rocks*			
'Rocks' are large, heavy, and jagged. If smaller, they are 'stones'. If smooth, they are 'pebbles' (11.1)	✓	✓	
Human-made materials such as brick or concrete are rocks (11.2)	✓	✓	
A boulder is not a rock because it is too big (11.1)	✓	✓	
A polished piece of marble is not a rock because it has been worked by humans and so is no longer natural (11.2)		✓	
All rocks were made billions of years ago when the Earth was first formed (11.2)		✓	
All rocks have been created by volcanoes (11.2)	✓	✓	
Very ancient rocks are always soft and crumbly (11.2)	✓	✓	
Minerals are precious small stones that are attractive, shiny, rare, and used in expensive jewellery (11.3)		✓	✓
Rocks are dull, commonly available, and inexpensive (11.3)	✓	✓	✓
A rock is only made up from one single substance (11.3)	✓	✓	
All rocks are heavy (11.3)	✓	✓	
Rocks or minerals that are attractive are called crystals (11.3)	✓	✓	✓
A mineral such as quartz is a type of vitamin that is essential in your diet (11.3)		✓	✓
The heaviest materials in the Earth are found at the South Pole (11.4)		✓	
There is no air in soil, so underground creatures need to come up to the surface to breathe (11.5)	✓	✓	
The soil in my garden has always existed (and not created over time by the erosion and weathering of rock) (11.5)	✓	✓	

(continued)

(continued)

Dinosaurs lived at the same time as humans ('Flintstones fallacy') (11.6)	✓		
Humans are responsible for the dinosaurs becoming extinct due to over-hunting (11.6)	✓		
All dinosaurs were very large creatures that lacked intelligence, lived in jungles, and were smooth-skinned (11.6)	✓	✓	
If there is a fossil of an organism, then the organism must now be extinct (11.6)	✓	✓	
Fossils are made from bone (not rock) (11.6)	✓	✓	
The older the fossil, the less sophisticated the organism was (11.6)		✓	✓
Difficulties conceptualizing deep time when learning about Earth's early history (11.6)	✓	✓	
All animals (including dinosaurs) were created at the same point in time, 6000 years ago (creationism) (11.6)		✓	
Year 5: *Earth and space*			
'Up' is always directly overhead, and 'down' is always in the direction of our feet (11.4)	✓	✓	

12

Climate change

Conceptual areas covered in this chapter:	*National Curriculum links:*
• Causes of global warming • How global warming is linked to climate change • Consequences of global warming • Climate change denial	Extra-curricular

12.1 What is climate change?

> **Misconception**
>
> *The climate is getting warmer because the Earth has moved closer to the sun.*

Scientific conception

Scientists agree that the Earth has become warmer over the past 150 years and is continuing to do so at an unrelenting pace, causing climate change. Although children are aware that this warming trend is happening and that the climate is changing, they often find it difficult to explain using scientific ideas what causes **global warming**. This is perhaps unsurprising since these concepts are not included in the primary National Curriculum for either science or geography.

To appreciate this underlying science we must look at how sunlight affects the Earth. First, consider what happens on the **moon**, which unlike the Earth, has no atmosphere (Figure 12.1a). Sunlight warms the moon's surface ①; however, because it has no atmosphere to retain this warmth, the moon is constantly

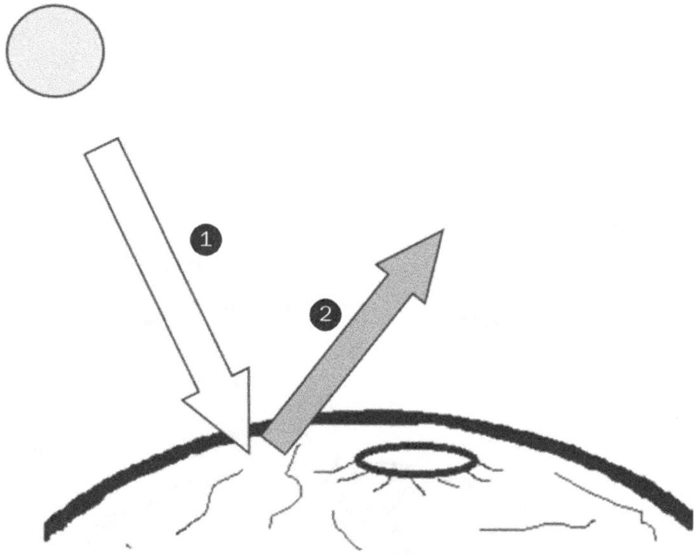

Figure 12.1a How the sun heats the moon (not to scale)

losing heat from its surface, with nearly all this energy escaping out into space ②. This makes temperatures on the surface of the moon very hot during the day, and very cold at night (maximum 120°C; minimum -247°C), and these extremes of temperature are one of the reasons why the moon is unable to sustain life.

Figure 12.1b shows that with the Earth, the fact that an atmosphere is present means that less heat escapes into space. The atmosphere can be thought of as a 'blanket of gases' surrounding the Earth that keeps much of the heat in. As was the case with the moon, sunlight warms the Earth ① and this warmth is continually being lost from the surface. Most of the heat from the surface is transferred into the atmosphere ②, which becomes warm itself in the process. Some of this heat from the atmosphere escapes into space ③, although most is retained, and as a consequence the Earth's surface is kept warm ④. Therefore, the surface of the Earth is heated by two different processes, ① and ④. Life is able to exist on Earth partly due to the fact there are no extremes of daily temperature as there are on the moon; like a blanket, the Earth's atmosphere keeps night temperatures relatively high by warming the surface, while temperatures during the day do not become excessively high because some sunlight is reflected away from the Earth by the upper atmosphere before it has a chance to reach the surface ⑤.

An overwhelming number of scientists accept that global warming, at least in part, is a result of human industrial pollution. Some gases in the atmosphere are very good at absorbing heat and then releasing that heat back to the surface of the Earth. They are called **greenhouse gases**, the most important of

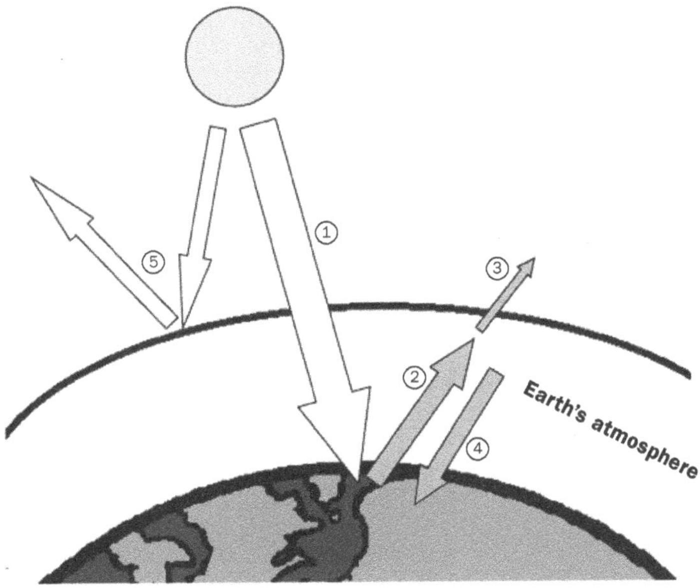

Figure 12.1b Explaining the greenhouse effect (not to scale)

which are carbon dioxide (CO_2) and water vapour. The amount of carbon dioxide in the atmosphere has increased since the late 1700s due to the burning of fossil fuels such as coal, wood, oil, and petrol during industrial and other processes, which release carbon dioxide when they burn. Therefore, the increasing levels of carbon dioxide mean that more heat is retained by the Earth's atmosphere, which makes temperatures rise (Figure 12.1b, arrow ④). In effect, the atmosphere is becoming a more efficient 'blanket'.

Children can become confused about what causes global warming and incorrectly cite reasons such as radioactive waste, acid rain, the extinction of endangered species, not picking up litter, and as the misconception statement above suggests, the Earth being closer to the sun. Scientifically acceptable interventions that will help the problem of global warming centre around the burning of fewer fossil fuels to limit further excessive releases of carbon dioxide into the atmosphere. The phenomenon of ozone layer depletion is frequently confused with global warming, and children may say that one is a cause of the other.

Aside from human pollution, over history, natural processes have also been responsible for the climate changing; these include volcanoes, how active the sun is, and erosion of rocks that releases carbon dioxide or methane into the atmosphere. A very small minority of scientists believe that human activity is *not* the cause of global warming and that temperatures are increasing as part of these natural cycles of warming and cooling. The final misconception entry in this chapter deals with other fallacies about climate change that children may be exposed to, and further discusses these minority views and ways that KS2 teachers could address them (12.2).

Reconstruction

Even though the science of global warming is beyond the primary curriculum, since climate change is high on the social agenda, many schools do teach about why the Earth is becoming warmer and the consequences of not arresting the warming trend. Also, several National Curriculum science topics do contain concepts that help children understand climate change science, these include: the changing weather across the four seasons (Year 1, *Seasonal changes* and Year 5, *Earth in space*); how changing the environment can affect ecosystems (Year 4, *Living things and their habitats*); and how sunlight travels through space and heats the Earth (Years 3 and 6, *Light*). These concepts need to be firmly embedded prior to teaching any scientific models of global warming and climate change, and relevant chapters of this book deal with the misconceptions children construct during each of these topics

The potential problems of global warming are well documented, such as the melting of the polar ice caps, sea level rises, and climate change. In addition to learning about the causes of global warming, KS2 teachers could consider discussing the concepts that underlie the consequences as they are important for general scientific literacy. This is particularly relevant, given the number of potential misconceptions about global warming (also see 12.2). In Year 4 as part of the *Living things* topic teachers are required to explore the impact humans have had on the planet; lessons about climate change would fit in well here.

The idea that atmospheric gases can keep the heat in like a blanket can be introduced by asking children to compare how warm they feel when outside on cloudy and cloudless nights. Clouds consist partly of water vapour (a greenhouse gas) and during overcast nights, clouds help keep in heat lost by the Earth's surface, therefore cloudy nights tend to be warmer, and clear nights cooler. Some researchers have suggested that the traditional approach of teaching environmental issues holistically as 'saving the planet' can act as a barrier to teasing apart children's misconceptions behind phenomena such as global warming. There is an ample number of animations available on internet sites such as YouTube that would help children understand the sequence of events that bring about global warming, which should first be vetted by teachers beforehand for scientific accuracy.

Sources: Bhattacharya *et al.* (2021); Boyes and Stanisstreet (1993); Francis *et al.* (1993); Skamp *et al.* (2009).

12.2 Is human activity contributing to climate change?

Misconception

Humans are not responsible for climate change.

Scientific conception

As discussed in 12.1, there is an overwhelming consensus among scientists that the Earth has become warmer over the past 150 years. This warming trend, at least in part, is due to the atmospheric pollution generated by industrial development and technological advance. Global warming is seen as having a harmful effect on the climate; an average increase of even a few degrees centigrade could result in rising sea levels, extreme weather conditions and drought, with associated effects on the biosphere including extinctions of species, food shortages, and poverty and displacement of human populations. Scientists advise a move towards stabilizing and then reducing the levels of greenhouse gases in the atmosphere to limit the effects of a changing climate.

Most governments and a majority of laypeople have acknowledged the existence of climate change and the need to limit its consequences, based on acceptance of the scientific evidence that underpins the claims. This acknowledgement is based on a trust in science as a means of solving problems, which includes being confident that scientists will carry out their work using rational methods and then honestly report their findings. However, a vocal minority have rejected the scientific consensus. Climate change sceptics distrust what scientists have to say, claiming either that scientists have 'got it wrong' or that governments are conspiring with scientists to convey dishonest information to the populace. These conspiracy theories reflecting a rejection of the science are shared via the internet in the form of social media posts and blogs, and sceptics have a substantial online presence with their contributions receiving considerable attention.

Sceptics fall into two broad categories: (1) those who reject that the climate is changing at all, and (2) those who accept climate change but deny that human activity is a cause. Over the past decade the first group has been declining in numbers – media attention given to recent 'freak' weather events makes it more difficult to reject that climate change is real. However, the second group (**anthropogenic deniers**) has not declined; a recent US study found that 50% of people believe no clear link exists between human action and a changing climate. Table 12.2a summarizes some of the misconceptions that climate change sceptics purvey online. There is a potential problem in that children exposed to these ideas will similarly reject the science and become sceptical that climate change has an anthropogenic cause. Although there has been little

Table 12.2a Climate change misconceptions (adapted from Allen and Parry, 2023)

Climate change misconception
The Earth is not getting warmer
The Earth is getting warmer, but this is not causing climate change
Climate change is not happening
The pollution humans have made has nothing to do with climate change
Atmospheric carbon dioxide is irrelevant to climate change
Fossil fuels produced by factories, cars, and aeroplanes are not causing climate change
Deforestation has no effect on climate change
Nuclear power stations are causing climate change
Climate change is only caused by things happening in nature, such as erupting volcanoes
Climate change is happening because the sun is burning hotter
Climate change is a good thing because the weather will improve
We need to maintain high levels of carbon dioxide in the air because plants need it for photosynthesis
The recent cold snap is evidence that climate change is not happening
Scientists disagree that climate change is happening
Scientists know that climate change is real but they are not concerned about it
When scientists tell us that climate change is happening, they are not telling us the truth
When the Government tell us that climate change is happening, they are not telling us the truth
We should not worry about climate change because it is part of the Earth's natural cycles
We should not worry about climate change because scientists will think of ways to stop it happening
We can never stop climate change because of China's industrial output
Addressing climate change is too expensive, it will crash the economy
We have more important things to worry about than climate change
We should not worry about climate change because in the future, the sun will start to cool down
We should not worry about climate change because in the future, the Earth will start to cool down
We should not worry about climate change because it only affects countries very far away
Renewable energy sources such as wind power and solar power are too costly and unreliable

research into climate change scepticism in primary children, a 2023 UK study determined that up to 42% of Year 6 children were susceptible to the types of misconceptions detailed in Table 12.2a.

Reconstruction

Because of the current lack of research in this area, there are no clear evidence-based interventions that primary teachers can fall back on when looking to address these misconceptions in the classroom. That said, there are a number of key concepts children would need to grasp in order to appreciate the science underpinning climate change, which will put them in a better position to reject those fallacies that are based on bad science; these are summarized in Table 12.2b. Suggestions about how best to teach these ideas are found in the previous misconception entry (12.1) and these pedagogies could be combined with approaches designed to promote children's critical thinking faculties in a general sense.

Table 12.2b Key concepts in understanding climate change science

Key concept
The difference between weather (short-term events) and climate (long-term trends)
How sunlight travels through space and heats the Earth
The role of greenhouse gases in global warming (especially carbon dioxide and water vapour)
Human sources of atmospheric carbon dioxide (e.g. burning fossil fuels, destruction of forests)
How photosynthesis affects the balance of gases in the atmosphere
The effects of a changing climate on the planet (e.g. changes in the environment affect ecosystems, rising sea levels, human migration)

Sources: Allen and Parry (2023); Hayward and Gronland (2021); Kovaka (2021).

Planning and assessment sheet 12 Climate change

(For suggestions on how to use this sheet, see p. xxviii.)

Misconception	*Attainment re. expected standard*		
	Working towards	*Working at*	*Working above*
Extra-curricular			
The climate is getting warmer because the Earth has moved closer to the sun (12.1)	✓	✓	
Global warming is made worse by radioactive waste, acid rain, the extinction of endangered species, ozone layer depletion, or not picking up litter (12.1)	✓	✓	
Humans are not responsible for climate change (12.2)	✓	✓	✓
Climate change deniers' myths (Table 12.2a has a list) (12.2)	✓	✓	✓

PART FOUR
Physics

13

Forces and magnets

Conceptual areas covered in this chapter:

- Gravitational attraction
- The difference between mass and weight
- Frictional forces
- Balanced and unbalanced forces
- Magnetic attraction

National Curriculum links:

Year 3: *Forces and magnets*

Year 5: *Forces*

13.1 Does mass affect the speed of falling?

Misconception

Heavier objects fall more quickly than lighter objects.

Scientific conception

A learner who constructs this misconception may believe that if an adult and a young child were to jump from a diving board into a swimming pool at the same instant, the adult would make the first splash because they are heavier and so would have fallen more quickly. One reason offered for why heavy objects fall with a greater speed is that because they are heavy, gravity pulls them with a greater force, i.e. 'gravity has got more to get hold of'.

If several objects that have different mass are dropped simultaneously from the same height, they will all hit the ground at exactly the same time, if the effects of **air resistance** can be removed from the system (though see caveat in the *Did you know?* Box p. 203). It is true that with several objects of different mass as in Figure 13.1a, the heavier objects will be pulled by gravity with a greater force than the lighter ones. For example, the 1 kg ball will experience

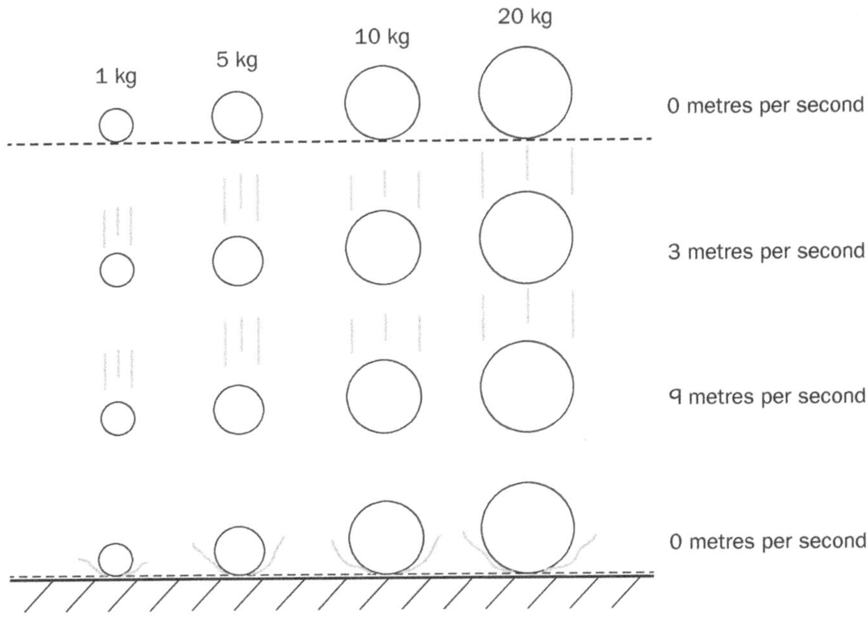

Figure 13.1a Objects of different mass fall at the same speed

a downward pulling force of 10 Newtons and the 20 kg ball a force of 200 Newtons – these forces are each object's *weight.*[1] However, how quickly the balls gain speed (**accelerate**) because of these gravitational pulls will be exactly the same for each ball. Therefore, their speed of falling will be the same at a given height and they will all hit the ground simultaneously. But the fact that all the balls in Figure 13.1a accelerate equally seems intuitively wrong because if they all have different weights, then why is gravity not pulling the heavier ones down more quickly?

To further understand this, an additional concept needs to be introduced, the idea of **inertia**, which is the resistance of an object to its present state of motion. It is difficult for one person to get a stationary, broken-down car moving by pushing it by themselves, but once they get the car in motion the effort required is less and it can be kept moving by applying a smaller pushing force. Inertia makes it difficult for the person to get the stationary car moving and it also prevents the person from stopping the car easily once it is moving – it is as if the car is consciously resisting any attempt to change its present state of motion. A similar situation occurs with the falling balls in Figure 13.1a. The heavier balls are indeed attracted to the Earth with a greater gravitational pull (weight) but because they have more mass, the effort required to get them moving in the first place is also greater because of their inertia, which 'tries to prevent' any greater acceleration. Simply put, with the heavier balls, the higher gravitational pull and higher inertia exactly cancel each other out, with the result that every ball is accelerated by the same amount and so falls with equal speed, no matter how heavy it is.

Sometimes the opposite view to this misconception is held, with children predicting that lighter objects will fall faster because they meet less air resistance. Indeed, the shape of an object can have a large effect on fall speed; for instance, a car falling while being suspended from a parachute may have a mass of 1000 kg but will fall more slowly than a 0.1 kg glass marble, due to the parachute having a greater air resistance than the marble.

Did you know?

A caveat. Even though we teach children the scientific view that all objects fall with equal speed regardless of their mass, an important caveat to falling objects is that within the Earth's atmosphere it is extremely difficult to eliminate air resistance, and so lighter objects do fall at a slower speed. If the experiment in Figure 13.1a were to be carried out in the school playground, there *would* be very slight differences in the falling speeds and the heavier balls would land first; whether observers would notice this would depend largely on the height from which they were dropped. If they were released from a point several stories high, the heavier balls would probably be seen to land first, but if dropped from a metre or so above the ground any difference would likely go unnoticed, although electronic apparatus such as datalogger light gates would be able to detect minor differences in speed. Therefore, the scientific view we teach is in fact idealized and bears little relation to the experiment that we carry out in the classroom.

Reconstruction

Although in reality heavier objects will fall slightly faster than lighter objects of the same shape because of the effects of air resistance (Box p. 203), the scientific view can still be taught successfully because experiments can be arranged so that any differences are undetectable by the human eye. Dropping different-sized glass marbles or ball bearings simultaneously from the same height will give reliable outcomes that show them appearing to land at the same time. Care must be taken to make sure they are released at exactly the same time, as things like sticky fingers can be a source of error. Attempts to eliminate the effects of air resistance can be made by performing other experiments, such as having a number of identically sized small plastic tubs, with each containing a different amount of mass.

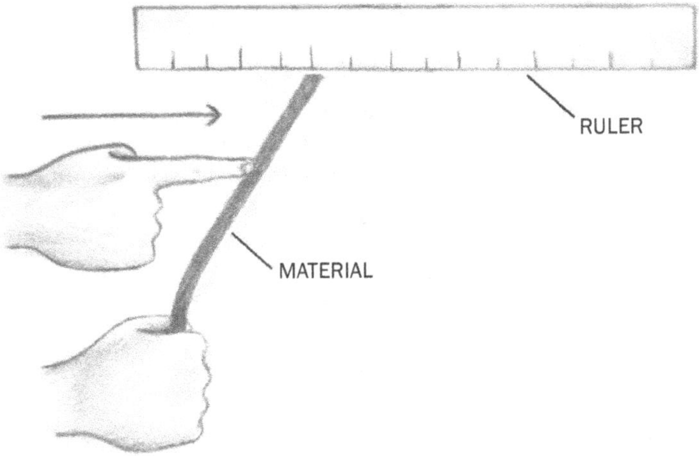

Figure 13.1b A simple Newton meter
Source: adapted from Rogers (2022).

The teacher can make a video recording of two objects of different mass being dropped at the same time from a short distance above a table that can be played back in slow motion to show that they land at the same time. A well-known video available on the internet shows the American astronaut David Scott dropping a geological hammer and a falcon's feather on the moon – where there is no atmosphere and so no air resistance – and both are seen to land at the same time. Trial and error will show that some objects are not suitable for experiments designed to address this misconception. I have found that with a golf ball and a ping pong ball, which are almost the same size but of different weights, the ping pong ball falls noticeably more slowly.

KS1 children can try marble painting using a box lid with a piece of A4 paper in the bottom. They dip a marble in paint and roll the marble around the lid so that coloured tracks are produced; adding different coloured paints leads to more attractive patterns. Using different-sized marbles will show children how objects of different mass move, with the larger marbles rolling more slowly due to their greater inertia. To introduce KS1 children to the idea of forces, read the story book *Oscar and the Cricket* by Geoff Waring. When talking to them about falling objects, *On the Way Home* by Gill Murphy is a good source.

Introducing the idea that forces act on objects at KS1 can also be done by showing how the shape of flexible materials can be changed. Start by asking children to manipulate plasticine or Blu Tack with their fingers to make different shapes, while they explain whether they are using twisting, squeezing, bending, or stretching forces. This can be extended by children making a simple Newton meter (Figure 13.1b), testing flexible, elastic materials such as wooden ice lolly sticks, plastic coffee stirrers, and plastic plant labels. They can discover patterns such as when they double their pushing force, the material will bend double the distance.

Sources: Bar *et al.* (2016); Frankel-Hauser (1998); Gunstone and White (1981); Howe *et al.* (2012); Murphy (1982); Rogers (2022); Waring (2007).

13.2 What forces are involved when an object is thrown through the air?

Misconception

A ball flying through the air has a force that constantly pushes it from behind.

Scientific conception

The idea that a constant force must be acting on anything that has been propelled forwards is extremely widespread. Children often think that if someone throws a ball in their direction, it only reaches them because it has been constantly 'pushed' throughout its flight by such a force (Figure 13.2a). They can feel this force when they catch a ball that is thrown at speed towards them, after which the pushing force ceases to exist.

In reality, there is no forward force on the ball during its flight. A force is a push or a pull, and the only time the ball is pushed is during the action of throwing. As soon as the ball leaves the thrower's hand it is no longer being pushed and during its flight it is actually slowing down due to the effects of air resistance – this is why when you catch a ball, the further you are away from the thrower, the slower the speed of the ball when it reaches you and so the 'softer' the catch.

Figure 13.2b shows the important forces that are in play when a ball is thrown. The thrower on the left of the diagram is applying a pushing force (P) to the ball during their throwing action. At the same time, the ball's weight (W)

Figure 13.2a A forward force pushes a ball throughout its flight (misconception)

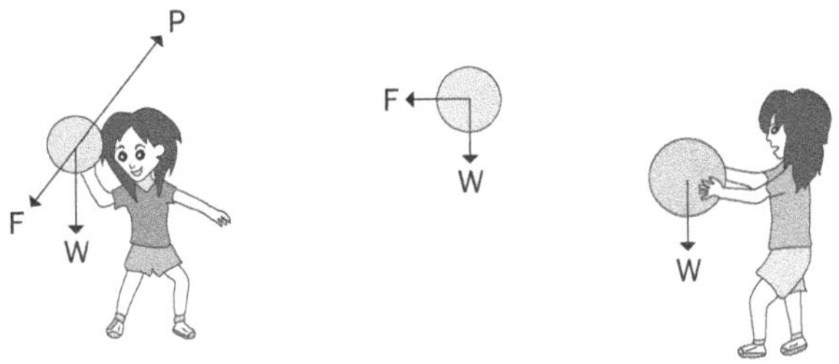

Figure 13.2b Forces acting on a thrown ball (see text for explanation)

is pulling it downwards and air resistance (**friction**, F) is pushing against the ball in the opposite direction to the pushing force. The middle picture of the ball shows that as soon as the ball leaves the thrower's hand, it no longer is being pushed forward by anything but continues on its path because the opposing air resistance (F) is not large enough to stop it moving forwards; however, this air resistance force which is pushing the ball in a backwards direction makes it **decelerate**, constantly slowing it down. This reflects Newton's first law of motion, which states that an object must continue moving (or remain still) unless acted upon by a force. While in flight, weight still pulls the ball down, which makes the ball fly in an arc-shaped path instead of a perfectly straight line. Once the catcher on the right of the diagram has the ball in their hands, it is no longer moving and so air resistance no longer applies, although weight is still pulling the ball downwards.

Although the flying ball has no forward force, our hands feel a pushing force when we catch it. This can be very confusing for children as it is an example where something that has no pushing force generates a pushing force by itself. Considering Newton's first law of motion again, when we catch a moving ball, we are applying a pushing force with our hands onto the ball in order to stop its motion. The force that we feel is the equal and opposite **reaction force** of the ball pushing back on our hands, similar to when we push down with our hand on the edge of a table – the table feels like it is pushing back into our hand and leaves a visible impression on our skin.

If the ball were to be thrown in **deep space**, once it left the thrower's hand there would similarly be no forward force acting on the ball. Also, because it wouldn't be near to the Earth or any other **celestial body**, it would not experience any weight force, or any air resistance, which means it would be travelling forwards in space in a perfectly straight line with no forces at all acting upon it. The ball would continue moving forward in this way for eternity at the same speed until another force was applied to it, according to Newton's first law of motion. Other surprising examples of moving objects that have no forward force acting on them are a moving car with the engine turned off, a freewheeling bicycle, and a bullet fired from a gun.

Famous scientists

Scientists can have misconceptions too. These misconceptions have their roots in older scientific theories that have now been discredited. Ancient Greek scientists thought that an object such as a thrown spear stays in flight because tiny air currents cause external forces to push and support it. In the fourteenth century CE, the French thinker Jean Buridan challenged this view, insisting that a special force within a spear was pushing it along and propelling it forwards during its flight; this force was *impetus*. Based on the more recent work of scientists such as Isaac Newton, we now accept that a thrown object has no forward force acting upon it.

Related misconceptions include when young children give human feelings to objects (anthropomorphism), such as 'I threw the ball up, but it fell back down because it wanted to', and that the ball keeps flying because it is supported by forces in the air around it. Some learners think that something flies because it contains a force inside it that is greater than gravity, and when this force has been used up, it begins to fall back down (see also 13.5). This idea can manifest itself in a wider sense with children thinking that all forces are present *within* objects, for example, a skydiver has gravity inside them which makes them fall, and once they land, the gravity has run out. With forces generally, children believe that the greater the force applied, then the greater the effect produced, which is not always the case; for instance, with levers, gears, and pulleys, a small input force results in a greater output force.

Reconstruction

Since forces are invisible and we can only see their effects, it is often difficult to address any misconceptions, which is one reason why they are so commonplace. One starting point would be to push a toy car across the floor and ask the children to name the forces acting on the car once it had been released from your hand but is still travelling forwards; this would elicit the misconception. Then remind children that a force must be either a constant push or a pull so that once your hand stops pushing the car and lets it go on its own, there is no longer any forward force on the freewheeling car. After the initial push to propel it forwards, the car will start to slow down, and although the car appears to be being pushed along in a forward direction, it is actually being pushed backwards by friction. Because forces cannot be seen, asking children to habitually draw force arrows on diagrams of their experiments will help them visualize that forces act in different directions, and have different strengths.

When introducing the idea of forces to KS1 children, familiarize them with the concepts of 'push' and 'pull'. Ask them to do a series of physical activities where they decide whether they are applying a push or a pull; for instance, kicking a sponge ball, lifting up a teddy, and throwing a paper aeroplane. Note that children sometimes have limited understanding of what precisely is a push or a pull, such that opening a door when you enter a room is a push, but kicking a ball is not.

The word 'force' can be misconstrued by children and interpreted in non-science ways, e.g. a force is associated with the armed forces or the police force. Gradually building up children's science vocabulary by defining key words from the early years onwards will help them differentiate between the scientific and everyday meanings of terms such as resistance, friction, attraction, balanced, etc.

Sources: Blown and Bryce (2013); Driver *et al.* (1994); Monach and Turford (2019); Piaget (1970); Watts (1982).

13.3 What is friction?

Misconception

Friction only acts on moving objects.

Scientific conception

Children discover that when they pull an object such as a toy car on a string over different surfaces, it is easier to pull the car over some surfaces than others. With a smooth laminate floor it takes little effort to pull the car, but over a carpet more pulling force is required. We teach them that with the carpet there is something called 'friction' involved. However, they typically do not consider friction to be at work with objects that are not moving, such as a book sitting on a sloping ramp. This might partly be to do with the fact that when they pull a moving object, they can physically 'feel the friction' over rough surfaces like a carpet, which they are unable to experience with stationary objects.

Friction can be defined as *a resisting force that acts in the opposite direction to another force.* When you travel down a slide in a children's playground, you can feel friction pushing back on your legs, feet, and bottom, opposing your downward sliding movement and trying to slow you down. With large slides where you pick up a good speed, large frictional forces can generate heat and cause minor burns or blisters if bare skin comes into contact with the slide. However, something does not have to move for friction to be present. You can park a car safely on a hill by leaving the handbrake on because friction opposes the car's weight and stops it rolling downhill. All these are examples of *contact friction* between solid surfaces that are touching, but friction also is present in other situations. Air resistance and water resistance (also called drag) involve friction forces that slow down an object's motion and are examples of *non-contact friction*. Vehicles such as cars and boats are designed to minimize this friction by having a streamlined shape that cuts through the air or water, allowing them to accelerate more quickly and have higher top speeds.

Other misconceptions relate to difficulties in understanding that friction works in a particular direction; children may know that an object has this general effect called friction slowing it down, but are not able to provide any more detail. The misconception that friction acts on an object placed on a flat, horizontal surface such as the floor is very common, such that when a person is standing up, friction stops them falling over. However, contact friction is only present when two objects are touching each other, and one surface is potentially trying to slide over the other. When a person is standing up and not moving, there are no sliding surfaces and so no friction. But if they were to start walking, the soles of their feet would be pushing the floor so friction would come into play (if there was no friction, walking would be impossible). Children may also believe that friction forces are always problematic and need minimizing, not considering that friction is useful in many everyday contexts, e.g. walking, brakes on a bicycle, holding a pen, etc.

Reconstruction

The Year 5 Programme of Study states that children should learn about friction acting between moving surfaces, and some examples of equipment used to teach friction concepts are shown in Figure 13.3. It is one of the forces that children find easiest to understand because its effects can be readily reproduced in the classroom. Friction can be studied using an experiment where children pull an object across horizontal surfaces covered with different materials such as sandpaper, glass, rubber, corrugated cardboard, and carpet. An empty margarine tub weighted down with some 100 g masses makes a good pulling vehicle. Attach some string to the tub and pull it using a Newton meter, recording how much pulling force is needed to get the tub moving over the different surfaces. Explain that the greater the force needed to pull the object, the more friction is acting with each surface. Ask children to brainstorm how unwanted friction can be reduced using the example of a bicycle (I bring a real bike into the classroom to use as a prop). For instance, friction at the chain is helped by lubricating oil, and air resistance is minimized in racing bikes by making the frontal area as small as possible.

A common primary science experiment to demonstrate air resistance is for children to construct parachutes from fabric, paper, or plastic bags, then time their drop from a good height using a stopwatch (e.g. down an open

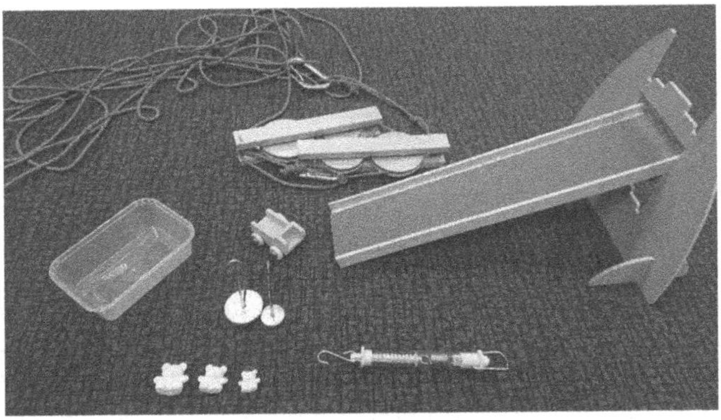

Figure 13.3 Examples of equipment used to teach friction concepts

stairwell – under close supervision). They compare the drop times of parachutes of different diameters, variable shapes, heavy vs. light loads, etc. Water resistance can be explored using a tall container such as a glass vase or measuring cylinder filled with water. Children make Blu Tack pellets of different shapes, then drop them one-by-one into the container, timing how long it takes for them to sink to the bottom. The more streamlined pellets should sink more quickly. Ask children to relate their conclusions to how drag is minimized in vehicles (e.g. Formula One racing cars, hydrofoil ships), and also in nature (e.g. birds of prey, sailfish). Children find this experiment tricky because the pellets sink very quickly through the water, so they will need fast reactions to operate their stopwatches accurately. To help make their measurements easier, add glycerol (available from chemists) to thicken the water and slow down the speed of the sinking pellets.

When children pull a heavy object like a large book using a Newton meter over the different surfaces, direct their attention to the fact that the book will only start to move when they pull with the necessary amount of force. Ask them to start pulling with very little force, then increase their pull a bit at a time until the book starts to slide. The book does not move with small pulling forces because friction is acting in the opposite direction to their pull – encourage them to try to *feel* how strong this resisting force is. Look at the reading of the Newton meter just at the point when the book begins to slide – this is the strength of the friction force acting on the book. Remind them that once the book is moving, friction continues to push the book in the opposite direction. This can be reinforced with the example of a tug of war where each side pulls with exactly the same force, helping children appreciate that forces are at play with non-moving objects also (13.4). There are websites that offer free interactive games for children that deal with concepts related to friction, as well as other forces, e.g. www.sciencekids.co.nz

Sources: Canlas (2021); Stead and Osborne (1980a); Tomara *et al.* (2017).

13.4 Does every force always have an opposite force?

Misconception

Forces always operate in pairs that are in the opposite direction to one another, and these two forces are always equal in strength.

Scientific conception

In Year 5, children learn in some detail about how different forces push or pull on objects, and a common approach is to have children draw force arrows on diagrams that show exactly where these forces are being applied and how strong they are. Force arrows should be drawn as straight lines with a ruler, touch the object where the force is being applied to show the direction of the force, and the length of the arrow ought to reflect the strength of the force (e.g. see Figure 13.2b).

Teachers typically introduce the idea that forces operate in pairs alongside the concept of balanced and unbalanced forces, with pairs of forces usually acting in opposing directions, as in a tug of war (see Figures 13.5b and 13.5c). When they are presented in this way, the two opposing forces can sometimes be of different strengths, which means it is an unbalanced system. However, and although beyond the primary curriculum, teachers are generally aware that for every force there is an equal and opposite reaction, known formally as Newton's third law of motion. These two different ideas can be merged into an incorrect hybrid concept: *all forces act in pairs that are equal and opposite*. Because of this, when children include two opposing force arrows on a diagram, they are routinely drawn as being equal in strength.

Leaving aside reaction forces, it is true that two forces involved in the same situation frequently act in opposite directions; however, these two opposing forces do not always have to be equal in strength. For instance, when a skydiver first jumps out of an aircraft, because they are falling relatively slowly through the air, their downwards weight force is greater than the upwards air resistance force acting in the opposite direction (Figure 13.4a). Because the downwards force is stronger than the upwards force, this is an unbalanced system so they accelerate downwards, gaining speed. As they fall faster and faster, the air resistance increases bit by bit and eventually the two forces become equal (Figure 13.4b). The system is now balanced, no further acceleration can take place and the skydiver falls at constant speed (**terminal velocity**). For other situations where opposing pairs of forces can be unbalanced, see Figures 13.2b, 13.5c, and 14.5c.

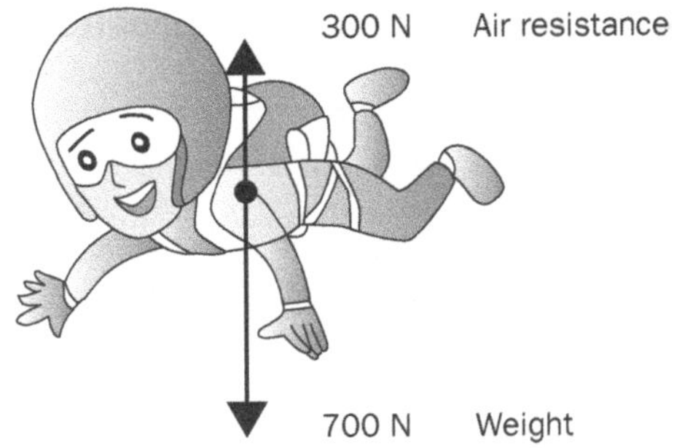

Figure 13.4a Opposing pairs of forces can be unbalanced (accelerating downwards)

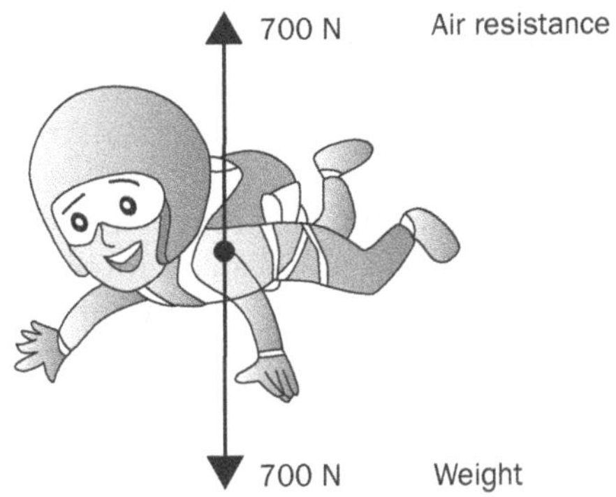

Figure 13.4b Equal and opposite forces on a skydiver (constant speed)

Reconstruction

The simple statement that forces always act in pairs is confusing for children, as it can mean two different things: either an unbalanced situation where opposing forces have different strengths, or that every force has an equal and opposite reaction. It is easy to see how the misconception can arise from a merging of these two dissimilar concepts. Although it could be argued that presenting as examples forces as pairs that act on a system maintains a simplicity that is appropriate to the study of physics at primary level, making the statement that forces *always* act in pairs should be avoided, and instead consider presenting examples where more than two forces apply, e.g. Figure 13.2b. The concepts surrounding Newton's third law of motion and reaction forces are beyond the primary curriculum, and in the context of the present discussion about the difficulties children have understanding the nature of opposing forces, the potential confusion created by including them at the primary phase would probably outweigh any advantages.

Giving a variety of examples from unbalanced systems will remind children that opposing forces need not always be equal in size. For example, with the common experiment of running toy cars down a slope, ask children to draw a picture of the system including force arrows on the car before and after release from the top of the slope.

KS1 children can see the effects of balanced forces by piling plastic bricks on top of each other. Run a competition to see who can make the tallest pile of bricks.

Sources: Hast and Howe (2015); Jones (1983).

13.5 A moving object experiences a large forward force and a small backward force

Misconception

If an object is moving, this means there is a stronger force in the forward direction.

Scientific conception

Children in Year 5 are introduced to the concept of forces as being balanced or unbalanced, e.g. in a 1-vs.-1 tug of war each person pulls the rope in the opposite direction. If both people pull with the same amount of force, then no movement takes place and the forces are balanced (Figure 13.5b); however, if one person pulls with more force than the other, there is movement in their direction because the forces are unbalanced (Figure 13.5c).

The simple tug-of-war system is a good way to illustrate the basic idea of forces being either balanced or unbalanced. However, children often apply this line of thinking to other contexts and assume that if an object is moving, then the forces always need to be unbalanced, which is incorrect (see Figure 13.5a). Using the example of cyclists experiencing different kinds of movement, Figure 13.5d shows how forces can be balanced or unbalanced depending on the strengths of the forward and backward forces. Note that for clarity, other forces such as weight and reaction forces have been ignored.

Figure 13.5a Forces on a cyclist travelling forwards at constant speed (misconception)

Figure 13.5b Balanced forces in a tug of war

Figure 13.5c Unbalanced forces in a tug of war

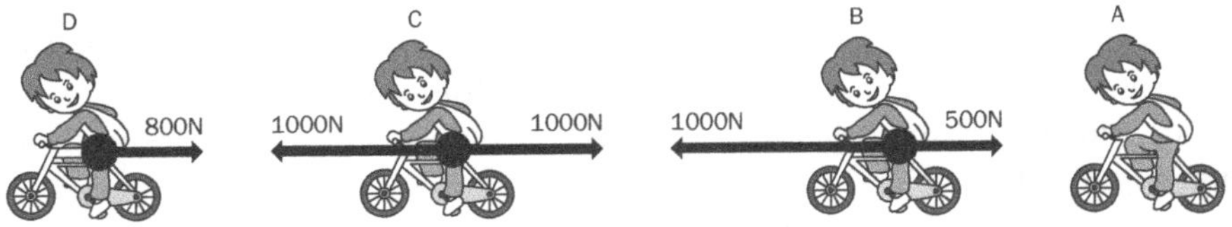

Figure 13.5d Balanced and unbalanced forces with a cyclist's motion

In Figure 13.5d, Cyclist A is not pedalling. There are no forward or backward forces. Forces are balanced (at zero), so there is no movement.

Cyclist B has just started pedalling with a force of 1000 N and experiences air resistance/friction at 500 N. Forces are unbalanced, so the cycle accelerates and moves forwards.

Cyclist C pedals with a force of 1000 N but they are travelling faster than Cyclist B, so experiences a larger air resistance/friction of 1000 N. Forces are balanced, so no more acceleration is possible and the cycle travels at constant speed. Cyclist C can try to accelerate again by pedalling with more force, or reducing air resistance by placing their body into more of a racing tuck, which will create a new unbalanced system.

Cyclist D stops pedalling and applies the brakes. They are still moving forwards and experience air resistance/friction of 800 N (including brake friction) but zero forward force (no pedalling), so forces are unbalanced. The cycle decelerates and eventually comes to a stop.

To summarize, Cyclist C shows that balanced forces can indeed be present with a moving object, which in this case is travelling at constant speed. Also, if forces are unbalanced, this will always result in either acceleration or deceleration in accordance with Newton's first law of motion (13.2). Note that the braking Cyclist D is still moving forwards although there is no forward force, a situation that is difficult for children to appreciate; 13.2 discusses this further.

A related misconception is that at a constant speed there are no forces acting on an object, when in fact forces do exist but cancel each other out to create a balanced system.

Reconstruction

This misconception is a variant of 13.2 and so the pedagogies described in that section can be applied here too.

Sources: Blown and Bryce (2013); Driver (1983).

13.6 Is there gravity in space?

Misconception

There is no gravity on the moon.

Scientific conception

When children watch scenes of floating astronauts in science fiction films or TV programmes, they tend to conclude that there is zero gravity on the moon,

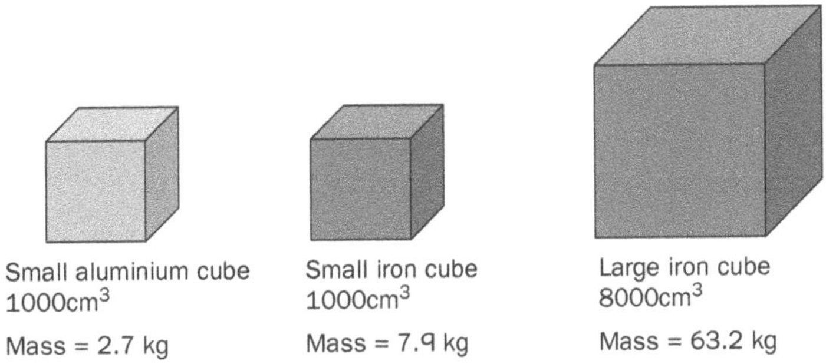

Figure 13.6a Masses of iron and aluminium cubes. When the two small cubes are compared with each other, the iron cube has more mass because (a) iron particles are heavier than aluminium particles, and (b) there are a greater number of iron particles in the cube (they are packed closer together)

on other planets, and in space generally. They can believe that gravity only exists on Earth because of the presence of an atmosphere, and once a spacecraft leaves the atmosphere, gravity suddenly disappears. For the same reason, children think that gravity is caused by air pressing down on objects within the atmosphere (see Box p. 218), or that things float in water because there is no air, so no gravity. All of these are misconceptions.

To understand the basic nature of gravity requires us to think about the concept of *mass*. Every material in the universe, including liquids and gases, is made from atoms, molecules, or ions – for the sake of simplicity in primary science, we call them particles (see Chapter 9). When two small solid cubes of identical size, one made of aluminium and the other iron, are placed on scales, their masses are found to be different (Figure 13.6a). The small iron cube has more mass for two reasons: first, an iron particle is heavier than an aluminium particle; and second, there are more iron particles present than aluminium particles.[2] The larger iron cube has a greater mass than the smaller iron cube because the larger one contains more iron particles. Therefore, the mass of an object depends on how heavy each particle is, and also how many particles there are – put simply, how much 'stuff' there is. Mass cannot be changed unless the object itself is changed, e.g. chipping a piece off an iron cube will reduce the mass of the cube because there will be fewer particles in what remains.

If the two small aluminium and iron cubes were taken into deep space, held about a metre apart and then released, they would start to move slowly towards each other until they were touching. This is gravitational attraction and is experienced by every object in the universe; note that it is nothing to do with magnetism. Children are surprised to learn that everything in the universe is attracted to everything else. The bigger the mass, the more intense the attraction, so on Earth if the two small metal cubes are placed on the floor, despite the same gravitational attraction still being present between the cubes, they do not move towards each other because there is a far larger object that is

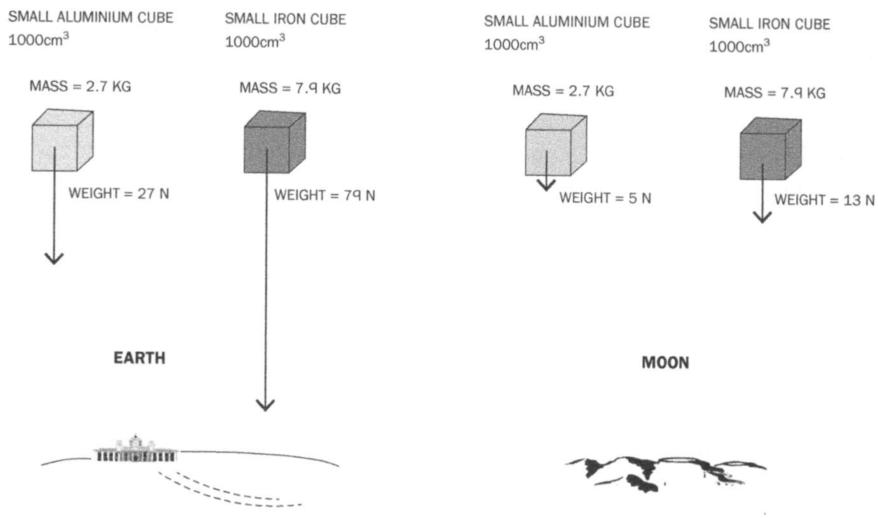

Figure 13.6b Masses and weights of metal cubes on the Earth and the moon

attracting them instead – the Earth. Also, the further the distance between masses, the less the attraction between them, which is why if you were to travel into deep space, far away from any celestial bodies, you would experience approximately zero gravity. Gravity behaves according to a mathematical relationship known as an *inverse square law*, meaning that if the distance that separates two objects is halved, then the gravitational strength is quadrupled. Another aspect of this relationship is that as distance is increased, gravity reduces very quickly, so over long distances its effects are extremely weak.

Objects in space such as the planets, the moon, and the sun attract each other constantly with large amounts of force. These celestial bodies are huge, so gravitational attraction is immense, especially from the sun, although the planets do not hurtle into the sun and burn up because they are skirting around the sun at high speed in **orbit**. A useful analogy is a ball circling a roulette wheel while bets are placed – it continues to circle smoothly and freely because it has enough speed to overcome being pulled towards the centre of the wheel. After a while, the ball loses speed because of friction and falls into the wheel, eventually landing in a number pocket. Because space is a near-vacuum, there is very little friction to slow the planets down, which, like the roulette ball, maintain enough orbital speed to avoid being pulled into the sun.

Earth's gravitational attraction applies a large pull on all objects close to its surface; this pulling force is called their weight. As discussed, this weight force is greater with objects that have more mass, and also when objects are closer to the Earth's centre (13.7); the approximate weights of our two small metal cubes on Earth are given in Figure 13.6b. Weight is measured in Newtons (N) and can be roughly calculated by multiplying the mass of an object by 10.

If the two cubes were to be shipped to the moon, their weights would be reduced (Figure 13.6b). This is because the mass of the moon is only 17% of that of the Earth and so would attract the cubes with only 17% of the gravity force experienced on Earth. Note that the *mass* of the cubes does not change on the moon because the cubes themselves have not changed and are still made of the same 'stuff'. Because the cubes weigh less on the moon, astronauts could throw them much further across the lunar surface than they could on Earth. In contrast, at the gaseous surface of the giant planet Jupiter, gravity is 2.5 times that of Earth, so if a person weighed 700 N (70 kg) on Earth, they would weigh 1750 N on Jupiter (equivalent to 175 kg on Earth).

To summarize, gravitational attraction exists between any two objects because they have mass. Particularly large objects such as planets, moons, and stars exert huge gravitational forces and so all relatively close objects will experience a significant and noticeable gravitational pull. Only in deep space far away from these celestial bodies will gravity be approximately zero. Since the weight of an object is the force it experiences due to gravity, weight can change depending on where the object is; on the other hand, its mass can never change unless the object is changed in some way.

Related misconceptions include the idea that gravity occurs due to the Earth's magnetic field exerting a force. Alternatively, some learners think the fact that the Earth is spinning causes gravity to occur; when the idea of **centripetal force** is introduced to **KS4** secondary physics students, this misconception may be reinforced.

I think . . .

Air causes gravity. *'Down here there is air . . . there is air on the floor. Gravity is just like air. There is no air in space. Air keeps you down'* (Year 4 child; Russell *et al.*, 1998, p. 87).

Reconstruction

To help address the misconception that there is no gravity in space, use video clips available on internet sites such as YouTube that show American Apollo astronauts walking on the moon and experiencing gravity forces – they do not just float around, they have to walk on the surface. The videos also show that gravity forces on the moon are clearly less than those on Earth. The idea that air must be present in order for gravity to work can be difficult to change. A video clip of the same astronauts inside their spacecraft journeying to and from the moon will show that even though air is present inside the craft, the astronauts can still experience weightlessness.

If children see videos of astronauts who are weightless orbiting the Earth inside space shuttles or space stations, this can reinforce the misconception that gravity disappears just beyond the atmosphere. In fact, because they are not that far away from the Earth, gravity is still powerful inside these spacecraft but the act of orbiting will create a feeling of weightlessness in spite of one's body still experiencing a large weight force (see 13.7 and 14.5).

Sources: Bar *et al.* (1997); Bar *et al.* (2016); Driver (1983); Russell *et al.* (1998).

13.7 Can gravity change?

Misconception

Gravity becomes stronger the further you are from the ground.

Scientific conception

Children can appreciate that if an object falls from 20 metres above the ground, it will land with more force than if dropped from a height of 1 metre. This can lead to the belief that at 20 metres high, the force of gravity must be stronger to create the extra landing force. The idea is reflected in a well-known folk tale that a dime dropped from the top of the Empire State Building in New York City would land with enough force to injure a passer-by on the pavement below. Other examples of the misconception include that if a car was pushed up a slope, it would become more difficult to push as it came closer to the top of the hill because gravity increases with height.

These beliefs go against how gravity actually works. Gravity creates an attractive pulling force on objects in the direction of the centre of the Earth; scientifically this is known as the object's weight. As an object moves further away from the centre of the Earth, gravity weakens, making the object weigh less. For instance, if a person who weighs 800 N at sea level boards an airliner which then climbs to 30,000 feet, they would weigh 1 N less (equivalent to 100 g). If the same person were then to be launched into deep space, because there would be (approximately) zero gravity, their weight would be 0 N because they would be distant from the centre of the Earth, as well as from other celestial bodies, so they would be weightless and able to float freely. In other words, an object must be raised to great heights above the Earth before there is any noticeable change in gravity. In everyday contexts, close to the Earth's surface, the weight of an object remains nearly the same no matter how high you lift it.

The reason why an object dropped from a tall building lands with such force is not because gravity is stronger. Throughout an object's fall, it is being pulled by a force (its weight) that constantly speeds up its descent (acceleration). This acceleration equates to approximately 10 metres per second for every second the object is falling: 1 second after release, its speed is 10 m/s, 2 seconds after release, its speed is 20 m/s, and so on. So the higher that an object is dropped from, the more time it will spend falling and the greater its final speed when it lands (though see terminal velocity, 13.4).

A variant of the misconception is the belief that gravity increases the further away you are from the Earth's surface until you leave the atmosphere, when gravity immediately drops to zero. This suggests that gravity has something to do with air pressure (see 13.6). Incidentally, it is very common, though incorrect, to think that astronauts in Earth's orbit are weightless because there is no gravity – in fact, gravity is strong at altitudes where spacecraft orbit the Earth and so the astronauts' weights are just slightly less than their weights on the Earth's surface. The reason why they can float around is due to something called *apparent weightlessness* – this occurs because astronauts are constantly falling when in orbit, similar to being in a runaway lift that has had its cables cut. The falling lift's occupants would be able to float freely inside and experience apparent weightlessness because both lift and occupants are in a state of freefall, like a skydiver. The situation of a spacecraft in orbit is different than the real weightlessness found in deep space where gravity would be truly absent (or insignificant) due to the immense distances from the Earth and other celestial bodies. In all these examples of apparent weightlessness, all objects will still have a significant weight force acting on them.

Secondary pupils can confuse an object's weight with its potential energy, which does increase with height. Some learners think that gravity becomes zero at the Earth's surface, because an object is no longer falling, again an idea that is similar to potential energy (related to 13.6). Others argue the opposite and say that gravity is only present on the surface of the Earth and objects not in contact with the surface are free of its influence, which is why birds are able to fly, although in aeroplanes, gravity is trapped inside.

Reconstruction

The misconception can be elicited by asking the class *at which point on a slope would gravity be at its most powerful?* A simple way to address this is to have children use a stopwatch to time a toy car running down a sloping ramp at a fixed angle. Carry out one timed run at table-top level and another at floor level – if the angle is fixed, there should be no difference in the times. Make the argument that if gravity were greater at higher elevations, then the car would run faster down the slope on the table top than it would at floor level. This could be extended by repeating the experiment on different floors of a multi-storey building. Reinforcement might involve suspending an object by a Newton meter at different heights above the ground to show there is no change in the measured weight of the object, so gravity must be constant. Of course, if the difference in heights was great enough, then differences in weight *would* be observed owing to a weakening of gravity. This could potentially be demonstrated using an accurate pair of scales to weigh a person at sea level and again in an airliner at cruising altitude.

Sources: Bar *et al.* (2016); Driver (1983); Ruggiero *et al.* (1985); Watts (1982).

13.8 Are all metals magnetic?

Misconception

All metals are magnetic.

Scientific conception

When children play or experiment with magnets, they soon realize that only metallic objects are attracted. Sometimes they over-generalize and think that magnets attract all metals; in fact, magnets can only attract three – iron, nickel, and cobalt – called the magnetic metals. This includes any **alloy** that contains any of these metals, e.g. a steel paper clip is magnetic because steel is an alloy made mostly from iron. If a magnet can attract a piece of metal, this also means that, if you use the right technique, you can turn that piece of metal itself into a magnet. Perhaps surprisingly, there are some materials that are non-metals but are still magnetic, such as iron oxide, which does not contain elemental iron. These materials can be turned into *ceramic magnets.*

Other misconceptions include the ideas that a barrier such as a piece of paper will stop the attraction of a magnet, a magnet would not work if there was no gravity, the bigger the magnet – the stronger the force, and only one small region of a magnet is magnetic (single pole misconception)

Reconstruction

Attempting to attract a variety of different metals using a magnet can serve as a useful exercise for addressing this misconception. Be sure to include common non-magnetic metals such as aluminium (drinks cans), brass (a door key), and tin metal. Lead metal should be used with care and only with classes where there is no possibility of hand-to-mouth contact, and hands should be washed after use.

One unexpected outcome is that tin metal is not magnetic but a tin can is. What we call 'tin' cans are actually made mostly of steel, which is magnetic, and only have a thin tin coating to prevent rusting. An interesting activity is to have a collection of 2 pence coins of different ages; children will find that only some are magnetic – those dated after 1992. This is because after 1992, 2 pence coins began to be made with a steel core whereas before they were made from solid bronze, which is a non-magnetic metal.

The magnetic metal nickel is present in 5 pence and 10 pence coins – with coins struck prior to 2011, nickel exists as an alloy with copper, and after that date the coins are steel-plated with pure nickel. With the pre-2011 coins the nickel content is low so these coins are non-magnetic; the post-2011 coins *are* magnetic, but this is more due to their steel core and not their nickel plating. Cobalt, the third magnetic metal, is not commonly available for experiments in the primary classroom because of its toxicity, though is present in trace amounts in everyday products such as paints, **batteries**, and stainless steel.

One advantage of teaching magnetism concepts is that unlike some other forces covered by the Programme of Study, it enables children to directly feel invisible forces in action. Rare Earth magnets are small, inexpensive, and exert powerful magnetic forces that children can readily experience – encourage them to feel for the push of magnetic repulsion, as well as the pull of attraction. Magnetism is an example of a force that acts at a distance, not requiring objects to be touching for a force to be exerted. Gravity similarly acts as a distance and upper KS2 children can be asked to compare and contrast magnetism with gravity, but it must be emphasized that these are two completely different types of force (children can believe that gravitational pull is a kind of magnetic attraction). Electrostatic forces such as those seen with **static electricity** experiments also act as at distance (see Chapter 15), although similar emphasis would be needed to clearly differentiate static electricity from magnetism.

There is scope with this topic to set KS1 children practical homework in which they have to solve problems using fridge magnets – for instance, 'write a list of ten objects that a fridge magnet will stick to'. One way to remember the three magnetic metals is the acronym 'FeNiCo', which represents the chemical symbols for iron, nickel, and cobalt respectively.

Sources: Grigorovitch and Nertivich (2017); Meyer (1991); Rogers (2022); Stepanović *et al.* (2023).

Notes

1 Children usually call this gravity, which is acceptable.

2 One analogy of these differences: an adult *rugby union* team of 15 players plays a game against a children's *rugby league* team of 13 players. This is an uneven match due to the combined mass of the adult team being greater than that of the children's team –adults are heavier and there are more of them.

Planning and assessment sheet 13 Forces and magnets

(For suggestions on how to use this sheet, see p. xxviii.)

Misconception	*Attainment re. expected standard*		
	Working towards	*Working at*	*Working above*
Year 3: *Forces and magnets*			
All metals are magnetic (13.8)	✓	✓	
A barrier such as a piece of paper will stop the attraction of a magnet (13.8)	✓		
A magnet would not work if there was no gravity (13.8)		✓	✓
The bigger the magnet, the stronger the force (13.8)	✓	✓	
Only one small region of a magnet is magnetic (single pole misconception) (13.8)	✓	✓	
The Earth's gravitational pull is a kind of magnetic attraction (13.8)		✓	
Year 5: *Forces*			
Heavier objects fall faster than lighter objects (13.1)	✓	✓	✓
Lighter objects fall faster than heavier objects because they meet less air resistance (13.1)		✓	
A ball flying through the air has a force that constantly pushes it from behind (13.2)	✓	✓	✓
Giving human feelings to objects (anthropomorphism), such as 'I threw the ball up but it fell back down because it wanted to' (13.2)	✓		
A thrown ball flies because it is supported by forces in the air around it (13.2)		✓	✓
A thrown ball flies because it contains a force inside it that is greater than gravity, but when this force has been used up, it begins to fall back down (13.2)		✓	✓
A skydiver has gravity inside them which makes them fall, and once they land, the gravity has run out (13.2)		✓	✓
The greater the force applied, the greater the effect produced (i.e. not considering levers, gears, and pulleys) (13.2)	✓	✓	✓
The word 'force' can be misconstrued and interpreted in non-science ways, e.g. 'a force' is associated with the armed forces or the police force (13.2)	✓		

(continued)

(continued)

Friction only acts on moving objects, not stationary ones (13.3)	✓	✓	✓
When a person is standing up and not moving, friction stops them falling over (13.3)	✓	✓	
Friction forces are always problematic so need minimizing, e.g. by lubrication (13.3)	✓	✓	
Forces always operate in pairs that are in the opposite direction to one another, and these two forces are always equal in strength (13.4)		✓	
If an object is moving, this means that there is a stronger force in the forward direction (13.5)	✓	✓	✓
There are no forces acting on an object at a constant speed (13.5)	✓	✓	
There is no gravity on the moon, on other planets, or in space generally (13.6)	✓	✓	
Gravity exists because of the Earth's atmosphere, and disappears immediately as soon as you leave the atmosphere (13.6)	✓	✓	
Gravity is caused by air pressing down on objects within the atmosphere (13.6)	✓	✓	
Gravity occurs due to the Earth's magnetic field exerting a force (13.6)			✓
Gravity is caused by the Earth spinning (13.6)		✓	✓
Gravity becomes stronger the further you are from the ground (13.7)	✓	✓	
If a car was pushed up a hill, it would become more difficult to push as it came closer to the top of the hill (because gravity increases with height) (13.7)	✓	✓	
Gravity increases the further away you are from the Earth's surface until you leave the atmosphere, when gravity immediately drops to zero (13.7)	✓	✓	
Astronauts in Earth's orbit are weightless because there is no gravity (13.7)	✓	✓	✓
Gravity is zero at the Earth's surface (because objects can no longer fall) (13.7)	✓	✓	✓
Gravity is only present on the surface of the Earth – objects not in contact with the surface are free of its influence, which is why birds are able to fly (13.7)	✓	✓	

14

Floating and sinking

Conceptual areas covered in this chapter:

- Scientific definitions of floating and sinking
- The density of materials
- Apparent weightlessness
- Upthrust forces

National Curriculum links:

Year 3: *Forces and magnets*

Year 5: *Forces; Properties of everyday materials and reversible change*

14.1 Why do some objects float and others sink?

Misconception

All light objects float, all heavy objects sink.

Scientific conception

When predicting whether a material will float or sink, children will often think its weight is the only factor. But it is impossible to decide if a material is 'heavy' or 'light' when there is no further point of reference. That is to say, you cannot simply claim that gold is heavier than feathers because the amount of each material needs to be considered – a barrel of feathers would weigh more than a single gold ring. Therefore, to make fair comparisons of heavier/lighter we also need to think about how much material is there – in science, this is done by measuring the amount of space each object takes up, i.e. its volume. The scientific concept of density gets around the problem by taking into account how much an object weighs (its mass to be precise) as well as its volume (Figure 14.1a). For example, a 1 cm^3 cube of steel has a mass of 8 g, so its density would

$$\text{density (g/cm}^3\text{)} = \frac{\text{mass (g)}}{\text{volume (cm}^3\text{)}}$$

Figure 14.1a The equation for calculating the density of a material

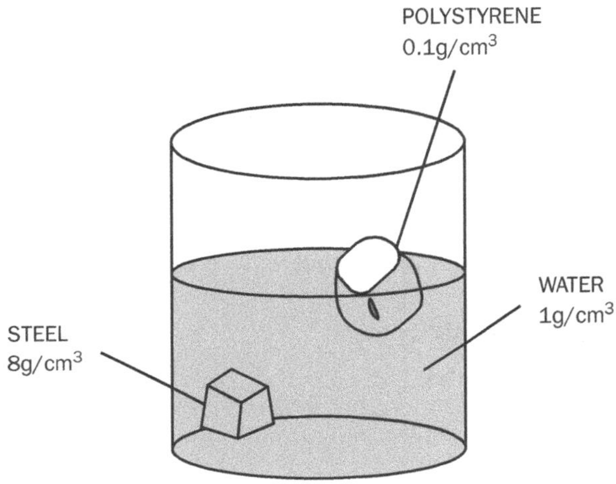

Figure 14.1b Objects denser than water sink; those less dense than water float

equal 8 ÷ 1 = 8 g/cm^3, while a 1 cm^3 cube of expanded polystyrene has a mass of 0.1 g, so its density would equal 0.1 g/cm^3.[1]

A simple way to address the question of whether something will float or not is to compare its density with that of water. Pure water has a density of approximately 1 g/cm^3 at room temperature, and materials with densities greater than 1 will sink in water (e.g. steel = 8 g/cm^3); those with densities less than or equal to 1 will float (e.g. expanded polystyrene = 0.1 g/cm^3) (Figure 14.1b). In 14.3, the idea that objects of different densities either float or sink is taken further and applied to different situations.

If the steel cube from Figure 14.1b was hammered very flat, then shaped into a hollow ball, it could float on the surface of the water (Figure 14.1c). This is because although its mass is still 8 g, its volume has been greatly increased and so its density has been reduced to a point that is below the density of water (i.e. 1 g/cm^3). This is the reason why a steel ship that weighs thousands of tonnes can float – it has lots of empty space inside, so its overall density is less than 1 g/cm^3. Another, more sophisticated way of looking at why objects float is discussed in 14.5 and uses the concept of **displacement**.

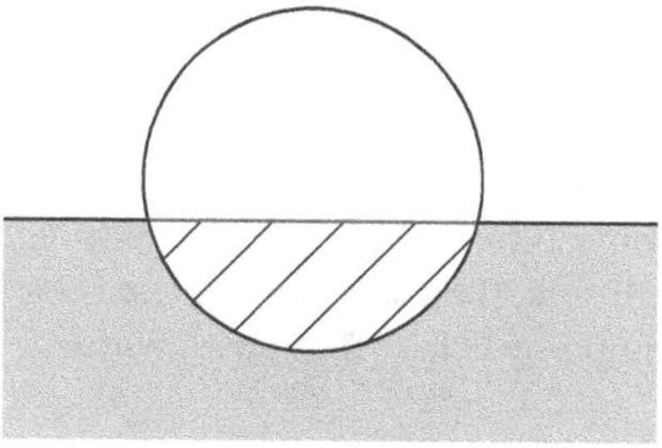

Figure 14.1c Floating hollow ball made from steel (shaded area shows displacement

Seeing objects floating and sinking are phenomena encountered in their daily lives by children from an early age and so they come to the classroom with their own ideas. Children can be drawn to irrelevant qualities of an object when deciding whether it will float, and ignore a material's physical properties. Objects that are flat or wide are thought more likely to float, as are smaller items – a good way to elicit this latter misconception is to show two candles of different length and ask the class which they expect to float and which they expect to sink (both will float). Some children believe that hard or sharp objects are more likely to sink, or that all objects that float must contain air within them. They can also predict that if an object has holes, such as a plastic sieve, then it will sink because water can enter inside.

To summarize, whether an object floats or sinks in water depends on its density. A solid object with no air spaces inside such as a 1 cm^3 cube can only float if the density of its material is less than or equal to that of water (i.e. 1 g/cm^3). However, a material such as steel whose density is greater than water can be made to float if it can be shaped in a way that increases its volume so that its density becomes less than 1 g/cm^3.

Reconstruction

The misconception can be addressed by having children experiment with a collection of 'heavy' things, some of which sink (e.g. 100 g mass) and some of which float (e.g. Thermos flask filled with water), as well as 'light' objects that sink (e.g. paper clip) and float (e.g. inflated balloon). Ask children to make a single piece of plasticine first sink and then float by remoulding its shape. The concept of densities, although beyond the primary curriculum, is a useful way to explain why some objects float and others sink, and should be within the capabilities of higher-attaining upper KS2 children. It has been demonstrated that, generally, children who understand a particle model of matter are more able to grasp the concept of density and apply it to floating and sinking problems; the pedagogies described in Chapter 9 would be applicable here. If teachers want to extend their own knowledge of the forces involved in floating and sinking, there are useful websites that are aimed at GCSE level; for a fun introduction to forces, and physics in general, try *Physics for Kids* at www.ducksters.com

KS1 children can explore whether a variety of objects float or sink as part of a messy play session. Collect 10 objects and ask children to predict which will float and which will sink, then ask them to test their predictions by placing the objects in washing-up bowls half-filled with water.

Sources: Carr *et al.* (1994); Elmali and Laçin Şimşek (2021); Hewson (1986); Liu *et al.* (2017); Schwichow and Zoupidis (2024).

14.2 Can something be floating and sinking at the same time?

Misconception

An iceberg is both floating and sinking at the same time.

Scientific conception

As discussed in other parts of this book, some scientific words have different meanings in other contexts that learners can find confusing. In everyday parlance, it might be acceptable to say that the submerged part of a floating object such as an iceberg has sunk because it has 'gone underwater' (Figure 14.2a). However, in primary science there is a clear distinction as to whether an object is floating or sinking – it can never do both at the same time. In the case of the iceberg, it is floating because it 'hangs' (is suspended) in a fluid.

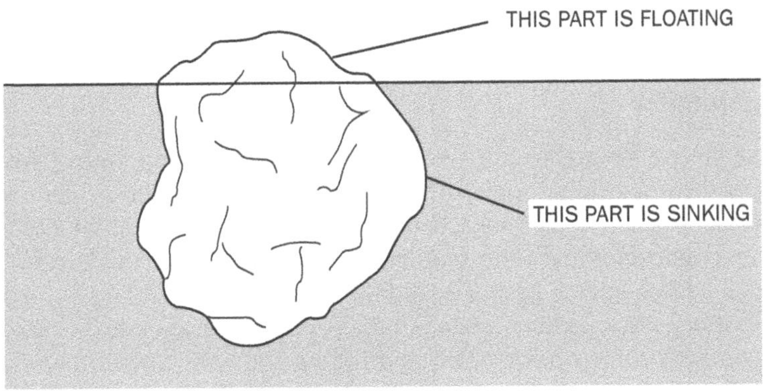

Figure 14.2a The underwater part of a floating iceberg is sinking (misconception)

Suppose, for instance, that the iceberg is relatively small and a helicopter lands on top of it – the extra weight of the helicopter causes the small iceberg to become totally submerged and continue to move downwards underwater because it can no longer be supported by the water it floats in, until both iceberg and helicopter rest on the sea bed (see 14.5). During its descent through the water, the iceberg is no longer technically floating because its downward movement means that it is not 'hanging' (being suspended) in a fluid, and instead is sinking.

Consider a submarine that is submerged 50 metres below the surface of the sea, neither rising nor descending in the water (Figure 14.2b, submarine 3). Is it floating? The answer is yes, because even though it is below the water's surface, it is still suspended in a fluid. Learners who think that the submarine is not floating would be applying a non-scientific understanding that assumes a floating object must be on the surface of a liquid. If the same submarine starts to rise towards the surface, it is still floating (submarine 2); if it begins to dive towards the sea bed, it is sinking, and no longer floating (submarine 4); when it comes to rest on the seabed, it is no longer sinking because it is being supported by a solid surface (submarine 5) (see Table 14.2).

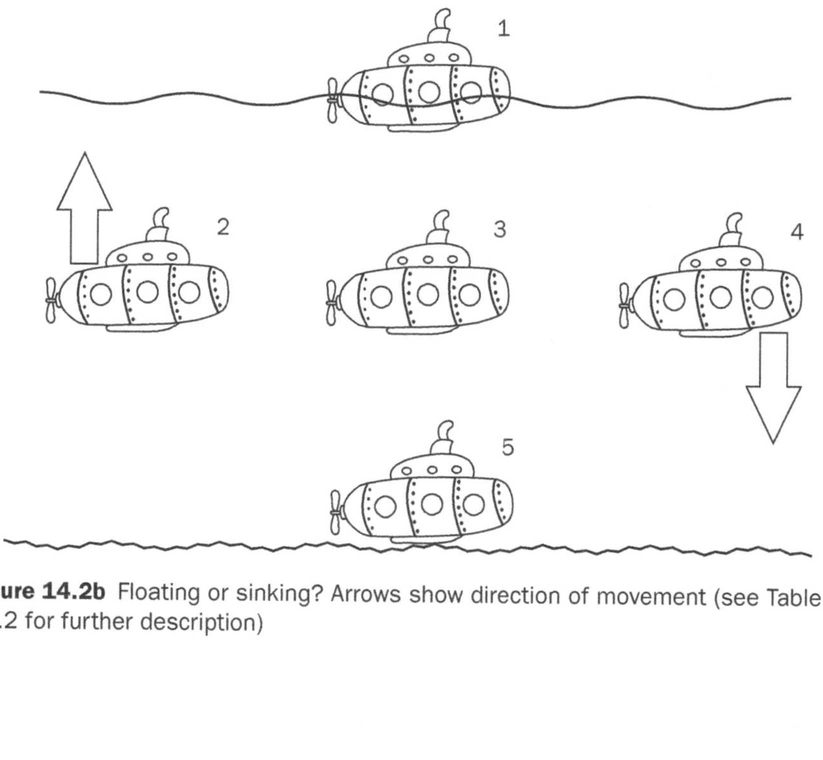

Figure 14.2b Floating or sinking? Arrows show direction of movement (see Table 14.2 for further description)

Table 14.2 Is the submarine floating or sinking?

Submarine	*Circumstance*	*Floating*	*Sinking*
1	Stationary on the surface of the sea	Yes	No
2	Ascending	Yes	No
3	Stationary at a constant depth of 50 metres	Yes	No
4	Diving	No	Yes
5	Stationary on the seabed	No	No

We can also think about this using the idea of densities – a sinking object is denser than water, and a floating object is less dense or has the same density as water. Beyond scientific definitions of floating and sinking, 14.1, 14.3, and 14.4 discuss the reasons why certain objects float and others sink.

A fluid is the scientific name for a liquid or a gas. Since air is a fluid, all the above examples also apply, for example, to a rising hot air balloon (floating) and a skydiver (sinking). Confusion may also arise when everyday meanings clash with scientific ideas. It would be acceptable for a child to write in a story during an English lesson that a leaf falls from a tree and floats gently down to the ground, but scientifically the leaf is sinking, not floating.

Related misconceptions include that a person in the sea wearing an inflated life jacket is sinking but the life jacket itself is floating, and if people on the water's surface are swimming, they are floating but if they are panicking, they are sinking. With submerged objects, children may correctly think that something that is maintaining a constant depth just below the surface of the water is floating, but if an object is holding its depth near to the sea bed it is sinking.

Did you know?

Icebergs. The iceberg in Figure 14.2a is approximately 90% underwater because ice has a density of just over 0.9 g/cm^3. This is a problem for shipping, as it is difficult to know how close one can sail to an iceberg since its large, submerged part tends to be invisible from the surface. The RMS *Titanic* infamously sank after colliding with an iceberg below her waterline.

Reconstruction

It is important that children consider what the whole object is doing when judging whether it is floating or sinking, instead of its different parts. In Figure 14.2a, considering the entire iceberg, instead of the parts above and below the water's surface, we can conclude that the object as a whole is clearly not sinking. Encourage children to think about the vertical movement of an object, i.e. whether it is moving upwards (floating), downwards (sinking) or keeping the same depth/height (floating). Using sets of closed questions as part of a dialogue to challenge the thinking of children could help them to construct meanings that are more scientific, for example:

Teacher:	*Is an iceberg sinking or floating?*
Child:	*The top bit floats and the bottom bit sinks.*
Teacher:	*If you drop a coin into water, will it be sinking or floating?*
Child:	*Sinking, because it's moving down.*
Teacher:	*Is a ship that is damaged and taking in water, slowly disappearing under the surface, floating or sinking?*
Child:	*Although a bit is showing above the surface, it's moving down, which means it's sinking.*
Teacher:	*How about an iceberg then?*
Child:	*Well, it isn't moving down, so it must be floating.*

Teachers can reinforce the scientific meanings of floating and sinking during traditional practical activities such as investigating if objects of different weights float or sink in tap water and salt water – salt water is denser than tap water, and things that normally sink can be seen to float. If children are encouraged to make and use physical props such as a **Cartesian diver**, this should help them understand more clearly definitions of floating and sinking. Note that a model iceberg can be made by freezing a carton of milk.

Sources: Biddulph and Osborne (1984); Carr *et al.* (1994); Joung (2009).

14.3 More about floating

Misconception

Wood is denser than water.

Scientific conception

The concept of density that children construct can differ from the scientific definition. As discussed in 14.1, the density of an object is its mass divided by its volume. Imagine a variety of materials were available to you as equally sized solid cubes exactly 1 cm^3 in volume. Some of these cubes, such as gold (density 19.3 g/cm^3) and lead (11.3 g/cm^3), would feel heavier than the rest because they are high-density materials. The cubes of low-density materials would feel lighter: soap (0.8 g/cm^3), rubber (0.4 g/cm^3), and expanded polystyrene (0.1 g/cm^3). Medium-density materials include glass (2.6 g/cm^3), concrete (2.4 g/cm^3) and aluminium (2.7 g/cm^3).

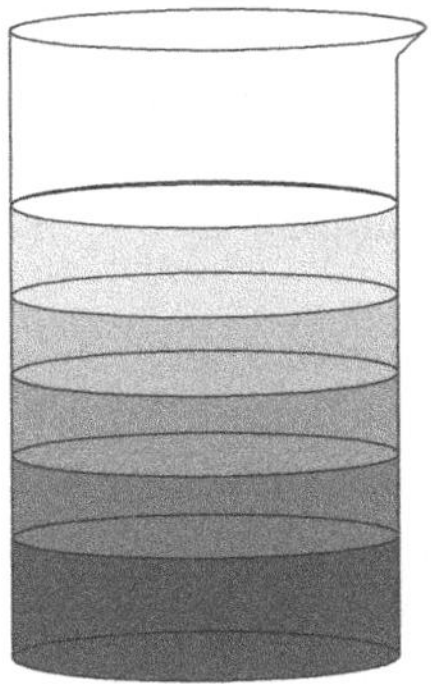

Figure 14.3a Liquids of different densities form layers (for illustration purposes only)

Children may correctly appreciate that a dense material is something that is heavy for its size, but if asked to imagine whether a piece of wood is more dense than a sample of water, they commonly think that the wood is more dense. The reasoning behind this decision might include the fact that wood is solid and hard while water is less substantial and soft. Experience with lifting a heavy wooden piece of furniture would strengthen this association. However, if we look at the density values, water (1.0 g/cm^3) is much more dense than common woods such as pine (0.4 g/cm^3) and elm (0.6 g/cm^3). Even fairly heavy woods like teak (0.7 g/cm^3) and mahogany (0.8 g/cm^3) are less dense than water, and very light woods such as balsa (0.1 g/cm^3) have a low density.

A simple way to discover whether a material is more dense or less dense than water is to see if it floats. If liquids that do not mix with each other are shaken together in a container, they will eventually separate out into different layers, with the denser liquids at the bottom and the less dense ones on top (Figure 14.3a).[2] Similarly, all of the woods mentioned in the previous paragraph will float on water, showing that water must be the denser material because it has formed a 'layer' underneath the wood, pushing the wood upwards. That said, a few types of wood are denser than water and will sink, such as ebony and leadwood. Also, if some porous woods are given time to become soaked with water, they can eventually sink; bogwood found in peat layers is very waterlogged and so is ideal for home aquariums because it sinks to the bottom of a tank without the need to be weighted down.

Reconstruction

Children can carry out an activity where they predict what would happen if a variety of woods were to be placed in water and then test their predictions practically. When discussing the results, explain how the woods that float must have a lower or equal density to water, and any that sink have a higher density. Samples of ebony can be secured from commercial collections of different cuboid

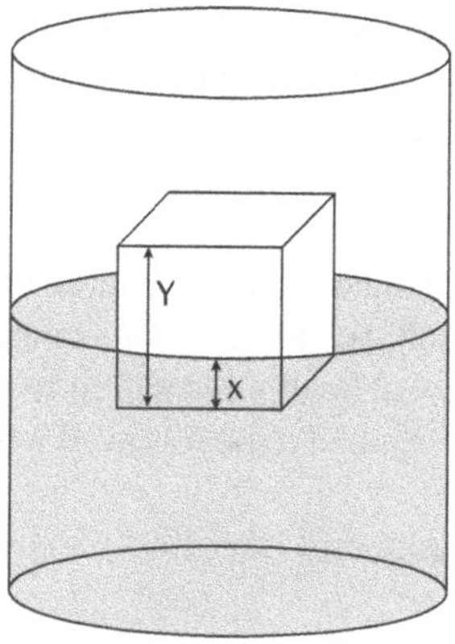

Figure 14.3b Density and floating ability

materials that can be sourced from educational suppliers, or in a classroom cupboard containing apparatus used in static electricity experiments, since it has been traditionally used as an insulator that is capable of holding a charge (see Chapter 15). Old black piano keys would be another source of ebony.

This activity can be extended by asking children to measure with a ruler the proportion of wood that lies below the waterline (x) and the total height of the wood (y). After dividing x by y, the wood samples can then be placed in rank order of 'floating ability' and compared to the actual density values, since the less dense woods will be more buoyant and have a greater proportion of their bulk above the water line (Figure 14.3b). Note that some children believe that the depth of water underneath an object affects the level at which it floats.

A more child-friendly version of the cylinder depicted in Figure 14.3a can be made by using safer liquids such as cooking oil, treacle, honey, corn syrup, and water, though the layers will not be as clear because they are able to mix together to some extent. An alternative demonstration is to pour a layer of corn syrup into the container, then slowly and carefully add a layer of water so that the two layers do not mix. Posing questions about why there are two distinct layers can act as a prompt for discussions about the relative densities of liquids. If you add a small piece of ebony (1.1 g/cm^3) to the container, it floats exactly between the layers of corn syrup (1.4 g/cm^3) and water (1.0 g/cm^3). Ask children to predict what might happen if you add olive oil to the mixture; some children might be able to correctly predict oil floats on water, recalling experiences such as washing up water at home having a greasy film on the surface, or from watching news reports of oil spill disasters on the ocean. Pour the cooking oil into the container to show that it does indeed form an upper layer, because its density (0.9 g/cm^3) is less than water's (1.0 g/cm^3). Misconceptions relating to oil being thicker than water as a reason for the two layers not mixing would need to be addressed, and might include a simple explanation of how some liquids like oil (hydrophobic) find it very difficult to mix with water. If you shake the mixture well and leave it to settle, there will now only be two layers since the water and corn syrup (hydrophilic) will mix together, but the oil layer remains separate.

To help address the misconception that water is a low-density material, ask upper KS2 children to carefully try to lift a substantial amount of it, say, a filled 15-litre water cooler bottle. Local health and safety regulations regarding the lifting of heavy objects will, of course, need to be followed when carrying out this activity.

Sources: Bar *et al.* (2016); Galili and Bar (1997); Pierratos and Koumaras (2022).

14.4 Is size important for floating and sinking?

Misconception

If two objects are the same size, the two will behave in the same way; they will either both float, or both sink.

Scientific conception

When children are predicting whether an object will float or sink, some believe the size of the object is the most important factor. It is a common misconception that small objects float while large objects sink (see 14.1). Therefore, when two small objects are the same size, if one floats, it is predicted that the other one will too, even if they are made from completely different materials. Children do not consider that one object might weigh more than the other, which is more of a determining factor as to whether something floats.

This is an example of over-generalization, especially among young children, whereby they link the behaviour of one thing with that of something else just because it looks similar. They tend to be fixated on the obvious perceptual properties of objects, such as size, shape, and colour, and ignore more abstract qualities such as weight. Therefore, young children may not appreciate that if two objects of equal size are made from different materials, one might float and the other sink. As discussed in other sections in this chapter, if an object is denser than water, it will sink. Density is an object's mass divided by its volume, so as well as considering the size of an object, how much it weighs is also an important factor.

A similar misconception is that if two objects have the same *weight*, then both will either float or sink, regardless of their size. There are links to other misconceptions in the current chapter, including if an object is made flatter or wider, it can be made to float (14.1). One explanation that children give to make sense of floating and sinking is that if an object floats, it must have air inside it somewhere.

Reconstruction

If your school has a commercially available set of cuboid materials this misconception can be addressed in a straightforward way. The cuboids are exactly the same size but made of a variety of different materials such as wood, polythene, glass, lead, expanded polystyrene, wax, Perspex, and aluminium. Ask children to discuss in groups which cuboids will float and which will sink, thus eliciting the misconception that all objects of the same size behave the same, by either floating or sinking. Children can then try out their ideas practically and it will quickly become apparent that some cuboids float while others sink, depending on the weight of material they are made from. Encourage children to try to explain to other members of their group why different cuboids of the same size are of different weights, which is a socio-constructivist way to direct their thinking towards a concept of density. If you do not have a set of cuboids, use two identical plastic photographic film canisters; fill one with sand and leave the other empty, then test them in the same way.

An alternative experiment is to place unopened cans of diet cola and ordinary cola in water. Children will be surprised to see that the diet cola can floats while the ordinary cola can sinks, which occurs because ordinary cola is heavier owing to its sugar content and so is denser than water.

Sources: Carr *et al.* (1994); Wei and Karpudewan (2018).

14.5 Can an object lose its weight?

> **Misconception**
>
> *When an object floats in water, it becomes weightless.*

Scientific conception

Activities such as swimming can lead children to believe that an object floats because its weight disappears when placed in water. If asked to name the forces acting on a floating ship, they might say that there are no forces present. As explained in 13.7, every object is constantly being attracted towards the centre of the Earth by a pulling force called weight (gravity), so even a swimming or floating object will have a downwards weight force acting on it. The feeling of weightlessness we have when swimming is due to the water supporting our body; in fact, water will push upwards on any object placed in it, even if only a small part dips into the water– this force is called **upthrust** (also called **buoyancy**). With a stationary floating object such as a boat, because there is no up or down movement, the forces are balanced, so weight is equal to upthrust (Figure 14.5a).[3]

Figure 14.5a The forces acting on a stationary floating object are balanced

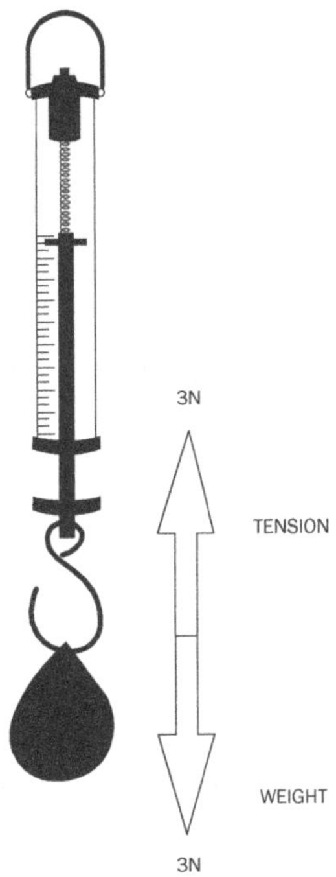

Figure 14.5b Forces acting on a metal object weighed in air using a Newton meter

The misconception can emerge during experiments that use Newton meters to investigate the forces at play when objects are placed into water. When a 3 N metal object is weighed in *air*, two forces are acting: the weight of the object pulls downwards, while the tension ('tightness') of the spring inside the Newton meter pulls upwards by an equal amount (Figure 14.5b). The scale on the Newton meter shows this tension and reads 3 N.

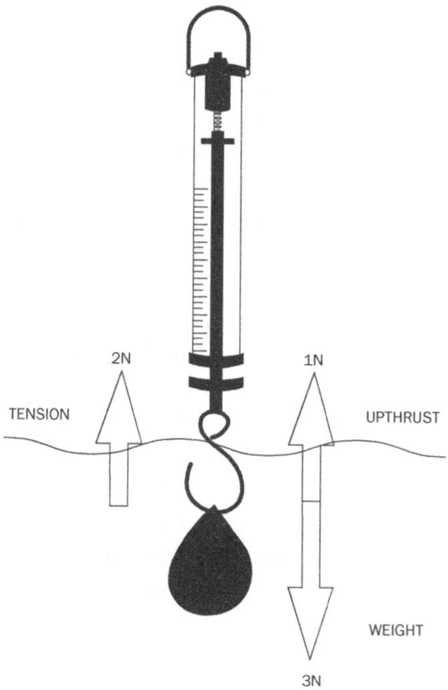

Figure 14.5c Forces acting on a metal object dipped in water

When the same metal object is immersed completely underwater, the Newton meter now reads only 2 N and the whole apparatus feels less heavy – this is called an 'apparent loss in weight'. Children may conclude that the water has made the object become lighter (Figure 14.5c). However, because the object has not changed in any way, it is still attracted towards the Earth by the same amount of force, so its weight remains the same at 3 N. Water supports the object by providing an upthrust of 1 N; therefore, there are two forces acting upwards, and one acting downwards, that cancel each other out (2 N + 1 N – 3 N = 0), resulting in a balanced system.

Thus, the reason why an object feels lighter when partly or completely submerged is that the water's upthrust pushes up against its weight. It is easier to pick up a heavy stone from the seabed than from the beach, although a submerged stone does not weigh any less than it does on the beach because it is the same object whether in or out of the water – the only way to make it weigh less would be to break it into smaller pieces. Note that in the case given in Figure 14.5c, weight is greater than upthrust and this is why the metal object would sink if we released it from the Newton meter (i.e. the upward tension force of the spring is removed). If, instead, the upthrust were equal to the weight as in Figure 14.5a, the object would be able to float on the surface due to balanced forces.

In 14.1, we discussed how whether an object floats or sinks depends on whether it is more dense or less dense than water. A more sophisticated way of looking at this is by thinking about upthrust using the concept of displacement. When we take a bath, as we enter the water the level in the bath rises because our body has pushed (displaced) some of the water out of the way. Similarly, as a hollow steel ball settles onto the surface of water, it pushes aside a volume of water equal to the shaded area in Figure 14.1c – this is the ball's displacement. The displacement can easily be measured by lowering the ball into a dish that has been filled to the very brim with water, and catching the overflow with a washing-up bowl. This displaced volume of water (the overflow) is then weighed. If the displaced water weighs, say, 80 N, then we could predict with absolute accuracy that the metal sphere on its own would also weigh 80 N. The fact that we can make such an exact prediction is due to the work of the Greek scientist Archimedes who, in the third century BCE, discovered that any floating object displaces water with a weight equal to the object's own weight, thus the 80 N steel sphere would displace 80 N of water. Furthermore, the upthrust force provided by the water is exactly equal to the weight of displaced water, i.e. 80 N, and considering the points made earlier in this section, this is why a balanced system exists with floating objects. If the hollow sphere were instead made of the heavy metal lead, it would sink lower into the water. If the lead sphere became completely submerged and began to sink, this would be because, for instance, the displacement of water is 200 N and the metal itself weighs 300 N, which creates unbalanced forces and downwards movement. To summarize, if the displaced water weighs *less* than the weight of an object, the water will not be able to support it and it will sink; if the displaced water weighs *the same* as the object, then it will float.

There are other misconceptions that relate to upthrust. Some children believe that a ship floats because it is supported by constant upward water currents, or by the force of its oars or engine. Others think that the depth of water beneath a floating object is a deciding factor as to whether an object floats or sinks, e.g. something that floats in shallow water will sink in deeper water. Some learners confuse the concept with water pressure and think that the upthrust force increases the deeper an object sinks because the pressure is higher. Other misconceptions include the idea that the upthrust increases as either the width of an object increases, or its weight increases.

Famous scientists

Archimedes and the King's golden crown. The King of Syracuse asked Archimedes to prove whether or not the royal crown was indeed made of pure gold. Gold has an unusually high density, and a simple way was to first weigh the crown, then melt it, and finally reshape it into a cube so its volume could be calculated, and so its density. Of course, the King forbade this, though after lengthy consideration an alternative solution eventually came to Archimedes while taking a bath. He realized that the submerged crown would displace its exact volume when placed in water, famously crying 'Eureka!' ('I've found it'). To this day, in science we still call the special vessel used to measure an object's displaced volume a 'Eureka can'.

Reconstruction

If children already understand the idea of balanced forces, a useful way to elicit the misconception is to ask the class which forces they think act on a stationary floating ship – they may instinctively believe that either no forces exist, or just weight is present. Remind them that since the ship is stationary, there must be balanced forces acting, i.e. something pushing up the ship with a force equal to the ship's weight, otherwise it would sink, and that this force is called upthrust. Using Newton meters to demonstrate the presence of upthrust is useful, and although such an activity lies outside the primary curriculum, it will help upper KS2 children construct a deeper understanding of why objects float or sink.

Because air is a fluid it also provides upthrust and higher attainers in upper KS2 can be set the challenge of calculating how much upthrust the air around them is pushing up on their body, using as a basis the equation:

$$\text{density} = \text{mass} \div \text{volume}.$$

First, calculate the volume of their body; the density of the human body is approximately the same as that of water (1 000 kg/m^3), therefore:

$$\text{The volume of their body (in m}^3\text{)} = \text{their body mass (in kg)} \div 1\,000\ \text{kg/m}^3.$$

Next, work out the mass of air that their body is displacing; the density of air is 1.2 kg/m^3, therefore:

$$\text{The mass of air their body displaces (in kg)} = \text{volume of their body (in m}^3\text{)} \times 1.2\ \text{kg/m}^3.$$

Finally, convert the mass of air their body displaces to *weight* (in N) by multiplying by 100.

Archimedes' principle states that the weight of air their body displaces = upthrust; I calculated the upthrust force on my own body as being 0.78 N, approximately equivalent to 78 g. Since my weight (650 N) is much greater than my upthrust, my body naturally sinks to the bottom of the 'sea of air'.

Having KS1 children push down an inflated party balloon (or an empty 2-litre plastic bottle with its lid on) into a bowl of water is a tried-and-tested method of showing the powerful nature of some upthrust forces. Because they will be pushing down against a weight of water equal to the balloon's large volume, they will find it difficult to completely submerge the balloon. This can be extended by repeating the task with a similar-sized ice balloon, where less effort is required on the part of the child because the weight of the ice balloon is greater and so assists their downward push. The ice balloon can also be used to show that 'heavy' objects can float as well as lighter objects, such as ice cubes from the freezer (14.1).

Sources: Bar *et al.* (1994); Parker and Heywood (2000); Potvin and Cyr (2017).

Notes

1 Density values in the book are given in grams per cubic centimetre (g/cm^3) unless otherwise stated. These values are equivalent to the **relative density** of an object or material.

2 Note that this diagram is for information only. Creosote and mercury are hazardous and should not be used in the classroom in this way.

3 Note that with the figures in this section, force arrows are not touching the object that is experiencing the force. This goes against convention but has been done to make the diagrams clearer.

Planning and assessment sheet 14 Floating and sinking
(For suggestions on how to use this sheet, see p. xxviii.)

Misconception	*Attainment re. expected standard*		
	Working towards	*Working at*	*Working above*
Year 5: *Forces*			
All light objects float, all heavy objects sink (14.1)	✓	✓	
Objects that are flat or wide will float (14.1)	✓	✓	
Smaller objects are more likely to float than larger objects (14.1)	✓	✓	
Hard or sharp objects sink (14.1)	✓		
All objects that float must contain some air within them (14.1)	✓	✓	
If an object has holes, such as a plastic sieve, then it will sink (because water can enter inside) (14.1)	✓		
An iceberg is both floating and sinking at the same time (14.2)	✓	✓	
A person in the sea wearing an inflated life jacket is sinking, but the life jacket itself is floating (14.2)	✓	✓	
If people on the water's surface are swimming, they are floating; if they are panicking, they are sinking (14.2)	✓		
A submerged submarine near to the surface of the sea is floating; when near to the sea bed, it is sinking (14.2)	✓		
Wood is more dense than water (14.3)	✓	✓	
The depth of water beneath an object is a deciding factor as to whether an object floats or sinks, e.g. something that floats in shallow water will sink in deeper water (14.5)	✓		
If there is more depth of water in a container, floating objects will have more of their bulk submerged (14.3)	✓		
Oil floats on top of water because oil is thicker (14.3)	✓	✓	
If two objects made of different materials are the same size, the two will behave in the same way; they will either both float, or both sink (14.4)	✓		

(continued)

(continued)

If two objects have the same weight, then both will either float or sink, regardless of their size (14.4)	✓		
When an object floats in water, it becomes weightless (14.5)	✓	✓	✓
There are no forces acting on a floating, stationary ship (14.5)	✓	✓	
A ship floats because it is supported by constant upward water currents, or by the force of its oars or engine (14.5)	✓	✓	
The upthrust force on an object increases the deeper an object sinks because the water pressure is higher (14.5)			✓
The upthrust force on an object increases as either the width of an object increases, or its weight increases (14.5)		✓	✓
Year 5: *Properties of everyday materials and reversible change*			
Hard or sharp objects sink (14.1)	✓		
Wood is more dense than water (14.3)	✓	✓	
Oil floats on top of water because oil is thicker (14.3)	✓	✓	

15

Electricity

Conceptual areas covered in this chapter:

- The nature of electricity
- Defining current and voltage
- Differences between conventional current and electron flow
- Three classic circuit misconceptions

National Curriculum links:

Year 4: *Electricity*

Year 6: *Electricity*

15.1 What is electricity?

> **Misconception**
>
> *When you buy an electrical item from a shop, the electricity is already inside it.*

Scientific conception

Younger learners especially can have naïve ideas about what **electricity** is. Despite children understanding that appliances such as kettles, TVs, and computers are powered by electricity, some think that the electricity is stored inside the appliance; therefore, when you buy the appliance, you are also buying the electricity that comes with it. They see electricity as a mysterious, immovable thing that is within an appliance and vital to making it work, similar to an engine underneath a car bonnet. To them, although electricity makes appliances work, it is never used up – you can never run out of electricity. Children know that many household appliances need to be plugged into the mains which then supplies electricity to make them function. However, battery-powered devices such as toy cars and torches requiring batteries, may not be thought as electrical.

The idea that electricity is immovable is true in the case of *static electricity*. If you rub a party balloon on a woollen sweater, it picks up static electricity – we say that the balloon is now charged – and you can use the charged balloon to attract things like small bits of tissue paper, or someone's hair. This type of electricity occurs due to the build-up (or removal) of electrons and can be stored on the balloon where it does not move, hence the word 'static'. However, the electrical devices mentioned in previous paragraphs do not work with static electricity; they are instead powered by **current electricity**, which like static occurs due to electrons, but instead of staying still, the electrons move around. When an appliance such as a TV is plugged into the mains and switched on, current electricity flows from the mains and around the TV to make it work. When the TV is bought from a shop, it does not contain electricity within it, and the same applies to battery-powered devices. A common misconception with all ages is to think that batteries store electricity – they cannot – they instead store chemical energy. When the battery is connected to a circuit, this chemical energy is transferred to the circuit and only then becomes electricity.

These misconceptions can link to beliefs that electricity is only found in the home or in school. Because of their limited experience, children do not always consider non-domestic uses of electricity, such as street lighting, factories, and trains. They also tend not to give electrical causes to natural phenomena such as thunder and lightning, or the transmission of electrical impulses through nerves inside the human body responsible for the knee-jerk reflex.

Reconstruction

Electrical concepts can be difficult for children to understand because they cannot see electricity moving through a circuit, although its effects are visible, such as a lit bulb. An engaging way to introduce the topic is with an *energy stick*, a children's toy that has a self-contained circuit that lights up or makes a sound when you touch both terminals with your hands (the sweat in your skin helps to make the connection). Several children can hold hands together in a circle to activate a single energy stick.

At KS1, a traditional activity is for the teacher to bring in a variety of electrical appliances from home and ask children to name them and describe what they are used for. A next step is to sort the appliances into those that need to be plugged into the mains and others that are battery-powered. The opportunity can be taken at this point to talk about the nature of electricity. Explain that electricity is something that moves around from one place to another: in the case of a TV, it moves from the mains socket into the TV itself, then returns back into the socket; similarly, with a torch, it moves from the battery, through the torch, then back into the battery. Emphasize that there is no electricity within an appliance when it is switched off, and that when you buy a TV or a torch from a shop, again there is no electricity within the device.

Experiments with fruit batteries are fun and can be used to show that electricity is found in nature as well as in the home. Source two nails (or pieces of wire), one copper and the other zinc ('galvanized' nails are zinc-coated). Insert the nails about 5 cm apart in your fruit then connect them to a light emitting diode (LED) using wire – the LED lights-up due to a chemical reaction inside the fruit, similar to that taking place within a normal battery. Children can compare the effectiveness of different fruits (citrus fruits work best due to their acidity), and even try vegetables such as potatoes, gherkins, and cucumbers. Connecting a household **multimeter** to measure the **voltage** generated by each fruit or vegetable provides quantitative data that can be converted into charts and graphs.

When children first build simple circuits during science lessons at school, they start to think about electricity as something that can move around, and the rest of this chapter deals with ideas that can emerge when children use electrical circuit components in school.

Sources: Lin (2016); Markwick and White (2022); Redhead (2018); Solomonidou and Kakana (2000).

Did you know?

When is a battery not a battery? In everyday life we talk about AA batteries, watch batteries, and mobile phone batteries, but technically none of these are true batteries. They are instead **cells**, and are essentially made from three components – an anode (**positive terminal**), a cathode (**negative terminal**) and an electrolyte (a material that separates anode and cathode). When a cell is connected to a circuit, a chemical reaction takes between the anode and cathode that produces electrons that leave the cathode and move around the circuit, making it work. Once the electrons have passed through the circuit, they re-enter the cell at the anode. A battery, on the other hand, is several cells joined together doing the same job, similar to batteries of medical tests, chickens, or artillery. If a torch is powered by two AA cells, those two cells together comprise the torch battery. It is important to familiarize children with the correct terminology in science lessons and encourage them to use the word 'cells' when describing what in everyday life they would call 'batteries'. The following sections of this chapter will refer to 'cell' in this correct scientific way.

15.2 What are the different ways that a bulb can be connected to a cell?

Misconception

Electricity works by simply coming out of one end of a cell.

Scientific conception

Based on experience with electrical toys, preschool children understand that cells ('batteries') do something vitally important in making devices work (although they are unlikely to understand that this is anything to do with electricity). People of all ages may find it a challenge to explain how cells do this, although some construct explanations similar to the idea of energy, whereby a cell gives up some of its 'stuff' to an appliance which is then used up. When the stuff has run out, the appliance no longer works and the cell is dead. Everyday expressions such as *it has run out of juice* reflect this simple analogy. Some children think the stuff is a kind of fluid inside the cell, which when connected to something like a bulb, pours into it in the same way that water flows through a hosepipe. For these learners the misconception statement above would be a rational explanation – it is called the *unipolar model of electrical flow* (Figure 15.2a and Figure 15.2b).

Of course, the unipolar model is incorrect. Electricity *can* be thought of in simple terms as a flow of water but the flow must occur in a continuous loop, called a circuit. In the next section, Figure 15.3b will show how electricity leaves the positive terminal of a cell, travels through wires around the circuit, passes through a bulb, goes through more wires before finally re-entering the negative terminal of a cell. If the positive and negative terminals are not connected in a continuous loop, the electricity cannot flow around, the bulb does not light, and the circuit is said to be 'broken' or disconnected.

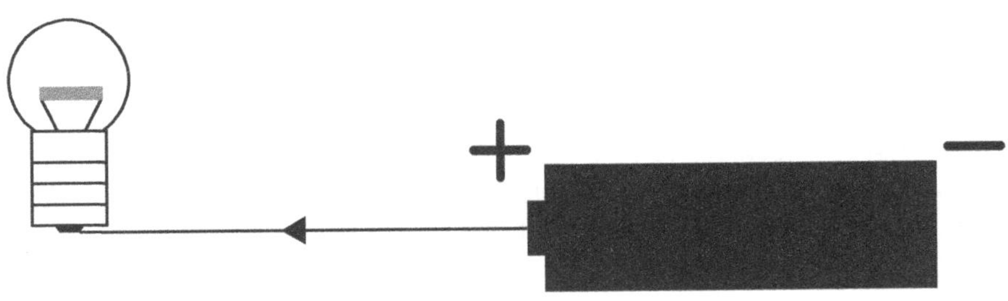

Figure 15.2a The unipolar model of electrical flow (misconception)

Figure 15.2b Child's drawing (aged 10 years) possibly depicting the unipolar model (misconception)

Source: Osborne *et al.* (1991), p. 32.

As electricity travels around a circuit and passes through wires, bulbs, or other components, the circuit as a whole transfers energy to its surroundings. Over time, a connected cell runs down because the circuit is constantly losing energy typically as heat, light, kinetic, or sound, and will eventually need to be replaced with a fresh cell.

Be safe!

Working with electrical circuits. The circuits used by primary children are usually quite safe and there is little, if any, danger of electrocution. This is because the source is normally low voltage cells ('batteries') or in some cases **direct current** (**DC**) power units that plug into the mains electricity but convert it to a safe level with low voltage and current. Overheating due to children accidentally building a short circuit is more of a risk. This is quite common, especially with beginners, as they connect the terminals of the cell directly together by mistake, with no other components such as bulbs or buzzers in between. This creates very low resistance within the circuit, as the current only has electrical wires to push its way through, and all the wires and connections can quickly become hot. This can be accompanied by the smell of burning and in some cases the plastic covering the connecting leads begins to melt, potentially creating a fire hazard. It is good practice before the lesson to ask the class to let you know immediately whenever they smell burning, at which point you need to try to find where the short circuit is and disconnect it. A different risk is the danger of cutting fingers on broken glass bulbs. Ask children not to screw them down into their plastic holders too firmly, which is the main cause. Finally, it might seem obvious but it is worth mentioning to the children that they are not allowed to use the mains supply. During one science lesson I spotted a child trying to connect two crocodile clips directly into the mains plug socket, a situation which had potentially serious consequences.

Reconstruction

Year 4 children can carry out a practical activity where they are given a bulb, two wires, and a cell, then set the challenge of making the bulb light up with a minimum of teacher help. This activity is suitable for eliciting the unipolar misconception, as some children may first attempt to the make bulb light using only a single wire attached to one cell terminal. Trial and error will help them realize that both ends of the cell need to connect to the bulb for it to light up, and so enable them to construct an understanding of how an electrical circuit works. Note that although this activity is excellent for addressing the unipolar misconception, other approaches are necessary for the clashing current and current consumption misconceptions (15.3 and 15.4).

Children may need some direct teacher guidance to make the bulb light up, as the wires need to touch the bulb in two distinct places: the outer metal screw casing and the metal 'blob' on the underside (Figure 15.2c). Some children may attempt to touch the wires to the glass surface of the bulb, and this can be linked to a discussion about whether glass is a conductor or an insulator. In a similar way, when joining together the different components on a circuit board, children may try to construct the circuit by clipping onto inappropriate parts, such as the plastic board itself, or the plastic covering on an electrical lead. There is perhaps an argument for teaching children which materials conduct electricity, prior to the building of any circuits. Use a visualizer or a webcam linked to an IWB when carrying out a close-up demonstration of exactly where the wires need to go, so that the whole class will be able to see the arrangement as depicted in Figure 15.2c.

Although the Programme of Study states that electricity should first be introduced in Year 4, most KS1 children are quite capable of building their own circuits. Providing a cell, bulbs, motors, buzzers, LEDs, etc., and allowing some time for exploration will allow younger children to see what happens when different components are connected into a simple circuit. A good way to introduce the idea of electricity to KS1 children is to read the story books *The Lighthouse Keeper's Lunch* by Ronda Armitage, and *Oscar and the Bird* by Geoff Waring.

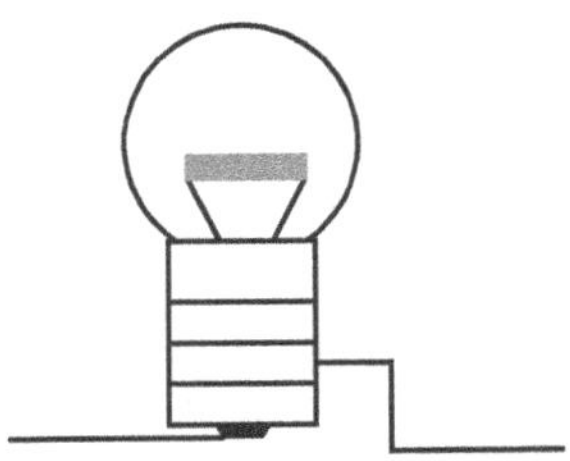

Figure 15.2c How wires connect to a bulb

Sources: Armitage (2007); Kada and Ravanis (2016); Kaliampos *et al.* (2020); Waring (2009).

15.3 How does electricity move around a circuit?

Misconception

Electricity is pushed out of both ends of a cell at the same time.

Scientific conception

As discussed in 15.2, children commonly believe that cells introduce some 'stuff' into a circuit, a kind of fluid that leaves the cell, flows through the wires, and then finally enters a component such as a bulb making it light up. This simple idea of a 'hosepipe' is the unipolar model (see Figure 15.2a). Children can develop this further by constructing the misconception that "stuff' is pushed out from both ends of the cell simultaneously, thus feeding a device. This more advanced 'double hosepipe' representation can arise because a learner (correctly) understands that both terminals of a cell need to be connected for a component to work. Since the electricity is imagined to meet in the middle of the circuit with nowhere else to go, this is termed the *clashing currents model of electrical flow* (Figure 15.3a). Some children think that this clash of currents causes friction, which makes the bulb light up and become hot, or that the currents in the two wires each take turns to light the bulb (crossing current model).

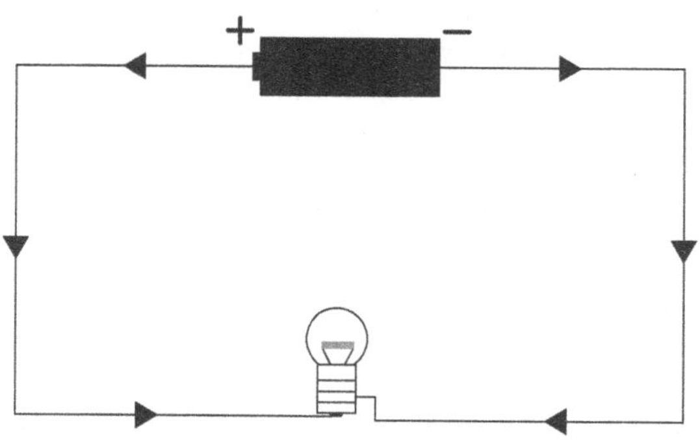

Figure 15.3a The clashing currents model of electrical flow (misconception)

Although a water flow analogy can help children understand how electricity moves around a circuit, it is better to think of the water/electricity as travelling in a continuous loop in a similar way to cars driving one-way around a racetrack. The electricity leaves the cell from the positive terminal only,

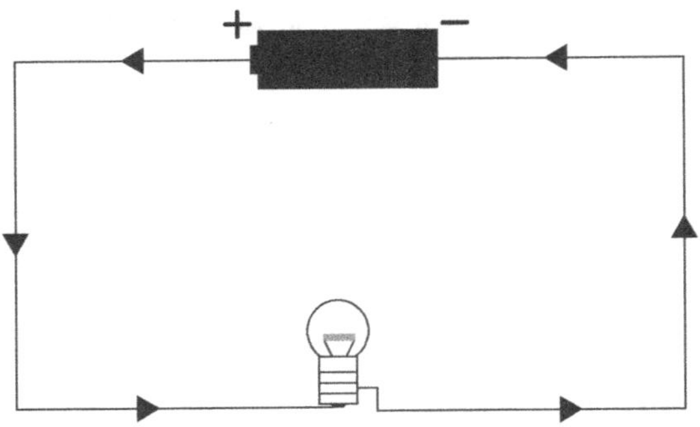

Figure 15.3b Scientific model of conventional electrical flow

travels around the wires, through components, then back into the cell at the negative terminal (Figure 15.3b). As explained in 15.2, the cell eventually runs down as the circuit transfers energy to its surroundings.

Reconstruction

Although an understanding of the direction of electrical flow is beyond the primary curriculum, it is important to recognize and correct misconceptions such as the clashing currents model should they arise. A practical way to illustrate which path electricity is taking through a circuit is to connect a household multimeter in series to different parts of a circuit. Since this piece of apparatus will indicate positive or negative readings depending on the direction of electrical flow, you can show children that no matter where in the circuit you connect the multimeter, the electricity always flows in the same direction.

Asking children to connect LEDs or buzzers to different parts of a circuit will result in the LEDs lighting up in some places and not in others. This is because LEDs will only turn on when electricity flows through them in one direction – they are a kind of one-way street (which can be a source of frustration to children because unless they know this, they think their circuit is broken). Using these observations, children can draw a diagram of the circuit that shows which way they think the electricity is flowing. Free interactive circuit builders are available on the internet that allow children to drag-and-drop different components and see what effect they have on, for example, the brightness of bulbs. The Top Marks website has links to animations that are easy to use and can also be manipulated by children on the IWB: www.topmarks.co.uk; there is evidence that animations explicitly showing electrons travelling through the components in a circuit are particularly helpful.

Sources: Chiu and Lin (2005); Lin (2016); Preston *et al.* (2022).

15.4 What is current?

Misconception

A circuit uses up electric current.

Scientific conception

Figure 15.4a shows how some children might draw electricity travelling in a simple circuit.[1] They may understand that the electricity (more correctly, *current*) comes out of one cell terminal, travels around the circuit passing through bulbs and wires, then re-enters the cell at the opposite terminal (which is the scientific model). However, they may also believe that bulbs actively use up current so that it becomes weaker during the journey around the circuit, represented by the size of the arrows on the diagram. Also, because there is less current available in the right-hand side of the circuit, bulb B is dimmer than bulb A. These conclusions are due to the incorrect idea that current is constantly being used up by a live circuit, called the *current consumption model of electrical flow.*

This misconception has been repeatedly seen in a variety of age groups and is difficult to address. Within a simple circuit such as Figure 15.4a, the current is not used up but remains the same strength throughout; to fully understand this we need to think about what current actually is. Within the atoms of a metal conductor such as the copper wire in a circuit, there are tiny subatomic particles called electrons, which carry a negative charge. These

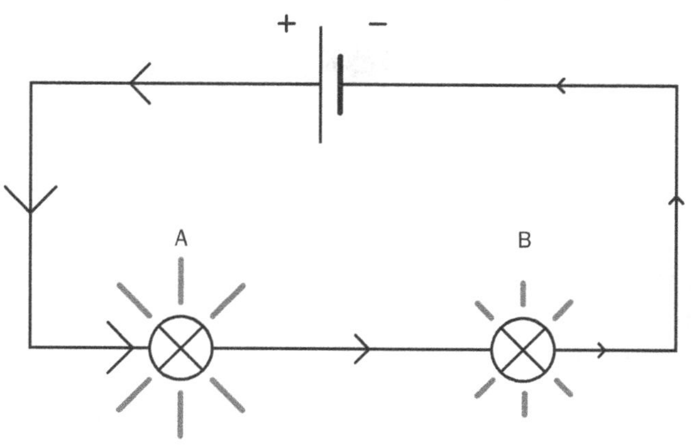

Figure 15.4a Current consumption model (misconception)

electrons are not tied to any one atom, instead being able to randomly wander up and down the wire; they are known as *free electrons*, and collectively as a *sea of electrons*. When the two terminals of a cell are connected by wires to make a circuit, the negatively charged sea of electrons is attracted towards the positive cell terminal (opposites attract) and so they move all together through the wire towards that terminal, causing electrical flow (Figure 15.4b). During their journey the moving electrons pass through the very thin bulb filament wire and cause it to glow because of 'friction' as they collide with the atoms in the filament, and the bulb lights up. The electrons then come out the other side of the bulb and enter the wire on their way back to the cell. When the electrons reach the positive cell terminal, they enter the cell; at the same time, more electrons leave the cell at the opposite, negative terminal and enter the wire, with this replenishment keeping the number of electrons in the circuit constant. This one-way movement of electrons around a circuit is called direct current (DC).

Therefore, the electrons that make up current are in a kind of self-contained system and so cannot be lost from the circuit (see 15.4b).[2] Because of this, bulbs A and B in Figure 15.4c will have an equal strength of current; if you were to use a multimeter to measure the current at any point in the circuit, you would always get the same reading, and the two bulbs would be equally bright.

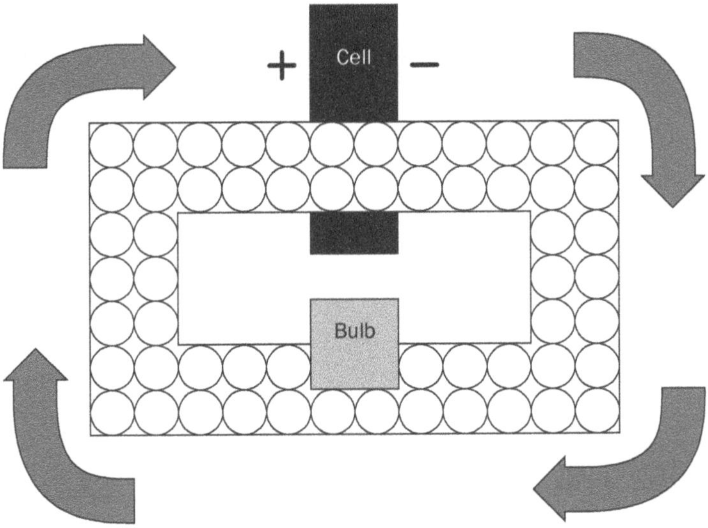

Figure 15.4b A simple model of electron flow in a series circuit (electrons are represented by the white circles, and are not to scale)

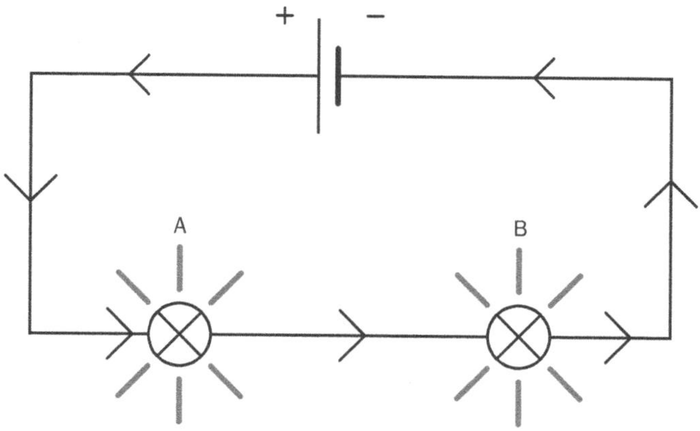

Figure 15.4c The direction of conventional current flow (as taught in primary science)

Within a domestic household electric circuit the situation is different, as the electricity is **alternating current (AC)** where the flow of current is not always in the same direction but instead switches direction very rapidly, 50 times a second. The electrons in an AC circuit are pushed along a wire first one way and then the opposite way, which ends up with them only moving a few millimetres each way through the wire. Although individual electrons do not travel very far through the wires, a bulb can be lit up because the sea of electrons as a whole is pushed in the circuit in alternate directions.

You might have noted that the directions of flow in Figures 15.3b and 15.4c are opposite to each other – this is not an error. In diagrams of electrical circuits, current is usually drawn as arrows travelling from positive to negative, i.e. anticlockwise in Figure 15.4c. This is termed *conventional current*, and although recognized and accepted worldwide by electricians, its direction of flow is actually not scientifically correct. As discussed, electrons are negatively charged, so travel in the other direction away from the negative terminal and towards the positive terminal, i.e. clockwise in Figure 15.4d (opposites attract, likes repel). There are historical reasons why the direction of conventional current is incorrect and is a source of perennial confusion for students at all levels of education. To avoid unnecessary confusion in the primary classroom, the conflicting directions of flow tend not to be shared with children, who are usually shown the conventional direction only, i.e. from the positive terminal to the negative terminal.

Reconstruction

Although the word 'current' does not appear in the primary Programme of Study, children need to appreciate that a cell supplies some kind of 'stuff' to a circuit to

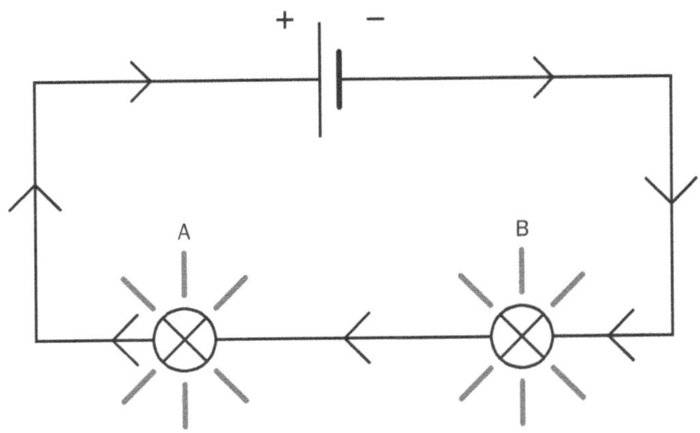

Figure 15.4d The direction of electron flow

Did you know?

A circuit loses energy, not current. A cell does not last forever, eventually running down because it 'gives' something to the circuit that it cannot get back – but what exactly is it losing? As explained in the main text, electrons leave the negative terminal of the cell, travel around the circuit and enter the positive terminal. A cell is a kind of pump that recycles electrons in the circuit by transferring energy, and gradually this pump loses its ability to do this because it loses energy that cannot be recovered. Chemical energy within the cell drives this process, which during the life of a cell such as in Figure 15.4c is transferred as electrical energy in the wires, then heat and light energy in the bulbs, which is finally lost from the circuit. So this circuit does not lose current in the form of electrons (they cannot leave the self-contained system – see Figure 15.4b) but transfers energy to the surroundings as heat and light, which makes the cell gradually run down, making the electrons circulate more slowly. When the chemical energy within a cell is exhausted, it can no longer drive electrons around a circuit and becomes flat. With rechargeable cells, the chemical energy can be restored by using the mains electricity to reverse the chemical processes within the cell.

make things work. Teachers can extend the thinking of higher attainers by introducing the idea of a travelling entity called current that is present in the wires and components of a circuit. A good way to elicit the current consumption misconception is to ask the class to predict the brightness of a string of several bulbs in a series circuit arranged as in Figure 15.4c. A common prediction is that the bulbs furthest away from the cell's positive terminal will be dimmer because electricity has been used up by the time it gets to them. Children then build circuits to test their predictions and will be able to see that all the bulbs actually have the same brightness, so helping to address the misconception. Teachers can reinforce this by using a household multimeter to demonstrate that the current when measured at any point in the circuit is of exactly the same strength.

There are technical aspects to this experiment which can prevent these misconceptions being addressed, or even reinforce them. The bulbs the children use should all be of the same rating (e.g. 2.5 V) and ideally need to be tested by the teacher prior to the lesson so that they indeed have the same brightness, because there are sometimes small variations due to manufacturing tolerances of cheaper bulbs – in particular, watch out for the odd rogue bulb of a higher rating that is much brighter. If children find there are minor variations in brightness, ask them to swap bulbs around in the circuit to show that the variation is due to the bulbs themselves, not their positions or order within the circuit.

A popular KS2 role-play activity is to have children pretend to be electrons travelling around a large room, such as the school hall, to represent different parts of a DC circuit. A simpler alternative is to have children in a circle each holding their own screwed-up piece of paper (electron) which they pass to the person next to them, creating a continuous stream of electrons. To show that electrons cannot escape and that they move around more slowly as the cell runs down, a bicycle chain is a good model of how a circuit runs in a self-contained loop.

The current consumption misconception is known to be very resistant. Children may persuade themselves that there is indeed a difference in bulb brightness when none exists, to preserve their own theory. Others may reason that their string of bulbs does have equal brightness but the current re-entering the cell is reduced at some point after leaving the last bulb. The concept of energy is not introduced in primary science and is perhaps best avoided in this context. When energy is introduced in secondary school at KS3, it becomes a regular source of further confusion for children who find it difficult to remember the difference between electrical current and electrical energy.

Sources: Glauert (2009); Lin (2016); Redhead (2018); Shipstone (1984).

15.5 What is voltage?

Misconception

Voltage makes a circuit work by travelling around the wires.

Scientific conception

Although primary teachers commonly use the words *volts* and *voltage* when describing the 'strength' of cells, to keep things at a simple level they tend to avoid any further explanation of these terms. Children can therefore construct their own ideas as to what volts and voltage actually are. They appreciate that different cells have different voltages and that the higher the voltage, the more 'stuff' a circuit receives, making bulbs brighter and buzzers noisier. Children can imagine that the voltage runs around the wires and components making everything work. However, as discussed in 15.4, although there are indeed tiny subatomic particles called electrons that travel around the circuit, this movement of electrons is termed current, not voltage.

Voltage is a poorly understood and difficult concept for learners at all levels of science education. Once children grasp the basic idea that voltage is something that a cell supplies to a circuit to make the components work, their thinking can be extended by understanding that *voltage is a kind of pushing force generated by a cell that causes current (electrons) to flow around the circuit.* The more volts a cell can provide, the greater the pushing force, so making the bulbs in a circuit brighter. As a cell runs down over time, its pushing force will decrease.

The cell in Figure 15.5a is using 6 V to drive the circuit containing two bulbs; in addition to the cell's voltage, the diagram, which is typical, shows that there are also volts present within the circuit itself, across each bulb. Note that the sum of the volts associated with each bulb approximately equals the total number of volts delivered by the cell, as if the bulbs have shared the cell's voltage between them, i.e. 2.9 V + 2.9 V = 5.8 V; the missing 0.2 V represents the 'share' taken by the wires in the circuit.[3] However, when the bulbs' voltage is shown on the diagram in this way, it can be a source of confusion that encourages learners to believe that volts have been sent around the circuit when actually *the circuit does not contain any moving volts.*

To clarify this, we need to think about voltage not as something physical and moving like current, but as a measure of difference between two different

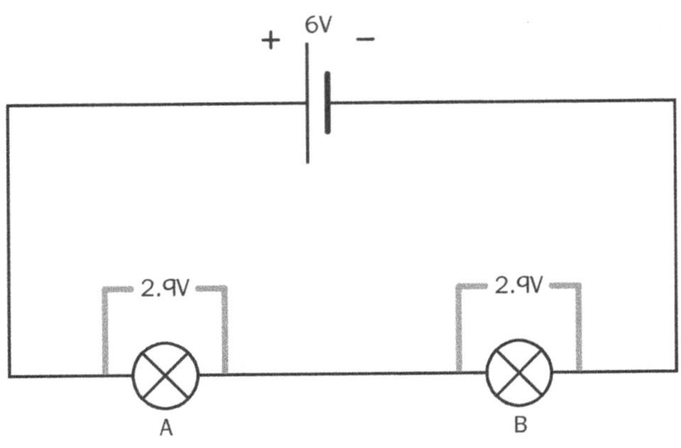

Figure 15.5a Voltage measurements within a simple DC circuit

points in a circuit. The voltage differences within the circuit in Figure 15.5a are shown in Figure 15.5b as a slope or hill, with the volts in the column on the left of the diagram representing the height of the slope. Voltage starts high when current leaves the cell at the positive terminal (6 V) and gradually falls to zero when current enters the cell at the negative terminal. Each bulb has caused a drop in voltage of 2.9 V, and each long wire a drop of 0.1 V, explaining why by the time the current enters the cell on the far right of the diagram, the voltage has become zero. As current passes through each bulb, the voltage drops significantly, so voltage is not something present within each bulb; instead, it is a measure of the drop in 'height' on either side of a bulb. Current can be imagined like a ball that is only able to move if there is a downhill slope for it to roll down – from left to right in Figure 15.5b. As current passes through each bulb, there is a large drop in height (voltage), and as it runs through each long wire there is another, smaller drop. As the current re-enters the cell at the negative terminal, it is at the lowest point on this imaginary slope, and the job of the cell is to boost it back up to the highest point, ready to leave the positive terminal for another trip around the circuit. If a bigger 12 V cell was to be substituted into the same circuit, the drop in voltage across the bulbs would be greater, approaching 6 V for each bulb, and they would glow much more brightly.

If a circuit contained one small bulb and one buzzer, the voltage across the buzzer would be much higher than the voltage across the bulb. It is as if the buzzer is greedy and takes nearly all the cell's voltage for itself, leaving little for the bulb, which glows very dimly, if at all. This can be described more scientifically as the voltage drop across the buzzer being massive compared with the voltage drop across the bulb.

In summary, volts are not something that travel around a circuit. Instead, they are a measure of the driving force that causes current to move, just as a slope causes a ball to roll downhill; the scientific name for this driving force is **potential difference**. If there was no difference in volts within the circuit, current would not be able to flow.

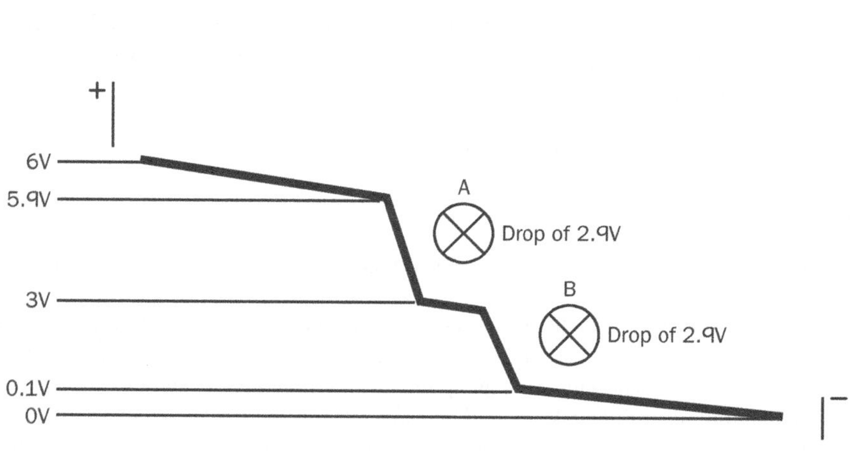

Figure 15.5b Voltage drops across a simple DC circuit (also refer to Figure 15.5a)

This misconception can be reinforced if children notice that the small bulbs used in school experiments each have a voltage rating stamped on them (e.g. 2.5 V), which may suggest that volts are something physical that travel through bulbs. This value merely lets the user know what cell voltage is required to light the bulb, and if a much higher voltage is supplied to the bulb by mistake, the filament may melt and the bulb blows.

Related misconceptions include the idea that voltage is the amount of electricity stored in a cell. As discussed in the Box on p. 254, cells do not contain electricity but instead are a source of chemical energy that can be converted into electrical energy. Therefore, a 'fully charged' cell actually contains no charge until it is connected to a circuit. Another common error is to think that voltage is a part of the current within a circuit. Although current needs a voltage to flow, the current and voltage are two separate things – the voltage enables the current to flow. In this section, voltage has been described as a 'driving force', although no mechanical push or pull exists within circuits during current flow. These 'forces' are attractions between positive and negative charges that have been created by chemical processes within cells (see 15.4).

Reconstruction

At primary level the concept of voltage is usually kept simple, being related to how bulbs are brighter when more cells are connected into a circuit. As with the concept of current (15.4), if misconceptions of voltage do arise, it is preferable if teachers try to address them, so laying better foundations for future study of circuits at secondary school. One way to explain voltage without using the more complex idea of potential difference is to say that when current leaves a cell, it is given a 'kick' and sent on its way around the circuit. To illustrate this, draw a cartoon foot that kicks circular objects (current) out of one terminal of a cell and gives them a reason to move around the circuit. The bigger the cell's voltage, the larger the foot, and so the bigger the driving force.

With higher-attaining KS2 children, teachers may consider introducing the idea of voltage dropping at different points in the circuit. A household multimeter can be used to show how volts drop across components, with these voltage losses then being drawn by children as a slope (as in Figure 15.5b).

Sources: Shipstone (1985); White and Gunstone (2014).

Notes

1 To provide clarity, conventional circuit symbols are used to represent components in 15.4 and 15.5.

2 Over time the cell will run down, making the electrons in the circuit slow down. Note that current is not a measure of the total amount of electrons within a circuit, but the number of electrons passing a certain point in the circuit in a given time.

3 Also note that in reality a 6 V cell will probably provide a little less than its stated voltage when measured with a meter because a small amount of voltage is needed to overcome the cell's own internal resistance.

Planning and assessment sheet 15 Electricity

(For suggestions on how to use this sheet, see p. xxviii.)

Misconception	*Attainment re. expected standard*		
	Working towards	*Working at*	*Working above*
Year 4: *Electricity*			
When you buy an electrical item from a shop, the electricity is already inside it (15.1)	✓		
The electricity that makes appliances work is never used up (they can never run out of electricity) (15.1)	✓		
Unlike mains-powered appliances, battery-powered devices are not thought to be electrical (15.1)	✓		
Batteries store electricity (15.1)	✓	✓	
Electricity is only found in the home or in school (not considering non-domestic uses of electricity such as street lighting and trains) (15.1)	✓		
Natural phenomena such as thunder and lightning do not involve electricity (15.1)	✓		
Year 6: *Electricity*			
Electricity works by simply coming out of one end of a battery (unipolar misconception) (15.2)	✓	✓	
Electricity is pushed out of both ends of a battery at the same time (clashing currents misconception) (15.3)	✓	✓	
When two currents meet, this causes friction which makes the bulb light up and become hot (clashing currents misconception) (15.3)	✓	✓	
Two currents in the two wires each take turns to light the bulb (crossing current misconception) (15.3)	✓	✓	
A circuit uses up electric current (current consumption misconception) (15.4)	✓	✓	✓
Voltage makes a circuit work by travelling around the wires (15.5)	✓	✓	✓
Voltage is the amount of electricity stored in a battery (15.5)	✓	✓	
Voltage is a part of the current within a circuit (15.5)	✓	✓	

16

Light

Conceptual areas covered in this chapter:	*National Curriculum links:*
• Light as a travelling wave • Differences between sources of light and reflectors of light • The nature of shadows • Coloured light	Year 3: *Light* Year 6: *Light*

16.1 Where is light present?

Misconception

Light is only found in bright areas.

Scientific conception

In everyday contexts when we talk about 'light' we are usually referring to how bright a particular place is, e.g. *we need some more light in here*, or *is it light outside yet?* Because of this, primary children's understandings conflict with the scientific idea of light as a form of energy that travels from one place to another. Figure 16.1a shows a light source (a torch) producing an illuminated circle on a flat wall in a dark room, where children believe that light is present only at the source and the illuminated wall because these are the only areas that are visibly lit up. In fact, because light travels from the torch bulb towards the wall, light is also present in the area in between, in the form of a beam (Figure 16.1b). To help children understand this, the beam that is normally invisible

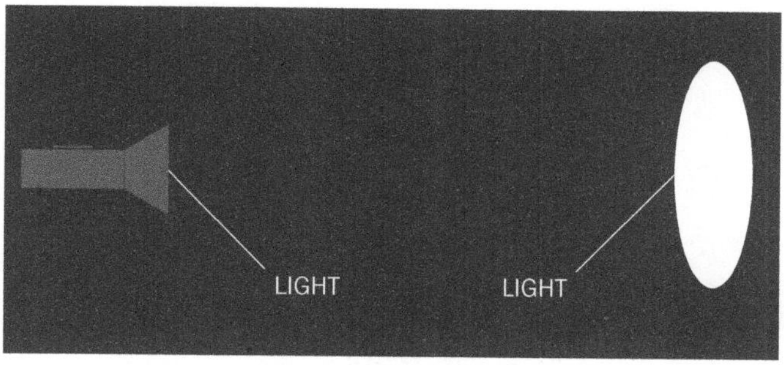

Figure 16.1a Light is only present in bright areas (misconception)

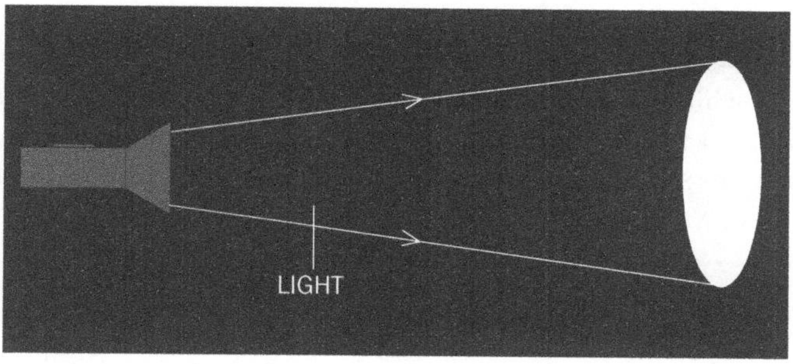

Figure 16.1b Light is also present within a torch beam

can be made to appear (see *Reconstruction*). However, we are not able to see the beam making its way across the room because light travels at an extremely high speed, approximately 300,000 km per second.

In diagrams, we draw light using arrows that show the path taken by the travelling light and also its direction – these are light rays, and are shown in Figure 16.1b. Even if children understand that light is made up of travelling rays, they can still have the misconception that light only exists in bright areas. For instance, in a room lit by a single candle, they might say that light only travels as far as the objects that are lit by the candle and does not penetrate into the dark corners of the room (Figure 16.1c). They believe that light travels outwards a short distance until it fills an area immediately around the candle and then stays still. However, the fact that a person is still able to see the candle even if they stand in a dark corner of the room means that light rays must have flooded the entire room. The person standing in the dark corner is still able to see the candle because light rays are travelling from the candle to their eyes. Returning to the torch example above, light therefore is not only present at the source, within the beam and on the illuminated wall, but will fill the entire room. Another manifestation of this misconception is the belief that light is a material-like substance emitted by a source which then sticks to objects, illuminating them, and travels no further.

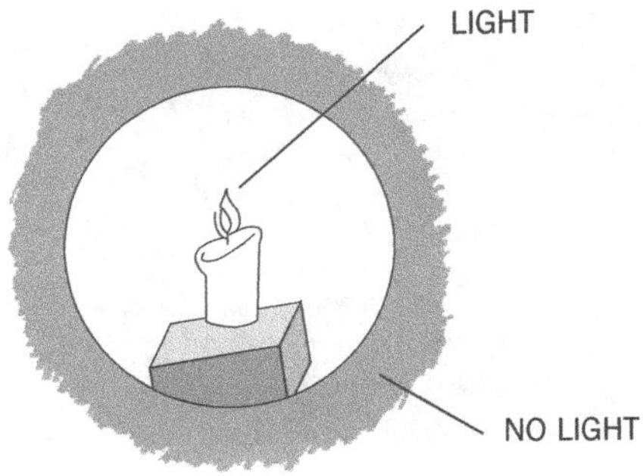

Figure 16.1c Candle illuminating a dark room (misconception)

Other non-scientific ideas about travelling light include light does not travel at nighttime, which is why it becomes dark. On the other hand, some children believe that light travels further at night, which explains how, during daytime, artificial sources such as car headlights and torches are more difficult to see.

Be safe!

Using a laser pointer in the classroom. These devices (also called laser pens) transmit laser radiation, which is high-intensity light directed in a narrow red beam. They can potentially cause permanent eye damage if the beam is shone directly into the eye. That said, laser pointers have been used by teachers in the UK for many years without any reported injury. Many laser pointers are classified as low risk and the likely result of the laser beam accidentally entering the eye is a dazzling flash with temporary blindness (spots before the eyes). Other pointers are more powerful, such as lasers that produce a green beam, and so must be used with greater care. In the primary classroom, let common sense prevail. They are useful tools but use them when teaching a light topic only if you are sure the beam will not be shone directly into children's eyes.

Reconstruction

Experiments that deal with the concept of travelling light require a room that can be blacked out, for instance, using thick dark curtains or blinds. Children can make a torch beam visible by sprinkling a little flour in the path of the beam. Teachers can show this more effectively by substituting the torch with a laser pointer, using appropriate safety precautions (see *Be safe!* Box above). Doing these activities, children begin to understand that light does not simply refer to how bright it is at a particular location, but it is something that moves from one place to another. Another example is how we are able to see a projector beam in a dusty cinema, and for a dramatic demonstration of the same principle ask children to shine a bright torch at home outside in a dark garden on a foggy or misty night. Drawings of torch beams are often over-emphasized in cartoons and animations, so these can serve as a reminder that light travels from a source to an illuminated object.

Light a candle in a dark classroom and ask the class to draw how far they think the light has travelled. Send some children into the dark corners of the room, then ask them if they can still see the candle. Explain that if they can, some of the light must still be reaching these dark areas because seeing the candle means its light has entered their eyes. If they draw a simple ray diagram of the candlelight and its penetration into dark corners, this will help reinforce the scientific concept. Also mention that if light did not travel very far from its source, we would be unable to see distant stars, which are billions of kilometres away from Earth.

Another approach known to be effective is to make a small hole with a sharpened pencil through a piece of card, then place the card close to a lit candle. Then place a second piece of card (without a hole) about 10 cm away from the first piece of card, so that light from the candle passes through the hole and produces an illuminated spot on the second piece of card. Asking children, *is there any light in between the two pieces of card?* will help them appreciate that firstly, that light travels from one place to another away from the source, and secondly, that light does not necessarily illuminate the space through which it travels. Introduce KS1 children to light by reading the story book *Oscar and the Moth* by Geoff Waring.

Sources: Driver *et al.* (1994); Fliegauf *et al.* (2022); Galili and Hazan (2000); Rodriguez and Castro (2016; 2020); Waring (2006).

16.2 How do we see things?

Misconception

We see things because light travels from our eyes towards an object.

Scientific conception

Children commonly draw light rays in a way that suggests they believe the reason we see things is because light travels outwards from our eyes and connects with the object – the *active eye model* (Figure 16.2a). In fact, the reverse is true. We see an object because the eye is able to absorb light rays travelling from the object; these light rays create electrical and chemical

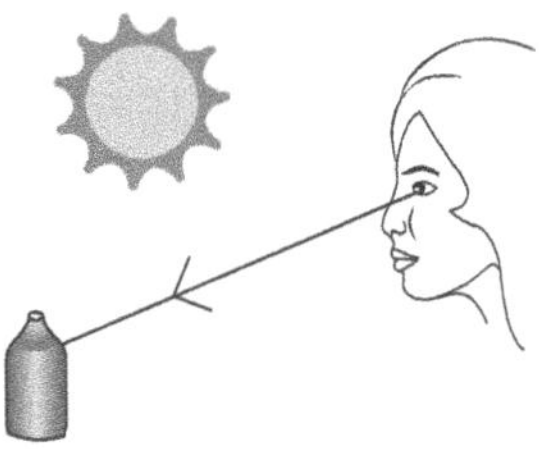

Figure 16.2a Light travels from eye to object (misconception)

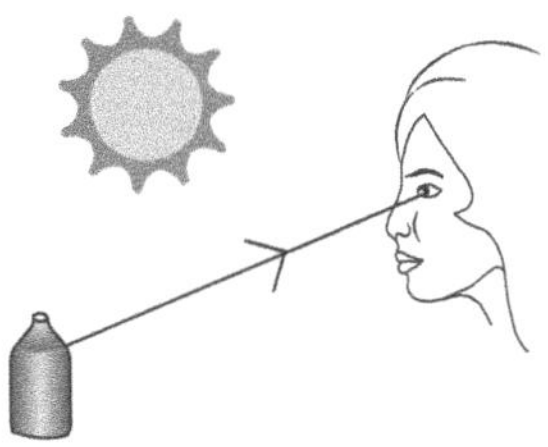

Figure 16.2b Light travels from object to eye

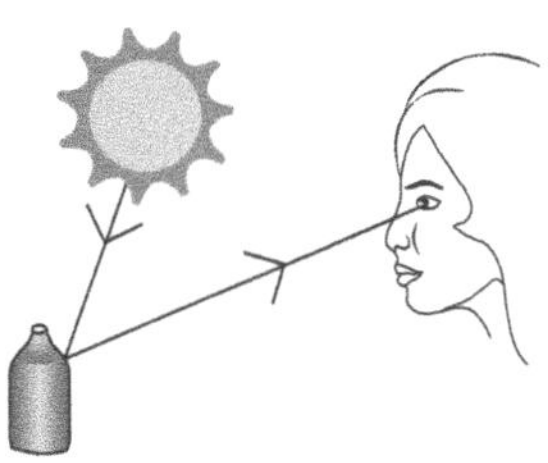

Figure 16.2c A light source illuminating an object makes it visible

signals within the eye that are sent to the brain. Therefore, the correct way to draw light rays is moving *away* from an object and *towards* the eye (Figure 16.2b).

However, this is only part of the story. We can only see an object when it is illuminated by a light source such as an electric bulb or the sun, since the object cannot generate light rays on its own (unless the object itself is a source). So there are two stages involved in this process: first, light travels from the source to the object, then light reflects off the object and into the eye (Figure 16.2c).

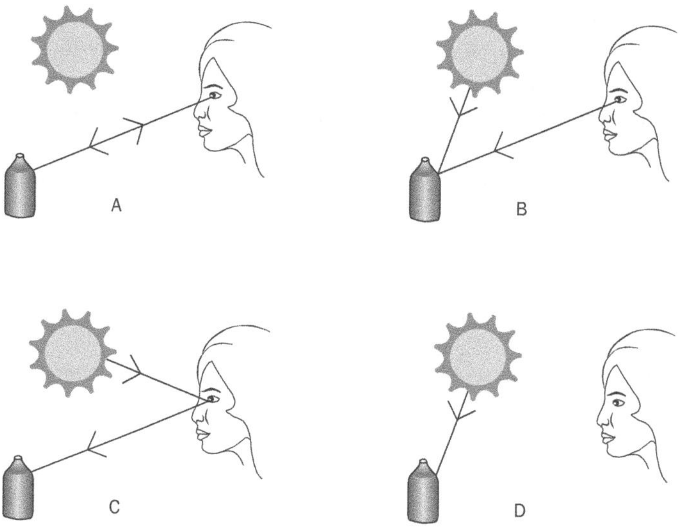

Figure 16.2d Four light misconceptions (see text for explanation)

There are several variations on the original misconception, each of which is discussed next and illustrated by the ray diagrams in Figure 16.2d:

Misconception A: Although the child correctly understands that light travels from object to eye, there are leftover elements of the original misconception resulting in a model of a light ray that continuously travels back and forth (*oscillating model*).

Misconception B: The way in which the sun has illuminated the object has been correctly drawn. However, the original misconception persists; the everyday expression *looking at things* may act as a trigger for this, possibly indicating the belief that we can only see things if we consciously look for them (see 17.1 for a similar misconception children have about sound).

Misconception C: The drawing might suggest that the child believes it is the eye that requires illumination in order to 'send' light rays towards the object and allow it to be seen (see Box p. 266).

Misconception D: Since the object is illuminated but no light then leaves the object towards the eye, this could be an example of the misconception that light is only present in bright areas (16.1).

Some children have problems with the idea that light can reflect off non-shiny surfaces, thinking that reflection only takes place with mirrors, **plane glass**, the surface of a pond, etc. There are also several misconceptions related to sources of light (16.3), including that no source is required in order to see an object, thus humans can (just about) see things in total darkness.[1] When drawing light rays from a source such as a candle directly to the eye, children may correctly draw the ray as in Figure 16.2b, but when drawing rays from a non-source, they may revert back to the original misconception (Figures 16.2a and 16.2e). Children can also have non-scientific ideas of how mirrors work, thinking that you can see your face simply because the mirror somehow reproduces an image of your face, and do not consider reflecting light rays.

I think . . .

Light and seeing. '*[When] the light is on our eyes we can read the words*' (10-year-old child; Osborne *et al.*, 1990, p. 23).

Reconstruction

The misconception that we can see things because light travels from our eyes towards objects is not helped by everyday expressions such as, '*I will look out for you around 4 o'clock*' or '*I was looking directly at her*'. Also, in cartoons when a character has spotted an object, the artist may draw an arrow from the eye to show what is being observed. Early in the topic, get children into the habit of including the light source in their ray diagrams. This will underline the idea that the reason why we can see something is that light *from* a source reflects *from* the object's surface and *into* our eyes. Children need to think of this journey being taken by one continuous ray of light from source to eye (via object), as shown in Figure 16.2c.

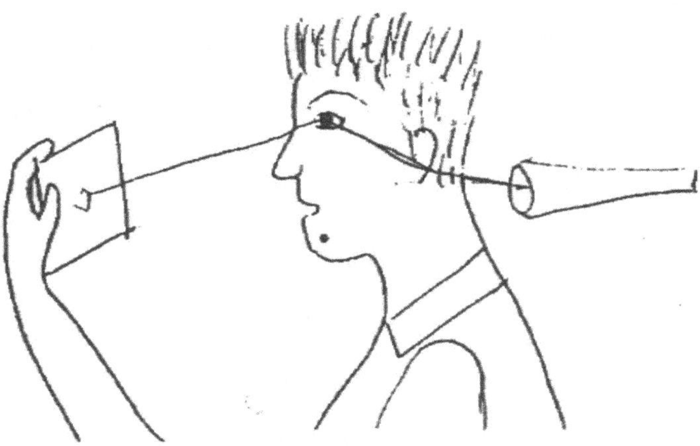

Figure 16.2e Child's drawing (aged 11 years) showing light entering the eye from a torch, and light travelling from the eye to an object (misconception variant C, Figure 16.2d)

Source: Osborne *et al.* (1990), p. 25.

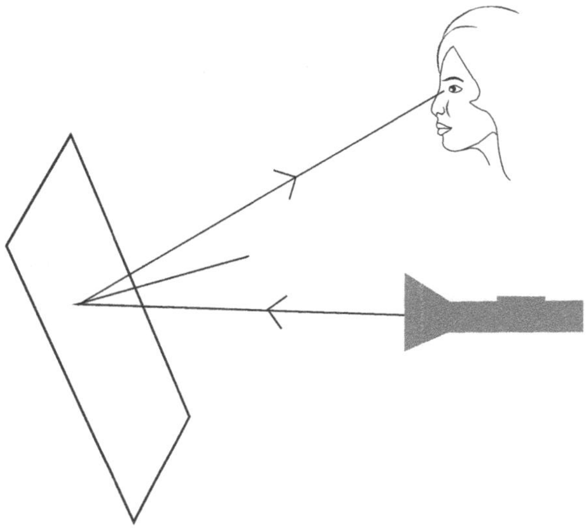

Figure 16.2f Using a torch and a mirror to help address the misconception

Research has shown that children can understand the scientific model more easily if the object is replaced by a mirror and they are asked to draw the journey of the light rays; use a torch or candle as the source, not the sun (Figure 16.2f).[2] The teacher can demonstrate more clearly if a laser pen is used as the source and the beam sprinkled with flour, but it is obviously important for safety reasons *not* to view the beam's reflection as shown in Figure 16.2f and instead to direct the beam towards a safe area of the room (see 16.1 for more on this technique).

KS1 children are capable of learning the differences between sources and non-sources of light. Ask children to draw and colour examples of things that can make their own light, and things that cannot. Optical illusions are fun ways to engage children of all ages when first introducing a light topic; they can be sourced from the internet, and for KS2 children, related to how the brain sometimes misinterprets what the eyes see. On a similar theme, children can make flip-books, which like animations, fool the brain by giving the false impression that objects are moving; without this capability to mentally construct a continual action scene, we would be unable to watch TV sets or films at the cinema.

Sources: Grigorovitch (2015); Osborne *et al.* (1990); Watts (1985).

16.3 Why does the moon shine?

Misconception

The moon is a source of light.

Scientific conception

In Year 3, children learn that objects such as a torch, fire, and the sun create their own light and are called *sources*. However, children sometimes over-generalize and can end up thinking a light source is anything that is bright or shines, such as a mirror, a glass window, a bicycle reflector, or the moon. These objects are not sources because they do not generate their own light: if no source were available to illuminate them, they would not be visible – they are instead good *reflectors* of light. The moon is a very bright object when viewed in the night sky because it is reflecting light from the sun and directing some of it down towards the Earth. The moon is therefore not a light source and if the sun were to suddenly stop shining, the moon would likewise fall into darkness.

There are other misconceptions that relate to light sources. Some children have difficulties understanding that dim light such as from glowing embers in a fire counts as a source. When asked to list sources of light, electrical devices such as light bulbs and street lights are more likely to be mentioned than natural sources such as the sun.

Reconstruction

Ask the class to investigate whether objects are light sources or not by looking at them while the room is in darkness; sources will appear brighter than they do in a normally lit room, and non-sources will be darker. A good way to elicit the misconception is to hold up a piece of reflective clothing in a dark room and shine a bright torch onto it – the reflective areas will glow very brightly – and ask children whether the clothing is a source of light. Switching the torch off will show that the clothing becomes dark; it is not making its own light so cannot be a source, it is merely an excellent reflector. Revising the idea of reflecting light using ray diagrams will remind children that light is able to bounce off objects and that materials that are shiny will reflect more light into our eyes than others that are dull. Using glow-in-the-dark toys can raise interesting questions because they are only temporary sources of light, and when they stop glowing, they become just reflectors.

Showing children pictures of the **phases of the moon** can help address the misconception, since if the moon were a light source like the sun, then parts of it would never be in shadow (18.7). Photographs of the Earth and other planets from space will demonstrate that all objects in the solar system shine to a certain degree because, like the moon, they reflect light from the sun. On the other hand, stars like the sun are sources of light; children experience feelings of awe, alongside development of their concept of deep time (see 11.6) when we tell them that many stars are so far away that the light that we see now, first left the star's surface when the dinosaurs were alive on Earth.

Sources: Ayvaci and Candaş (2018); Şahin *et al.* (2008).

16.4 Does light always travel in straight lines?

Misconception

Light does not travel in straight lines when it bounces off a mirror.

Scientific conception

A fundamental concept that underlies the teaching of light is that it always travels in a straight line. This helps explain phenomena such as shadows, reflections, and the **dispersion** of light to produce a **spectrum** (16.6). The misconception statement above is correct in the sense that light travels towards a mirror, hits its surface, then bounces away from the mirror in a different direction, and this is the reason why we can see objects in a mirror (see Figure 16.2f). However, throughout this journey the light rays are travelling in perfectly straight lines. When they hit the mirror surface, the path of the rays usually deviates, i.e. the rays leave the mirror at an angle – this is like how a snooker ball can be made to bounce off a cushion and change its direction of travel. Therefore, even though the mirror has changed the direction that the light was originally travelling in, during each stage of its journey the light still travels in perfectly straight lines.

Another version of the same misconception is the idea that a lens 'bends' light that passes through it as a result of **refraction**. Like a mirror, a lens *does* change a light ray's path but in between each change of direction, the light ray travels in straight lines. Something that does not help the situation is the fact that teachers commonly use the term 'bending light' when describing refraction, implying that light does not always take a straight path.

Although beyond KS2, one exception to this rule is when light travels through space and passes close to a very large mass such as a cluster of galaxies. The gravity of the cluster is so immense that it attracts light rays towards it, bending them slightly and making them take a curved path. This is called *gravitational lensing* and allows astronomers to 'see around corners' at what lies behind the galaxy cluster.

Reconstruction

The Year 6 Programme of Study requires children to understand that light travels in straight lines but, as already mentioned, practically all light concepts are underpinned by this assumption and so children will have encountered this fundamental idea earlier in their primary education. Provide children with everyday examples of light travelling in straight lines, including pictures of sunbeams shining through a forest, a projector beam in a dusty cinema, and science fiction films that show laser beams. To address the misconception that

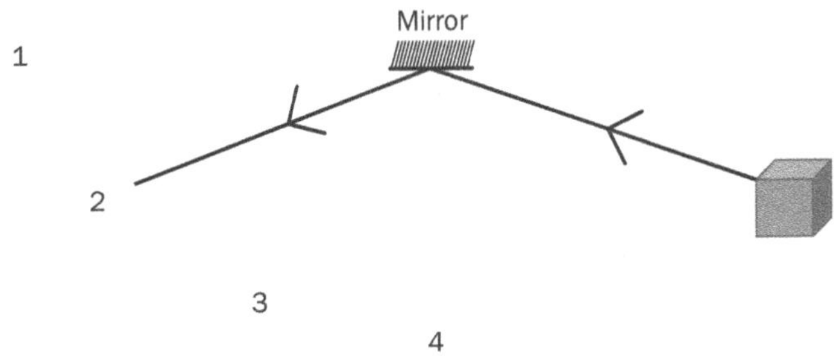

Figure 16.4 Where do you need to stand to see the box in the mirror?

mirrors cause light *not* to go in straight lines, show Figure 16.4 and ask where would you need to stand to see the box in the mirror, at position 1, 2, 3 or 4? This helps children understand that the angle the light ray hits the mirror (**angle of incidence**) is the same as the angle it leaves the mirror (**angle of reflection**) (also see Figure 16.2f).

There is a simple practical activity called *light snooker* where children can work out puzzles similar to Figure 16.4 by using a mirror and a light source such as a torch that can produce a very narrow beam of light. In a darkened room, make sure the torch is switched off and place it in front of the mirror, but off to one side (like the box in Figure 16.4). Children predict the path of the light ray after it reflects from the mirror by placing their finger on a spot where the ray will touch (position 1, 2, 3, or 4 in Figure 16.4). Turning the torch on will reveal if they have guessed correctly. Note that in Figure 16.4, a common misconception is to predict position 4 due to the belief that any light rays always reflect from a mirror at right angles. This activity can be extended by children drawing the light rays and then measuring the angles with a protractor to show the angles of incidence and reflection are equal. Watching a video clip of a game of real snooker or pool provides good analogies of the way that light reflects from all objects, including mirrors.

A simpler activity demonstrating the same principle involves throwing a bouncy rubber ball at the surface of a flat table, while asking a child to predict the direction it will bounce off by holding a small hoop, the aim being to get the ball to travel through the hoop. This can be extended by duct-taping a muffin tray to the table then throwing the ball at the tray, making it bounce off in unpredictable directions. Explain that the bare tabletop is like a smooth reflective surface such as mirror, where light predictably reflects off at the same angle as it hits, which allows us to see a clear image of our faces. However, the muffin tray is like an object with a rough surface, where the angles of reflection vary, so an image is never formed – this is an example of *scattering light* (which is beyond the primary science Programme of Study).

Children can make card periscopes using small plastic mirrors and then draw how the light rays travel to help them see around opaque barriers such as a wall (templates for periscopes are available free on the internet, e.g. www.webinnate.co.uk/science). KS1 children can be encouraged to think about how mirrors work by making kaleidoscopes (again, templates are available from the internet).

Sources: Ayvaci and Candaş (2018); Driver (1983); Shallcross (2017).

16.5 Where do shadows come from?

Misconception

My shadow is always there inside me and bright light can push it out.

Scientific conception

Primary children often hold non-scientific ideas about what shadows are and how they behave. In line with the misconception statement above, they sometimes believe that a shadow is a part of every object but cannot always be seen. They might even think that because a shadow belongs to an object, the shape of a shadow is always a perfect replica of the object itself. This 'Peter Pan' model of a shadow is not consistent with scientific concepts that explain the passage (**transmission**) of light through objects.

An object broadly falls into one of three categories depending on the amount of light that can pass (be transmitted) through it. A *transparent* object such as a clear pane of glass allows the passage of all light (or nearly all light), which is why we can clearly see things on the other side. A *translucent* object allows only the passage of some light, so when looking through frosted glass, things appear undefined and lack detail. An *opaque* object does not allow any light to be transmitted. Because opaque objects block light completely, there is an area behind the object where no light is present – this area does not contain light so appears black to us – a shadow (Figure 16.5). Translucent objects can also cast shadows but because they allow some light to be transmitted, these shadows are hazy with no sharply defined edges, and they are never completely black. Note that although Figure 16.5 shows an opaque cube absorbing the central light ray, this is not a completely true representation, as some light will be absorbed and some will be reflected from the cube (see 16.6).

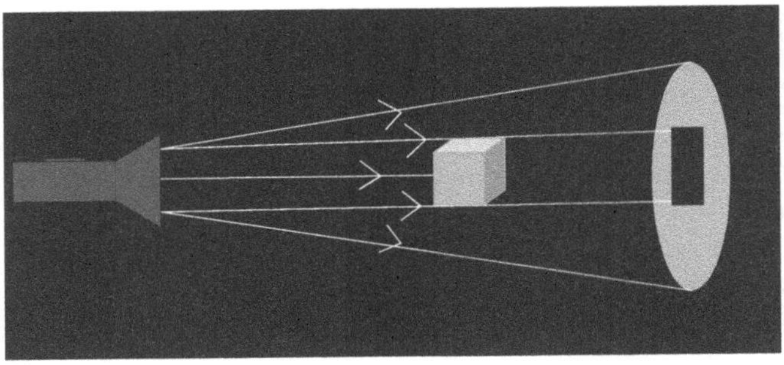

Figure 16.5 Shadows are formed when opaque objects block light

Linked to the idea that a shadow belongs to an object, is the confusion some children experience regarding the concepts of 'reflection' and 'shadow'. They will sometimes say 'shadows are reflections', meaning that an object's shadow is an accurate representation of that object, similar to an image that can be seen in a mirror. Children frequently draw shadows as mirror images complete with details included within the shadow itself; for instance, when drawing a person's shadow they include facial features, details of clothing, etc. (see Box p. 272).

Other misconceptions about shadows include the brighter the light source, the taller the shadow, and shadows only appear in the presence of bright light. Although children are usually correct when predicting where their own shadow would be in relation to a light source such as the sun, they are less successful when attempting similar predictions with the shadows of other objects. When coloured light is shone onto an object, some children will predict that the shadow will be the same colour as the illuminating light (the shadow will be black).

I think . . .

Shadows and reflections. *'I think a shadow is a reflection from the sun. Sometimes when you look in a pond you see a reflection. When you go somewhere where it can reflect, you see your shadow'* (child [age unknown], Guest, 2003, p. 15).

Reconstruction

Shadows are covered in Years 3 and 6 as part of the *Light* topics. Children are required to understand that shadows are created when a light source is blocked, and carry out experiments that investigate which factors can change the size, shape, sharpness, etc. of shadows. As discussed, if children are asked to draw their own shadows, some include details within the shadows such as faces, and these ideas can be easily challenged by examining real shadows, ideally outside in the playground on a sunny day.

Misconceptions relating to shadows' size, shape, etc. can be tested using traditional investigations that will be familiar to primary teachers where the distances between a light source, object, and screen are systematically changed to see how the shadow changes. Making shadow puppets is a fun exercise for younger children and can lead to discussion about the nature of shadows, so helping them construct simple though scientifically acceptable ideas at a young age, such as which kinds of objects block light to cast a shadow, and which do not. Also, on a sunny day in the playground, in pairs children can draw around their partner's shadow using chalk and then compare the shape and size of their shadow with those of others in the class.

The concept of translucency can be developed by asking children to bring sunglasses to school and discovering how much light is able to pass through them (Box p. 273). Use a freely available tablet app that can measure light intensity and test how effective different sunglasses are using a torch as the source, or natural sunlight from the window. Children's thinking can be extended by discussing the fact that despite sunglasses being able to stop the transmission of some visible light, this experiment does not test their ability to stop ultraviolet light, which can be damaging to eyesight.

Children tend to be able to understand transparency and opacity (probably because they are opposites) better than translucency. A handy comparison is to show two A4 plastic punched pockets, one transparent type and another frosted type, to demonstrate the difference between transparency and translucency. Shining a laser pen through the transparent A4 pocket will allow the beam to pass through nearly unchanged, while with the frosted example the beam is scattered and so no longer visible.

Sources: Galili and Hazan (2000); Grigorovitch and Nertivich (2017); Guest (2003); Watts and Gilbert (1985).

Learning technologies

Dataloggers. In the 1990s, UK educational institutions underwent an IT revolution that saw powerful personal computers introduced into primary schools. Initially, their use was limited to word processing in English lessons and working with spreadsheets in mathematics. However, the potential usefulness of PCs as aids to practical work during science lessons was quickly realized and companies started to manufacture electronic apparatus that was capable of generating experimental data.

These *dataloggers* connected to a PC and were able to carry out a variety of tasks including measuring light intensity, sound intensity, temperature, heart rate (see 3.4), the speed of a toy car, and how quickly an object was falling after it had been dropped. The data were processed by the PC and displayed on the monitor as a results table that children could print off. The use of dataloggers in primary schools became popular as children enjoyed using the new technology that took some of the tedium out of data collecting and also helped reduce experimental error to give them more valid results. Dataloggers are still available today and have increased in sophistication from the early models. Modern versions can be disconnected from the PC and used remotely, even taken outside to measure the temperature at different habitats around the school grounds, for instance. One type of datalogger has a motion capture camera that can be set up overnight to photograph wildlife that visit the school during the hours of darkness. The disadvantage of dataloggers has always been their cost; the price of a complete set typically runs into hundreds of pounds. With some datalogger sets, manufacturers recommend that a representative comes into school to train staff in their use, although others are more user-friendly and easier to operate. Although dataloggers are well worth the initial outlay, cheaper alternatives exist that allow children to collect data using electronic devices. There are many free apps available for tablets and mobile phones that are capable of, for instance, measuring light and sound intensity, temperature, and speed. A common activity during a light topic is to ask children to bring sunglasses to school and use a light sensor to measure how effective they are at blocking sunlight (see 16.5). Note, however, that they rely on the tablet's or phone's inbuilt sensors, which are rather basic compared with those found in dataloggers, so data will be less accurate and reliable.

16.6 Why do we see the colours of the rainbow when light passes through a prism?

Misconception

White light is pure; coloured light is white light with impurities in it.

Scientific conception

We depend on sunlight and electric lighting to provide illumination so that we can operate normally in our everyday lives. These sources produce **white light**, and what might not be immediately obvious is that white light consists of

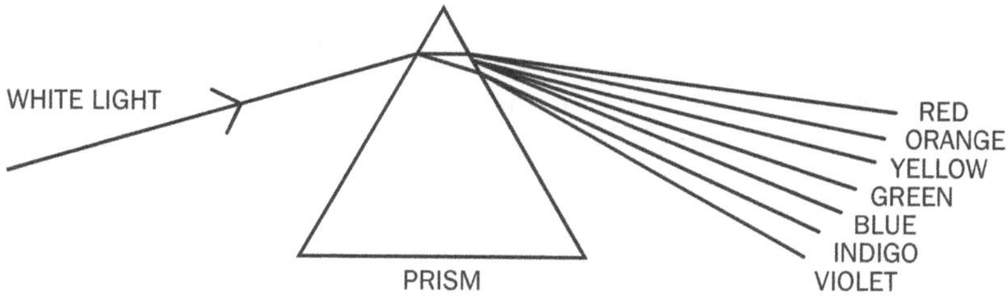

Figure 16.6a Using a prism to disperse white light into its constituent colours

several types of different coloured light mixed together. These different colours can be seen by using a prism to split white light into its constituent parts; this is called dispersion (Figure 16.6a). These colours are the visible spectrum and this method of splitting light was first described by Sir Isaac Newton in 1671. Newton noted that there were seven distinct colours in the spectrum (which can be remembered by the acronym ROYGBIV), although it is debatable whether indigo and violet can truly be differentiated from one another. Rainbows are spectra produced when there is rain in the air and tiny water droplets act like individual prisms to reflect and disperse white light, creating a bow-shaped image in the sky.

The human eye contains light-sensitive cells within the **retina** that can detect colour. These cells are called *cones* and there are three different types: red, green, and blue: red cones detect only red light, green cones only green light, and blue cones only blue light. There are no cones that detect other colours such as pink or brown, and for this reason red, green, and blue are termed the three **primary colours**. Objects that we see around us have a particular colour for two reasons; first, it depends on which colour light they absorb and, second, it depends on the colour of light that the object is illuminated with. Looking at the examples in Figure 16.6b that have been illuminated with white light, if we see a white cube, then the object must have reflected all the white light back towards our eyes, and absorbed no light (Figure 16.6b (i)). If a different cube appears red, then it has reflected red light towards our eyes, but where have the green light and the blue light gone that were within the original white sunlight? The cube must have absorbed the green and blue light, and reflected only red (Figure 16.6b (ii)). When objects appear black, no light is reflected towards the eyes, so the cube must have absorbed all the white sunlight (i.e. red, green, and blue) and reflected no light at all – when we perceive black, this means the absence of any reflected light (Figure 16.6b (iv)). These phenomena can be linked to everyday experience for instance, in summer, white clothing feels cooler because it reflects all visible sunlight, whereas black clothing feels warmer because it absorbs all sunlight.

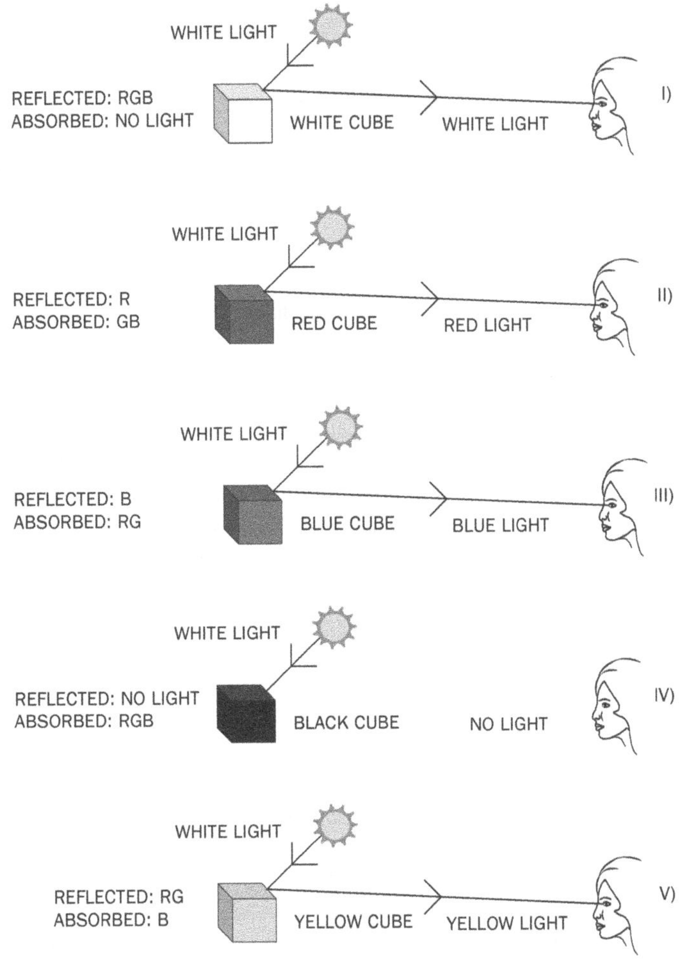

Figure 16.6b Why objects appear as a particular colour

Of course, we are also capable of perceiving a wide range of colours other than simply red, green, and blue. Figure 16.6c shows that when light of the primary colours is mixed, **secondary colours** can be made: these are yellow, magenta (purple), and cyan (turquoise). For example, red and green light mix to produce yellow light, so a daffodil flower appears yellow because it is reflecting both red and green light (see Figure 16.6b (v)). We see other hues apart from the primary and secondary colours because different coloured light mixes in different proportions. If mixed light is 90% red and 10% green, this would appear more orange than yellow. Note that in the art world, the primary colours are traditionally red, blue, and yellow. These are different to the scientific primary colours because they are concerned with the mixing of paints on a palette, which produce different colours to when beams of light are mixed.

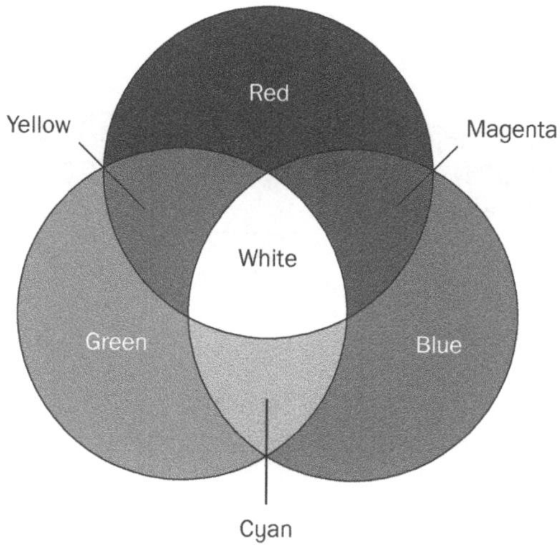

Figure 16.6c Mixing the primary colours of light

Other colour misconceptions include the belief that when light of different colours is mixed, a darker light is always produced, and that when an object is illuminated with coloured light, the light adds its own colour to the object, or the light stops certain colours within the object from escaping (instead of the object reflecting and absorbing different colours). Younger children whose experiences involve only white light produced by everyday sources such as electric lighting in the home, and the sun, may think that light has only one colour.

Reconstruction

Colour theory is beyond the primary curriculum and children in Year 6 are required only to experience simple phenomena such as rainbows and the colours of soap bubbles, and practise using prisms to disperse white light. This usually includes teaching the idea that white light is a mixture of many colours, and children can be extended by mixing light beams of different colours themselves using coloured cellophane stretched over torches. To be effective, though, these activities require reasonably powerful torches and a darkened room.

When dispersing light using a prism, it is tricky to achieve the correct angle for a spectrum to appear and readers are referred to Figure 16.6a as a rough guide – the incoming beam should just clip one corner of the prism, and place an A4 white card screen where you expect the spectrum to appear. Once a spectrum is produced, a second prism can be introduced close to the spectrum beam that will recombine it back into white light again, so reinforcing the idea that white light is a mixture. To demonstrate the same principle, children will enjoy constructing a coloured card spinner with a small pencil pushed through the centre; when it is spun, the colours merge and the whole spinner appears white – this is Newton's disc (Figure 16.6d).[3]

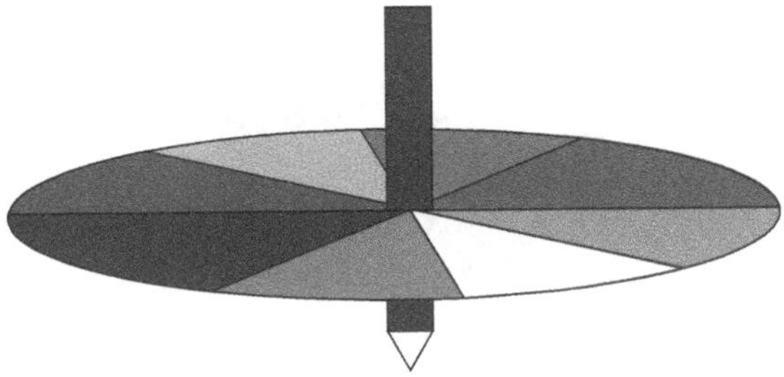

Figure 16.6d Newton's disc spinner

Simple spectra can be produced by using a CD and holding a torch just above its shiny surface at a slight angle, then placing a white card screen also above the surface to catch the spectrum. Even simpler, if children peer through a prism directly at a light source such as an overhead light or table lamp (never the sun), an attractive spectrum can be seen with the prism held close to the eye. Finally, a laser pen is a powerful source of light that teachers can use with care to demonstrate reflection and absorption of light due to colour. When shone onto white card, the laser light looks very bright as close to 100% of the light is reflected, while on black card there is practically no reflected beam due to the near total absorption of light.

Sources: Feher and Meyer (1992); Galili and Hazan (2000); Guesne (1985); Martinez-Borreguero *et al.* (2013).

Famous scientists

Sir Isaac Newton. It could be argued that Newton (1642–1727) was the most prolific and versatile scientist in Western history. He is renowned for formulating many different laws and theories about the physical world that explain the phenomena of light, sound, gravity, planetary motion, and mechanics. Many of his ideas are still accepted by scientists today. He is, however, less well known for his achievements in the field of mathematics, which include the development of modern calculus.

Notes

1 One study found that this misconception was more common with city children who, because of environmental light pollution, had little experience of total darkness; with a sample of rural children this misconception was less common.
2 Note that the angle of incidence is equal to the angle of reflection (see 16.4).
3 Carry out an internet search to help determine the colours of the disc using the search terms 'Newton's disc' or 'Newton's spinner'.

Planning and assessment sheet 16 Light

(For suggestions on how to use this sheet, see p. xxviii.)

Misconception	*Attainment re. expected standard*		
	Working towards	*Working at*	*Working above*
Year 3: *Light*			
Light is only found in bright areas (general illumination misconception) (16.1)	✓	✓	
If a person is standing in a shadow, they cannot see any light (16.1)	✓	✓	
Light is a material-like substance given out by a candle which sticks to nearby objects, illuminating them, and travels no further (16.1)	✓		
Light does not travel at night – this is why it becomes dark (16.1)	✓		
Light travels further at night, which explains how during daytime, artificial sources such as car headlights and torches are more difficult to see (16.1)	✓	✓	
My shadow is always there inside me and bright light can push it out (16.5)	✓		
The shape of a shadow is always a perfect replica of the object itself (16.5)	✓		
Shadows are reflections, i.e. an object's shadow is an accurate representation of that object, like an image that can be seen in a mirror; when children draw shadows they include details such as facial features, buttons on clothing, etc. (16.5)	✓		
The brighter the light source, the taller the shadow (16.5)	✓	✓	
Shadows only appear in the presence of bright light (16.5)	✓		
When coloured light is shone on an object, the shadow will be the same colour as the illuminating light (16.5)	✓	✓	
Year 6: *Light*			
We see things because light travels *from* our eyes *towards* an object (active eye misconception) (16.2)	✓	✓	
A light ray continuously travels back-and forth-between the object and our eyes (oscillating misconception) (16.2)	✓	✓	

(continued)

(continued)

A light ray travels from a source to illuminate an object (correct), and we see the object because a different light ray travels *from* our eyes *towards* the object (misconception) (16.2)	✓	✓	
A light ray travels from a source into our eye, then *from* our eye *towards* the object (16.2)	✓	✓	
A light ray travels from a source to illuminate an object, then no further (general illumination misconception) (16.2)	✓		
Light can only reflect off shiny surfaces (e.g. mirror, metal spoon, the surface of a pond) (16.2)	✓	✓	✓
Humans can see things in total darkness (because a source is not required to see an object) (16.2)	✓	✓	
Light rays travel from a source into our eyes which allows us to see the source, but no light rays are involved when we see things that are not sources (16.2)	✓		
You see your face in a mirror because the mirror reproduces an image of your face (reflecting light rays are not considered) (16.2)	✓		
The moon is a source of light (16.3)	✓	✓	
Dim light, such as from glowing embers in a fire, is not considered a true source (16.3)	✓		
When listing sources of light, electrical devices such as light bulbs and streetlights are mentioned in preference to natural sources such as the sun (16.3)	✓		
Light does not travel in straight lines when it bounces off a mirror (16.4)	✓	✓	
Light does not travel through a lens in straight lines, because the lens bends the light as it passes through (16.4)		✓	
Light has only ever one colour – white (16.6)	✓		
White light is pure; coloured light is white light with impurities in it (16.6)		✓	✓
When light of different colours is mixed, a darker light is always produced (16.6)	✓	✓	
When an object is illuminated with coloured light, the light adds its own colour to the object, or the light stops certain colours within the object from escaping (instead of the object reflecting and absorbing different colours) (16.6)		✓	

17

Sound

Conceptual areas covered in this chapter:

- Sound as a travelling wave
- A source needs to vibrate to create a sound
- Transmission of sound through different materials
- Pitch of sound and frequency of sound waves

National Curriculum links:

Year 4: *Sound*

17.1 How does sound travel?

Misconception

For a sound to be heard, the listener must concentrate on it first.

Scientific conception

Some primary children have a concept of sound that is quite different from the scientific model. They correctly understand that a sound such as a ringing telephone has a source but believe that the sound itself is only present inside their ears, and do not appreciate that sound is a wave that travels from one place to another. Children who do think of sound as travelling between the source and a listener often believe that the person doing the listening needs to be consciously focusing on the sound before it can be heard – this is the *active listener model* (Box p. 282). If no listener is present, then there is no sound to be heard, and some children can even think that if a sound is being made by a person playing a musical instrument, the player themselves cannot hear it unless they actively concentrate on the sound they are producing. This misconception has parallels with a philosophical riddle: if a lonely tree falls in the forest with no one around, does it make a sound? The scientific answer to this mystery is, yes, it would still generate a sound wave that travels outwards from the source and is capable of being heard.

I think . . .

Active listener. *'The noise goes through the air to people who are listening. If they're not listening, they'll only hear a bit of it...'* (7-year-old child; Watt and Russell, 1990, p. 16).

The misconception is like the idea that we must actively look at something with our eyes in order to see it, as when children draw ray diagrams that show light travelling *away* from the eye towards the object being viewed (16.2). Young children in particular tend to draw sound waves travelling *from* listener to source, and the everyday phrase *listening to* suggests that people need to be actively and consciously involved before they hear a sound. Another indication of the active listener misconception is drawing sound as travelling only from the source directly to the listener and nowhere else (Figure 17.1); drawn correctly, the wave should be shown as travelling in all directions from the source, like ripples in a pond. Some young children, however, are capable of constructing scientific models of how sound travels (Box p. 283). Related misconceptions include the idea that sounds never travel very far from their source because they always 'die out' over distance, and that whenever a sound from a single source is heard, all other sounds in the environment are lost.

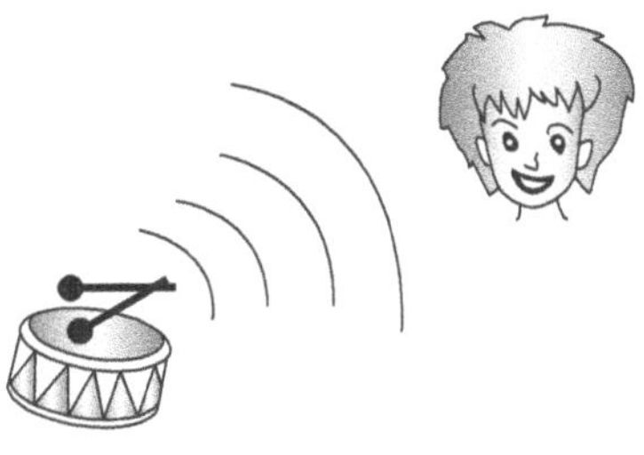

Figure 17.1 Sound travels only to people who are listening (misconception)

Reconstruction

Elicit the misconception by asking the class to draw a picture that shows the journey of a sound. Also pose the question, *if everybody leaves the room, will a ticking clock – or a ringing mobile phone – still be making a sound?* Test the idea by audio-recording the sound with the room empty of people.

The misconception that conscious listening is required for a sound to be heard can be challenged by surprising the class with an unexpected noise such as a tinkling bell while they are working quietly. As the bell gets their attention, explain that even though no one was 'ready' for the sound, they were able to hear it anyway. Therefore, sound will reach them even if they are not concentrating on the source. Extend children's thinking by introducing the concept of sound as a travelling wave by demonstrating echoes in a suitable location in the school grounds – a large open area just in front of a flat, tall wall is ideal, and a school whistle will make a suitable brief, sharp note. This will also address the misconception that sound waves cannot reflect off objects, e.g. are just 'absorbed' by a listener.

Take KS1 children around the school on a 'listening walk'. Back in the classroom after the walk, ask them to list as many sounds as they can remember, try to name the source of each sound, then describe the sound itself: whether it was loud, pleasant, high **pitched**, etc. The story book *Oscar and the Bat* by Geoff Waring, and Roger McGough's poem *The Sound Collector*, provide a good introduction to basic sound concepts.

I think . . .

Correct model of sound perception. '*In the playground it gets to you because you listen ... it would get to you if you didn't listen because your ears don't stop listening. They're listening all the time even at night. You hear them with your ears*' (7-year-old child explaining how we hear a sound; Watt and Russell, 1990, p. 29).

Sources: Batlolona and Jamaludin (2024); McGough (2005); Sarioğlan (2016); Waring (2007); Watt and Russell (1990).

17.2 Can sound waves be stopped?

Misconception

Sound cannot pass through a solid material.

Scientific conception

This belief seems to contradict common experiences such as sitting inside a classroom and being able to hear noises from outside in the playground. Children can rationalize this by arguing that even if windows and doors are closed, sound is able to seep into the room through tiny unseen gaps. They believe that if they sat in an airtight box, they would be completely insulated from sounds on the outside.

When a sound wave hits a barrier such as a glass window, some of the sound does not pass into a room because it is either reflected off the surface of the window or absorbed into the glass. However, a good deal of the sound is able to enter the glass material and come out of the other side, entering the room. In fact, sound travels quite well through solids such as glass and wood, which enables us to can hear sounds from outside while in a room with all the windows and doors sealed. Therefore, a person in an airtight box would still be able to hear sounds from the outside providing the walls of the box were not too thick, e.g. 1 metre of concrete (although tapping directly on thick concrete from the outside would transmit sound through to the inside). 'Soundproofing' a house involves removing most of the energy from incoming sound waves by building barriers that absorb the sound as much as possible, such as placing lead metal or foam into wall cavities, and using double or triple glazing.

A related misconception is that muffling a sound such as a ringing mobile phone tightly with a pillow makes the sound wave slow down as it travels from the pillow, through the air to our ears, which quietens the sound. In this case, the speed of transmission through the air would be the same as its speed without muffling, although the energy of the sound wave would be reduced, which is why the sound is quieter. Because sound needs a medium to travel in (solid, liquid, or gas), a sound wave can never pass through a vacuum. Science fiction films that show loud explosions in space are therefore scientifically incorrect. The misconception that sound can be heard through a window only because it seeps through gaps can be linked to a view of sound itself being a material thing that cannot pass through solid objects.

Reconstruction

A simple practical activity to help address the misconception involves a box such as a Tupperware container, which you can prove to the class is airtight by submerging it in a bowl of water. Put the bowl and the water aside and place a mobile phone inside the Tupperware container, seal it, then make it ring – many children will be surprised at how loud the sound is. This can be developed into an investigation where layers are added to the outside of the container to determine how well different materials can muffle sound. The loudness of a sound can be measured using free apps for tablets or mobile phones, or science dataloggers (see Chapter 16, Box p. 274).

Another way to demonstrate that sound can travel quite easily through solid materials is to use a string telephone made from two plastic cups and a piece of taut string, although some children may argue that the sound does not pass through the solid string, but through the hole in the cup and then to their ear. An activity that addresses this same issue is scratching on a desk while holding your ear flat against its surface – the scratching will be much louder when heard through the desk than when heard normally as the wave travels through the air. If your school has metal railings, tapping them with a hammer will produce sound waves inside the railings that travel surprising distances, which can be heard by pressing your ear against the railings; distance travelled by the sound wave can be measured by positioning children at different points along the railings away from the source of the tapping. Link this to anecdotes of people who have been lost in the desert sending out Morse code messages over long distances by banging on a metal pipeline. A similar experiment can be carried out inside the school using heating pipes or radiators that link two classrooms (taking care to ensure they are not hot), mimicking a method of secret communication supposedly used by occupants of prison cells. Further anecdotal examples include North American Indians listening for approaching horses by putting their ears to the ground, and the Western outlaw Jesse James using metal rail tracks to listen for an approaching train, both of which show that sound tends to travel further through solid material than through the air.

Explain that sound can travel in water too. Whales and dolphins can communicate over long distances across the ocean; recordings of these haunting calls can be sourced from the internet. A good demonstration of this is for children to put their head underwater in a swimming pool and then drop a coin – the sound as it hits the bottom is quite loud and sharp, showing that sound waves travel very well through water.

Sources: Asoko *et al.* (1991); Eshach *et al.* (2018).

17.3 Where do sounds come from?

Misconception

A sound is resting inside a musical instrument waiting to be let out when people play it.

Scientific conception

Although they may understand that sound is something that travels away from its source to other places, children can find it difficult to explain how the sound is generated at the source in the first place. They can rationalize that a source is a 'sound container' that always has sound stored inside it, waiting for someone to come along and release the sound, such as when beating a drum, strumming a guitar, or blowing into a recorder.

For a sound to be generated, an object must vibrate. When a drum is hit, this causes the skin to move up and down very quickly (i.e. vibrate); typically, a drum skin vibrates 100 times per second – this is the **frequency** of the sound. However, vibrations do not just happen at the drum. A layer of air just above the drum also starts to vibrate 'in tune' with the drum skin, at 100 times a second, and these new vibrations then spread out through the air away from the drum to create a sound wave (the wave travels at about 330 metres per second, the speed of sound). When the sound wave reaches a person, there is a thin flap of skin inside the ear called the eardrum which reacts to the vibrating air by expanding inwards and outwards. This vibration is passed on via tiny bones and fluid-filled tubes housed within the skull before being converted into electrical signals that are sent to the brain – it is then that the person becomes conscious that a sound has been made. Therefore, a musical instrument cannot store sound inside it; before the instrument vibrates, no sound exists.

Children sometimes get cause and effect mixed up when they think about how sounds are generated; for example, they imagine that when a guitar string vibrates, the sound has made the string vibrate instead of the other way around (reverse causality bias). A drum vibrating at 100 times per second makes quite a low-pitched sound and other sources vibrate at different speeds. When a small bell tinkles, a high-pitched sound is made that vibrates very quickly, typically 2000 times per second. When children use the phrases 'high note' and 'low note', they may not be referring to the pitch of the sounds, but instead think that the former is a loud noise, and the latter a quiet noise. This is not surprising, since we employ this meaning when we ask the class to 'whisper in a low voice' or 'keep the noise down'.

Reconstruction

Allowing children to play with a variety of musical instruments and then naming the part of the instrument that is making the sound helps develop a conceptual link between vibration and sound generation. These could include toy guitars (vibrating strings), xylophones (bars), recorders (column of air), cymbals (metal body), and bells (metal body of the bell itself, not the clapper/clanger inside). Young children may be stuck on the idea that the sound is simply being produced by the person and not the instrument, so it will need to be explained that a sound can only be generated when something vibrates. If a person playing a guitar, for example, is not vibrating, something else must be – the player makes the strings vibrate, and it is they that produce the sound. Also show how sounds can be generated when everyday objects vibrate, e.g. plucking an elastic band, or holding a ruler on the edge of a desk and 'twanging' it. A vibrating tuning fork touching the surface of a cup of water produces a surprisingly powerful splash. With these examples, the source of the sound is quite clear as the material visibly vibrates. Other ways of demonstrating vibrations are to place rice on the skin of a drum and then beat it, putting your hand on an inflated party balloon and talking close to the balloon, and feeling your larynx as you vocalize high-pitched then low-pitched noises (the larynx moves up and down as you go from low to high, and back again). The reverse can be demonstrated by simply plucking a guitar string then placing your finger on the vibrating string to make the sound immediately stop. Although sound is a part of the Year 4 POS, KS1 children can make home-made guitars using elastic bands and a shoe box, which will help them think how a vibrating source links to a sound they can hear. 'Brian Cox School Experiments' are Royal Society webpages that include suggestions of how to make musical instruments at home.

Children can think about the pitch of sounds by playing the game *higher or lower.* The teacher plays a bar on a xylophone or glockenspiel and then a second, different bar. The class have to guess whether the second bar is at a higher or lower pitch than the first, which will encourage them to use these terms correctly when talking about the pitch of sounds instead of using them to describe how loud or quiet a sound is.

An interesting puzzle to set children involves three identical glass bottles with different amounts of water in each. If you hit the bottles with a rubber beater, the bottle with the most water will make the lowest pitched sound. However, if you blow across the top of the bottles to make a whistling sound, the opposite is true – the bottle with the most water now produces the highest pitched sound. This happens because as the mass of a vibrating source increases, slower vibrations are created. When you hit the bottles with a rubber beater, you are vibrating the glass bottle itself plus the water inside, so bottles with more water will have the bigger mass and vibrate more slowly, producing lower pitched sounds. But when you blow across the top of the bottles, what vibrates is the air inside the bottle that sits above the water. So with the bottle that contains the most water, the mass of this column of air is less and the sound will be of a higher pitch. Although this may be conceptually challenging for many KS1 children, they can still make sounds of different pitch using a set of identical bottles containing different quantities of water. Blowing across the mouth of the bottles produces a variety of musical notes and the class could cooperate to become an orchestra, playing simple tunes such as *Frère Jacques.* If children cannot blow hard enough to produce a note, they can use a bicycle pump or a party balloon pump instead.

With KS2 children, introduce the idea that humans cannot hear every pitch of sound, only frequencies within the range of about 20 to 20,000 vibrations per second. Other animals can hear much higher frequencies; for instance, dogs can hear sounds of up to 60,000 vibrations per second. There are websites you can visit that produce high pitched sounds that test the upper frequency limit of what we can hear (the *Times Educational Supplement* website has useful links: https://www.tes.com/teaching-resources). What children are able to hear is highly dependent on age, with younger children better able to hear the higher frequencies.

Upper KS2 children can investigate *which is the crunchiest biscuit?* Have packets of several biscuit types available for children to find out which makes the loudest sound when they break each biscuit. They can use free tablet or mobile phone apps such as *Decibel X* to measure the loudness of each crunch. Independent variables include biscuit type, method of breaking (by hand or by biting), biscuit shape, and biscuit size (home-bake the same biscuit in different shapes and sizes). With younger children, the dependent variable of measured loudness of sound could be replaced by subjectively judging each crunch, e.g. giving it a mark out of 10.

Did you know?

Elephants can 'hear' through their feet. Humans cannot hear sounds that vibrate less than about 20 times per second, but elephants are capable of hearing very low frequencies, down to 5 vibrations per second. Sounds below the level of human perception are in the **infrasound** range (and those above, in the **ultrasound** range). Elephants can 'talk' to each other in the infrasound range by making very low-pitched rumbling noises that humans are unaware of. As well as using their ears to pick up these sounds as they travel through the air, elephants can also feel them in their feet as the sound waves move through the ground. The waves move up from the feet through the elephant's leg bones to their skull and are eventually detected in the ears. Since sound travels further through solids than through air, this means that elephants can communicate over long distances, up to 10 kilometres (see 17.2).

Sources: Asoko *et al.* (1991); Linfield and Ireland (2022); Poole (2021); Royal Society (2024); Sarioğlan (2016).

Planning and assessment sheet 17 Sound

(For suggestions on how to use this sheet, see p. xxviii.)

Misconception	*Attainment re. expected standard*		
	Working towards	*Working at*	*Working above*
Year 4: *Sound*			
Before a sound can be heard, the listener must be consciously focusing on it first (active listener misconception) (17.1)	✓		
If a person plays a musical instrument, they cannot hear it unless they actively concentrate on the sound they are producing (active listener misconception) (17.1)	✓		
Sound is only present inside the ears (i.e. not a wave that travels from one place to another) (17.1)	✓		
Sound waves travel *from* the listener *to* the source (17.1)	✓		
Sound waves travel only *from* the source directly *to* the listener and nowhere else (sound waves actually spread out from a source in all directions) (17.1)	✓	✓	
Sounds never travel very far from their source because they always 'die out' (17.1)	✓	✓	
Whenever a sound from a single source is heard by a person, they cannot hear any other sounds (17.1)	✓		
Sound waves cannot reflect off objects, they are just 'absorbed' by a listener (17.1)	✓		
Sound cannot pass through a solid material (17.2)	✓	✓	
Sound can be heard through a closed window only because it seeps through invisible gaps (17.2)	✓	✓	
With quiet sounds, the sound wave travels more slowly (17.2)	✓	✓	
Muffling the sound of a ringing mobile phone with a pillow makes the sound wave slow down, as it travels from the pillow through the air to our ears, which quietens the sound (17.2)	✓	✓	

(continued)

(*continued*)

You would be able to hear loud explosions in space (common in science fiction films) (17.2)	✓	✓	✓
A sound is resting inside a musical instrument waiting to be let out when people play it (17.3)	✓		
When a guitar string vibrates, the sound has made the string vibrate (instead of vice versa – reverse causality bias) (17.3)	✓		
When a musical instrument is played, the sound is being produced by the person and not the instrument (i.e. some part of the person is vibrating) (17.3)	✓		
A 'high' note is a loud noise, and a 'low' note a quiet noise (i.e. not relating these terms to the pitch of the sound) (17.3)	✓	✓	

18

Earth and space

Conceptual areas covered in this chapter:

- The solar system and wider universe
- Day and night
- Comparative sizes of the Earth, sun and moon
- The moon's phases
- The seasons

National Curriculum links:

Year 1: *Seasonal changes*

Year 5: *Earth and space; Forces*

18.1 Flat Earth

Misconception

The Earth is flat.

Scientific conception

There are several different versions of the flat Earth misconception, five of which are presented here, starting with the simplest idea of a completely flat Earth and ending with the most 'scientific' of them (although still essentially a flat Earth construct).

1 *We live on a flat planet that has never-ending sides and bottom* (Figure 18.1a). This simple model of the Earth is based on everyday impressions that tell us that the surface of our planet must be flat, and the Earth is an

infinitely long, horizontal object. With this construction there is no end to the Earth underground below our feet, sideways, or above our heads until it meets the sky. A related misconception is that space starts at the Earth's flat surface and continues above our heads, upwards and outwards for infinity.

2 *We live on a flat, cylindrical planet where the bottom is never-ending* (Figure 18.1b). Children who have heard that the Earth is round may think of it as a cylinder, which is a cross between a flat Earth and a more scientific construction. To these children the surface of the Earth is flat, although its sides are not infinite as in model 1 – instead there are boundaries. However, beneath our feet the bottom of the cylinder-Earth is never-ending, or connected like a statue's pedestal to a fixed point a vast distance below the surface, i.e. the Earth is not an object that floats freely in space. It would be possible to walk/sail off the edge of the Earth.

Figure 18.1a Model 1: Infinite Earth (misconception)

Figure 18.1b Model 2: Earth as an infinite cylinder (misconception)

3 *We live on a flat disc* (Figure 18.1c). The Earth is a flat, round object that is free, disconnected from the rest of space (its bottom has limits). This is a version of the idea that celestial bodies such as the Earth, sun and moon are flat, two-dimensional objects like coins. Drawings and photographs of planets and stars in textbooks are two-dimensional, and some children may not automatically think of them as being three-dimensional spheres. In popular fiction, Terry Pratchett's Discworld is a mixture of models 2 and 3.[1]

4 *Earth is a ball and we live inside it* (Figure 18.1d). Learners accept that the Earth is three-dimensional and spherical, although all life and space exists inside the ball itself, and we live on a flat area within the middle of the Earth. For a child, this model still allows them to believe that we live on a flat Earth and is consistent with the idea that where the Earth ends at the horizon, the heavens (i.e. space) begin. The idea that the heavens exist on the inside of a rounded surface reflects how the sky appears to an observer, as a huge dome, and was accepted as fact in some ancient cultures.

Figure 18.1c Model 3: Earth as a flat disc (misconception)

Figure 18.1d Model 4: Spherical Earth that contains all of space (misconception)

Figure 18.1e Model 5: Spherical Earth with a flat part where we live (misconception)

5 *Earth is a ball, although there is a flat part at the top where we live* (Figure 18.1e). This is a compromise whereby children accept that the Earth is a sphere but part of them still believes the Earth must be flat. In the minds of these learners, this misconception fully explains how photographs and video clips from space can show a spherical Earth because we either live on the flat opposite side to that which is being photographed, or the flat bits are too small to be picked up on the picture. Another variant where the scientific concept has been only partly accepted is the view that the planet Earth is spherical and exists out there in space, while where we live is a flat area, unrelated to that planet.

These misconceptions are examples of how some ideas in science go against what our everyday perceptions clearly tell us – that the Earth's surface is flat terrain that extends out to the horizon. Because of the Earth's large size, we cannot easily see that our planet is actually a ball (Figure 18.1f) when we stand on its surface. However, the Ancient Greeks were able to understand that the Earth is a sphere and even made a fairly accurate estimation of its circumference. Despite this early work, the idea that the Earth was flat has persisted through the centuries in several cultures and even as recently as the seventeenth century Chinese sailors 'knew' that they had to be careful when in certain waters otherwise they would fall off the edge into oblivion (model 3).

In contemporary times, most adults in developed societies believe the scientific, spherical Earth model, although a tiny minority of people such as the members of Flat Earth Society still argue the opposite.

Figure 18.1f The Blue Marble (photographed by the crew of Apollo 17, December 1972). Image: NASA.

Reconstruction

Ask the class to show you where we live on a three-dimensional **globe map** of the Earth, as younger children may have seen a globe map but not yet made the connection that it represents our planet. Providing video images that show the Earth as a three-dimensional entity and spherical can reinforce the scientific view. For instance, clips from modern science fiction films offer outstanding **CGI** effects that render planets and other celestial bodies as three-dimensional objects. Following a journey that involves the film's characters landing on a planet from space may show that the journey ends on the planet's surface and not its interior (as with model 4). Allowing children to handle 3D inflatable models of the Earth (and other planets) would also help to address the various flat Earth misconceptions.

It might be difficult to challenge children who accept that the Earth is a sphere but the little area where we live is a flat bit. Classical stories of sailors

Figure 18.1g A ship travelling towards the observer crosses the horizon

who spotted approaching ships by first observing their masts over the horizon before the hull appeared help children to appreciate that the whole of the Earth's surface is curved, including 'our bit' (Figure 18.1g). Flat Earth misconceptions can be believed by the same children who find it difficult to imagine which way is 'down', so the pedagogies described in 11.4 are relevant here also.

Sources: Arnold *et al.* (1995); Nussbaum and Novak (1976); Özsoy (2017); Vosniadou and Brewer (1990).

18.2 What is at the centre of the solar system?

Misconception

The Earth lies at the centre of the solar system, with the sun and the planets orbiting around it.

Scientific conception

Some primary children believe that the Earth is at the centre of space and every other celestial body orbits around it (Figure 18.2a).[2] The way that the sun appears to move across the sky during the course of a day can easily give the impression that the sun is circling the Earth (18.3).

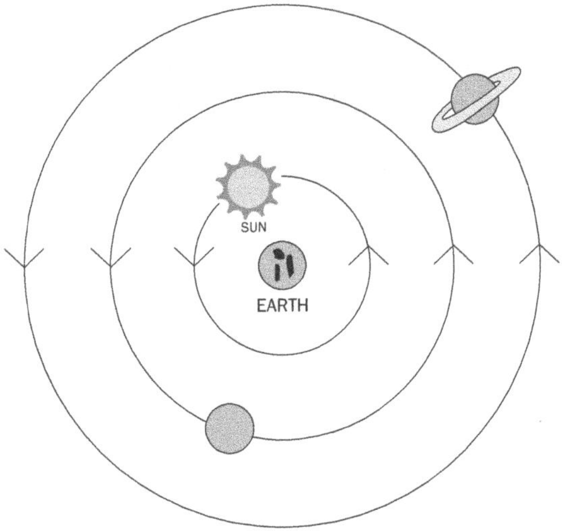

Figure 18.2a Classic geocentric model of the solar system, showing three orbiting bodies (misconception)

For many centuries, because of these observations of the sun's daily motion across the sky and also religious teachings, the Earth-centred (**geocentric**) model (Figure 18.2a) was widely acknowledged to be the correct view. During the mid-1500s, the Polish astronomer Nicolaus Copernicus proposed an alternative theory that had the sun at the centre of the solar system (**heliocentric** model), the accepted scientific view today. The modern heliocentric model has the sun being orbited by the eight planets, their moons, and other smaller bodies such as comets, asteroids, and **dwarf planets** (Figure 18.2b).

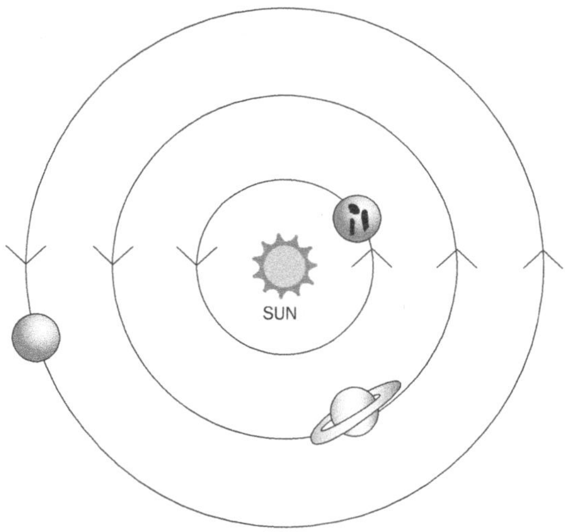

Figure 18.2b Modern heliocentric model of the solar system, showing three orbiting bodies, including Earth

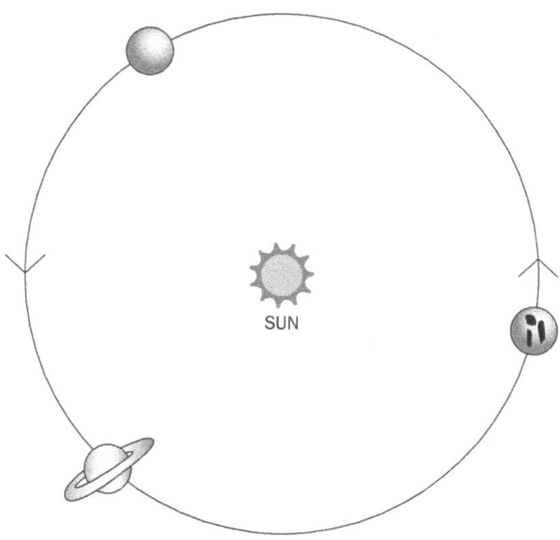

Figure 18.2c All the planets have a single shared orbit (misconception)

There are other non-scientific models of the solar system based on both geocentric and heliocentric beliefs. The heliocentric model shown in Figure 18.2c assumes that all the planets are found at around the same distance from the sun and share the same orbit path. In reality, the outermost planet Neptune is 75 times further away from the sun than the closest planet, Mercury.

Famous scientists

A dangerous idea. In the time of Copernicus, the heliocentric belief that the sun was at the centre of the universe went against biblical teachings and was ruthlessly persecuted by the Catholic Church. His heliocentric theory was published shortly before he died, supposedly so he could avoid the attentions of the Inquisition. Galileo was an outspoken supporter of heliocentrism and helped Copernicus's ideas survive his death. As a result, Galileo was vigorously pursued by the Church and eventually charged with heresy. Contemporary accounts report that he was lucky to escape execution, being sentenced instead to life-long house arrest.

Reconstruction

Practically all the ideas that children learn during a space topic depend on first having a correct understanding of the solar system's layout, so it is important that any geocentric misconceptions are challenged early on. An effective way to teach that the sun (and not the Earth) is at the centre of the solar system is to use diagrams and video images of space sourced from internet websites such as YouTube. With this particular misconception, an effective constructivist strategy would be to elicit children's non-scientific ideas and then challenge them using engaging videos such as the journey of a spaceship across the solar system, which will help children construct a scientific heliocentric model. Role play can be used with children pretending to be the Earth and other planets, the moon, comets, etc., and moving in circles around an inflatable model of the sun, or a large beach ball. A planetarium visit is a great way to help children overcome geocentric misconceptions.

Discussions of celestial bodies' orbits can be linked to forces concepts, especially the effects of gravity (see 13.6 and 13.7). To give children some idea of the immense distances between the planets, they can make a toilet paper solar system (search online for further details). They will need one roll of toilet paper (200 sheets) and use the scale of 1 sheet of paper = 30 000 km. Spread out the entire roll across a large area such as the school hall. Using gel pens, mark on the paper where the planets lie; e.g. Mercury at 2 sheets, Earth at 5 sheets, and Neptune at 153 sheets. Pluto is no longer considered a planet (see 18.9) but can be marked at 200 sheets.

Sources: Dunne (2019); Parker and Heywood (1998); Sharp (1996); Taylor *et al.* (2003).

18.3 Why does day become night?

Misconception

The sun moves around the Earth; this is what causes daytime and night-time.

Scientific conception

As part of a space topic, the class can fix an upright stick into the ground and then record the position and length of the stick's shadow over the course of a sunny day. Using these shadows helps children understand that the sun appears to move slowly across the sky from east to west. To explain this movement, some children may believe that the sun completes one circle (orbit) of the Earth once every 24 hours (Figure 18.3a). If a person stood at X on Earth and the sun was at position 1, then it would be daytime for that person; 12 hours later when the sun reaches position 2, it would be night-time for that person because the Earth is directly blocking any incoming sunlight. During this time the Earth is still, remaining fixed in position, and does not spin.

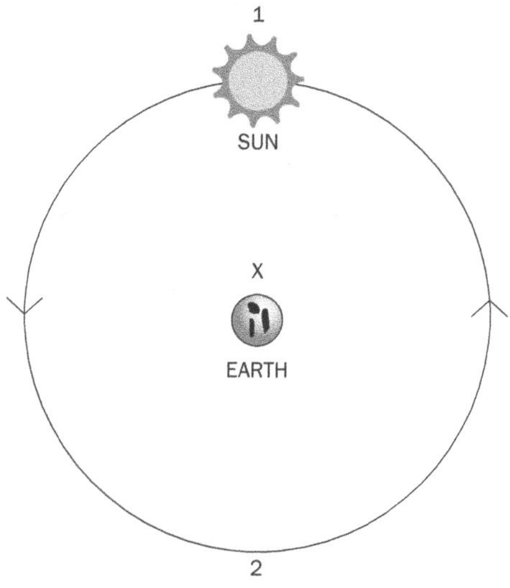

Figure 18.3a A geocentric model of day and night (misconception)

Although this geocentric model might make perfect sense to children, as discussed in 18.2 it is scientifically incorrect. The correct heliocentric model has the sun lying at the middle of the solar system while the planets, including Earth, orbit around it. However, what causes day and night cannot be explained by reference alone to the heliocentric model – children also need to understand that the real reason why day and night occur is because the Earth is spinning on its axis.

Figures 18.3b and 18.3c represent a correct heliocentric model where the Earth follows a roughly circular path (orbit) around the sun – it makes one complete orbit every 12 months (365¼ days). At the same time, a completely different kind of movement takes place – the Earth spins on its axis once every 24 hours. The sun is only able to shine on half of the Earth at any one time, with the other half being in darkness, shown shaded on the diagrams. In Figure 18.3b, it would be daytime for someone at position X because they are standing on the lit-up half of the Earth. Twelve hours later the Earth has spun halfway around and for the person at X it would be night (Figure 18.3c). Note that although 12 hours have passed, the Earth has not moved along its orbit path to any noticeable degree – the Earth is indeed orbiting the sun, but day and night occur only because the Earth is spinning on its axis. Children are often confused by the fact the Earth both orbits and spins at the same time, two completely separate motions that occur independently of each other, and they will incorrectly say things such as *day and night are caused by the Earth orbiting the sun.* They may also confuse the times taken for each motion, stating that *the Earth orbits the sun once every 24 hours.*

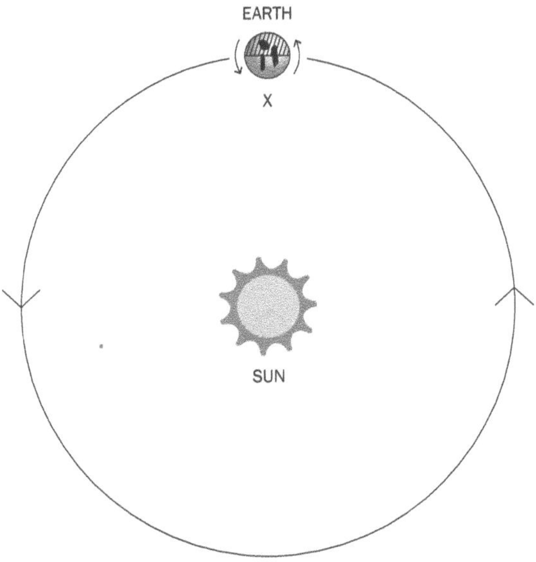

Figure 18.3b Daytime at X

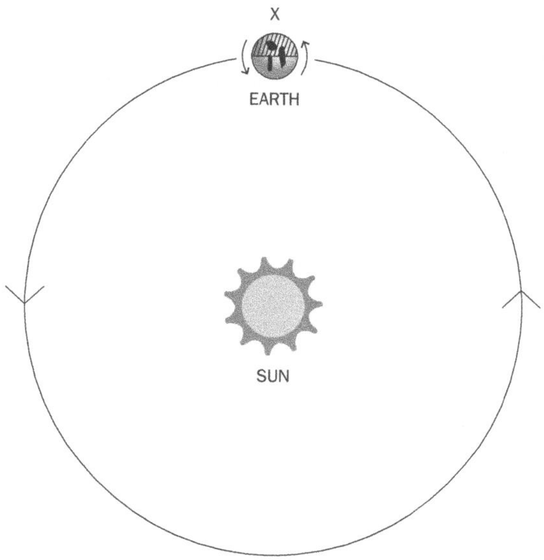

Figure 18.3c Night-time at X

There are several related misconceptions concerning the causes of day and night.

1 *Night comes because the moon blocks sunlight.* Although this is based on a correct heliocentric model, the moon does not have an orbit path around the sun that is separate from the Earth's orbit (Figure 18.3d). This misconception is related to the belief that the moon only appears in the sky at night, an idea perpetuated in children's story books that depict the moon as a cartoon anthropomorphic figure dressed in a night cap, carrying a candle, is asleep, etc.
2 *Clouds are responsible for day and night.* Some children believe that when the sun disappears at night, it is hiding behind clouds. During the day the moon cannot be seen because it too is now hiding behind clouds.
3 *The sun and moon swap places to cause day and night.* This geocentric model represents another attempt to explain the incorrect idea that the sun comes out during the day and the moon during the night. One source of this confusion might be the analogue wristwatches that show a tiny sun rising at daytime and a tiny moon rising at night. A variant of this misconception is that although the sun and moon are in positions as shown by Figure 18.3e, they do not orbit the Earth and instead remain fixed in place, with day and night occurring instead due to the Earth spinning. This is an interesting blend of correct (Earth spins) and incorrect (geocentric) science (see also Figure 18.2c, and the child's comment in the Box below). Further

variants include that the sun disappears during the night because it has travelled into space, the sun is hiding underneath the Earth, and the sun is still there in the sky but it becomes dark at night time.

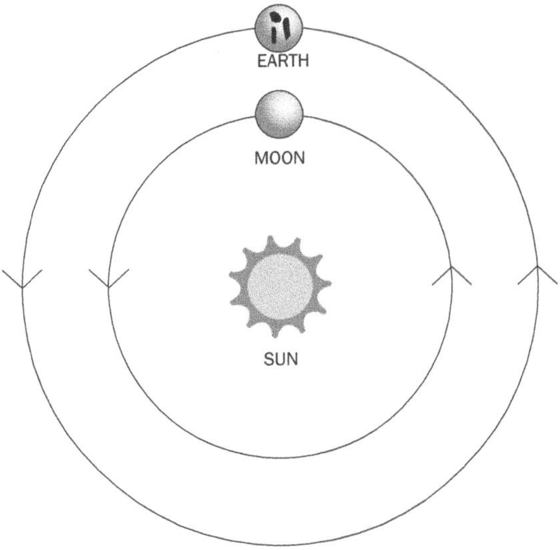

Figure 18.3d The moon blocks the sun to cause night-time (misconception)

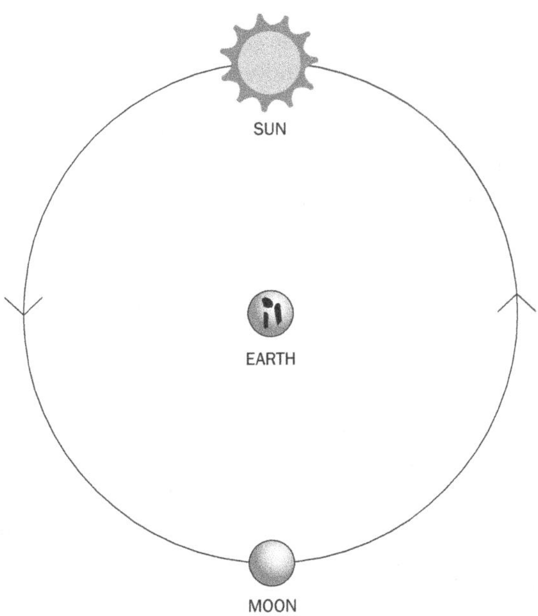

Figure 18.3e Sun and moon swap positions and the Earth stays still (misconception)

I think . . .

Day and night. '*[At night the sun] changes into a moon*' (9-year-old child; Osborne *et al.*, 1993, p. 37).

Reconstruction

In the primary classroom, the scientific view of the cause of day and night can be taught by demonstration in a darkened room using a globe map of the Earth and a light source. Quite a strong light source (e.g. a 150 W bulb or halogen lamp) is required to show a clear line between light and shade on the globe. Using an IWB projector as the source would not be suitable because of reflections from the whiteboard itself. If the lamp is kept still on a table and the globe placed a couple of metres away fully within its glow, the globe should be half in light and half in shadow. If a small sticker or some Blu Tack is then placed where the UK is located and the globe then spun on its axis, this will correctly show why we experience daytime, then night-time, then daytime again, and so on, as well as how the sun appears to move across the sky from east to west from the point of view of an observer in the UK. Remember to spin the globe in an anticlockwise direction as you look down onto the North Pole.

Variations of this approach use role play, with children taking the part of the sun and the spinning Earth (be careful they do not get too dizzy as they spin around). Several of the misconceptions discussed in this section are linked with the idea that the moon only comes out at night, so addressing this is a good starting point.

Sources: Nikolopoulou *et al.* (2024); Nobes *et al.* (2023); Osborne *et al.* (1993); Sharp (1996); Vosniadou and Skopeliti (2017).

18.4 How does the sun rise and set?

Misconception

The sun rises straight up into the sky in the morning, stays still in the sky, then moves back down at night.

Scientific conception

Some children believe that the sun rises up above the horizon in the morning, stays in exactly the same position in the sky during the day, and then sets below the horizon at night at the same spot from which it appeared that morning (Figures 18.4a, 18.4b, and 18.4c). This simple model of sunrise and sunset does not consider how the sun is seen to move across the sky. During the course of a sunny day, if you were to record the position of the sun in the sky every couple of hours, it would become clear that it moves in an arc shape (Figure 18.4d).

Figure 18.4a Sunrise (misconception)

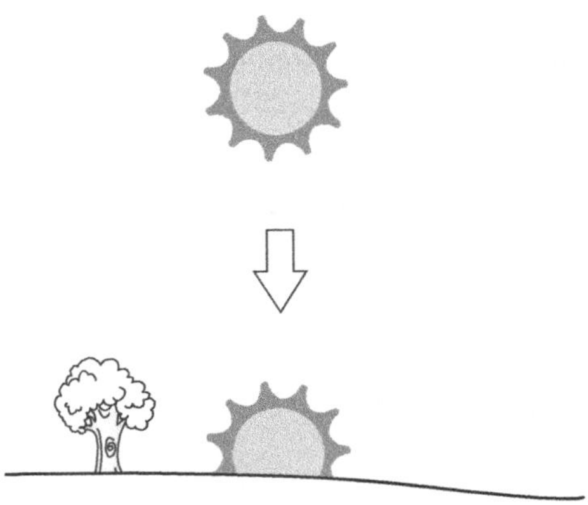

Figure 18.4b Sunset (misconception)

Figure 18.4c Child's drawing showing the position of the sun at: morning (a), midday (b), and afternoon (c) (misconception)

Source: Osborne *et al.* (1993, p. 43).

Figure 18.4d The sun's apparent motion across the sky during the course of a day

The sun rises in the east then sets towards the west. In the northern hemisphere, the sun is seen to move from left to right across the sky, while in the southern hemisphere the reverse is true. At midday, the sun will be at the highest point in its arc, and people of all ages commonly believe that at this time the sun is directly overhead; however, this is only the case nearer the equator between the Tropics of Cancer and Capricorn on the day of the **summer solstice**. In the UK, the sun is never directly overhead – even in the middle of summer it reaches an angle of only around 60° in the sky. Note that because they are drawn in two dimensions, pictures such as Figure 18.4d might reinforce the misconception that the sun is directly overhead at midday.

The sun only *appears* to travel in an arc across the sky – the Earth's rotation is responsible for giving this false impression and the sun actually remains in the same position in space (18.3). This misconception can exist together with the idea that when the sun sets, the moon is seen to rise in the same place in the sky in a similar vertical way, replacing the sun, so is a variant of the misconception shown by Figure 18.3e.

> ***Be safe!***
>
> **Staring directly at the sun.** Warn children that if they stare directly at the sun, even for very short periods or when wearing dark sunglasses, this will likely result in permanent eye damage. The possibility of eye injury increases greatly if the sun is viewed directly through a telescope, binoculars, or any other optical instrument.

Reconstruction

Daily records of a stick's shadow as described in 18.3 demonstrates that the sun does not stay still in the sky during the course of the day; instead, it is constantly moving in an arc-shaped path. A quicker way to show this is to ask children on a sunny day to go outside and draw chalk marks on the floor around the shadows made by the edges of buildings, fence posts, and other fixed features. Returning to the chalk marks 20 minutes later will show that the shadows have moved, and these observations can be linked to the sun's apparent motion across the sky. Inside the classroom the teacher can demonstrate using a torch as the sun and a vertical rod. When the torch (sun) moves in an arc from left to right, the rod's shadow moves in the opposite direction, and also becomes shorter at midday and longer in the mornings and evenings when the sun has just risen or is about to set.

Another idea is to sit a child in a swivel chair (the spinning Earth) and have a volunteer stand still a couple of metres away shining a torch beam (the sun) in the chair's general direction. As the chair is slowly spun anticlockwise, from the seated child's position the torch will appear to move from left to right, which is like how an observer on Earth sees the sun move across the sky during daylight hours. The familiar saying *the sun rises in the east and sets in the west* is useful to encourage the understanding that the sun does not rise and set in the same place.

Sources: Schoon and Boone (1998); Sharp (1996); Vosniadou and Skopeliti (2017).

18.5 How big are the Earth, sun, and moon?

> **Misconception**
>
> *The Earth, sun and moon are all about the same size.*

Scientific conception

As part of a space topic, children need to know how the sizes of these three celestial bodies compare with each other. Books commonly show the solar system as the eight planets, the sun, and occasionally other objects such as comets, asteroids, and dwarf planets. Because of the vast distances between these bodies in real space, pictures of the solar system in books (including this book) are never drawn to scale, and instead are squeezed onto either one page or a double-page spread. Similarly, there are huge differences between the sizes of celestial bodies, so again for convenience textbooks sometimes incorrectly show them as all being the same size. For many children, this could be the source of the misconception.

Some textbooks, however, use a more realistic scale and depict the sun as being much larger than other bodies in the solar system, although the planets and moons are usually still shown as being of similar diameters. Children therefore may correctly conclude that the sun is very large, but incorrectly think that the Earth and moon are the same size.

The moon is smaller than the Earth, at around a quarter its size (Figure 18.5a); the sun is much bigger at about 109 times the size of the Earth (Figure 18.5b). Children therefore tend to believe that the moon is bigger than it actually is, and that the sun is smaller than it actually is.

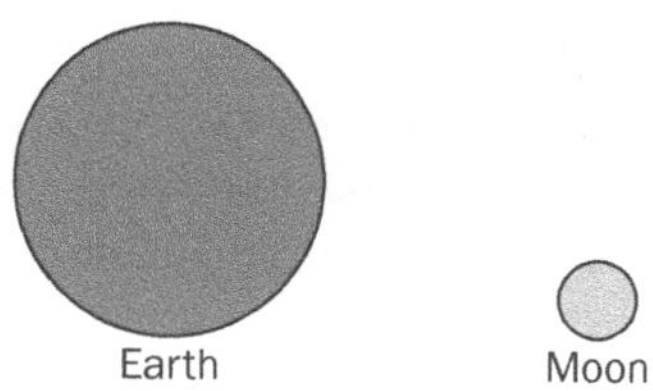

Figure 18.5a Comparative sizes of the Earth and moon, drawn approximately to scale

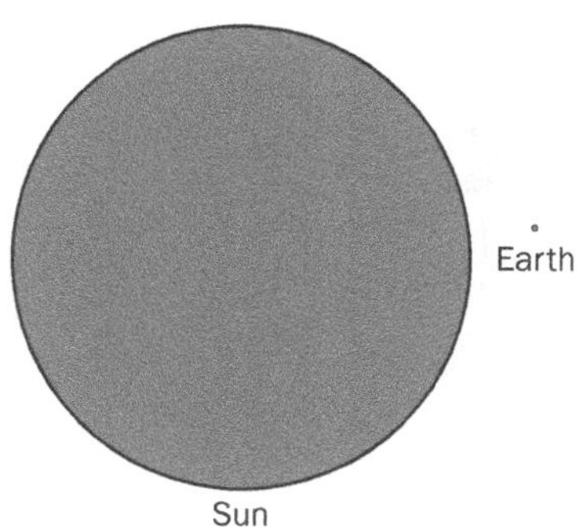

Figure 18.5b Comparative sizes of the Earth and sun, drawn approximately to scale

Reconstruction

Use three-dimensional models to show how the sizes of the Earth, sun and moon compare with each other. If the Earth were the size of a football, then the moon would be a tennis ball. On a much larger scale, if the sun were a basketball, the Earth would be a peppercorn and the moon the size of a handwritten full stop on a piece of paper.

Sources: Bryce and Blown (2012); Dankenbring and Capobianco (2016).

18.6 The moon's orbit

Misconception

The moon orbits 'around' the Earth.

Scientific conception

Although on the face of it the above statement could be correct, Figure 18.6a shows how children can construct a different understanding of the moon's orbit that is non-scientific. In this case, the word *around* has been misinterpreted to mean that the moon circles the sun around the outside of the Earth's orbit.

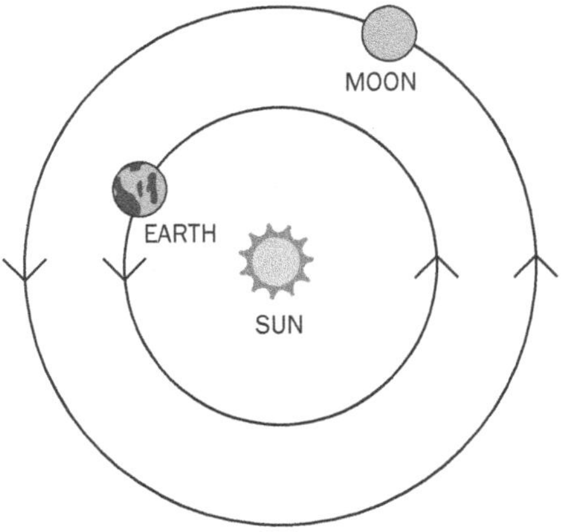

Figure 18.6a The moon has its own dedicated orbit around the sun (misconception)

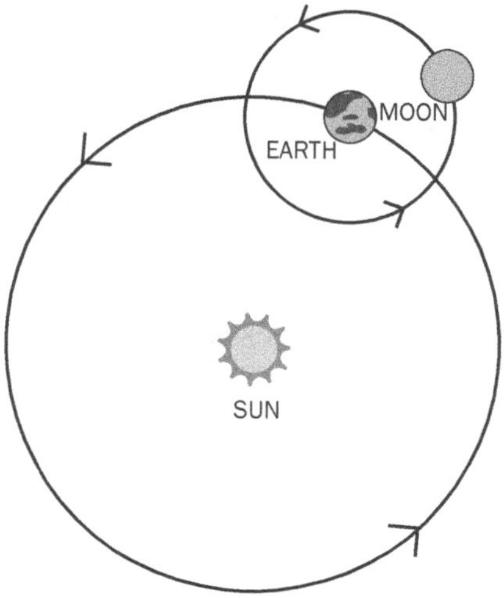

Figure 18.6b The scientific view

Figure 18.6b shows the correct arrangement, with the Earth orbiting the sun, while at the same time the moon orbits the Earth. The moon orbits the Earth approximately once every 28 days – the Ancient Romans observed and recorded the moon's phases to measure the passage of time and divided the year into 12 parts, or *months* (both *moon* and *month* have the same linguistic source). Note that it is correct to say that the moon is going around the sun, but incorrect to say that it is *orbiting* the sun (at primary school level, at least).

The belief that the moon is a planet can also be a cause of the misconception that it occupies its own orbit around the sun; however, the moon is not a planet, it is a satellite of the Earth. Other misconceptions about the moon include that its surface was formed when moon rock melted and boiled, which created bubbles that then burst to make craters.

Reconstruction

Since this misconception reflects a non-scientific model of the solar system, it could be addressed in similar ways to those discussed in 18.2, e.g. role play with one child being the Earth and circling the sun, while another plays the moon and circles the Earth. When teaching children, it is best to avoid expressions along the lines of *the moon orbits/goes around the sun*; it is preferable to say *the moon orbits the Earth, and the Earth orbits the sun.*

When teaching the Earth and space in primary schools it can sometimes be difficult to think of science investigations relevant to the topic. One experiment can be linked to **meteorites** that have collided with the moon's surface, where children have to discover the factors that might have influenced the size and shape of the moon's craters. A variety of plasticine balls (meteorites) are dropped into a sand tray to make impressions in the sand (craters). Independent variables include the diameter of the balls, their mass, and the height they are dropped from, Dependent variables can be measured such as crater depth, size, and shape. The investigation can be linked to the 'dinosaur killer', a huge meteorite that hit the Earth 66 million years ago off the coast of modern-day Mexico, leaving a 170 km-wide crater. Note that the everyday phrase for a **meteor** is 'shooting star', and it may need to be explained to children that meteors are not stars, merely chunks of rock entering Earth's atmosphere.

Source: Kara (2022); Sharp (1996).

Learning technologies

Virtual reality headsets. In the mid-1990s, a new way to interface with computers was developed that allowed video game players to imagine that they were physically present in a virtual world. An early virtual reality (VR) headset comprised a large helmet that covered the eyes, ears, and the top of the head. It was essentially a visual interface that projected an image inside the helmet that gave a 360° view of a scene when playing a game; for example, it allowed the user to have an all-round view from the top of a mountain – as the person turned their head around, the headset sensed this and provided different images that gave them an impression that they were actually on a mountain and seeing the view in real life. Modern gaming versions of these headsets are smaller than the originals but expensive to buy, with even the basic types costing several hundred pounds. Fortunately, there are cheaper VR headsets available that are ideal to use in the classroom and cost less than £10 each. They consist of a cardboard or thin plastic frame containing lenses that are designed to be used with an ordinary mobile phone placed inside and worn over the eyes like an oversized pair of goggles. The attitude sensors in the phone mean that when you turn your head, the view changes accordingly, giving you a 'virtual' experience of being in a certain place. Free VR applications (apps) can be downloaded from the internet and when used together with the headsets, offer virtual experiences such as walking through an African rainforest, being in the crowd at a music concert featuring your favourite artist, exploring the seabed surrounded by sharks, dolphins, etc., as well as a host of gaming apps. Although not cost-free, collections of VR experiences for use in schools are commercially available from companies such as Nearpod. In recent years, primary schools have begun to realize the educational benefit of the cheaper VR headsets and in the context of the current chapter, there are apps available that allow children to make virtual journeys through space, experiencing the universe in apparent 3D. These will likely help address many of the misconceptions described in this chapter, including confusing the Earth's orbit with its spin. There are also VR headsets available for tablets but at the moment these are less common and more expensive. A simpler, non-VR option is to download a free app onto a tablet, such as *Skymap* (many others are available), which enables children to point the tablet to an area of the sky and identify stars and planets. If budget allows, your school may consider purchasing educational VR kit such as CLASSVR that comes with VR headsets plus supporting software (this costs several thousand pounds).

18.7 What causes the moon's phases?

Misconception

The Earth's shadow causes the different phases of the moon.

Scientific conception

Over the course of several days and nights, the white part of the moon gradually changes shape (Figure 18.7a); these shapes are the phases of the moon. It is commonly believed that part of the moon is in darkness because the Earth casts its own shadow onto the surface of the moon. However, it is relatively rare for the moon to be in the Earth's shadow (and vice versa), an event we call a lunar **eclipse**. The dark part on the moon that is visible with the different phases is not due to another celestial body such as the Earth casting its shadow; it is merely because of the particular way that any sphere is lit up by a light source.

Figure 18.7b shows how a strong source shone towards a white ball in a dark room causes one half of the ball to be illuminated. Because light travels in straight lines, the torch beam is unable to 'go around the corner' and reach the far side of the ball, so it remains in darkness. This is precisely what happens when the moon is lit by the sun in space. The dark areas associated with the phases of the moon are therefore not caused by the Earth's shadow; in fact, the moon is in its own shadow.

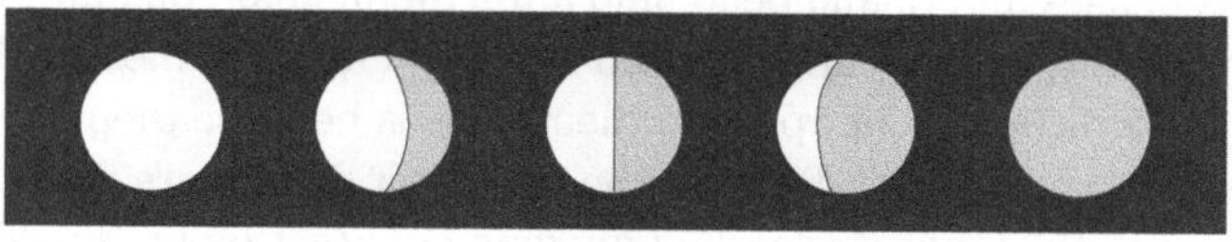

Figure 18.7a Phases of the moon: full, gibbous, half, crescent, new

Figure 18.7b Illuminated ball

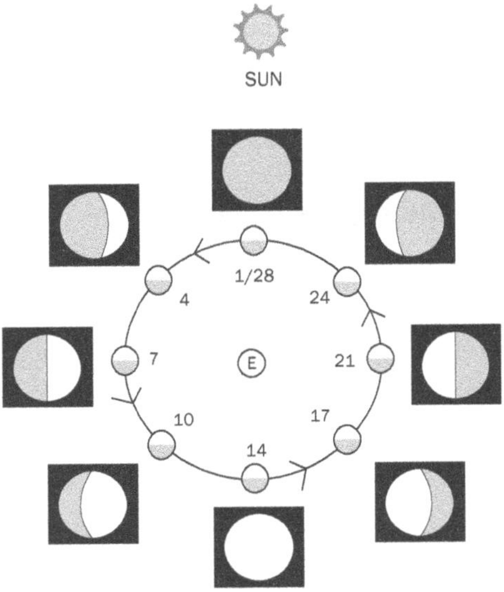

Figure 18.7c How the moon's phases relate to its orbit around the Earth (see main text for explanation)

The moon makes one complete orbit of the Earth approximately every 28 days, as shown on the inner circle of Figure 18.7c. The different pictures of the moon within this inner circle show how the moon is lit up in space by the sun at different stages during its 28-day journey (note that the position of the sun is at the very top of the diagram). The outer pictures on Figure 18.7c show how the moon would look as viewed from Earth at each stage. A full moon is observed on day 14, then as the days pass, it will gradually become more covered in shadow until it is completely dark, becoming a new moon by day 28. The stages in between full and new moon are gibbous moon (days 15–18), half moon (days 19–23), and crescent moon (days 24–27). At day 28, the process starts again with the new moon becoming gradually less in shadow as the days pass, going through the crescent, half, and gibbous phases and finally becoming a full moon again by day 14. Although diagrams of this type are frequently used when teaching the moon's phases, children often have difficulty interpreting them. This is because they have to locate themselves at the position on Earth in the middle of the picture, look across at a specific moon in the inner circle, then imagine how that moon would appear to them in reality, and consider the appropriate phase (outer circle).

Note that the new moon is sometimes shown in textbooks as a very thin sliver of a crescent and not totally in shadow, since the ancients thought that the first bit of light that appears after being totally in darkness was the moon being reborn, or 'new'. In textbooks, the half moon is sometimes called either last quarter or first quarter, terms which should be avoided in the primary classroom because of the possible confusion with the gibbous or crescent phases.

Other reasons given by children to explain the moon's phases include passing clouds, the Earth turning on its axis during the night so we look at the moon from a slightly different angle (associated with the misconception that the moon passes through all of its phases during the course of a single night), and as the moon gets further away from the sun, less light reaches it so there is more shadow. Young children tend to be able to recognize the moon when in the full or crescent shape more than the other phases, perhaps because story books usually depict the moon as being in one of these two phases.

Reconstruction

It is a good idea to start by showing how a sphere is illuminated in a darkened room. A white hockey ball makes a good moon, and a strong light source must be used such as a powerful torch or a table lamp with a bright bulb. It helps if the beam is made as narrow as possible to cut down on reflected light from other parts of the room, which helps to make a sharp line between light and darkness on the ball. This will clearly show that the part of the 'moon' in darkness is not a result of the shadow of another object – instead, the moon is in its own shadow. This can be extended to demonstrating how different phases of the ball can be seen depending on the angle at which children look at the ball (as shown in Figure 18.7c), and then related to the moon's orbit around the Earth.

Diagrams such as that shown in Figure 18.7c can be confusing if presented alone and so are commonly used in combination with a class practical activity. A ping pong ball that has been painted half black makes a good model of an illuminated moon. It will help if you ask children to imagine that their head represents the Earth with the 'moon' held at eye level, and a fixed point in the room such as the teacher's desk is the sun. Children then orbit the ball around their heads in a circle, looking at the different amounts of light and darkness at different stages of the journey; these can then be directly connected with the moon's phases. Children can have difficulty pointing the moon in the right direction as it moves around their heads, as the white half always needs to point towards the part of the room that is the 'sun'.

To support the learning associated with this practical task, one activity is to ask children to record how the phases of the moon change over the course of several days and nights. This is one reason why space topics have traditionally been taught during the winter months, when the sun sets before children go to bed. Note that when the moon is observed during daylight hours, the phases are much less visible.

Sources: Sharp (1996); Turkmen (2017).

18.8 What causes the seasons?

Misconception

It is hotter in summer because the Earth is closer to the sun.

Scientific conception

The idea that variations in the distance between the Earth and the sun are responsible for the change in seasons is a common misconception. Figure 18.8a shows that at different times of the year, the Earth and sun are indeed different distances apart because the sun is offset, and not exactly at the centre of the Earth's orbit (greatly exaggerated in this figure). It makes sense that during the time that the Earth is closest to the sun it receives more heat and therefore this means it must be summer, and when the Earth is furthest away it must be winter. However, the real reasons for the changing seasons are more complex.

The Earth's axis is an imaginary line running through the North and South Poles. The Earth, like all planets, spins on its axis in the same way that you can spin a globe map of the Earth. However, the Earth does not spin 'straight' in space with its axis at right angles to its orbit around the sun; instead, the Earth

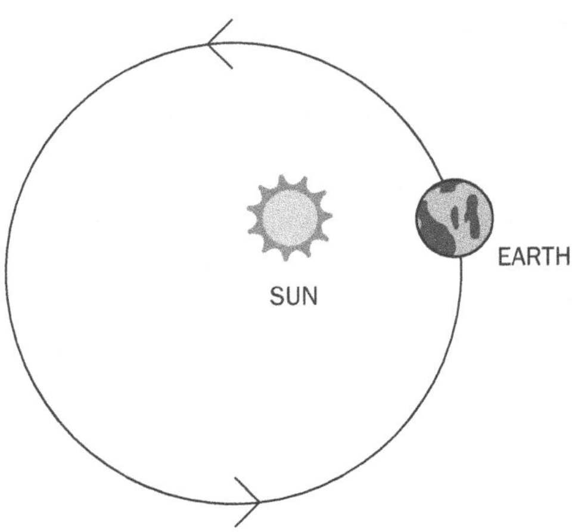

Figure 18.8a When the Earth is close to the sun, it is summer (misconception)

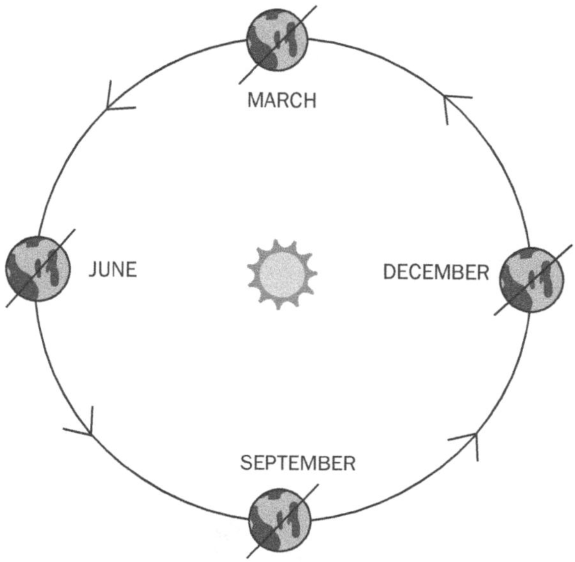

Figure 18.8b The changing seasons and the Earth's tilted axis (the central circle is the sun and the four outer circles represent the Earth at different times of the year)

is tilted on its axis at an angle of 23.5°, and this is why globe maps are manufactured with a lopsided angle to their axis. This tilt is seen in Figure 18.8b but for clarity has been exaggerated.

Referring to Figure 18.8b, in December, the Earth's northern hemisphere is facing more away from the sun when compared with the southern hemisphere – we say that *the northern hemisphere is tilted away from the sun.* For this reason, it is winter for northern hemisphere countries in December, including the UK. Six months later in June the opposite situation applies, with the northern hemisphere tilted towards the sun, making it summer in the UK. Australia, on the other hand, being a country in the southern hemisphere, experiences summer in December and winter in June, because the southern hemisphere is tilted towards and away from the sun at these times of the year respectively. In March the northern hemisphere is half-way between being tilted towards and away from the sun, so spring weather in the UK is intermediate between summer and winter. The same can be said for September (autumn).

But why should having the hemisphere where you live tilted towards the sun create hotter weather? Perhaps surprisingly, this is little to do with the fact that because of the tilt, the northern hemisphere is slightly closer to the sun. The real reason is due to differences in sunlight strength. Figure 18.8c shows how light from the sun travels through space and hits the Earth. Looking more closely at the surface of the Earth at points A and B (Figures 18.8d and 18.8e), the angle of the Earth's surface affects the concentration of sunlight hitting each

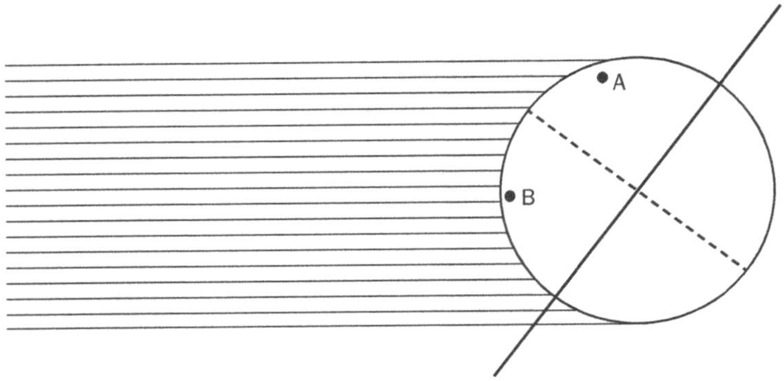

Figure 18.8c Sunlight strength at two different points on the Earth's surface

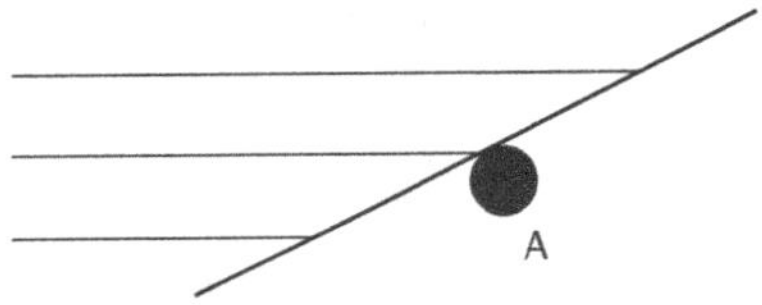

Figure 18.8d Sunlight strength at point A

Figure 18.8e Sunlight strength at point B

point. The length of the drawn line representing the Earth's surface at A and B is the same, as is the denseness of the light travelling from the sun (distance between 'beams') but more beams of sunlight can hit at B than at A. Since sunlight carries energy, the length of the Earth's surface at B will be warmer than at A because the sunlight is more concentrated at B, and more spread out at A.

In Figure 18.8c, the Earth's northern hemisphere is tilted away from the sun, so as discussed earlier, it will be winter at point A (December). At the same time, since the southern hemisphere is tilted towards the sun, it will be summer at point B (also December). Nearer the equator there are typically two seasons, wet and dry, because the sunlight strength does not change enough over the year to cause the temperature changes required for there to be four separate seasons. Something else that contributes to higher temperatures in summer is the fact that days are longer. More hours spent in daylight during the summer months means the Earth is heated for a longer period, and so becomes warmer.

Other misconceptions children have for why summer temperatures are hotter include the sun spending less time behind the clouds, the sun burning hotter during the summer months, changes in plant life causing seasonal change (instead of vice versa –reverse causality bias), the cold outer planets stopping the Earth taking heat from the sun, and the angle of the Earth's tilted axis has changed.

To summarize, temperatures are hotter in summer mainly due to differences in the strength of sunlight hitting the Earth's surface (Figures 18.8c–e). These differences cause seasonal change because the Earth lies on a tilted axis, which makes the northern and southern hemispheres take turns at being tilted towards and away from the sun over the period of a year (Figure 18.8b). Another contributing factor is longer daylight hours in the summer.

Reconstruction

Understanding the concepts behind seasonal variation is beyond the primary curriculum. However, children are likely to express ideas reflecting this misconception during a space topic and ask questions about the causes of seasons, and attempting to address it during the primary years would be time well spent. Using the same set-up as described in 18.3, an illuminated globe in a darkened room is a useful visual tool. Physically carrying the globe around the light source in a circle (i.e. making the Earth orbit the 'sun') but keeping the direction of its axis the same will show exactly how the northern hemisphere changes between tilting towards and away from the sun over the course of one year – it works best if you can make the globe completely orbit the light source (although someone may need to keep readjusting the direction of the light beam). At the same time, you could even delve into the sunlight strength explanation by placing a piece of A4 white card on the Earth at different points on the surface. It will be clear to children that when one hemisphere is tilting away from the 'sun', the card looks quite dim because of a low light strength, which causes winter temperatures (Figure 18.8f).

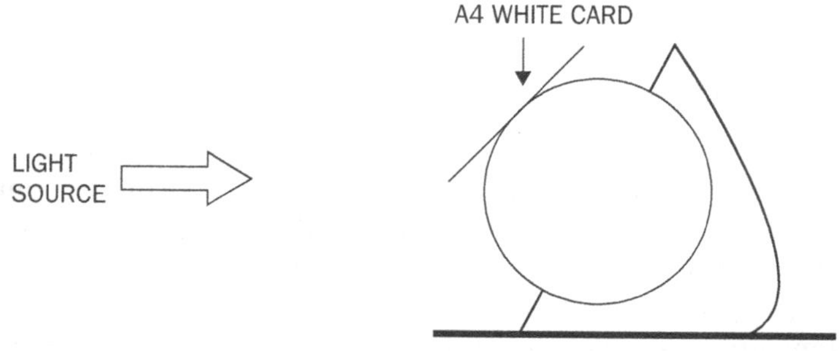

Figure 18.8f Holding an A4 white card at various points on a globe map to show differences in light strength

KS1 children can consider seasonal changes by asking them to think about the different things that happen in summer and in winter, such as how local wildlife varies with the seasons (especially birds and flowering plants), the clothes they wear, how long they can play outside, how dark it gets, and differences in types of weather.

If you suspect that some children believe that summer is caused by the Earth being closer to the sun, tell them that the Earth is actually at its closest point to the sun at the beginning of January, which, of course, is winter in the UK.

Did you know?

Distance really can make a (small) difference. A caveat must be mentioned at this point. When the Earth becomes closest to the sun in January, this does in fact have a warming effect on the Earth, but it is very small compared with the effect of light strength. It is debatable whether this should be shared with children, since although it is scientifically acceptable, it may act as a source of confusion and later trigger a return to the misconception that the distance between the Earth and sun causes seasonal change.

Sources: Baxter (1989); Parker and Heywood (1998); Sharp (1996).

18.9 How many planets are there in the solar system?

Misconception

Pluto is a planet.

Scientific conception

Since the 1930s, astronomers have believed that there were nine planets in the solar system, with Pluto the planet furthest away from the sun. In the 1990s, celestial bodies began to be discovered that lay beyond the orbit of Pluto but were not classified as planets because they were thought to be too small (they were much smaller than Pluto), and were instead called **trans-Neptunian objects (TNOs)**. In 2003, the TNO *Sedna* was discovered, which is almost as large as Pluto, and was briefly classified as the tenth planet. The later discovery of numerous more TNOs of a similar size to Pluto presented a dilemma – should all of these small objects be regarded as 'planets'? In 2006, the TNO *Eris* was discovered, which was actually larger than Pluto, and prompted the International Astronomical Union to decide that only the innermost eight bodies were worthy of the name 'planet' – that is, Mercury, Venus, Earth, Mars, Jupiter, Saturn, Uranus, and Neptune. TNOs such as Pluto and Eris were no longer classified as planets and were renamed dwarf planets.

Reconstruction

Traditionally, children have rote-learned the names and order of the planets using mnemonics such as *My Very Eager Mother Just Served Us Nine Pizzas.* New mnemonics reflect the fact that Pluto is no longer considered a planet, e.g. *My Very Eager Mother Just Served Us Nachos.*

It does not help that some sources such as textbooks, library books, and videos still present Pluto as a planet, and for this reason children need to be advised to be on the lookout for these, and given a simple explanation as to why Pluto is no longer considered to be a planet.

Source: Broughton *et al.* (2012).

18.10 How do the planets move?

Misconception

The planets and stars do not move – they are part of the unchanging background of the night sky.

Scientific conception

Many upper KS2 children correctly understand that the Earth orbits the sun, while the stars do not. They sometimes include all the other planets in this model, thinking them to be like the stars, not orbiting the sun, instead existing as non-moving celestial bodies that form a natural backdrop to the night sky (Figure 18.10). In fact, all objects within the solar system are pulled by the sun's gravity and celestial bodies such as planets travel in regular orbits around the sun at high speeds. However, the movement of planets across the night sky is very slow, though can be observed and recorded over a period of weeks and months as they journey through the star **constellations**. The English word *planet* has roots in the Greek *planēs*, meaning 'wanderer', which reflects how they travel across the night sky.

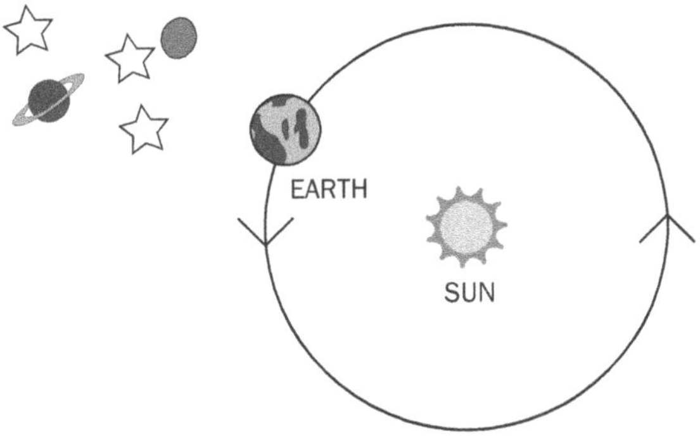

Figure 18.10 The Earth orbits the sun while planets and stars do not move (misconception)

The stars, on the other hand, exist outside of the solar system and so are not influenced by the sun's gravity, therefore they do not orbit the sun. Instead, stars appear fixed in position to an observer on Earth and this is why over many days and weeks, planets can be seen to gradually move across a motionless backdrop of stars. Note that the movement of the planets described here is not the same as the *apparent* movement of the whole night sky due to the Earth's rotation. In the same way that the sun appears to move from east to west during the course of a day, because the Earth spins (18.4), at night-time the Earth is still spinning and so the night sky appears to move in the same way.

Related misconceptions include the belief that planets are so far away they can only be seen using a telescope or binoculars, when in fact several planets are very bright at certain times of the year and can be seen with the naked eye. Children may have little understanding of the sizes of planets and stars, thinking that they are smaller than the Earth and moon because they appear tiny in the sky – in fact, the Earth is one of the smaller planets in the solar system.

Reconstruction

Animations and videos sourced from the internet are useful and engaging visual tools for showing that the planets move around the sun, as are commercially available DVDs about the solar system. Together with activities and games for learning the names of the planets (see 18.9), have children role-play the solar system in a large space such as the playground or school hall with individual children taking the roles of celestial bodies and moving around a central sun. They will need to be reminded that the model is not to scale, as the distances between planets would in reality be much larger (see the toilet paper solar system in 18.2).

During times of the year when planets such as Mars, Venus, Jupiter, or Saturn can be seen with the naked eye, upper KS2 children can make weekly drawings at home in a logbook to show the movement of one or more of these planets through the constellations over a period of a couple of months. Websites such as www.skyandtelescope.com give useful information about where planets can currently be seen in the night sky. For instance, at the time I was writing this book, Jupiter appeared bright and was visible as it passed through the constellation *Aries*.

Sources: Sharp (1996); Schoon and Boone (1998).

18.11 What is the universe?

Misconception

The universe is just all the planets in the solar system.

Scientific conception

Children generally enjoy learning about space and typically know that the Earth where we live is one of a group of similar bodies called planets. Many also understand that our group of planets exists in the same area in space, and that this area is called the solar system. Although they can readily name better-known planets such as Mars and Saturn, children rarely know what else, apart from planets, is to be found in the solar system, or what, if anything, lies outside the solar system. Many children are also familiar with the word universe but believe that it is just another name for the solar system; when asked to describe the universe, because they do not know what lies beyond the solar system, they say that the universe consists solely of the sun and the planets and nothing else. If they include the stars as part of the universe, this can link with the misconception that the stars are inside the solar system, lying almost within touching distance in the sky just above the Earth, as a backdrop to the heavens (18.1 and 18.10). Even if children understand that the universe is very big, they often believe its size has limits (it is not infinite) and that the Earth is at its centre.

As discussed in other sections of this chapter, the solar system consists of the sun, the eight planets, plus smaller bodies such as dwarf planets, asteroids, and comets. It extends a good distance beyond Neptune (the furthermost planet) and includes huge, mysterious regions of space where no planets are to be found – the Kuiper Belt, the Scattered Disc, and the Oort Cloud. The solar system does, however, have a boundary and is thought to be 20,000 billion kilometres across. In contrast, the size of the universe is difficult to measure and scientists debate about how big it really is. One problem is that because the universe is so immense, we can see little of it from Earth and so we can never be certain about its true size. It may be the case that the universe is infinitely large, having no boundaries; however, one estimate of the size of the part of the universe that we are able to see is 900,000 billion billion kilometres, a truly unimaginable distance.

Related misconceptions include that stars exist outside the solar system but all lie the same distance from the Earth, stars in the same constellation are always close to each other, and all stars are the same size.

Reconstruction

The fact that children usually think the universe is much smaller than it actually is, can be difficult to address. This is especially the case with younger age groups, whose cognitive faculties are not yet developed enough to overcome their natural egocentrism that prevents them viewing the world too far outside of themselves. That said, some older children know that 'the universe' means everything that exists, and are able to imagine things that lie great distances out into space, beyond their immediate sphere of experience on Earth. Children may be aware that astronomers have discovered objects that exist beyond Neptune, e.g. dwarf planets (see 18.9), and comets, and so space is probably much larger than they first think it is. It is rarely appreciated that the stars exist billions of kilometres away, outside of our solar system, so the knowledge that each star in the sky is like our sun and may have its own solar system would help children construct a model of more appropriate size. At the least, children should know that the solar system is a very small part of the larger universe and these two entities are not the same thing.

Learning technologies

Infrared cameras. Space telescopes orbiting the Earth produce spectacular images of objects outside the solar system that can be found online and used to enthuse and inform children about the variety of galaxies, star clusters, nebulas, supernovas, etc. The recently launched James Webb Space Telescope is predicted to be the best source of these images in the coming years, capturing pictures in the infrared range of light. Discussions of these images can be linked to practical activities using infrared cameras in the classroom (also known as thermal imaging cameras). These devices can display images of, for instance, temperature changes within a kettle as it boils, a cup of tea as it cools, rubbing your hands together, and putting on/taking off items of outer clothing. However, these cameras are expensive (at least £200), but you may be able to borrow one from the science department of a local secondary school or university.

A fun activity to help children become familiar with entities in the wider universe is *Smaller to Larger*. Create a set of card labels of the following: *the moon, Mercury, Earth, Jupiter, star, solar system, nebula, galaxy, universe.* Give one child a card each then ask the nine children to line up in what they think is size order. If they get the order incorrect, tell them how many children are in the wrong place; e.g. if just Earth and Jupiter are incorrectly sequenced, say 'two'. Continue until they discover the correct order, and later discussion can include defining any unfamiliar labels, and showing pictures of how the objects vary in size in relation to each other. Many of the pedagogies described elsewhere in this chapter present visual evidence to children of how the solar system and beyond are arranged and are suitable when addressing these issues – for example, videos of imaginary journeys through space, travelling from Earth outwards to points beyond our solar system and into the wider universe. Discussion of the universe outside of the solar system is not part of the primary Programme of Study although older children would be stimulated by the immense distances involved, as well as the metaphysical ideas that might crop up, especially concerning the origins of the universe (what was there before the Big Bang?), the possibility of an infinite universe, and that there may be other universes as well as our own.

Sources: Fairhurst and Tyler (2022); Jang and Nam (2012); Spiliotopoulou-Papantoniou (2007).

Notes

1 It would be interesting to know to what extent reading Pratchett's books contributes to children's flat Earth misconceptions.

2 In the diagrams in this chapter, note that the distances between bodies, and the sizes of the bodies themselves, are not to scale unless otherwise stated.

Planning and assessment sheet 18 Earth and space
(For suggestions on how to use this sheet, see p. xxviii.)

Misconception	*Attainment re. expected standard*		
	Working towards	*Working at*	*Working above*
Year 1: *Seasonal changes*			
Summer temperatures are hotter because changes in plant life cause the seasons to change (instead of vice versa; reverse causality bias) (18.8)	✓		
Year 5: *Earth and space*			
Earth is a flat planet that has never-ending sides and bottom (18.1)	✓		
Earth is a flat, cylindrical planet where the bottom is never-ending (18.1)	✓		
Earth is a flat disc (18.1)	✓		
Earth is a ball and we live inside it (18.1)	✓		
Earth is a ball, although there is a flat part at the top where we live (18.1)	✓		
Space starts at the Earth's flat surface and continues above our heads, upwards and outwards for infinity (18.1)	✓		
It is possible to walk/sail off the edge of the Earth (18.1)	✓		
'Planet Earth' is spherical and exists out there in space, while where we live is a flat area, unrelated to that planet (18.1)	✓		
The Earth lies at the centre of the solar system, with the sun and the planets orbiting around it (geocentric model) (18.2)	✓	✓	
The planets orbit the sun, but are all the same distance away from the sun, sharing the same single orbit path (18.2)	✓		
The sun moves around the Earth – this is what causes daytime and night-time (i.e. the Earth does not spin) (18.3)	✓	✓	
The sun completes one orbit of the Earth once every 24 hours (18.3)	✓	✓	
Day and night are caused by the Earth orbiting the sun (i.e. ignoring the Earth's spin) (18.3)	✓	✓	
The Earth orbits the sun once every 24 hours (18.3)	✓	✓	

(continued)

(continued)

The moon only comes out at night (18.3)	✓	✓	
Night comes because the moon blocks sunlight (18.3)	✓		
At night, the sun is hiding behind clouds; during the day, the moon is hiding behind clouds (18.3)	✓		
The sun and moon swap places to cause day and night (18.3)	✓		
The sun and moon are fixed in position in space; day and night occur due to the Earth spinning which gives us changing views of the sun and moon (18.3)	✓	✓	
The sun disappears during the night because it has travelled into space (18.3)	✓		
At night, the sun is hiding underneath the Earth (18.3)	✓	✓	
At night, the sun is still there in the sky but it becomes dark (switches off) (18.3)	✓		
The sun rises vertically up into the sky in the morning, stays still in the sky, then moves vertically back down at night (18.4)	✓	✓	
When the sun sets, the moon rises in the same place in the sky, replacing the sun (18.4)			
At midday in the UK the sun is directly overhead (18.4)	✓	✓	✓
The Earth, sun, and moon are all about the same size (18.5)	✓	✓	
Like a planet, the moon orbits the sun (18.6)	✓	✓	
The moon's surface was formed when moon rock melted and boiled, which created bubbles that then burst to make craters (18.6)			✓
A shooting star (meteor) is a star like the sun (18.6)	✓	✓	
The Earth's shadow causes the different phases of the moon (18.7)	✓	✓	✓
The moon's phases are caused by passing clouds (18.7)	✓		
The moon's phases are caused by the Earth turning on its axis during the night so we look at the moon from a slightly different angle (associated with the misconception that the moon passes through all of its phases during the course of a single night) (18.7)			✓

(continued)

(continued)

As the moon gets further away from the sun, less light reaches it so there is more shadow, which causes the moon's phases (18.7)		✓	✓
The full or crescent moon phases are more easily recognized (and named) than the gibbous, half, or new moon phases (18.7)	✓	✓	✓
It is hotter in summer because the Earth is closer to the sun (18.8)	✓	✓	✓
Summer temperatures are hotter because the sun spends less time behind clouds (18.8)	✓	✓	
Summer temperatures are hotter because the sun burns more fiercely during the summer months (18.8)	✓	✓	
Summer temperatures are hotter because the cold outer planets stop the Earth taking heat from the sun (18.8)		✓	
Summer temperatures are hotter because the angle of the Earth's tilted axis has changed (18.8)		✓	✓
Pluto is a planet (18.9)	✓	✓	
The planets and stars do not move – they are part of the unchanging background of the night sky (18.10)	✓	✓	✓
The stars exist within the solar system (18.11)	✓	✓	
The planets are so far away they can only be seen using a telescope or binoculars (18.10)	✓	✓	✓
The universe is another name for the solar system (18.11)	✓	✓	
The Earth lies at the centre of the universe (18.11)	✓	✓	
Stars exist outside the solar system, but all lie the same distance from the Earth (18.11)		✓	✓
Stars in the same constellation are always close to each other (18.11)		✓	✓

Science glossary

Abdomen The part of an animal's main body furthest from the head; in humans, between the bottom of the ribs and the top of the pelvis

AC *See* Alternating current

Accelerate Move faster

Adaptation (biology) A feature arising due to natural selection that helps a living thing to survive in its environment

Air resistance A type of friction that opposes the movement of an object through the air

Alloy A mixture of two or more metals

Alternating current (AC) Electric current that switches its direction of travel around a circuit very rapidly. Most domestic electricity supplies are AC

Alveoli Air sacs found deep within the interior of the lungs; the site of gaseous exchange

Angle of incidence Angle at which a light ray meets a surface

Angle of reflection Angle at which a light ray reflects from a surface

Anthropogenic deniers Sceptics who despite accepting that climate change is real, reject the idea that human activity is responsible

Anthropomorphism Attributing human qualities (e.g. emotion) to things that are non-human

Apex predator *See* Top predator

Arterial/artery Refers to blood carried away from the heart and towards other body tissues

Arthropods Invertebrates with a hard external skeleton and jointed limbs, e.g. insects, spiders and crustaceans

Atom The smallest 'bit' of an element that can exist

Battery Several cells connected together

Boiling A liquid changing into a gas; occurs at or above the material's boiling point. *See also* Evaporation

Breathing The actions of inhaling and exhaling; ventilates the lungs to allow gaseous exchange

Buoyancy *See* Upthrust

Capillary Tiny blood vessels, a single cell thick

Carbon cycle The recycling of carbon atoms through living things, rocks, the soil, ocean, atmosphere, etc.

Cartesian diver Device, often home-made, that allows an object (e.g. an eye-dropper) to descend and ascend in a water-filled bottle subject to external pressure (see internet for further details)

Celestial body A natural object that exists in space, e.g. star, planet, moon

Cell 1. (electricity) Uses chemical energy to create voltage differences within a circuit, so allowing current to flow. 2. (biology) Building block of living things; many contain a nucleus, cell membrane and cytoplasm

Cellular respiration Glucose and oxygen react together to become carbon dioxide and water, releasing energy. Takes place within cells

Centripetal force Inward force on an object travelling a curved path acting towards the centre of rotation

CGI Computer-generated images

Chemical change A material changes into something completely different, losing its chemical identity; also known as a chemical reaction

Chlorophyll Green pigment found in plant cells that is important for photosynthesis

Chromosome Cellular structure made from DNA, proteins, etc.; contains the genes

Climate change Long-term transformations in temperature and weather patterns

Colloid A mixture where tiny 'bits' of one material are dispersed within a different material

Combustion Burning – material reacts with oxygen, producing heat and light (flames are not necessarily generated)

Community (ecology) All populations of species living in the same ecosystem

Compressed air Air at a pressure greater than atmospheric pressure

Condensation A gas changing into a liquid

Conduction The passage of heat or electricity through a (usually solid) material

Constellation A group of stars forming an imaginary arrangement in the night sky, e.g. Scorpio

Convection current The circular movement of a fluid due to changes in density caused by heating and cooling

CPR Cardiopulmonary resuscitation (heart massage); first aid for a patient whose heart has stopped beating

Current electricity Electricity that moves around a circuit; measured in amps (symbol A)

DC *See* Direct current

Decelerate Slow down

Decomposition The process of breaking down dead organic matter by bacteria and fungi

Deep space An empty area of space that is distant from celestial bodies

Density The mass of a material per unit volume

Dew point The temperature at which water vapour starts to condense to form dew

Digestion The breakdown of foodstuffs into simpler units before absorption

Direct current (DC) Electricity moving in a single direction through a circuit

Dispersion (wave) The separation of white light into different colours using, for instance, a prism

Displacement The volume of fluid pushed aside by an object that is immersed in that fluid

DNA Deoxyribonucleic acid

Dormant Alive but in a resting and inactive state, e.g. seed, bacterial spore, volcano

Drag *See* Air resistance

Dwarf planet Celestial body that is of sufficient size to exert enough gravity to become approximately spherical, but has not cleared its neighbouring space, and is not a moon. Smaller than a true planet, e.g. Pluto, Eris

Eclipse Occurs when one celestial body moves into the shadow of another

Ecology The study of how living things interact with their natural environment

Ecosystem A discrete area where living things and non-living things interact as part of a complete system

Electricity (current) A flow of charge

Electron Subatomic particle found outside the nucleus of an atom; carries a negative charge

Element A material that cannot be broken down into anything simpler without losing its chemical identity. The periodic table is a list of all known elements

Embryo A developmental stage that occurs after fertilization

Energy The capacity to do work. Can exist in different forms, e.g. heat, light, kinetic, sound

Epigenetics The study of inheritable changes in gene function that occur without a change in the DNA sequence

Evaporation A liquid changing into a gas below its boiling point. *See also* Boiling

Evolution Theory that organisms developed from earlier, different species, usually via the process of natural selection

Exoskeleton A rigid protective covering found on the outside of the bodies of some invertebrates

Fertilization When a male and female sex cell meet to produce a new individual

Floating Suspended in a fluid

Flora The entire plant life of an ecosystem

Fluid A liquid or a gas

Food A substance that supplies energy to an organism during cellular respiration

Food spoilage Process that results in a food product becoming inedible

Force A push or a pull; measured in Newtons (symbol N)

Force arrow Diagrammatic way to show the direction and size of a force

Freezing A liquid changing into a solid

Frequency (wave) The number of vibrations that occur every second; measured in Hertz (symbol Hz)

Friction A force that opposes the forward movement of an object

Gaseous exchange Occurs at surfaces where gases are swapped, e.g. lungs, leaf

Gene The unit of inheritance; carries information in the form of a DNA sequence

Geocentric Earth-centred

Germinate When a seed or spore first starts to grow (sprout)

Gestation Development of the embryo/foetus inside the womb

Global warming The gradual rise in atmospheric temperature that has been taking place over the past 150 years.

Globe map Map of the world superimposed on a sphere

Glowing splint Thin taper of wood that is set alight and then blown out, leaving a glowing ember; often used to test for the presence of oxygen

Greenhouse gases Gases in the atmosphere that absorb heat and are thought to contribute to global warming; notably carbon dioxide, water vapour, and methane.

Habitat The specific place where an organism lives

Heat A type of energy that can be transferred from hotter to cooler places

Heat equilibration Movement of energy that disperses heat equally throughout a system

Heliocentric Sun-centred

Homo sapiens The taxonomic name for the human species

Hydroponics Artificially growing plants in a liquid solution of nutrients in the absence of soil

Inertia The resistance of an object to its present state of motion

Infrasound Sound at too low a frequency for humans to hear; < 20 vibrations per second

Interdependence (ecology) The dependence that organisms in an ecosystem have on each other for survival

Invertebrate An animal without a backbone

Ion A charged atom

Irreversible change An alteration to something that cannot be undone

IWB Interactive whiteboard

Keratin A protein found in body structures such as nails, claws, hair, fur, feathers, hooves, and scales

Key (biology) A table or flowchart that helps in the identification of unknown organisms

KS1 Key Stage 1 (Years 1–2)

KS2 Key Stage 2 (Years 3–6)

KS3 Key Stage 3 (Years 7–9)

KS4 Key Stage 4 (Years 10–11)

LED Light-emitting diode; small electronic bulb, often coloured

Macroscopic Visible to the naked eye; the opposite of microscopic

Mass The amount of matter that an object is made from

Matter Something consisting of particles

Meaningful erroneous conceptual network Several related misconceptions linked in a learner's mind that make perfect sense because they all seem to fit well together

Melting A solid becoming a liquid

Meteor A fragment of rock originating from space passing through Earth's atmosphere, often appearing as a bright streak of light; colloquially known as a 'shooting star'

Meteorite A meteor that has landed on the Earth's surface

Microbe A microscopic organism; sometimes called a micro-organism

Microscopic Something too small to be seen with the naked eye

Mineral 1. (geology) A naturally occurring 'pure' chemical that has been formed by geological processes. 2. (nutrition) A chemical element essential for a healthy diet

Molecule Several atoms chemically joined together

Moon A large, natural object that orbits a planet; the Earth has one moon

Multicellular Made of more than one cell

Multimeter A multi-function electrical device that can be used to measure current, voltage, resistance, etc.

Mutation A random change in a gene that may affect an organism's characteristics

Negative terminal The point where electrons exit a cell and enter a circuit; labelled with a minus sign

Neutron Subatomic particle found in the nucleus of an atom; carries no charge (is electrically neutral)

Orbit The circular or elliptical (oval) path taken when one object in space revolves around another

Ovum (plural *ova*) The female sex cell in animals and some plants

Particle 1. (fundamental chemical unit) Used in primary science to describe atoms, molecules, ions, and sometimes electrons. 2. (granular) A small grain of finely divided solid

Pedagogy Method of teaching

Pathogens Microbes that cause a disease

Phases of the moon The different shapes of the illuminated part of the moon as seen from Earth

Photosynthesis Synthesis of food and oxygen from carbon dioxide and water in the presence of light

Phylum (plural *phyla*) The taxonomic category immediately below Kingdom

Physical change A change that does not result in an alteration in the identity of a chemical, e.g. state change

Pitch (sound) How high or low a sound is; depends on the frequency of the sound wave

Plane glass A flat, non-curved piece of glass

Plant blindness The tendency for people to ignore the presence of plant species; for example, in food chains, plants are thought to be irrelevant

Plasma The liquid part of blood (does not include red and white blood cells)

Pneumatic Using air under pressure to do work

Population (ecology) The total number of organisms belonging to the same species in an ecosystem

Positive terminal The point where electrons enter a cell after leaving a circuit; labelled with a plus sign

Potential difference The driving 'force' provided by a cell that causes current to move around a circuit

Predator An animal that hunts another animal for food

Prey An animal hunted by a predator

Primary colours (science) Red, green and blue. All other colours can be derived when these three colours are mixed together in different proportions

Processes of life Activities that something must be capable of before it can be called 'living'

Producer (ecology) A green plant

Programme of Study (POS) The subject-specific statutory content that is required to be taught in English state schools; initially enshrined in the Education Reform Act (1988)

Proton Subatomic particle found in the nucleus of an atom; carries a positive charge

Pseudoscience A methodology that might claim to be scientific but is not, such as astrology

Pyramid of numbers A diagram comparing the numbers of each population in a food chain

Radiation Energy transmitted as a wave

Reaction force Equal and opposite force acting in accordance with Newton's third law of motion

Refraction A wave changing direction as it moves from one medium to another; e.g. when a light ray moves from air to glass

Relative density The ratio of the density of a substance to the density of water

Retina Layer of light-sensitive cells at the back of the eye

Reverse causality bias When a learner confuses cause with effect, e.g. overweight people eat more because they are bigger.

Reversible changes Situations where materials are altered but are able to change back later to their original form

Rock Any natural material that is a product of geological processes and consists of an aggregate of more than one mineral

Secondary colours Cyan, magenta and yellow. These are produced when two primary colours are mixed

Seed dispersal Transport of mature seeds away from a parent plant by wind, animals, water, explosion, etc.

Seedling An early stage of plant development; follows germination

Sinking An object descending through a surrounding fluid because it has a greater density than the fluid

Solar system The sun and all of its orbiting celestial bodies, e.g. planets, moons, comets, asteroids, dwarf planets

Spectrum The rainbow-like band observed when white light is dispersed into its constituent colours

Sperm cell Male sex cell in animals

State change When a material changes from one state of matter to another, e.g. solid to liquid (melting)

State of matter At primary science level, solid, liquid or gas

Static electricity Electricity that is not moving around a circuit

Steam Water in the gaseous phase at or above its boiling point (100°C with pure water at normal atmospheric pressure)

Stem cell Immature, undifferentiated cell that can potentially develop into one of a variety of cell types such as a muscle cell or a skin cell

Subatomic particle Extremely small particles that form atoms, i.e. electrons, protons and quarks

Summer solstice The day of the year when one hemisphere of the Earth is most tilted towards the sun; in the northern hemisphere, around 21 June

Taxonomy The study of biological classification

Terminal velocity The maximum velocity gained by an object freefalling through a fluid

Thorax The middle part of an animal's body; in humans, the chest

Top predator A predator that is not hunted by another predator; occupies the top level in a food chain/web

Transmission (wave) A wave travelling through a material

Trans-Neptunian object (TNO) Celestial body that orbits the sun beyond Neptune, e.g. Pluto, Sedna

Trophic level The position occupied by an organism in a food chain, e.g. producer, primary consumer

Ultrasound Sound at too high a frequency for humans to hear; > 20,000 vibrations per second

Universe Everything that exists; all of space (and time), including the galaxies and the areas in-between them

Upthrust Upward force applied to any immersed or partly immersed body in a fluid

Vacuum The absence of matter; a true empty space

Venous/vein Refers to blood carried towards the heart and away from other tissues

Vertebrate An animal with a backbone

Vestige A feature of an organism left over from distant ancestors; it was important to ancestors but now has little use

Viscosity The 'thickness' of a liquid, e.g. treacle is very viscous

Voltage The driving force that causes current to flow around a circuit; measured in volts (symbol V)

Volume The physical space occupied by a material

Water vapour Water in the gaseous phase below the boiling point (100°C for pure water at normal atmospheric pressure)

Wave A ripple of energy away from a source, e.g. sound, light, water, pulse

Weight (force) The gravitational pull exerted by the Earth (or another celestial body) on an object

White light Light from e.g. the sun, an electric light bulb or a torch. Appears to be colourless but is a mixture of different-coloured light

Bibliography

Part One: Introduction

Allen, M. (2010) Learner error, affectual stimulation and conceptual change. *Journal of Research in Science Teaching*, 47: 151–173.

Allen, M. and English, J. (2024) Can AI chatbots help us to become better teachers of science? *Primary Science*, 181: 25–28.

Avraamidou, L. and Zembal-Saul, C. (2005) Giving priority to evidence in science teaching: A first-year elementary teacher's specialized practices and knowledge. *Journal of Research in Science Teaching*, 42: 965–986.

Bennett, J., Dunlop, L., Atkinson, L., Compton, S., Glasspoole-Bird, H., Lubben, F., Reiss, M.J. and Turkenburg, M.G.W. (2023) *A Systematic Review of Approaches to Primary Science Teaching*. York: University of York.

Carle, E. (1969) *The Very Hungry Caterpillar*. London: Puffin.

Carter, L. (2008) Sociocultural influences on science education: Innovation for contemporary times. *Science Education*, 92: 165–181.

diSessa, A.A. (1993) Toward an epistemology of physics. *Cognition and Instruction*, 10: 105–225.

Driver, R. (1983) *The Pupil as Scientist?* Milton Keynes: Open University Press.

Ehrlén, K. (2009) Drawings as representations of children's conceptions. *International Journal of Science Education*, 31: 41–57.

Harlen, W. (2009) Enquiry and good science teaching. *Primary Science Review*, 106: 5–8.

Hayward, J. and Gronland, G. (2021) *Conspiracy Theories in the Classroom: Guidance for Teachers*. London: Institute of Education, UCL.

Joung, Y.J. (2009) Children's typically-perceived-situations of floating and sinking. *International Journal of Science Education*, 31: 101–127.

Keogh, B. and Naylor, S. (2014) *Concept Cartoons in Science Education*, Set 1, revised edition. Sandbach: Millgate House.

Oliveira, A.W. and Sadler, T.D. (2008) Interactive patterns and conceptual convergence during student collaborations in science. *Journal of Research in Science Teaching*, 45: 634–658.

Otero, V.K. and Nathan, M.J. (2008) Preservice elementary teachers' views of their students' prior knowledge of science. *Journal of Research in Science Teaching*, 45: 497–523.

Phethean, K. (2009) When are you too old to play in science? *Primary Science Review*, 105: 12–15.

Piaget, J. (1929) *The Child's Conception of the World.* London: Routledge & Kegan Paul.

Pintrich, P.R., Marx, R.W. and Boyle, R.A. (1993) Beyond cold conceptual change: The role of motivational beliefs and classroom contextual factors in the process of conceptual change. *Review of Educational Research*, 63: 167–199.

Posner, G., Strike, K., Hewson, P. and Gertzog, W. (1982) Accommodation of a scientific conception: Towards a theory of conceptual change. *Science Education*, 66: 211–227.

Ruiz-Gallardo, J.R. and Paños, E. (2018) Primary school students' conceptions about microorganisms: Influence of theoretical and practical methodologies on learning. *Research in Science and Technological Education*, 36: 165–184.

Sequeria, M. and Freitas, M. (1987) Children's alternative conceptions about 'mold' and 'copper oxide'. In J.D. Novak (ed.) *Proceedings of the 2nd International Seminar: Misconceptions and Educational Strategies in Science and Mathematics*, 26–29 July, pp. 413–423. Ithaca, NY: Cornell University Press.

Vygotsky, L.S. (1962) *Thought and Language.* Cambridge, MA: MIT Press.

Zembal-Saul, C., Krajcik, J. and Blumenfeld, P. (2002) Elementary student teachers' science content representations. *Journal of Research in Science Teaching*, 39: 443–463.

Part Two: Biology

1. What makes some things living and others non-living?

Allchin, D. (2017) Is an apple living? *The American Biology Teacher*, 79: 509–511.

Arnold, B. and Simpson, M. (1979) The concept of living things. *Aberdeen College of Education Biology Newsletter*, 33: 17–21.

Bell, B. and Barker, M. (1982) Towards a scientific concept of 'animal'. *Journal of Biological Education*, 16: 197–200.

Bell, B.F. (1981a) Animal, plant, living: Notes for teachers. LISP Working Paper #30. Hamilton, New Zealand: Science Education Research Unit, University of Waikato.

Bell, B.F. (1981b) When is an animal, not an animal? *Journal of Biological Education*, 15: 213–218.

Collins, R. (2005) *Germs*. London: Bloomsbury Paperbacks.

Edelsztein, V. (2023) Has the coronavirus pandemic changed students' conceptions of microorganisms? Evidence from elementary school. *International Journal of Science Education*, 46: 733–749.

Goldman, E.J., Baumann, A.E. and Poulin-Dubois, D. (2023) Preschoolers' anthropomorphizing of robots: Do human-like properties matter? *Frontiers in Psychology*, 13, 1102370.

Jewell, N. (2002) What's inside a seed? *Primary Science Review*, 75: 12–14.

Osborne, J.F., Wadsworth, P. and Black, P.J. (1992) *SPACE Research Report: Processes of Life.* Liverpool: Liverpool University Press.

Ozgur, S. (2018) A study on young Turkish students' living thing conception. *Educational Research and Reviews*, 13: 150–165.

Piaget, J. (1929) *The Child's Conception of the World.* London: Routledge & Kegan Paul.

Rodríguez, A.M. (2006) *Edward Jenner: Conqueror of Smallpox (Great Minds of Science)*. Buffalo, NY: Enslow Pub Inc.

Ruiz-Gallardo, J.R. and Paños, E. (2018) Primary school students' conceptions about microorganisms: Influence of theoretical and practical methodologies on learning. *Research in Science and Technological Education*, 36: 165–184.

Sequeria, M. and Freitas, M. (1986) 'Death' and 'decomposition' of living organisms: Children's alternative frameworks. Paper presented at the 11th Conference of the Association for Teacher Education in Europe (ATEE), Toulouse, France, 1–5 September.

Sere, M.G. (1983) Premiers pas et premiers obstacles à l'acquisition de la notion de pression. LIRESPT Working Paper, University of Paris VII, Paris.

Simard, C. (2023) Microorganism education: Misconceptions and obstacles. *Journal of Biological Education*, 57 (2): 308-316.

Stavy, R. and Wax, N. (1989) Children's conceptions of plants as living things. *Human Development*, 32: 85–94.

Tamir, P., Gal-Chappin, R. and Nussnovitz, R. (1981) How do intermediate and junior high school students conceptualize living and non-living? *Journal of Research in Science Teaching*, 18: 241–248.

Tang, J.W., Bahnfleth, W.P., Bluyssen, P.M., Buonanno, G., Jimenez, J.L., Kurnitski, J., ... and Dancer, S.J. (2021) Dismantling myths on the airborne transmission of severe acute respiratory syndrome coronavirus-2 (SARS-CoV-2). *Journal of Hospital Infection*, 110: 89–96.

Wynn, A.N., Pan, I.L., Rueschhoff, E.E., Herman, M.A. and Archer, E.K. (2017) Student misconceptions about plants: A first step in building a teaching resource. *Journal of Microbiology and Biology Education*, 18: 1.

2. How living things are classified

Alanazi, F. H. (2018) Saudi children's taxonomic knowledge of animal species. *Journal of Baltic Science Education*, 17: 395-413.

Allen, M. (2015) Preschool children's taxonomic knowledge of animal species. *Journal of Research in Science Teaching*, 52: 107–134.

Allen, M. and Choudhary, A. (2012) Animal classification by early years children. Paper presented at UK Science Education Research Conference, NSLC, University of York.

Bell, B.F. (1981) What is a plant? Some children's ideas. *New Zealand Science Teacher*, 31: 10–14.

Brass, K. and Jobling, W. (1994) Digging into Science – a unit developed for a Year 5 class. In P.J. Fensham, R.F. Gunstone and R. White (eds) *The Content of Science*, pp. 112–120. London: Falmer Press.

Braund, M. (1998) Trends in children's concepts of vertebrate and invertebrate. *Journal of Biological Education*, 32: 103–110.

Carle, E. (1969) *The Very Hungry Caterpillar*. London: Puffin.

Chen, S.H. and Ku, C.H. (1998) Aboriginal children's alternative conceptions of animals and animal classification. *Proceedings of the National Science Council (Part D)*, 8: 55–67.

Davies, N. (1997) *Big Blue Whale*. London: Walker Books.

Hast, M. (2022) Acquisition of naïve and scientific conceptions: How linguistic context matters in Singaporean children's understanding of "animal". *Eurasia Journal of Mathematics, Science and Technology Education*, 18: 1–9.

Inagaki, K. and Hatano, G. (1987) Young children's spontaneous personification as analogy. *Child Development*, 58: 1013–1021.

Jones, V. and Hill, M. (2023) Learning to love creatures that buzz and scuttle. *Primary Science*, 179: 18–20.

Leach, J., Driver, R., Scott, P. and Wood-Robinson, C. (1992) *Progression in Conceptual Understanding of Ecological Concepts by Pupils Aged 5–16*. Leeds: Centre for Studies in Science and Mathematics Education, University of Leeds.

Papadopoulou, P. and Athanasiou, K. (2015) Children ideas for 'animal' compared to teachers' conceptions. *International Journal of Innovation and Research in Educational Sciences*, 2: 2349–2371.

Patrick, P. and Tunnicliffe, S.D. (2011) What plants and animals do early childhood and primary students' name? Where do they see them? *Journal of Science and Educational Technology*, 20: 630–642.

Prokop, P., Prokop, M. and Tunnicliffe, S.D. (2008) Effects of keeping animals as pets on children's concepts of vertebrates and invertebrates. *International Journal of Science Education*, 30: 431–449.

Rittig, N. and Scheuch, M. (2022) Preschoolers' conceptions about frogs and toads. Paper presented at the 11th World Environmental Education Congress, Prague, Czech Republic, 14-18 March.

Schlegel, J., Breuer, G. and Rupf, R. (2015) Local insects as flagship species to promote nature conservation? A survey among primary school children on their attitudes toward invertebrates. *Anthrozoös*, 28: 229–245.

Shepardson, D.P. (2002) Bugs, butterflies, and spiders: Children's understandings about insects. *International Journal of Science Education*, 24: 627–643.

Stavy, R. and Wax, N. (1989) Children's conceptions of plants as living things. *Human Development*, 32: 85–94.

Tema, B.O. (1989) Rural and urban African pupils' alternative conceptions of 'animal'. *Journal of Biological Education*, 23: 199–207.

Trowbridge, J.E. and Mintzes, J.J. (1985) Students' alternative conceptions of animal classification. *School Science and Mathematics*, 85: 304–316.

Trowbridge, J.E. and Mintzes, J.J. (1988) Alternative conceptions in animal classification: A cross-age study. *Journal of Research in Science Teaching*, 25: 547–571.

Villarroel, J.D., Antón, A., Zuazagoitia, D. and Nuño, T. (2018) Young children's understanding of plant life: A study exploring rural–urban differences in their drawings. *Journal of Biological Education*, 52: 331–341.

Waring, G. (2009) *Oscar and the Frog*. London: Walker Books.

Yen, C.F., Yao, T.W. and Chiu, Y.C. (2004) Alternative conceptions in animal classification focusing on amphibians and reptiles: A cross-age study. *International Journal of Science and Mathematics Education*, 2: 159–174.

Yen, C.F., Yao, T.W. and Mintzes, J.J. (2007) Taiwanese students' alternative conceptions of animal biodiversity. *International Journal of Science Education*, 29: 535–553.

3. Blood circulation

Bartoszeck, A.B., Machado, D.Z. and Amann-Gainotti, M. (2011) Graphic representation of organs and organ systems: Psychological view and developmental patterns. *Eurasia Journal of Mathematics, Science and Technology Education*, 7: 41–51.

Chavan, R. and Khandagale, V. (2022) Intricacies in identification of biological misconceptions. *Scholarly Research Journal for Interdisciplinary Studies*, 9: 16810–16819.

Dameraua, K., Beudels, M.M., Börtitz, C., El Balti, N., Funk, L., Westerholt, D., ... and Preisfeld, A. (2022) The effect of teaching with anatomical models in science education on primary school children's understanding of human organs. *International Electronic Journal of Elementary Education*, 14: 539–555.

Loukas, M., Benninger, B. and Tubbs, R.S. (2018) *Gray's Clinical Photographic Dissector of the Human Body*. Philadelphia, PA: Elsevier Health Sciences.

Osborne, J.F., Wadsworth, P. and Black, P.J. (1992) *SPACE Research Report: Processes of Life*. Liverpool: Liverpool University Press.

Pasco, D. and Ennis, C.D. (2015) Third grade students' mental models of blood circulation related to exercise. *Journal of Teaching in Physical Education*, 34: 76–92.

Schoon, K. and Boone, W. (1998) Self-efficacy and alternative conceptions of science of preservice elementary teachers. *Science Education*, 82: 553–568.

Symons, A., Brass, K. and Odgers, S. (1994) Year 9 bodies. In P.J. Fensham, R.F. Gunstone and R. White (eds) *The Content of Science*, pp. 177–184. London: Falmer Press.

Westbrook, S.L. and Marek, E.A. (1992) A cross-age study of student understanding of the concept of homeostasis. *Journal of Research in Science Teaching*, 29: 51–61.

Westman, A.K. and Karlsson, K.G. (2016) Does every cell get blood? Young students' discussions about illustrations of human blood circulation. *European Journal of Science and Mathematics Education*, 4: 161–175.

4. Breathing

Adeniyi, E.O. (1985) Misconceptions of selected ecological concepts held by some Nigerian students. *Journal of Biological Education*, 19: 311–316.

Arnaudin, M.W. and Mintzes, J.J. (1985) Students' alternative conceptions of the human circulatory system: A cross-age study. *Science Education*, 69: 721–733.

Chavan, R. and Khandagale, V. (2022) Intricacies in identification of biological misconceptions. *Scholarly Research Journal for Interdisciplinary Studies*, 9: 16810–16819.

Dameraua, K., Beudels, M.M., Börtitz, C., El Balti, N., Funk, L., Westerholt, D., ... and Preisfeld, A. (2022) The effect of teaching with anatomical models in science education on primary school children's understanding of human organs. *International Electronic Journal of Elementary Education*, 14: 539–555.

Fokides, E. and Mastrokoukou, A. (2018) Results from a study for teaching human body systems to primary school students using tablets. *Contemporary Educational Technology*, 9: 154–170.

Garcia-Barros, S., Martínez-Losada, C. and Garrido, M. (2011) What do children aged four to seven know about the digestive system and the respiratory system of the human being and of other animals? *International Journal of Science Education*, 33: 2095–2122.

Gellert, E. (1962) Children's conceptions of the content and functions of the human body. *Genetic Psychology Monographs*, 65: 293–405.

Osborne, J.F., Wadsworth, P. and Black, P.J. (1992) *SPACE Research Report: Processes of Life*. Liverpool: Liverpool University Press.

Pasco, D. and Ennis, C.D. (2015) Third grade students' mental models of blood circulation related to exercise. *Journal of Teaching in Physical Education*, 34: 76–92.

Sarwanto, S., Fajari, L.E.W. and Chumdari, C. (2021) Critical thinking skills and their impacts on elementary school students. *Malaysian Journal of Learning and Instruction*, 18: 161.

Symons, A., Brass, K. and Odgers, S. (1994) Year 9 bodies. In P.J. Fensham, R.F. Gunstone and R. White (eds) *The Content of Science*, pp. 177–184. London: Falmer Press.

Tracana, R.B., Varanda, I., Viveiros, S. and Carvalho, G.S.D. (2012) Children's conceptions about respiration before and after formal teaching: Identification of learning obstacles. In *Proceedings of the XV IOSTE Symposium: The Use of Science and Technology Education for Peace and Sustainable Development.* 29 October–3 November, pp. 1–11. Hammamet, Tunisia.

Westbrook, S.L. and Marek, E.A. (1992) A cross-age study of student understanding of the concept of homeostasis. *Journal of Research in Science Teaching*, 29: 51–61.

Yip, D.Y. (1998) Erroneous ideas about the composition of exhaled air. *School Science Review*, 80: 55–62.

5. Plant and animal nutrition

Allen, M. (2017) Early understandings of simple food chains: A learning progression for the preschool years. *International Journal of Science Education*, 39: 1485–1510.

Allen, M., Harper, L. and Clark, Z. (2019) Preschoolers' concepts of digestive physiology and their links with body mass index. *Research in Science Education.*

Althea (1999) *Talking it Through: Lunch Boxes.* Bradfield: Happy Cat Books.

Barker, M. (1985) Teaching and learning about photosynthesis. LISP Working Paper #220-9. Hamilton, New Zealand: Science Education Research Unit, University of Waikato.

Bell, B.F. and Brook, A. (1984) *Aspects of secondary students' understanding of plant nutrition.* Children's Learning in Science Project. Leeds: Centre for Studies in Science and Mathematics Education, University of Leeds.

Bjornsdottir, I., Almarsdottir, A.B. and Traulsen, J.M. (2009) The lay public's explicit and implicit definitions of drugs. *Research in Social and Administrative Pharmacy*, 5: 40–50.

Boyes, E. and Stanisstreet, M. (1990) Pupils' ideas concerning energy sources. *International Journal of Science Education*, 12: 513–529.

Brinkman, F. and Boschhuizen, R. (1989) Preinstructional ideas in biology: A survey in relation with different research methods on concepts of health and energy. In M.T. Voorbach and L.G.M. Prick (eds) *Teacher Education 5: Research and Developments on Teacher Education in the Netherlands*, pp. 75–90. London: Taylor & Francis.

Bruce, L. (2000) *Fran's Flower.* London: Bloomsbury Paperbacks.

Cakici, Y. (2005) Exploring Turkish upper primary level pupils' understanding of digestion. *International Journal of Science Education*, 27: 79–100.

Cruickshank, M. (2012) *Fags, Booze, Drugs + Children.* Glendaruel: Argyll Publishing.

Dameraua, K., Beudels, M.M., Börtitz, C., El Balti, N., Funk, L., Westerholt, D., ... and Preisfeld, A. (2022) The effect of teaching with anatomical models in science education on primary school children's understanding of human organs. *International Electronic Journal of Elementary Education*, 14: 539–555.

Dreyfus, A. and Jungwirth, E. (1988) The cell concept of 10th graders: Curricular expectations and reality. *International Journal of Science Education*, 10: 221–229.

Equit, M., Sambach, H., Niemczyk, J. and von Gontard, A. (2013) Children's concepts of the urinary tract. *Journal of Pediatric Urology*, 9: 648–652.

Fraiberg, S. (1959) *The Magic Years.* New York: Scribner's.

Hernell, O., Timby, N., Domellöf, M. and Lönnerdal, B. (2016) Clinical benefits of milk fat globule membranes for infants and children. *Journal of Pediatrics*, 173: S60–S65.

Käpylä, M.K., Heikkinen, J.P. and Asunta, T. (2009) Influence of content knowledge on pedagogical content knowledge: The case of teaching photosynthesis and plant growth. *International Journal of Science Education*, 31: 1395–1415.

Linfield, R. (2021) Finding the fun in healthy living. *Primary Science*, 168: 9–10.

Lucas, A. (1987) Public knowledge of biology. *Journal of Biological Education*, 21: 41–45.

Mintzes, J.J. (1984) Naive theories in biology: Children's concepts of the human body. *School Science and Mathematics*, 84: 548–555.

Opitz, S.T., Blankenstein, A. and Harms, U. (2017) Student conceptions about energy in biological contexts. *Journal of Biological Education*, 51: 427–440.

Osborne, J.F., Wadsworth, P. and Black, P J. (1992) *SPACE Research Report: Processes of Life*. Liverpool: Liverpool University Press.

Ozbas, S. and Kilinc, A. (2015) School students' conceptual patterns about weight gain: A preliminary study for biology teaching focusing on obesity. *Journal of Biological Education*, 49: 339–353.

Provo, J., Lamar, C. and Newby, T. (2002) Using a cross-section to train veterinary students to visualize anatomical structures in three dimensions. *Journal of Research in Science Teaching*, 39: 10–34.

Smith, E.L. and Anderson, C.W. (1984) Plants as producers: A case study of elementary science teaching. *Journal of Research in Science Teaching*, 21: 685–698.

Smith, E.L. and Anderson, C.W. (1986) Alternative student conceptions of matter cycling in ecosystems. Paper presented at the National Association for Research in Science Teaching, San Francisco, CA, 28–31 March.

Stavy, R., Eisen, Y. and Yaakobi, D. (1987) How Israeli students aged 13–15 understand photosynthesis. Unpublished manuscript, Tel Aviv University, Tel Aviv.

Stears, M. and Dempster, E.R. (2017) Changes in children's knowledge about their internal anatomy between first and ninth grades. In P. Katz (ed.) *Drawing for Science Education*, pp. 147–154. Rotterdam: Sense Publishers.

Teixeira, F.M. (2000) What happens to the food we eat? Children's conceptions of the structure and function of the digestive system. *International Journal of Science Education*, 22: 507–520.

Temple Clothier, A. (2019) Curiosity, co-creation and constructing knowledge with hydroponics for sustainable wellbeing. *Primary Science*, 156: 11–13.

Turner, S.A. (1997) Children's understanding of food and health in primary classrooms. *International Journal of Science Education*, 19: 491–508.

Uskola, A., Zamalloa, T. and Achurra, A. (2022) Using multiple strategies in deepening the understanding of the digestive system. *Journal of Biological Education*, 58 (2): 364–382.

Wandersee, J.H. (1983) Students' misconceptions about photosynthesis: A cross-age study. In H. Helm and J.D. Novak (eds) *Proceedings of the International Seminar: Misconceptions in Science and Mathematics*, 20–22 June, pp. 441–446. Ithaca, NY: Cornell University Press.

Xu, T. and Jones, I. (2016) An investigation of children's understanding of food and nutrition. *Early Childhood Education Journal*, 44: 289–297.

Yong, C.L. (2017) Utilizing concept cartoons to diagnose and remediate misconceptions related to photosynthesis among primary school students. In M. Karpudewan,

A.N.M. Zain and A.L. Chandrasegaran (eds) *Overcoming Students' Misconceptions in Science*, pp. 9–27. Singapore: Springer.

6. Food chains and webs

Allen, M. (2017) Early understandings of simple food chains: A learning progression for the preschool years. *International Journal of Science Education*, 39: 1485–1510.

Barenholz, H. and Tamir, P. (1987) The design, implementation and evaluation of a microbiology course with special reference to misconceptions and concept maps. In J.D. Novak (ed.) *Proceedings of the 2nd International Seminar: Misconceptions and Educational Strategies in Science and Mathematics*, 26–29 July, pp. 32–45. Ithaca, NY: Cornell University Press.

Barman, C.R., Griffiths, A.K. and Okebukola, P. (1995) High school students' concepts regarding food chains and food webs: A multinational study. *International Journal of Science Education*, 17: 775–782.

Biffi, D., Hartweg, B., de la Fuente, Y., Patterson, M., Stewart, M., Simanek, E. and Weinburgh, M. (2016) Developing an educational tool to model food chains. *Electronic Journal of Science Education*, 20: 40–53.

Fradley, C. (2006) Welly-walks for science learning. *Primary Science Review*, 91: 14–17.

Gallegos, L., Jerezano, M.E. and Flores, F. (1994) Preconceptions and relations used by children in the construction of food chains. *Journal of Research in Science Teaching*, 31: 259–272.

Gotwals, A.W. and Songer, N.B. (2010) Reasoning up and down a food chain: Using an assessment framework to investigate students' middle knowledge. *Science Education*, 94: 259–281.

Griffiths, A.K. and Grant, B.A.C. (1985) High school students' understanding of food webs: Identification of a learning hierarchy and related misconceptions. *Journal of Research in Science Teaching*, 22: 421–436.

Kharrazi, A., Kudo, S. and Allasiw, D. (2018) Addressing misconceptions to the concept of resilience in environmental education. *Sustainability*, 10: 4682.

Leach, J., Driver, R., Scott, P. and Wood-Robinson, C. (1992) *Progression in Conceptual Understanding of Ecological Concepts by Pupils Aged 5–16*. Leeds: Centre for Studies in Science and Mathematics Education, University of Leeds.

Leach, J., Driver, R., Scott, P. and Wood-Robinson, C. (1996) Children's ideas about ecology 3: Ideas found in children aged 5–16 about the interdependency of organisms. *International Journal of Science Education*, 18: 129–141.

Maxted, M.A. (1984) Pupils' prior beliefs about bacteria and science processes: Their inter-play in school science laboratory work. Unpublished MA thesis, University of British Columbia, Vancouver, BC.

Melis, C., Wold, P.A., Billing, A.M., Bjórgen, K. and Moe, B. (2020) Kindergarten children's perception about the ecological roles of living organisms. *Sustainability*, 12: 9565.

Munson, B.H. (1994) Ecological misconceptions. *Journal of Environmental Education*, 25: 30–34.

Schollum, B. (1983) Arrows in science diagrams: Help or hindrance for pupils? *Research in Science Education*, 13: 45–49.

Shepardson, D.P., Wee, B., Priddy, M. and Harbor, J. (2007) Students' mental models of the environment. *Journal of Research in Science Teaching*, 44: 327–348.

Tyler, P. (2020) Rethinking how we teach about ecosystems in primary schools. *Primary Science*, 162: 5–7.

Yoon, S.A., Goh, S.E. and Park, M. (2018) Teaching and learning about complex systems in K-12 science education: A review of empirical studies 1995–2015. *Review of Educational Research*, 88: 285–325.

7. Reproduction, inheritance and evolution

Adeniyi, E.O. (1985) Misconceptions of selected ecological concepts held by some Nigerian students. *Journal of Biological Education*, 19: 311–316.

Amprazis, A. and Papadopoulou, P. (2023) Plant blindness intensity throughout the school and university years: A cross-age study. In *Shaping the Future of Biological Education Research: Selected Papers from the ERIDOB 2022 Conference*, pp. 137–146. Basingstoke: Springer Nature.

Biro, V. (2004) *Gumdrop and the Dinosaur.* Worksop: Award Publications.

Bishop, B.A. and Anderson, C.W. (1990) Student conceptions of natural selection and its role in evolution. *Journal of Research in Science Teaching*, 27: 415–427.

Budden, B. (2018) Common misconceptions: Evolution. *Why & How Magazine*, PSTT. Available at: https://pstt.org.uk/resources/common-misconceptions/ (accessed 14 March 2024).

Czekanski-Moir, J.E. and Rundell, R.J. (2020) Endless forms most stupid, icky, and small: The preponderance of noncharismatic invertebrates as integral to a biologically sound view of life. *Ecology and Evolution*, 10: 12638–12649.

Deadman, J.A. and Kelly, P.J. (1978) What do secondary school boys understand about evolution and heredity before they are taught the topics? *Journal of Biological Education*, 12: 7–15.

Deniz, H., Donnelly, L.A. and Yilmaz, I. (2008) Exploring the factors related to acceptance of evolutionary theory among Turkish preservice biology teachers: Toward a more informative conceptual ecology for biological evolution. *Journal of Research in Science Teaching*, 45: 420–443.

Dennis, M., Duggan, A. and McGregor, D. (2015) Evolution in action. *Primary Science*, 131: 8–10.

Engel-Clough, E. and Wood-Robinson, C. (1985) Children's understanding of inheritance. *Journal of Biological Education*, 19: 304–310.

Gormley, K., Birdsall, S. and France, B. (2022) Same, same but different! Exploring children's understandings of within-species variation. *Journal of Biological Education*, 58: 530–551.

Hackling, M.W. and Treagust, D.F. (1982) What lower secondary students should understand about the mechanisms of inheritance, and what they do understand following instruction. *Research in Science Education*, 12: 78–88.

Hooper, M. (1996) *Dinosaur.* Cambridge: Cambridge University Press.

Huxley, T.H. (1890) *Man's Place in Nature, and Other Anthropological Essays.* New York: Hurst and Company.

Ibourk, A., Williams, M., Opperman, A., Cisterna, D., Nazar, C.R. and Xie, Y. (2018) Young students' understanding of the relationship between inheritance and variation of traits using structural equation modeling. *Science Education*, 102: 1201–1238.

Jensen, M. and Finley, F. (1995) Teaching evolution using historical arguments in a conceptual change strategy. *Science Education*, 79: 147–166.

Kargbo, D.B., Hobbs, E.D. and Erickson, G.L. (1980) Student beliefs about inherited characteristics. *Journal of Biological Education*, 14: 137–146.

Meikle, W.E. and Scott, E.C. (2010) Why are there still monkeys? *Evolution: Education and Outreach*, 3: 573–575.

Nehm, R.H. and Schonfeld, I.S. (2008) Measuring knowledge of natural selection: A comparison of the CINS, an open-response instrument, and an oral interview. *Journal of Research in Science Teaching*, 45: 1131–1160.

Nicholson, C. (2009) The teaching of evolution in primary schools. *Primary Science Review*, 107: 13–15.

Russell, T. and McGuigan, L. (2019) Teaching and learning about evolution: A developmental perspective. *Primary Science*, 156: 33–35.

Schussler, E.E. (2008) From flowers to fruits: How children's books represent plant reproduction. *International Journal of Science Education*, 30: 1677–1696.

Stern, F. and Kampourakis, K. (2017) Teaching for genetics literacy in the post-genomic era. *Studies in Science Education*, 53: 193–225.

Taylor, N. and Jones, P. (2001) Animal adaptation through modelling. *Primary Science Review*, 66: 17–19.

Tsui, C.Y. and Treagust, D.F. (2007) Understanding genetics: Analysis of secondary students' conceptual status. *Journal of Research in Science Teaching*, 44: 205–235.

Tuomisto, H., Tuomisto, M. and Tuomisto, J.T. (2018) How scientists perceive the evolutionary origin of human traits: Results of a survey study. *Ecology and Evolution*, 8: 3518–3533.

Zacharia, Z.C., Lazaridou, C. and Avraamidou, L. (2016) The use of mobile devices as means of data collection in supporting elementary school students' conceptual understanding about plants. *International Journal of Science Education*, 38: 596–620.

Part Three: Chemistry

8. Chemical changes in materials

Ahtee, M. and Varjola, I. (1998) Students' understanding of chemical reaction. *International Journal of Science Education*, 20: 305–316.

Angeloudi, A., Papageorgiou, G. and Markos, A. (2018) Primary students' argumentation on factors affecting dissolving. *Science Education International*, 29: 127–136.

Bouma, H., Brandt, I. and Sutton, C. (1990) *Words as Tools in Science Lessons*. Amsterdam: Chemiedidactiek, University of Amsterdam.

Çalik, M. and Ayas, A. (2005) A comparison of level of understanding of eighth-grade students and science student teachers related to selected chemistry concepts. *Journal of Research in Science Teaching*, 42: 638–667.

Cosgrove, M. and Osborne, R. (1980) Physical change. LISP Working Paper #26. Hamilton, New Zealand: Science Education Research Unit, University of Waikato.

de Andrade, V., Freire, S. and Baptista, M. (2017) Constructing scientific explanations: A system of analysis for students' explanations. *Research in Science Education*, 49: 787–807.

Department of Education and Science (DES) (1984) *Science in Schools. Age 15: Report No. 2*. Assessment of Performance Unit. London: HMSO.

Driver, R. (1985) Beyond appearances: The conservation of matter under physical and chemical transformations. In R. Driver, E. Guesne and A. Tiberghien (eds) *Children's Ideas in Science*, pp. 145–169. Milton Keynes: Open University Press.

Fotou, N. (2014) Students' predictions in novel situations and the role of self-generated analogies in their reasoning. Unpublished doctoral dissertation, University of Leeds.

Hadenfeldt, J.C., Neumann, K., Bernholt, S., Liu, X. and Parchmann, I. (2016) Students' progression in understanding the matter concept. *Journal of Research in Science Teaching*, 53: 683–708.

Hand, B.M. and Treagust, D.F. (1988) Application of a conceptual conflict teaching strategy to enhance student learning of acids and bases. *Research in Science Education*, 18: 53–63.

Holloway, T. (2019) Common misconceptions: Time for a change! *Why & How Magazine*, PSTT. Available at: https://pstt.org.uk/resources/common-misconceptions/ (accessed 19 March 2024).

Knox, J. (1985) A study of secondary students' ideas about the process of burning. MEd thesis, University of Leeds.

Meheut, M., Saltiel, E. and Tiberghien, A. (1985) Pupils' (11–12-year-olds) conceptions of combustion. *European Journal of Science Education*, 7: 83–93.

Panagiotaki, M.A. and Ravanis, K. (2014) What would happen if we strew sugar in water or oil? Predictions and drawings of preschoolers. *International Journal of Research in Education Methodology*, 5: 579–585.

Papageorgiou, G., Grammaticopoulou, M. and Johnson. P.M. (2010) Should we teach primary pupils about chemical change? *International Journal of Science Education*, 32: 1647–1664.

Pattison, D. and Willis, P. (2016) *Burn: Michael Faraday's Candle*. Little Rock, AR: Mims House.

Schoon, K. and Boone, W. (1998) Self-efficacy and alternative conceptions of science of preservice elementary teachers. *Science Education*, 82: 553–568.

Watson, J., Prieto, T. and Dillon, J. (1997) Consistency of students' explanations about combustion. *Science Education*, 81: 425–444.

9. Particles

Bouma, H., Brandt, I. and Sutton, C. (1990) *Words as Tools in Science Lessons*. Amsterdam: Chemiedidactiek, University of Amsterdam.

Brook, A., Briggs, H. and Driver, R. (1984) *Aspects of Secondary Students' Understanding of the Particulate Nature of Matter*. Children's Learning in Science Project. Leeds: Centre for Studies in Science and Mathematics Education, University of Leeds.

Gómez, E.J., Benarroch, A. and Marín, N. (2006) Evaluation of the degree of coherence found in students' conceptions concerning the particulate nature of matter. *Journal of Research in Science Teaching*, 43: 577–598.

Hadenfeldt, J.C., Neumann, K., Bernholt, S., Liu, X. and Parchmann, I. (2016) Students' progression in understanding the matter concept. *Journal of Research in Science Teaching*, 53: 683–708.

Harrison, A. and Treagust, D. (1996) Secondary students' mental models of atoms and molecules: Implications for teaching chemistry. *Science Education*, 80: 509–534.

Lee, K.W.L. and Tan, S.N. (2004) Atoms and molecules: Do they have a place in primary science? *Primary Science Review*, 82: 21–23.

Liu, X. and Lesniak, K. (2006) Progression in children's understanding of the matter concept from elementary to high school. *Journal of Research in Science Teaching*, 43: 320–347.

Nakhleh, M.B., Samarapungavan, A. and Saglam, Y. (2005) Middle school students' beliefs about matter. *Journal of Research in Science Teaching*, 42: 581–612.

Novick, S. and Nussbaum, J. (1978) Junior high school pupils' understanding of the particulate nature of matter: An interview study. *Science Education*, 62: 273–281.

Nussbaum, J. (1985) The particulate nature of matter in the gaseous state. In R. Driver, E. Guesne and A. Tiberghien (eds) *Children's Ideas in Science*, pp. 124–144. Milton Keynes: Open University Press.

Papageorgiou, G., Stamovlasis, D. and Johnson, P.M. (2010) Primary teachers' particle ideas and explanations of physical phenomena: Effect of an in-service training course. *International Journal of Science Education*, 32: 629–652.

Piaget, J. and Inhelder, B. (1974) *The Child's Construction of Quantities*. London: Routledge & Kegan Paul.

Renstrom, L., Andersson, B. and Marton, F. (1990) Students' conceptions of matter. *Journal of Education Psychology*, 82: 555–569.

Rips, L.J. and Hespos, S.J. (2015) Divisions of the physical world: Concepts of objects and substances. *Psychological Bulletin*, 141: 786–812.

Samarapungavan, A., Bryan, L.A., Staudt, C., Sapkota, B., Will Pinto, H.E., Broadhead, J.M. and Kimball, N. (2023) Using technology-mediated inquiry to help young learners reimagine the visible world through simple particle models. *Journal of Research in Science Teaching*, 60: 390–422.

Sere, M.G. (1985) The gaseous state. In R. Driver, E. Guesne and A. Tiberghien (eds) *Children's Ideas in Science*, pp. 105–123. Milton Keynes: Open University Press.

Shallcross, D.E., Shallcross, N.K., Schofield, K.G. and Franklin, S.D. (2016) Why does jelly wobble? A workshop for primary school children on the structure and properties of solids. *Journal of Emergent Science*, 11: 38–44.

Skamp, K. (2005) Teaching about 'stuff'. *Primary Science Review*, 89: 20–22.

Smith, P.S. and Plumley, C.L. (2016) *A Review of the Research Literature on Teaching about the Small Particle Model of Matter to Elementary Students*. Chapel Hill, NC: Horizon Research, Inc. Available at: https://files.eric.ed.gov/fulltext/ED587209.pdf (accessed 30 May 2024).

Stains, M. and Talanquer, V. (2007) Classification of chemical substances using particulate representations of matter: An analysis of student thinking. *International Journal of Science Education*, 29: 643–661.

Stuart, I. (2021) Even the youngest children can learn atomic theory! *Primary Science*, 168: 21–26.

10. Solids, liquids, and gases

Adams, K. and Feagin, S. (2017) Describing matter. *Science and Children*, 54 (8): 52–57.

Ahtee, M. and Varjola, I. (1998) Students' understanding of chemical reaction. *International Journal of Science Education*, 20: 305–316.

Allen, M. and Kambouri-Danos, M. (2017) Substantive conceptual development in preschool science: Contemporary issues and future directions. *Early Child Development and Care*, 187: 181–191.

Baji, F. and Haeusler, C. (2022) Introducing Iranian primary children to atoms and molecules. *Research in Science Education*, 52, 1387–1418.

Bar, V. (1986) *The Development of the Conception of Evaporation*. Jerusalem: The Amos de Shalit Science Teaching Centre, The Hebrew University of Jerusalem.

Bar, V., Brosh, Y. and Sneider, C. (2016) Weight, mass, and gravity: Threshold concepts in learning science. *Science Educator*, 25 (1): 22–34.

Bar, V. and Galili, I. (1994) Stages of children's views about evaporation. *International Journal of Science Education*, 16: 157–174.

Brook, A. and Driver, R. (in collaboration with Hind, D.) (1989) *Progression in Science: The Development of Pupils' Understanding of Physical Characteristics of Air Across the Age Range 5–16 Years*. Leeds: Centre for Studies in Science and Mathematics Education, University of Leeds.

Dove, J. (1998) Alternative conceptions about the weather. *School Science Review*, 79: 65–69.

Ford, D.J. (2005) The challenges of observing geologically: Third graders' descriptions of rock and mineral properties. *Science Education*, 89: 276–295.

Frankel-Hauser, J. (1998) *Science Play*. Nashville, TN: Ideal Publications.

Galili, I. and Bar, V. (1997) Children's operational knowledge about weight. *International Journal of Science Education*, 19: 317–340.

Goodwin, A. (2003) Evaporation and boiling: Trainee science teachers' understanding. *School Science Review*, 84: 131–141.

Holloway, T. (2019) Common misconceptions: Time for a change! *Why & How Magazine*, PSTT. Available at: https://pstt.org.uk/resources/common-misconceptions/ (accessed 9 April 2024).

Jenkins, M. (2008) *The Emperor's Egg*. London: Walker Books.

Jones, B.L. and Lynch, P.P. (1989) Children's understanding of the notions of solid and liquid in relation to some common substances. *International Journal of Science Education*, 11: 417–427.

Leite, L., Mendoza, J. and Borsese, A. (2007) Teachers' and prospective teachers' explanations of liquid state phenomena: A comparative study involving three European countries. *Journal of Research in Science Teaching*, 44: 349–374.

National Physical Laboratory (2024) *Creating Impact from Science and Engineering*. Available at: https://www.npl.co.uk/ (accessed 9 April 2024).

Opitz, S.T., Harms, U., Neumann, K., Kowalzik, K. and Frank, A. (2015) Students' energy concepts at the transition between primary and secondary school. *Research in Science Education*, 45: 691–715.

Osborne, R.J. and Cosgrove, M.M. (1983) Children's conceptions of the changes of state of water. *Journal of Research in Science Teaching*, 20: 825–838.

Oversby, J. (2004) Science knowledge: Representing liquids. *Primary Science Review*, 83: 27.

Paik, S.H. (2015) Exploring the role of a discrepant event in changing the conceptions of evaporation and boiling in elementary school students. *Chemistry Education Research and Practice*, 16: 670–679.

Ross, K. and Law, E. (2003) Children's naive ideas about melting and freezing. *School Science Review*, 85: 99–102.

Russell, T., Longden, K. and McQuigan, L. (1991) *SPACE Research Report: Materials*. Liverpool: Liverpool University Press.

Russell, T. and Watt, D. (1990) *SPACE Research Report: Evaporation and Condensation*. Liverpool: Liverpool University Press.

Samarapungavan, A., Bryan, L. and Wills, J. (2017) Second graders' emerging particle models of matter in the context of learning through model-based inquiry. *Journal of Research in Science Teaching*, 54: 988–1023.

Shallcross, D.E., Shallcross, N.K., Schofield, K.G. and Franklin, S.D. (2016) Why does jelly wobble? A workshop for primary school children on the structure and properties of solids. *Journal of Emergent Science*, 11: 38–44.

Stavy, R. (1990) Children's conception of changes in the state of matter: From liquid (or solid) to gas. *Journal of Research in Science Teaching*, 27: 247–266.

Stavy, R. (1994) States of matter: Pedagogical sequence and teaching strategies based on cognitive research. In P.J. Fensham, R.F. Gunstone and R. White (eds) *The Content of Science*, pp. 221–236. London: Falmer Press.

Stavy, R. and Stachel, D. (1984) *Children's Ideas about Solid and Liquid*. Tel Aviv: Israeli Science Teaching Centre, School of Education, Tel Aviv University.

Stylos, G. and Kotsis, K.T. (2021) Hands-on experiments to teach basic heat concepts. *Primary Science*, 167: 32–34.

Tiberghien, A., Sere, M.G., Barboux, M. and Chomat, A. (1983) Étude des représentations préalables de quelques notions de physique et leur évolution. LIRESPT Working Paper, University of Paris VII, Paris.

Wang, T.L. and Tseng, Y.K. (2018) The comparative effectiveness of physical, virtual, and virtual-physical manipulatives on third-grade students' science achievement and conceptual understanding of evaporation and condensation. *International Journal of Science and Mathematics Education*, 16: 203–219.

11. The Earth

Bhattacharya, D., Carroll Steward, K. and Forbes, C. T. (2021) Empirical research on K-16 climate education: A systematic review of the literature. *Journal of Geoscience Education*, 69:, 223–247.

Brass, K. and Duke, M. (1994) Primary science in an integrated curriculum. In P.J. Fensham, R.F. Gunstone and R. White (eds) *The Content of Science*, pp. 100–111. London: Falmer Press.

Ennis, M. (2023) School of rock: Enthusing children by celebrating science curriculum links. *Primary Science*, 179: 24–26.

Ford, D.J. (2005) The challenges of observing geologically: Third graders' descriptions of rock and mineral properties. *Science Education*, 89: 276–295.

Frankel-Hauser, J. (1998) *Science Play*. Nashville, TN: Ideal Publications.

Frøyland, M., Remmen, K.B. and Sørvik, G.O. (2016) Name-dropping or understanding? Teaching to observe geologically. *Science Education*, 100: 923–951.

Guffey, S.K. and Slater, T.F. (2020) Geology misconceptions targeted by an overlapping consensus of US national standards and frameworks. *International Journal of Science Education*, 42: 469–492.

Happs, J.C. (1985) Mountains. LISP Working Paper #202. Hamilton, New Zealand: Science Education Research Unit, University of Waikato.

Kali, Y., Orion, N. and Eylon, B.S. (2003) Effect of knowledge integration activities on students' perception of the earth's crust as a cyclic system. *Journal of Research in Science Teaching*, 40: 545–565.

King, C., Fleming, A., Kennett, P. and Thompson, D. (2005) How effectively do science textbooks teach earth science? *School Science Review*, 87: 95–104.

Koba, S.B. and Mitchell, C.T.T. (2011) *Hard-to-Teach Science Concepts: A Framework to Support 3rd–5th Grade Learners.* Arlington, VA: NSTA Press.

Marques, L. and Thompson, D. (1997) Portuguese students' understanding at ages 10–11 and 14–15 of the origin and nature of the Earth and the development of life. *Research in Science and Technological Education*, 15: 29–51.

Most, B. (1978) *If the Dinosaurs Came Back.* Boston, MA: Houghton Mifflin Harcourt.

Nussbaum, J. (1985) The Earth as a cosmic body. In R. Driver, E. Guesne and A. Tiberghien (eds) *Children's Ideas in Science.* Milton Keynes: Open University Press.

Russell, T., Bell, D., Longden, K. and McGuigan, L. (1993) *SPACE Research Report: Rocks, Soil and Weather.* Liverpool: Liverpool University Press.

Russell, T. and McGuigan, L. (2015) Why are there still apes if apes changed into people? *Primary Science*, 139: 22–25.

Schoon, K. and Boone, W. (1998) Self-efficacy and alternative conceptions of science of preservice elementary teachers. *Science Education*, 82: 553–568.

Trend, R. (2001) Deep framework: A preliminary study of U.K. primary teachers' conceptions of geological time and perceptions of geoscience. *Journal of Research in Science Teaching*, 38: 191–221.

Turkmen, H. (2017) After almost half-century landing on the moon and still countering basic astronomy conceptions. *European Journal of Physics Education*, 6 (2): 1–17.

Whitburn, N. (2007) Earth science in the classroom. *Primary Science Review*, 96: 30–34.

12. Climate change

Allen, M. and Parry, S. (2023) Links between children's scientific understanding and their rejection of pseudoscientific claims indicative of climate change scepticism. In: *ESERA 2023: 15th Biennial Conference of the European Science Education Research Association*; 28 Aug.–1 Sept. 2023, Cappadocia, Turkey.

Bhattacharya, D., Carroll Steward, K. and Forbes, C.T. (2021) Empirical research on K-16 climate education: A systematic review of the literature. *Journal of Geoscience Education*, 69: 223–247.

Boyes, E. and Stanisstreet, M. (1993) The 'greenhouse effect': Children's perceptions of causes, consequences and cures. *International Journal of Science Education*, 15: 531–552.

Francis, C., Boyes, E., Qualter, A. and Stanisstreet, M. (1993) Ideas of elementary students about reducing the 'greenhouse effect'. *Science Education*, 77: 375–392.

Hayward, J. and Gronland, G. (2021) *Conspiracy Theories in the Classroom: Guidance for Teachers.* London: Institute of Education, UCL.

Kovaka, K. (2021) Climate change denial and beliefs about science. *Synthese*, 198: 2355–2374.

Skamp, K.R., Boyes, E. and Stanisstreet, M. (2009) Global warming responses at the primary secondary interface: 1 Students' beliefs and willingness to act. *Australian Journal of Environmental Education*. 25: 15–30.

Part Four: Physics

13. Forces and magnets

Alonzo, A.C. and Steedle, J.T. (2009) Developing and assessing a force and motion learning progression. *Science Education*, 93: 389–421.

Bar, V., Brosh, Y. and Sneider, C. (2016) Weight, mass, and gravity: Threshold concepts in learning science. *Science Educator*, 25 (1): 22–34.

Bar, V., Zinn, B., Goldmuntz, R. and Sneider, C. (1994) Children's conceptions about weight and free fall. *Science Education*, 78: 149–169.

Bar, V., Zinn, B. and Rubin, E. (1997) Children's ideas about action at a distance. *International Journal of Science Education*, 19: 1137–1157.

Bennett, R. (1996) An investigation into some Key Stage 2 children's learning of foundation concepts associated with geared mechanisms. *Journal of Design and Technology Education*, 1: 218–229.

Blown, E.J. and Bryce, T.G.K. (2013) Thought-experiments about gravity in the history of science and in research into children's thinking. *Science and Education*, 22: 419–481.

Canlas, I.P. (2021) Using visual representations in identifying students' preconceptions in friction. *Research in Science & Technological Education*, 39: 156–184.

Champagne, A., Klopfer, L., Solomon, C. and Cohen, A. (1980) *Interactions of Students' Knowledge with their Comprehension and Design of Science Experiments.* Technical Report. Pittsburgh, PA: Learning Research and Development Center, University of Pittsburgh.

Driver, R. (1983) *The Pupil as Scientist?* Milton Keynes: Open University Press.

Driver, R., Squires, A., Rushworth, P. and Wood-Robinson, V. (1994) *Making Sense of Secondary Science: Research into Children's Ideas.* London: Routledge.

Frankel-Hauser, J. (1998) *Science Play.* Nashville, TN: Ideal Publications.

Grigorovitch, A. and Nertivich, D. (2017) Introduction to magnets for lower primary school students. *European Journal of Education Studies*, 3 (3): 144–154.

Gunstone, R.F. and White, R.T. (1981) Understanding of gravity. *Science Education*, 65: 291–299.

Hast, M. and Howe, C. (2015) Children's predictions and recognition of fall: The role of object mass. *Cognitive Development*, 36: 103–110.

Howe, C., Taylor Tavares, J. and Devine, A. (2012) Everyday conceptions of object fall: Explicit and tacit understanding during middle childhood. *Journal of Experimental Child Psychology*, 111: 351–366.

Jones, A.T. (1983) Investigation of students' understanding of speed, velocity and acceleration. *Research in Science Education*, 13: 95–104.

Meyer, K. (1991) Children as experimenters: Elementary students' actions in an experimental context with magnets. Unpublished doctoral dissertation, University of British Columbia, Vancouver, BC.

Minstrell, J. (1982) Explaining the 'at rest' condition of an object. *The Physics Teacher*, 20: 10–14.

Monach, J. and Turford, B. (2019) Common misconceptions: Levers, gears and pulleys. *Why & How Magazine*, PSTT. Available at: https://pstt.org.uk/resources/common-misconceptions/ (accessed 11 April 2024).

Montanero, M., Suero, M.I., Pérez, A.L. and Pardo, P.J. (2002) Implicit theories of static interactions between two bodies. *Physics Education*, 37: 318–323.

Murphy, J. (1982) *On the Way Home.* London: Macmillan Children's Books.

Osborne, R. (1984) Children's dynamics. *The Physics Teacher*, 22: 504–508.

Pfundt, H. and Duit, R. (1994) *Bibliography: Students' Alternative Frameworks and Science Education.* Kiel: IPN.

Piaget, J. (1970) *The Child's Conception of Movement and Speed.* London: Routledge & Kegan Paul.

Reynoso, E., Fierro, E., Torres, G., Vicentini-Missoni, M. and Pérez de Celis, J. (1993) The alternative frameworks presented by Mexican students and teachers concerning the free fall of bodies. *International Journal of Science Education*, 15: 127–138.

Rogers, B. (2022) Forces and motion in a nutshell. *Primary Science*, 172: 8–10.

Ruggiero, S., Cartelli, A., Dupre, F. and Vicentini-Missoni, M. (1985) Weight, gravity and air pressure: Mental representations by Italian middle school pupils. *European Journal of Science Education*, 7: 181–194.

Russell, T., McQuigan, L. and Hughues, A. (1998) *SPACE Research Report: Forces.* Liverpool: Liverpool University Press.

Stead, K. and Osborne, R. (1980a) Friction. LISP Working Paper #19. Hamilton, New Zealand: Science Education Research Unit, University of Waikato.

Stead, K. and Osborne, R. (1980b) Gravity. LISP Working Paper #20. Hamilton, New Zealand: Science Education Research Unit, University of Waikato.

Stepanović, M.B., Balać, S., Gavrilović, B. and Kozoderović, G. (2023) How primary students understand the concept of magnetism. *Science International Journal*, 2: 203–208.

Terry, C. and Jones, G. (1986) Alternative frameworks: Newton's third law and conceptual change. *European Journal of Science Education*, 8: 291–298.

Tomara, M., Tselfes, V. and Gouscos, D. (2017) Instructional strategies to promote conceptual change about force and motion: A review of the literature. *Themes in Science and Technology Education*, 10: 1–16.

Vicentini-Missoni, M. (1981) Earth and gravity: Comparison between adults' and children's knowledge. In W. Jung, H. Pfundt and C.J. von Rhoneck (eds) *Proceedings of the International Workshop on Problems Concerning Students' Representation of Physics and Chemistry Knowledge*, 14–16 September, pp. 223–253. Ludwigsburg: Pädagogische Hochschule.

Viennot, L. (1979) Spontaneous learning in elementary dynamics. *European Journal of Science Education*, 1: 205–221.

Viennot, L. and Rozier, S. (1994) Pedagogical outcomes of research in science education: Examples in mechanics and thermodynamics. In P.J. Fensham, R.F. Gunstone and R. White (eds) *The Content of Science*, pp. 237–254. London: Falmer Press.

Waring, G. (2007) *Oscar and the Cricket.* London: Walker Books.

Watts, D.M. (1982) Gravity: Don't take it for granted. *Physics Education*, 17: 116–121.

14. Floating and sinking

Bar, V., Brosh, Y. and Sneider, C. (2016) Weight, mass, and gravity: Threshold concepts in learning science. *Science Educator*, 25 (1): 22–34.

Bar, V., Zinn, B., Goldmuntz, R. and Sneider, C. (1994) Children's conceptions about weight and free fall. *Science Education*, 78: 149–169.

Biddulph, F. and Osborne, R. (1984) Pupils' ideas about floating and sinking. Paper presented to the Australian Science Education Research Association Conference, Melbourne, VIC, May.

Carr, M., Barker, M., Bell, B., Biddulph, F., Jones, A., Kirkwood, V., Pearson, J. and Symington, D. (1994) The constructivist paradigm and some implications for science content and pedagogy. In P.J. Fensham, R.F. Gunstone and R. White (eds) *The Content of Science*, pp. 147–160. London: Falmer Press.

Elmali, S. and Laçin şimşek, C. (2021) Pre-school children's opinions about the concepts of floating and sinking and the effect of in-class interactions on their opinions. *Hacettepe University Journal of Education*, 36: 227–238.

Galili, I. and Bar, V. (1997) Children's operational knowledge about weight. *International Journal of Science Education*, 19: 317–340.

Hewson, M. (1986) The acquisition of scientific knowledge: Analysis and representation of student conceptions concerning density. *Science Education*, 70: 159–170.

Joung, Y.J. (2009) Children's typically-perceived-situations of floating and sinking. *International Journal of Science Education*, 31: 101–127.

Liu, C., Carraher, D.W., Schliemann, A.D. and Wagoner, P. (2017) Learning to quantify relationships among weight, size, and kind of material. *Cognition and Instruction*, 35: 20–54.

Mullet, E. and Montcouquiol, A. (1988) Archimedes' effect, information integration and individual differences. *International Journal of Science Education*, 10: 285–301.

Parker, J. and Heywood, D. (2000) Exploring the relationship between subject knowledge and pedagogic content knowledge in primary teachers' learning about forces. *International Journal of Science Education*, 22: 89–111.

Pierratos, T. and Koumaras, P. (2022) Teaching about density with a filmed experiment. *Primary Science*, 172: 23–26.

Potvin, P. and Cyr, G. (2017) Toward a durable prevalence of scientific conceptions: Tracking the effects of two interfering misconceptions about buoyancy from preschoolers to science teachers. *Journal of Research in Science Teaching*, 54: 1121–1142.

Rowell, J.A. and Dawson, C.J. (1977) Teaching about floating and sinking: An attempt to link cognitive psychology with classroom practice. *Science Education*, 61: 245–253.

Schwichow, M. and Zoupidis, A. (2024) Teaching and learning floating and sinking: A meta-analysis. *Journal of Research in Science Teaching*, 61: 487–516.

She, H.-C. (2002) Concepts of a higher hierarchical level require more dual situated learning events for conceptual change: A study of air pressure and buoyancy. *International Journal of Science Education*, 24: 981–996.

Wei, A.S. and Karpudewan, M. (2018) Effects of social and emotional learning on disadvantaged Year 1 pupils' understanding of sinking and floating concepts. *Eurasia Journal of Mathematics, Science and Technology Education*, 14: 2609–2622.

15. Electricity

Armitage, R. (2007) *The Lighthouse Keeper's Lunch.* London: Scholastic Books.

Bar, V., Zinn, B. and Rubin, E. (1997) Children's ideas about action at a distance. *International Journal of Science Education*, 19: 1137–1157.

Chiu, M.H. and Lin, J.W. (2005) Promoting fourth graders' conceptual change of their understanding of electric current via multiple analogies. *Journal of Research in Science Teaching*, 42: 429–464.

De Posada, J. (1997) Conceptions of high school students concerning the internal structure of metals and their electric conduction: Structure and evolution. *Science Education*, 81: 445–467.

Driver, R. (1983) *The Pupil as Scientist?* Milton Keynes: Open University Press.

Finley, F.N. (1986) Evaluating instruction: The complementary use of clinical interviews. *Journal of Research in Science Teaching*, 23: 635–650.

Fredette, N. and Lockhead, J. (1980) Student conceptions of simple circuits. *The Physics Teacher*, 18: 194–198.

Garnett, P.J., Garnett, P.J. and Treagust, D.F. (1990) Implications of research on students' understanding of electrochemistry for improving science curricula and classroom practice. *International Journal of Science Education*, 12: 147–156.

Glauert, E.B. (2009) How young children understand electric circuits: Prediction, explanation and exploration. *International Journal of Science Education*, 31: 1025–1047.

Kada, V. and Ravanis, K. (2016) Creating a simple electric circuit with children between the ages of five and six. *South African Journal of Education*, 36: 1–9.

Kaliampos, G., Kada, V., Saregar, A. and Ravanis, K. (2020) Preschool pupils' mental representations on electricity, simple electrical circuits, and electrical appliances. *European Journal of Education Studies*, 7: 596–611.

Lin, J.W. (2016) Do skilled elementary teachers hold scientific conceptions and can they accurately predict the type and source of students' preconceptions of electric circuits? *International Journal of Science and Mathematics Education*, 14: 287–307.

Markwick, A. and White, A. (2022) Working scientifically with fruit and vegetable batteries. *Primary Science*, 171: 11–14.

Osborne, J.F., Black, P.J., Smith, M. and Meadows, J. (1991) *SPACE Research Report: Electricity*. Liverpool: Liverpool University Press.

Osborne, R. (1985) Building on children's intuitive ideas. In R. Osborne and P. Freyberg (eds) *Learning in Science*, pp. 41–50. Auckland: Heinemann.

Osborne, R.J. (1982) Bridging the gap between teaching and learning. Paper presented at the New Zealand Science Teachers' Association Conference, Hamilton, New Zealand.

Osborne, R.J. (1983) Towards modifying children's ideas about electric current. *Research in Teaching and Technological Education*, 1, 73–82.

Paatz, R., Ryder, J., Schwedes, H. and Scott, P. (2004) A case study analysing the process of analogy-based learning in a teaching unit about simple electric circuits. *International Journal of Science Education*, 26: 1065–1081.

Preston, C.M., Hubber, P.J. and Xu, L. (2022) Teaching about electricity in primary school multimodality and variation theory as analytical lenses. *Research in Science Education*, 52: 949–973.

Redhead, K. (2018) Common misconceptions: Electricity. *Why & How Magazine*, PSTT. Available at: https://pstt.org.uk/resources/common-misconceptions/ (accessed 16 April 2024).

Shipstone, D.M. (1984) A study of children's understanding of electricity in simple DC circuits. *European Journal of Science Education*, 6: 185–198.

Shipstone, D.M. (1985) Circuits. In R. Driver, E. Guesne and A. Tiberghien (eds) *Children's Ideas in Science*. Milton Keynes: Open University Press.

Solomonidou, C. and Kakana, D.M. (2000) Preschool children's conceptions about the electric current and the functioning of electric appliances. *European Early Childhood Education Research Journal*, 8 (1): 95–111.

Tiberghien, A. and Delacote, G. (1976) Manipulations et représentations de circuits électriques simples par des enfants de 7 à 12 ans. *Revue Française de Pédagogie*, 34: 32–44.

von Rhoneck, C. (1981) Students' conceptions of the electric circuit before physics instruction. In W. Jung, H. Pfundt and C.J. von Rhoneck (eds) *Proceedings of the International Workshop on Problems Concerning Students' Representation of*

Physics and Chemistry Knowledge, 14–16 September, pp. 194–213. Ludwigsburg: Pädagogische Hochschule.

Waring, G. (2009) *Oscar and the Bird*. London: Walker Books.

White, R. and Gunstone, R. (2014) *Probing Understanding*. Abingdon: Routledge.

16. Light

Anderson, C.W. and Smith, E.L. (1983) Children's conceptions of light and colour: Developing the concept of unseen rays. Paper presented to the Annual Meeting of the American Educational Research Association, Montreal, QC, Canada, 11–15 April.

Ayvaci, H.ş. and Candaş, B. (2018) Students' understandings on light reflection from different educational levels. *Journal of Computer and Education Research*, 6 (11): 1–32.

Driver, R. (1983) *The Pupil as Scientist?* Milton Keynes: Open University Press.

Driver, R., Squires, A., Rushworth, P. and Wood-Robinson, V. (1994) *Making Sense of Secondary Science: Research into Children's Ideas*. London: Routledge.

Feher, E. and Meyer, K.R. (1992) Children's conceptions of colour. *Journal of Research in Science Teaching*, 29: 505–520.

Feher, E. and Rice, K. (1986) Showing shadow shapes: Activities to elicit and dispel some preconceptions. *Science and Children*, 24 (2): 6–9.

Fetherstonhaugh, T. and Treagust, D.F. (1990) Students' understanding of light and its properties following a teaching strategy to engender conceptual change. Paper presented to the Annual Meeting of the American Educational Research Association, Boston, MA, 16–20 April.

Fliegauf, K., Sebald, J., Veith, J. M., Spiecker, H. and Bitzenbauer, P. (2022) Improving early optics instruction using a phenomenological approach: A field study. *Optics*, 3: 409–429.

Galili, I. and Hazan, A. (2000) Learners' knowledge in optics: Interpretation, structure and analysis. *International Journal of Science Education*, 22: 57–88.

Grigorovitch, A. (2015) Teaching optics perspectives: 10–11 year old pupils' representations of light. *International Education and Research Journal*, 1 (3): 4–6.

Grigorovitch, A. and Nertivich, D. (2017) Représentations mentales des élèves de 10–12 ans sur la formation des ombres (Mental representations of students of 10–12 years old on the formation of shadows). *European Journal of Education Studies*, 3 (5): 150–160.

Guesne, E. (1978) Lumière et vision des objets: Un exemple de représentation des phénomènes physiques préexistant à l'enseignement. In G. Delacote (ed.) *Physics Teaching in Schools*, pp. 265–273. London: Taylor & Francis.

Guesne, E. (1984) Children's ideas about light. In E.J. Wenman (ed.) *New Trends in Physics Teaching*, Vol. IV, pp. 179–192. Paris: UNESCO.

Guesne, E. (1985) Light. In R. Driver, E. Guesne and A. Tiberghien (eds) *Children's Ideas in Science*, pp. 10–32. Milton Keynes: Open University Press.

Guest, G. (2003) *Alternative Frameworks and Misconceptions in Primary Science*. Bristol: University of the West of England.

Martinez-Borreguero, G., Pérez-Rodríguez, A.L., Suero-López, M.I. and Pardo-Fernández, P.J. (2013) Detection of misconceptions about colour and an experimentally tested proposal to combat them. *International Journal of Science Education*, 35: 1299–1324.

Osborne, J.F., Black, P.J., Smith, M. and Meadows, J. (1990) *SPACE Research Report: Light.* Liverpool: Liverpool University Press.

Ramadas, J. and Driver, R. (1989) *Aspects of Secondary Students' Ideas about Light.* Children's Learning in Science Project. Leeds: Centre for Studies in Science and Mathematics Education, University of Leeds.

Rodriguez, J. and Castro, D. (2016) Changing 8–9 year-old pupils' mental representations of light: A metaphor-based teaching approach. *Asian Education Studies*, 1 (1): 41–47.

Rodriguez, J. and Castro, D. (2020) Quality improvement in teaching and learning science in primary school settings: Using a metaphor to approach the concept of light. *Jurnal Ilmiah Pendidikan Fisika Al-BiRuNi*, 9: 185–194.

Şahin, Ç., Ipek, H. and Ayas, A. (2008) Students' understanding of light concepts in primary school: A cross-age study. *Asia-Pacific Forum on Science Learning and Teaching*, 9: 1 (article 7).

Settlage, J. (1995) Children's conceptions of light in the context of a technology-based curriculum. *Science Education*, 79: 535–553.

Shallcross, R. (2017) Common misconceptions: Seeing the light. *Why & How Magazine*, PSTT. Available at: https://pstt.org.uk/resources/common-misconceptions/ (accessed 17 April 2024).

Tiberghien, A., Delacote, G., Ghiglione, R. and Metalon, B. (1980) Conceptions de la lumière chez l'enfant de 10–12 ans. *Revue Française de Pédagogie*, 50: 24–41.

Waring, G. (2006) *Oscar and the Moth.* London: Walker Books.

Watts, D.M. (1985) Student conceptions of light: A case study. *Physics Education*, 20: 183–187.

Watts, D.M. and Gilbert, J.K. (1985) *Appraising the Understanding of Science Concepts: Light.* Guildford: Department of Educational Studies, University of Surrey.

17. Sound

Asoko, H.M., Leach, J. and Scott, P.H. (1991) A study of students' understanding of sound 5–16 as an example of action research. Paper prepared for the symposium on Developing Students' Understanding in Science at the Annual Conference of the British Educational Research Association, Roehampton Institute, London, 2 September 1990.

Batlolona, J.R. and Jamaludin, J. (2024) Students' misconceptions on the concept of sound: A case study about Marinyo, Tanimbar Islands. *Journal of Education and Learning*, 18: 681-689.

Eshach, H., Lin, T.C. and Tsai, C.C. (2018) Misconceptions of sound and conceptual change: A cross-sectional study on students' materialistic thinking of sound. *Journal of Research in Science Teaching*, 55: 664–684.

Eshach, H. and Schwartz, J.L. (2006) Sound stuff? Naïve materialism in middle-school students' conceptions of sound. *International Journal of Science Education*, 28: 733–764.

Linder, C.J. (1993) University physics students' conceptualisations of factors affecting the speed of sound propagation. *International Journal of Science Education*, 15: 655–662.

Linder, C.J. and Erickson, G. (1989) A study of tertiary physics students' conceptualisations of sound. *International Journal of Science Education*, 11: 491–501.

Linfield, R. and Ireland, E. (2022) Teaching the physics of sound creatively with young children, *Primary Science*, 172: 15–16.

McGough, R. (2005) *The Sound Collector*. Harlow: Longman.

Poole, A. (2021) Common misconceptions: Sound. *Why & How Magazine*, PSTT. Available at: https://pstt.org.uk/resources/common-misconceptions/ (accessed 22 April 2024).

Royal Society (2024) *Brian Cox School Experiments*. Available at: https://royalsociety.org/news-resources/resources-for-schools/brian-cox-experiments/ (accessed 22 April 2024).

Sarioğlan, A.B. (2016) Conceptual level of understanding about sound concepts: Sample of fifth grade students. *E-International Journal of Educational Research*, 7 (1): 87–97.

Waring, G. (2007) *Oscar and the Bat*. London: Walker Books.

Watt, D. and Russell, T. (1990) *SPACE Research Report: Sound*. Liverpool: Liverpool University Press.

Whittaker, A.G. (2012) Pupils think sound has substance – well sort of. *School Science Review*, 94: 109–111.

Wittmann, M., Steinberg, R. and Redish, E. (2003) Understanding and affecting student reasoning about sound waves. *International Journal of Science Education*, 25: 991–1013.

18. Earth and space

Arnold, P., Sarge, A. and Worral, L. (1995) Children's knowledge of the earth's shape and its gravitational field. *International Journal of Science Education*, 17: 635–641.

Baxter, J. (1989) Children's understanding of familiar astronomical events. *International Journal of Science Education*, 11: 502–513.

Broughton, S.H., Sinatra, G.M. and Nussbaum, E.M. (2012) 'Pluto has been a planet my whole life!' Emotions, attitudes, and conceptual change in elementary students' learning about Pluto's reclassification. *Research in Science Education*, 43: 529–550.

Bryce, T.G.K. and Blown, E.J. (2012) Children's concepts of the shape and size of the earth, sun and moon. *International Journal of Science Education*, 3: 388–446.

Dankenbring, C. and Capobianco, B.M. (2016) Examining elementary school students' mental models of sun–earth relationships as a result of engaging in engineering design. *International Journal of Science and Mathematics Education*, 14: 825–845.

Davies, R.W. (2002) There's a lot to learning about the Earth in space. *Primary Science Review*, 72: 9–12.

Dunne, M. (2019) Teaching about Earth in space: It's out of this world. *Primary Science*, 160: 5–7.

Ehrlén, K. (2009) Drawings as representations of children's conceptions. *International Journal of Science Education*, 31: 41–57.

Fairhurst, C. and Tyler, P. (2022) The James Webb Space Telescope: Using physics to explore the universe. *Primary Science*, 172: 11–14.

Jang, M.D. and Nam, Y. (2012) Pre-service elementary teachers' conceptions on the relative sizes of celestial bodies. *Journal of the Korean Earth Science Society*, 33: 645–657.

Jones, B.L., Lynch, P.P. and Reesink, C. (1987) Children's conception of the Earth, Sun and Moon. *International Journal of Science Education*, 9: 43–53.

Kara, F. (2022) The effect of reflective science diaries on achievement and removal of misconceptions of 5th grade students about the moon concept. *International Online Journal of Education and Teaching*, 9: 1545–1559.

Lias, S. and Thomas, C. (2003) Using digital photographs to improve learning in science. *Primary Science Review*, 76: 17–19.

NASA (2015) Earth in full view from Apollo 17. Available at: https://www.nasa.gov/image-article/earth-full-view-from-apollo-17/ (accessed 30 May 2024).

Nikolopoulou, A., Fili, S., Founta, M. and Starakis, I. (2024) Kindergarten students' and pre-service teachers' perceptions regarding the frequency of the Moon's appearance at night. *International Journal of Early Years Education*, 32: 137–157.

Nobes, G., Frède, V. and Panagiotaki, G. (2023) Astronomers' representations of the earth and day/night cycle: Implications for children's acquisition of scientific concepts. *Current Psychology*, 42: 17612–17631.

Nussbaum, J. (1985) The Earth as a cosmic body. In R. Driver, E. Guesne and A. Tiberghien (eds) *Children's Ideas in Science*, pp. 170–192. Milton Keynes: Open University Press.

Nussbaum, J. and Novak, J.D. (1976) An assessment of children's concepts of the Earth utilising structured interviews. *Science Education*, 60: 535–550.

Osborne, J.F., Wadsworth, P., Black, P.J. and Meadows, J. (1993) *SPACE Research Report: The Earth in Space*. Liverpool: Liverpool University Press.

Özsoy, S. (2017) Is the earth flat or round? Primary school children's understandings of the planet Earth: The case of Turkish children. *International Electronic Journal of Elementary Education*, 4: 407–415.

Parker, J. and Heywood, D. (1998) The earth and beyond: Developing primary teachers' understanding of basic astronomical events. *International Journal of Science Education*, 20: 503–520.

Plummer, J.D. (2009) Early elementary students' development of astronomy concepts in the planetarium. *Journal of Research in Science Teaching*, 46: 192–209.

Sadler, P.M. (1987) Misconceptions in astronomy. In J.D. Novak (ed.) *Proceedings of the 2nd International Seminar: Misconceptions and Educational Strategies in Science and Mathematics*, 26–29 July, pp. 422–425. Ithaca, NY: Cornell University Press.

Schoon, K. and Boone, W. (1998) Self-efficacy and alternative conceptions of science of preservice elementary teachers. *Science Education*, 82: 553–568.

Sharp, J.G. (1996) Children's astronomical beliefs: A preliminary study of Year 6 children in south-west England. *International Journal of Science Education*, 18: 685–712.

Shen, J. and Confrey, J. (2007) From conceptual change to transformative modeling: A case study of an elementary teacher in learning astronomy. *Science Education*, 91: 948–966.

Spiliotopoulou-Papantoniou, V. (2007) Models of the universe: Children's experiences and evidence from the history of science. *Science and Education*, 16: 801–833.

Taylor, I., Barker, M. and Jones, A. (2003) Promoting mental model building in astronomy education. *International Journal of Science Education*, 25: 1205–1225.

Trumper, R. (2006) Teaching future teachers basic astronomy concepts – seasonal changes – at a time of reform in science education. *Journal of Research in Science Teaching*, 43: 879–906.

Trundle, K.C., Atwood, R.K. and Christopher, J.E. (2007) A longitudinal study of conceptual change: Preservice elementary teachers' conceptions of moon phases. *Journal of Research in Science Teaching*, 44: 303–326.

Turkmen, H. (2017) After almost half-century landing on the moon and still countering basic astronomy conceptions. *European Journal of Physics Education*, 6 (2): 1–17.

Vosniadou, S. and Brewer, W.F. (1990) A cross-cultural investigation of children's conceptions about the Earth, the Sun and the Moon: Greek and American data. In H. Mandl, E. De Corte, N. Bennett and H.F. Friedrid (eds) *Learning and Instruction: European Research in an International Context*, pp. 605–629. Oxford: Pergamon Press.

Vosniadou, S. and Skopeliti, I. (2017) Is it the Earth that turns or the Sun that goes behind the mountains? Students' misconceptions about the day/night cycle after reading a science text. *International Journal of Science Education*, 39: 2027–2051.

Zeilik, M., Schau, C. and Mattern N. (1998) Misconceptions and their change in university-level astronomy courses. *The Physics Teacher*, 36: 104–107.

Index

Illustrated references are in *italics;* glossary references are in **bold.**